(continued from front flap)

contributions. Novelists such as Dreiser, Faul and Hemingway created images of man's situa All these thinkers made assumptions and gu that are signposts to a more complete and acc picture of the nature of man.

Modern biologists, anthropologists, and statisticians have applied scientific methods to the study of man, but there has not yet arisen a coherent science of man. The New World was a prodigious gamble on the unmeasured powers of the common man, a gamble uninformed then as now by any body of measurable certainties about genetic inheritance. The dynamics of equality in frontier America, of definitions of equality in the minds of Abraham Lincoln, Henry George, Mark Twain, Edward Bellamy, and others—these intellectual forces possess a nongenetic reality that biology neither denies nor attempts to measure: Anthropology has established an enormous body of factual data, but it has not yet initiated a controlled experiment to determine man's plastic response to the vision of uncommon achievement.

The author believes that a correlation of sciences is needed to measure the impact of these forces on American life. Until this measurement is made, he feels, we can know neither the effects of hereditary constants nor the full reach of man's most crucial variable—his plasticity, his teachability. Dr. Wolfe envisions and outlines a possible course for this "science of man," a science that would experiment in the nurture of genius and test our hope for new crops of uncommon men from the average soil of American life.

DON M. WOLFE is a professor of English at Brooklyn College and editor of the *Journal of Historical Studies*. After receiving his Ph.D. from the University of Pittsburgh, he held teaching posts on several faculties, including the College of the City of New York, New York University, and the American University in Washington, D.C. In 1957–58 he was a member of the Institute for Advanced Study at Princeton. Dr. Wolfe is general editor of the *Complete Prose Works of John Milton,* published by Yale University Press; editor of various anthologies, including *New Voices;* and author or coauthor of thirty-six books and articles on scholarly subjects.

THOMAS Y. CROWELL COMPANY

201 Park Avenue South · New York 10003

ESTABLISHED 1834

The Image of Man in America

The Image of Man
in America

SECOND EDITION

DON M. WOLFE

THOMAS Y. CROWELL COMPANY
Established 1834
New York

MANUFACTURED IN THE UNITED STATES OF AMERICA

L.C. CARD 77-106588

1 2 3 4 5 6 7 8 9 10

To Alvin Johnson
A Reach to Greatness from the American Earth

PREFACE

T HOUGH I have finished this volume of intellectual history with reluctance, it has been many years in the making. As long ago as 1944 I sent outlines of the book, together with copies of several chapters I had completed, to a number of friends and kindred minds. Among these were George P. Gooch, F. O. Matthies· sen, John Dewey, Lewis Mumford, Merle Curti, Howard Mumford Jones, Willard Thorp, Ruth Benedict, and Charles Beard. Ruth Benedict wrote: "The topic you have chosen . . . is one I've always hoped that someone would study seriously—with due reference to its contrast between European thought in the great reactionary period from, say, 1820 to 1880." Charles Beard wrote: "Your new proposal is, of course, beyond human attainment. . . . But isn't anything worth doing beyond human attainment? Can science answer? I doubt it. . . . Maybe a romantic illusion can become a scientific reality, and a scientific reality, a social illusion. Watch yr. step, young man." Similarly, each letter I received reflected a different bias, one I hoped to weave with many other conflicting biases into the pattern of my history. Howard Mumford Jones spoke for the insight of the literary and social critic: "I am sardonically skeptical enough to think that the biologists and anthropologists are not necessarily any wiser about human nature than Jefferson or Mark Twain." I do not agree with either Jones or Beard that science cannot answer. But science has not thus far equipped itself to answer, and part of its equipment must come from the poets, historians, philosophers, biographers, utopians, and novelists; from the guesses, the half-revelations, the bubble of metaphor, that always precede the formulae of physics and the drawing boards of the sociologist or the engineer.

As I probed more deeply, chapter by chapter, I found one bias lacking among representative American figures that would have

vii

given better balance to my pattern of treatment: No great American figure of the nineteenth or twentieth century, Dr. Holmes excepted, believed with Sir Francis Galton that human nature was relatively fixed by genetic determinants. To the intellectual historian nothing is more fundamental than to present a sympathetic analysis of all intellectual positions. Such a principle is most important in this volume, in which my own bias is environmentalist—a bias which has, however, suffered deterioration over the years before the mounting evidence of genetic forces at work but still largely untallied, or at least unlinked categorically to specific genetic determinants.

I am indebted to many scholars who have given me the benefit of their specialized knowledge: to Saul Padover, Ronald S. Crane, and George P. Gooch for analysis of the Jefferson chapter; to Carl Sandburg for reading the Lincoln chapters; to Van Wyck Brooks for comments on the Emerson and Lincoln chapters; to Emory Holloway, Gay Wilson Allen, Charles Glicksberg, and John Birss for commentary on the Whitman chapter; to Horace Kallen for reading the James chapter; to Florence Teagarden for timely assistance on the Terman chapter; to Ruth Benedict, Ashley Montagu, Alfred Kroeber, and S. Benton Talbot for assistance on the biology and anthropology chapters, and to Ashley Montagu also for his comments on the Kinsey chapter. I am further indebted to my friend Frederic Ewen for critical analysis of the whole manuscript in its original form. To my friend and colleague, Charles Glicksberg, I am grateful for a devotion to this project much beyond the call of scholarly duty. From its early stages he has shown me its main limitations and helped me to overcome them. He has, moreover, read the whole book in both first draft and galley proof. Two staunch friends of the idea of this book in its early stages were Henry Simon and Arnold Mitchell; their encouragement is green in the memory.

Finally I am indebted to Miss Ruth Popofsky, who has given me indispensable aid in research and critical analysis; and to Mrs. Margaret Hartley and Allen Maxwell of Southern Methodist University Press for their imaginative and consistent attitude toward the scope and purpose of this volume.

DON M. WOLFE

New York
September 15, 1957

Preface to the Second Edition

A history of American profiles of the nature of man, centering on the relative influence of environment and heredity, is more fraught with meaning now than in any preceding generation. While the impact of nature's genetic determinants remains largely inscrutable (except in quantitative patterns of sexual release), the enormous range of environmental impacts, whether benign or destructive, may be traced and tallied with varying degrees of certainty. A central problem of any civilization is to make the volume of benign impacts on its youth so overwhelming as to be irresistible. "There is a power in love," wrote Emerson, "to define another's destiny better than that other can, and, by heroic encouragements, hold him to the task." The events of the past decade have reduced rather than accelerated the commitment of benign example and persuasion to our youth. The limitations of such a commitment, as well as its immense range of beneficent possibilities, were not lost on Emerson. Every man to Emerson was "a golden impossibility"— a plastic creature awaiting the irresistible touch of the discerning friend, the magical teacher.

In preparing this second edition, I am indebted afresh to the scholars and friends named in the original preface—especially to Charles Glicksberg, my inspiring colleague at Brooklyn College, and to Merle Curti, for exciting hours of intellectual companionship in which the themes of this book were the focus. Dr. Lila Freedman, of Princeton, has also given incisive criticism and fruitful suggestions. Finally I am indebted to my brother, Glenn Wolfe, for his constant encouragement and initiation of plans for the second edition.

Don M. Wolfe

Princeton
November 1, 1969

Contents

List of Illustrations

The Image of Man in America

Introduction

WHATEVER may have been the barbarism of the enemy in World War II, in the Korean conflict, or in Vietnam (the longest war in American history), some American soldiers have witnessed in themselves and their comrades and officers a degradation of the nature of man beyond prior comprehension. Though it is true that many of these Americans acted under the inexorable pressure of war psychology, the roots of all cruelties may be traced to pressures of some kind. To what extent we can place blame for torture and cruelty, in war or out, remains a mystery to the thoughtful critic of human nature.

Consider, for example, the young southern captain mentioned in *The New York Times* after World War II—a soft-spoken leader well liked by his company, who found himself cut off in the Battle of the Bulge, with only forty men remaining and a large group of prisoners handicapping their chances of staying alive. Nothing was left, in a desperate situation, but to kill the prisoners, one of whom was a young lad of fifteen or sixteen. "He was crying and begging me to save him," said the captain later, "and I was kind of sorry I had to kill him." [1]

Consider another American, a marine on a South Pacific island whose buddy had raped a native girl and had been killed in turn by the girl's native lover. At dawn the marine's company surrounded the native's village—unofficially, of course—and destroyed it to the last man and child. Again: when American soldiers occupied North Africa, one of them chanced one night upon an Arab girl prostrate on the ground—bartered by her mother to a queue of the Americans.

3

Each of these stories, except the one in the *Times,* I have verified in personal conference with an eyewitness. But thousands of American soldiers can tell similar stories. We cannot assert that such extensions of man's capacity for cruelty are limited to abnormal people, any more than we can affirm that every member of a lynching mob is a fit subject for a mental hospital. Such degradation of the nature of man occurs among normal people: tender fathers, dutiful sons, conscientious church members, devout believers.

All wars, we may safely assert, have produced similar cruelties committed in frenzied moments by men otherwise normal. But at no time in the history of the world has man exhibited more imagination in the generation of mass hatred and the infliction of mass cruelty than in the last two decades. In that period the German people, with many honorable exceptions, were persuaded by their leaders to hate and torture, burn and kill six million defenseless men, women, and children, as in a righteous cause. The use of the latest science—of psychology, chemistry, electronics, medicine, engineering—to intensify suffering and prolong death, the torturers afterward stealing the gold of their victims' teeth and stuffing the hair of their heads into mattresses, has never before been exhibited on such a massive scale. Nor has it been demonstrated before with such devastating certainty how surely even the most idealistic temperament disintegrates in a concentration camp under the impact of slow starvation. It is impossible to think that the frenzy of Nazi hatreds, the delight in prolonged tortures, affected only those minds among the German people that were already diseased. People decent by any civilized standard succumbed to the infection, even as the witch-hunters in early New England, the lynchers with their nubs of Negro ears, the American soldiers over the prostrate girl.

How to explain the nature of man that will use his latest science to put out the eyes of his enemy, roast a newborn child, or drive his victim insane by pulling out his nails? Is the Jeeter Lester of *Tobacco Road* the end result of long years of malnutrition, or is his callous nature a genetic product? The death of his mother he receives with utter indifference: more important is the next meal of turnips, which he will steal from his children if necessary. In *A Farewell to Arms* the hero kills his sergeant in cold blood, merely to be rid of his presence. In *Sanctuary* an impotent gambler forces the act of coition between two people in his power, merely to satisfy his impulse of cruelty and hatred. In *Studs Lonigan* the author traces the depths to which a middle-class boy may descend; and how accurate much of his picture is there are millions to testify from their own lives. Man is on occasion infinitely more cruel, degraded, and murderous than any animal; to unspeakable ends he can direct a high intelligence, an imagination, an accumulation of science, that no animal can muster. Is this depravity in man rooted in his genetic structure, as suggested in such a novel as *Lord of the Flies?* Is he innately evil, as some philosophers contend? Or is this depravity merely the extension of the environmental pressures under which he lives?

To show how great American thinkers have answered these and similar questions is the purpose of this book. In an era of disillusionment with the nature of man, when as yet no co-operative scientific procedure has been established to demonstrate the upward reaches of man (the lower depths being already amply documented), when man is still groping to identify the fixed aspects of his nature, it is a fruitful task to retrace the portraits which American thinkers have bequeathed us of the nature of man. They made assumptions, they made guesses, as Jefferson did about the nature of the Negro, the Indian, and the emergence of genius; but these guesses are the signposts to a more complete and accurate portrait of the nature of man. Holmes with his amazing knowledge of medicine and psychology, Lincoln with his relentless logic, George with his grasp of economic history, each clarified a facet of human nature, preparing the way for Boas and his followers, and for the co-operative science of man yet to come.

II

Almost everyone, consciously or unconsciously, has shaped in his mind a portrait of the nature of man. Each thinker and writer somehow delineates his image of the composite inner man, as do Thomas Wolfe in *You Can't Go Home Again,* Plato in *The Republic,* Machiavelli in *The Prince,* More in *Utopia.* The portrait of man is usually painted in the maker's own image; it may be a simple portrait, with a few sharp, emphatic lines, like that of William Saroyan; it may be a complex, careful picture, like that of Holmes, Steffens, or Boas. "One thing Bellamy forgot in *Looking Backward,*" says the young intellectual, "is how to account for the change in man's nature from 1887 to the year 2000," meaning, of course, that in 1887 man was genetically egotistic and depraved. Only an immature grappler with man's portraits of man could venture such a criticism. What is the nature of man deep down—what are the fixed elements of his being that he shares with all mankind, in the darkness of his mother's womb? Is he then, before he sees the light, already branded with fear, greed, hatred, as Hobbes and Machiavelli picture him? Is his inmost soul, his genetic strain, closer akin to the sadism of the gas chamber executioner than to the compassion of the democratic citizen? Despite the centuries of guesswork, no science yet exists that can identify in the embryo the traits of hatred, fear, sympathy, that later are so common as to be thought genetic. "What is man?" asks the Psalmist, and answers, "a little lower than the angels." "What is man?" asks Milton in *Samson Agonistes,* and paints an image of himself, rejecting for that name the masses, "the common rout, that wandring loose about, grow up and perish as the summer flie."[2] The man on the street paints his portrait of man with these words: "Everybody is out to get the other fellow," or "You can't change [the depravity of] human nature." The psychologist in his laboratory, the biologist in his fruit-fly experiments, Pavlov with his dogs, the anthropologist on his distant island, the sociologist in his Middletown, all are seeking to delineate the true nature of man.

Not only these seekers, but philosophers, economists, and logicians as well have their uses in pushing back the boundaries of intellectual chaos which circumscribe the subject of human nature. Until science, or a correlation of sciences, can bring to the study of man the same objectivity that Agassiz brought to the study of porpoises, as Holmes pointed out long ago, then no portrait of man, even the simplest and most superstitious ones, can be totally without value. When a man says, "Just like a Jew," he means, in effect, "Jewish greed and Jewish aggressiveness are passed on *genetically* from generation to generation." Similarly, when a man says, "Negroes are like children," he means that a set of genes peculiar to Negroes transmits from one generation to another the quality of childishness. Such statements, believed by millions of Americans, imply that man's character is largely shaped at the moment of conception. This image, so widely held, is instructive to those who would present more mature definitions of human nature. Aristotle was one of the few men who was not tempted to guess what human traits, if any, are transmitted by the genes. In the *Ethics* he wrote: "The formation of a virtuous character some ascribe to Nature, some to Custom, and some to Teaching. Now Nature's part, *be it what it may*, obviously does not rest with us."[3] Hence, concludes Aristotle, we must work with what we know, with laws, with precept, with example, to shape the ideal citizen.

III

Over the centuries we may trace three or four persistent assumptions about man's essential nature. The first is that man is depraved and evil, prone to selfishness and hatred as the sparks fly upward. Though this theory is deeply rooted in the Christian and Hebraic theological traditions, especially in Calvinism, it is also a persistent force among relatively irreligious thinkers. Machiavelli wrote that any man setting up a constitution must start by assuming that "all men are bad and ever ready to display their vicious nature."[4] To the same analysis Thomas Hobbes brought the support of the mathematics and psychology of his day, describing man as a selfish, competitive animal. "Life it selfe is but Motion," he wrote, "and can never be without Desire, nor without Feare, no more than without Sense."[5] To this general view Darwin's *The Origin of Species* gave decisive impetus.[6] To the extent to which man's sexual nature is regarded as unstable, capricious, or as a remnant of the chimpanzee, as Emerson said, even man's procreative machinery testifies to his innate depravity. The researches of Sigmund Freud, in the minds of some esteemed critics of human nature, point to man's genetic sexual structure as the source energy of his maladjustments and frustrations, driving him unknowingly to irrational resolutions of his conflicts. In *The Mind in the Making* James Harvey Robinson traces the origin of man's irrational behavior to the overlapping instincts he has inherited from his animal and savage ancestors.

The obverse of this portrait of man is that man is by nature noble and good, and is corrupted, not by genetic poison, but by circumstance or choice. To many liberal theologians each man is born in the image of God, even as was Adam himself. Arminius and Milton, as well as the great Catholic thinker St. Thomas Aquinas, asserted the theory of innate nobility. Such was the view also of the pagans Cicero and Plutarch. "The soul has a principle of kindness in itself," wrote Plutarch, "as well as to perceive, think, or remember." The first book of More's *Utopia* pictures sound Englishmen corrupted by circumstance, forced by society to thievery if they would live, and then punished for society's crimes. More, like all great Renaissance utopians, viewed man as essentially noble, awaiting only the social impetus to unfold his capacity for becoming his brother's keeper.

American utopians, such as Bellamy and Henry George, were to strike much the same strain of reasoning. "Call it religion, patriotism, sympathy, the enthusiasm for humanity, or the love of God— give it what name you will," wrote Henry George, "there is yet a force which overcomes and drives out selfishness; a force which is the electricity of the moral universe. . . . To be pitied is the man who has never seen and never felt it."[7] Emerson, Whitman, Channing, Alcott, and Ripley held also to the view of man's essential goodness, that man is a divine participant of the Universal Soul, with truth and righteousness implanted in his being before his birth. To such men as Whitman and Sherwood Anderson even man's sexual nature is an expression of his essential nobility. In this tradition of human nature, as in the theory that man is essentially evil, we have the secular and the religious interpreters, both denounced as utopians and idealists by their ideological enemies. Even in such a scientific thinker as Jefferson we find a conviction of man's innate function of kindness and sympathy.

A variant of these two positions is that man's nature is (even before birth) the repository of both evil and virtuous tendencies. Conceived in sin (his organism rooted in animal and savage psychology), he is sure to be egotistic, selfish, predatory. On the other hand he is made in the image of God (unlike other animals, he can think and speak); therefore he has a tendency to noble and virtuous action. Which of these two general modes of life becomes habitual depends upon man's free will and free choice. How free will can be separated from both heredity and environment the philosophers who take this view fail to explain.

This position is taken not only by most religious groups, but also by laws and institutions, which hold a man responsible for his actions whether or not he has had an opportunity to read and understand the requirements of the law under which he lives. Whatever the forces arrayed against a criminal, both the church and the law court, as Holmes points out, assume his freedom of choice and pronounce judgment accordingly. If such assumptions are necessary to law and order and moral uprightness, it is clear that their truth is far from scientific acceptance; it is also clear that even the church and the state recognize the necessity for their modification. If a man murders, the circumstances under which he acted—even a temporary frenzy—may reduce the area of his responsibility in the eyes of the court and the jury. In the quiet of the confessional, a man may explain the circumstances of his sin and thus provide a justification for mitigating his penance.

Another general view of human nature, adopted by only a few

thinkers before the twentieth century, is that man at birth is as ethically neutral as a bag of salt or a glass of water. Such a view assumes neither inherent evil nor inherent goodness, nor a combination of the two. Whatever traits may be ascribed to man's nature are only, in this third conception, projections of the influences of his environment. This concept of man's nature is inherent in the belief of Socrates that evil is only ignorance, virtue knowledge. Since knowledge and ignorance are environmental in origin, proponents of this view assume that man's nature in the darkness of the womb is ethically neutral and infinitely plastic.

The first reasoned defense of this theory was set forth by William Godwin in his *Enquiry Concerning Political Justice*. According to Godwin, virtuous as well as evil influences, when applied with sufficient pressure, are irresistible—a view that Comenius had anticipated in his *Great Didactic*. If we believe only free choice guides man, asked Godwin, why do we have schools and churches and parental guidance? Man's character is mechanistically determined by the forces, constructive or destructive, brought to bear upon his youth. As Robert Owen said in his *New View of Society*, "The character of man is . . . always formed for him." Further: "Any general character, from the best to the worst, from the most ignorant to the most enlightened, may be given to any community, even to the world at large, by the application of proper means; which means are to a great extent at the command and under the control of those who have influence in the affairs of men."⁸

In recent decades it has been commonly believed that criminals are the product of a slum environment—that, as Father Flanagan said, "There is no such thing as a bad boy"; but it is less commonly believed that exceptionally able and remarkable men are the products of their peculiar advantages and opportunities. Any pressure on the human organism, whether beneficent or destructive, cannot fail to make a change in normal personality in proportion to its intensity and duration. Many educators accept this aspect of the plasticity theory of human nature. To this principle almost everyone assents in some degree; otherwise he would take no trouble to train his children, send them to school, or surround them with beneficent influences of church or neighborhood. In general the social worker of today adopts this point of view in dealing with his clients, saying to himself, "There, but for the grace of God [my parents, my community, my playmates, none of which I chose], go I." Likewise the anthropologist, in making his researches, tacitly assumes that before birth the human organism is ethically neutral but endlessly plastic. What man inherits is not traits, but the plasticity by which he may be molded into an infinite number of patterns.

It is obvious that no man holds rigidly to one of these general assumptions about human nature without at times slipping into a contradictory intellectual position. If one believes that human nature is genetically evil, he nevertheless sees all around him men and women who are exceptions to the rule; in fact, he is unlikely to regard himself as the embodiment of depravity. His heroes of history—Jesus, Socrates, Joan of Arc, George Washington, Abraham Lincoln—show profound tendencies toward an organic nobility. Notwithstanding his position, one who believes in inherent depravity usually supports his church and school because he believes that some change in human nature is possible, perhaps with the aid of a personal God. He would not claim that an American newborn infant brought up in a cannibal tribe would speak English or prefer the Presbyterian church to his tribe's medicine man.

Those who believe that man is essentially noble cannot deny the existence of cruelty and torture, notwithstanding the image of God in the souls of the perpetrators. If one believes that all man has to do is to choose between the good and evil that he inherited, that man has a free will to make of his life a glorious summation or a bitter frustration, he nevertheless sees that his son attends the best schools, plays with companions of his own race and social position, reads good books, and meets girls of good repute; he also wants schools for other boys and is in favor of maintaining the churches and all beneficent pressures on the young.

Those holding that man inherits neither evil nor good but only a plastic, responsive mechanism are likely to be less surprised by any human aberration than their fellow-philosophers of human nature. Like Robert Owen and William Graham Sumner, they interpret all of man's moral choices as projections of his environment; that is, what society has taught him is right, however wrong that choice may be to another society. "The mores," said Sumner, "can make anything right." Owen was even more emphatic: "By judicious training the infants of any one class in the world may be readily formed into men of any other class, even to believe and declare that conduct to be right and virtuous, and to die in its defence, which their parents had been taught to believe and say was wrong and vicious."[9] Unlike their fellow-philosophers, men who hold this assumption of human nature as infinitely plastic believe not at all in inherited traits. Even sex to them is ethically neutral in its origin; its constructive or destructive use is determined by the milieu in which its owner lives and grows. To the philosopher of plasticity no cruelty is contrary to human nature; cruelty does not spring from the genetic structure, but from determinants which no man, however well trained, can ultimately resist. Nor can one holding the plasticity theory be surprised at the emergence of kindness, generosity, or the sudden flowering of many geniuses; all of these are to be explained not by genetic structure, but by the fluid forces of society.

IV

Through all the persistent assumptions about human nature runs the timeless and still largely unanswered question: What is inherited and what is acquired? The philosopher of plasticity answers, in effect, all behavior patterns are acquired, not inherited; though in this he is supported by the anthropologist, the biologist has not yet brought forth his conclusive evidence. It is the fashion among some psychologists today and some intellectuals inexperienced in the literature of human nature to say that it is an absurd and silly question to ask what is acquired and what is inherited. "Are not both necessary to man's growth?" they ask. "Each is impotent without the other." But the moot question is the most pertinent one of all, as hundreds of books testify, among them the most complete study yet made of identical twins.[10] Yet only the anthropologist has as one of his avowed aims' the solving of this problem. "One of the fundamental aims of scientific anthropology," writes Boas, "is to learn which traits of behavior, if any, are organically determined and are, therefore, the common property of mankind and which are due to the culture in which we live."[11] The great thinkers about human nature, from Plato and Aristotle to Mark Twain, James, and Dewey, have all concerned themselves with this question; and to trace the stream of American answers to it is the central problem of this book.

The facets of the question of what is inherited and what is acquired touch life at many controversial points. That man inherits the color of his skin and the physical structure of his body at birth is a point of common agreement. That his being born Italian, Finnish, Jewish, Norwegian, French, Chinese, Brazilian, Negro, Choctaw, has any relation whatever to the language he learns, the sexual habits he exhibits, his behavior as son, student, citizen, father, lover, husband, worker, soldier, is vehemently denied. A blonde-haired boy born in Texas and transported at birth to inland China, adopted by a Chinese family, would grow up Chinese in language, religion, eating habits, patriotism, and ideas of sex, marriage, and American imperialism. So affirms the philosopher of plasticity. If this is true, then discrimination against a Negro, an Italian, a Japanese, all born in America, is an act of delusion, an intellectual monstrosity. On this point Lincoln's logic is memorable: "You say A is white and B is black. It is color, then; the lighter having the right to enslave the darker? Take care. By this rule you are to be slave to the first man you meet with a fairer skin than your own."[12]

Another facet: within any relatively homogeneous group, such as the farm population of New Hampshire, runs a wide diversity of temperament, desire to achieve, accomplishment, education, income, ideals of marriage, from which a jury of educators might select the relatively constructive (for our society) and the relatively undesirable. Now to what extent is a man's position in society, or his position in any of the categories listed above, determined by his genetic structure? Some would say that a man's position in each category would depend upon his intelligence, which is largely a genetic product. To this other critics, among them Otto Klineberg, would reply that the I.Q. is not static, but changes with each year of favorable educational opportunity; and such authorities as Margaret Mead would maintain that temperament itself is in the main a product of childhood environment.

If such plasticity exists, then the achievement of men in constructive effort—in advances in education, democratic ideals, creative power—is as yet only a tiniest fraction of their capacity. The philosopher of plasticity affirms that uncommon men can be made as rapidly as the environment of common men is charged with the electricity of civilized opportunity and stimulation. He points to the environment of Jefferson, Franklin, Emerson, Horace Mann, Lowell, Whitman, Mark Twain, William James, Theodore Dreiser, John Dewey, Woodrow Wilson, and says, in effect: The genius of these men is only the fruit of peculiar advantages and opportunities denied to other men. Reconstruct these advantages a thousand fold, advantages of the same intensity and duration, and you will create a thousand men of similar stature. To this statement the geneticist replies: Your assumption is ridiculous. You cannot make bread out of stones, or a hickory tree out of lettuce seed. The poor and the weak are always with us. Man is born to fame or obscurity. His limitations are rooted in his genetic inheritance.

V

Each age, like man himself, traces a portrait of human nature in its own image. Thus in aristocratic countries, where men remained, as in England, for many generations in the same social and economic position, it was thought that the aristocrat, by virtue of his birth alone, inherited superior gifts and temperament. A cobbler could inherit from his father only a cobbler's intelligence, no more; a peasant had a peasant's soul implanted in him before his birth. Whatever his struggles, therefore, it was assumed that only in a few cases could a bricklayer's son presume to attend Oxford or Cambridge. Now and then, it is true, as Tennyson was to write later, a peasant was to be found in a palace, a king in a peasant's hut; but nature was not often so capricious. In the typical English novel, if a man of lowly station made his way upward to renown and heroic action, it was found at the end that he was the illegitimate son of a great lord. Blood would finally tell. In general, aristocratic societies believed implicitly in the analysis of human nature that Plato traced in *The Republic:*

Citizens, we shall say to them . . . you are brothers, yet God has framed you differently. Some of you have the power to command, and in the composition of these he has mingled gold, wherefore also they have the greatest honor; others he has made of silver, to be auxiliaries; others again who are to be husbandmen and craftsmen he has composed of brass and iron; and *the species will generally be preserved in the children.* But as all are of the same original stock, a golden parent will sometimes have a silver son, or a silver parent a golden son.[13]

It is even possible, continues Plato, that a golden or silver parent will have a brass or iron son, or at least one tinged with brass and iron. In such situations the state must be very firm; it must see that such a son is given the job of an artisan, which befits his talents. Such is the aristocratic picture of human nature, which by and large is the accepted view throughout the world today, so strong is the traditional concept that "blood will tell."

With the rise of the trading classes, however, recruited in the main from peasants and yeomen, a new image of man was promulgated side by side with the march of the democratic impetus. The poorer the sectarian group in the English Civil Wars, the more drastic its economic and social demands, and the more insistent its elevation of the common man's powers and dignity. From the assumption of spiritual equality before the Lord, it was but a short step to the assumption that the common man deserved political and even economic equality. Nowhere were the crucial questions debated more strenuously than in Cromwell's army, where for the first time in English history rank was determined by fighting ability alone, and many a butcher's son—among them Major General Harrison—commanded platoons, companies, or regiments in the field. Was not the suffrage, declared Colonel Rainsborough in the Leveller debates with Cromwell's officers, merely an exercise of human reason? It should not be denied to "the meanest man in the Kingdome." As for biblical sanction, asserted Rainsborough, "I doe not finde any thinge in the Law of God, that a Lord should chuse 20 Burgesses, and a Gentleman butt two, or a poore man shall chuse none."[14]

A century later, in his "Elegy Written in a Country Churchyard," Thomas Gray traced a revolutionary portrait of man in keeping with the assumptions of Rainsborough and his fellows, both English and American. The humble villagers beneath the stones, asked Gray, why did they die obscure? Why was there no Milton, no Cromwell or Hampden among them? Gray's answer is categorical: They were too poor and too ignorant. To them were denied the magic and the majesty of books. Poverty battered their bodies and stunted their spirits: "Chill Penury repress'd their noble rage,/ And froze the genial current of the soul." They died without flowering, without having known the comfort and leisure to create, or having grasped the rich heritage of the ages in their minds. No more revolutionary poetic tribute had yet been paid to the undeveloped powers of the common man. The "Elegy" was a precursor to the portraits of Rousseau, Godwin, Shelley, Paine, Franklin, and Jefferson. If the great poem's central meaning was only "romantic nonsense," as many literature professors were later to teach, then the new portraits of men etched in the American and French Revolutions were a lamentable delusion.

It was inevitable that the New World should produce images of man in keeping with the revolutionary changes it made in the lives of the colonists. The restraints and values of an aristocratic society, built up over centuries of refinements and reinforcements, no longer availed. In a wilderness society, where no one was rich and everyone could own land, titles were absurd, fine clothes and powdered wigs were superfluous, social rank was meaningless. Only in the larger towns and cities could the stratifications of Europe find a new foothold, to be weakened by every step of the westward march. Only those who had lived in both the New and the Old Worlds, as had Thomas Paine, could appreciate the contrast. "So deeply rooted were all the governments of the old world," he wrote in *The Rights of Man*, ". . . that no beginning could be made in Asia, Africa, or Europe, to reform the political condition of man. Freedom had been hunted round the globe; reason was considered as rebellion; and the slavery of fear had made men afraid to think." But in the New World, beginning a new society, forced to throw off the customs of the old, men from various nations of Europe, of differing religious faiths, met "not as enemies, but as brothers." "In such a situation," asserted Paine, "man becomes what he ought. He sees his species, not with the inhuman idea of a natural enemy, but as kindred."[15]

No doubt Paine was too sanguine in his evaluation of American attitudes; but soon thousands of men who had been obscure, even penniless, in Europe rose in America to positions of trust and eminence, not only in government but in intellectual attainments as well, some of their descendants destined to write the Constitution and establish the American Republic. "Our ancestors who migrated hither," wrote Jefferson, "were laborers, not lawyers." They saw in themselves an embodiment of human nature expanded to powers unattainable in the restraints of the Old World. It was natural for such leaders to look upon the common man with a confident eye. For the first time in the history of the West, as Tocqueville was later to discover, the spirit of equality was not accidental and spasmodic, but pervasive. Cromwell's army had been but a little island of democratic agitation; now the principle of equality in habits and customs had infected a continent.

In America, then, the concept of plasticity, the infinite malleability and teachability of the human organism, was to be tested as never before. From the mass of farmers and tradesmen and pioneers, uncommon men were in the making, not at the prodigious rate of ancient Athens but, as Jefferson was to insist, in proportion to the population and the duration of their civilization. "Mr. Burke talks of nobility," wrote Paine, scornfully; "let him show what it is. The greatest characters the world has known have arisen on the democratic floor."[16] The New World was in essence a prodigious gamble on the unmeasured powers of the common man, a gamble scornful of nature's unique boundaries, and uninformed, then as now, by any body of measurable certainties about genetic inheritance.

I
Jefferson and the Science of Man

> *All eyes are opened, or opening, to the
> rights of man. The general spread of the
> light of science has already laid open to
> every view the palpable truth, that the mass
> of mankind has not been born with saddles
> on their backs.*
>
> —Jefferson

I N the age of Jefferson, as in our own, the science of
man was shackled by a great chain of myths centuries old. Hamilton
and Jefferson made assumptions about human nature that cannot
be proved or disproved even today by criteria that the mathematician or the chemist or the biologist would accept as indisputable.
As does every science, the science of man began with hunches and
hypotheses rather than with laboratory facts. In his approach to the
nature of man Hamilton denominated the people as a "great beast."
If this assumption was mythical, Jefferson assumed what to many
scholars is still another myth; namely, that the reasoning apparatus
of the ordinary human mind could be indefinitely extended. To
place political power in the hands of the average man would be a
test of his reasoning faculties.

One difference between Hamilton and Jefferson was that while
Hamilton remained confident in his assumptions about the nature
of man, Jefferson was a constant seeker of the sensory evidence that
would justify or banish his assumptions. In the history of American
assumptions about the nature of man nothing has been more needed
or less sought after than a scientific method that would qualify or
dispel the hopes of both the scoffers and the believers in the potential greatness of the common man.

About the nature of man Jefferson exhibited a lifelong curiosity, a curiosity heightened by the dynamic society about him, by the growth of the great men of his age, and by his immense reading in the rationalistic literature of the eighteenth century. Like all thinkers about the science of man, he was curious about what is inherited and what is acquired. Though he believed the Negroes inferior to whites by nature, he recognized the paucity of evidence and was eager for proof, as he wrote to Banneker, that their inferiority was only the effect of the degrading circumstances of their lives. Whence came, Jefferson wondered, the genius of the Indians for compassion and eloquence? As a boy he had heard the great Cherokee Outasseté speak his farewell to the assembled warriors around the campfires. "The moon was in full splendor," wrote Jefferson,

and to her he seemed to address himself in his prayers for his own safety on the voyage, and that of his people during his absence; his sounding voice, distinct articulation, animated action, and the solemn silence of his people at their several fires, filled me with awe and veneration, although I did not understand a word he uttered.[1]

Was this greatness inherited? Did it somehow pass from father to son? The hereditary aristocracy of England had assumed for centuries that virtue and distinction flowed in the bloodstream; and many of the leading families of Virginia emphatically concurred. Indeed, as late as 1926 a biographer of Jefferson accounted in part for his subject's distinction in a similar manner, asserting that Mendel's law might yet account for the transmission of genius. On this topic Jefferson himself was sufficiently categorical: genius by and large is made, not born. Though his mother's family, the Randolphs, could claim a distinguished line of ancestors, Jefferson wrote of his maternal pedigree with an ironical note in his *Autobiography:* "To which let every one ascribe the faith & merit he chooses."

Nevertheless, Jefferson wondered; he was a cautious, a scientific thinker, with knowledge too limited, especially in this field, for closing his mind and imprisoning his conclusion in a tight little bottle. Every year he saw Virginians of relatively undistinguished antecedents, like Patrick Henry and Dabney Carr, and most conspicuously himself, developing in one or more areas of life into uncommon men. Could the common man, the mass man, really grow decisively? Could his reason expand to a capacity for self-government, to deserve the power of the ballot? "Our ancestors ... who migrated hither," wrote Jefferson, "were laborers, not lawyers." Yet these men, in carving farms out of the wilderness, had begun to read, had bought books, perhaps forty, perhaps even a hundred. A few at a time their children came to William and Mary College. A new life of the mind expanded in Virginia that in England would have remained in these families shuttered for centuries on end.

II

A man's destiny often lies buried in the images of his youth—some will say in the darkness of the womb that bore him. But before greatness comes the image of greatness, before compassion human tenderness, before resourcefulness a breathing man. For grappling with frontier realities, for embodiment of the fierce energy of man's expanding powers, none could have served more dramatically than Peter Jefferson, the father of Thomas. Of prodigious strength; carrying in his huge frame the power of three laborers; surveyor, farmer, woodsman, naturalist, canoer, swimmer, reader of Addison, Shakespeare, Swift, and Pope, Peter Jefferson carved out of the wilderness a thousand acres for his family, lending confidence and friendship to lesser men, providing for Thomas a joyous, invigorating childhood, assuring him by example the bountiful fruits of disciplined energy, both physical and intellectual.

Even as a boy Thomas was proud of his father's rise from humble origins, slightly scornful of his mother's aristocratic forebears. The democratic impress of the frontier, lending dignity not to man's birth but to his personal resources, was a daily reality in Jefferson's childhood. He grew strong and self-disciplined, his skin reddened by sun and wind, at Shadwell riding and swimming almost daily. Turning to Homer and Virgil on his long canoe rides, delighting in the violin, the young Jefferson, unlike many immature democrats, saw no contradiction between the elegance and grace and charm of Randolph manners and the rough democratic impetus of the frontier man. Every activity of great men had its gifts to offer; he would reject none, would make them all his own. Like Leonardo before him (a kindred mind in the scope of life's fascinations), Jefferson early learned that life unwasted gives time enough for the fulfilment of all persistent dreams.

In his fourteenth year when his father died, young Thomas was already a well-organized human being, systematic in his searches, delighting in the day's changes, the shift from nature to books, from practical action to music and reverie, from the sounds of hammer and anvil and ax to the elegance of the dining room. After two years of classical studies among the four hundred books of the Reverend Mr. Maury (and in the images of the greatness of Greece and Rome lies one of the keys to Jefferson's genius), the young man entered William and Mary College. Then a school of only one hundred students in a town of a thousand souls, William and Mary had served for several decades as the center of Virginia's aspirations and the training ground of its leaders. Almost all of Jefferson's associates there achieved fame of a kind in the stirring decades to follow. In the expansion of Jefferson's amazing intellectual faculties, his experiences at William and Mary were decisive. "It was my great good fortune," wrote Jefferson,

and what probably fixed the destinies of my life that Dr. William Small of Scotland was then Professor of Mathematics, a man profound in most of the useful branches of science, with a happy talent of communication, correct and gentlemanly manners, & an enlarged & liberal mind. He, most happily for me, became soon attached to me & made me his daily companion when not engaged in the school; and from his conversation I got my first views of the expansion of science & of the system of things in which we are placed.[2]

Unfortunately for comprehension of Jefferson's intellectual growth, the particulars of Dr. Small's teachings (later also ethics, rhetoric, and literature) were never committed to type, either in his own books or in Jefferson's jottings. But Jefferson's emphasis on the *expansion* of science in this passage provides a key to the broad outline: to his mastery of the classics Jefferson now began to add, like Condorcet, an acquisition of the scientific outlook as broad and deep as that of Bacon himself; applying the scientific method not only to the narrow spheres of botany, biology, horticulture, architecture, physics, astronomy, statistics, but also to the quest of reality in the nature of man and the pragmatic test of the democratic idea. When Bacon wrote, "Government is not founded upon demonstration," he spoke the scientific outlook of Jefferson, who believed that social experimentation only could provide conclusive answers to those who denied or supported the capacity of the common man to govern himself.

At Williamsburg Jefferson made the most of new intellectual worlds opening to him. Gifted with enormous energy, he often read and studied fifteen hours a day, neglecting after his first year the social diversions he loved so well. His closest friend, John Page, testified that Jefferson "could tear himself away from his dearest friends, and fly to his studies." Though only seventeen, Jefferson was already a discriminating thinker in his own right, a worthy stimulant to the well-stocked mind of William Small, and soon a companion also to Governor Fauquier and George Wythe, the leading lawyer of the Virginia colony. Professor Small, wrote Jefferson,

introduced me to the acquaintance and familiar table of Governor Fauquier, the ablest man who had ever filled that office. With him, and at his table, Dr. Small & Mr. Wythe, his *amici omnium horarum*, & myself, formed a *partie quarree*, & to the habitual conversations on these occasions I owed much instruction.[3]

Long afterward Jefferson gave these discussions an even higher place in the scale of his development: "At these dinners I have heard more good sense, more rational and philosophical conversations, than in all my life besides. They were truly Attic societies." Coming from a man steeped as Jefferson was in the literature of Greece and Rome, as well as the conversations of Paris intellectuals, this evaluation shows not only the intellectual intensity of Williamsburg life, but also the amazing quality of Jefferson's own mind in his seventeenth and eighteenth years. If it is true that expectations of greatness, images by friends and parents and comrades, are an inevitable prelude to the appearance of the jewel itself, then in these dinners with the flower of Virginia minds, nurtured on two continents, some of Jefferson's own expectations must have had their birth. By the near great he was admitted as a peer and colleague; in their minds it was but a natural step to colonial and national stature.

After two years at William and Mary Jefferson turned to the study of law under the guidance of George Wythe. Setting himself a requirement of fifteen hours a day, he applied himself not less rigorously than had John Milton in the fruitful years at the Horton estate. The books that he recommended to his friend Bernard Moore, and long afterward to John Minor, are guideposts to the growth of Jefferson's beliefs; his subdivisions of a day's labor furnish a hint of the productivity of his intellectual quests. From dawn until eight o'clock, advised Jefferson, the young law student should read the physical and natural sciences, ethics, religion, and philosophy. In these fields he preferred the empiricists and materialists: John Locke he twice recommends, for his *Essay Concerning Human Understanding* and *Conduct of the Mind in Search after Truth;* also Dugald Stewart's *Elements of Philosophy of the Human Mind,* Condorcet's great *Outlines of an Historical View of the Progress of the Human Mind,* and Kames's *Essays on the Principles of Morality and Natural Religion.* From eight o'clock until noon, Jefferson advised the reading of law, the young student concentrating on Coke's *Institutes*—a book reverberating and inflammatory in the 1640's, when John Lilburne cited endless legal arguments against the maltreatment and extralegal imprisonments of commoners like himself.[4]

For the third period of the day, from twelve until one, Jefferson advised political studies, especially Locke, Sidney, Priestley, and Malthus. In the afternoon, continued Jefferson, for the moment forgetting all need of nourishment and relaxation, the young man should concentrate on history, the Greek and Latin authors in the original, Gibbon's *Decline and Fall,* Robertson and Burke on American annals. Lastly, in the evenings, the young student should turn to literature, rhetoric, and oratory, giving ample time to the art of speaking and writing with ease and polish, setting down criticisms of style in felicitous phrasing, imitating the oratorical effects of Cicero and Demosthenes, and at last speaking one's creations to a friendly listener. Interspersed with music and dancing, with canoeing and swimming, with the delights of graceful talk, some such daily program was Jefferson's pathway not only to the capacious riches of his young mind, but also to its poised and pigeonholed order. Behind the man who at thirty-three was to write the great Declaration of Independence lay twenty years of disciplined and purposeful self-expansion. His belief in the immense potential of the common man, first fired in early youth, was now not a faith to him, but a certainty, buttressed not by the Puritan belief in spiritual equality, but by a sober examination of the nature of man in the light of the latest science the world could muster.

III

In Jefferson's day, as in later decades, skepticism about the success of self-government in America was rooted in a pervasive and traditional distrust of the common man's capacity for rational and disinterested action. In Hamilton's mind the interior of man was a tyranny swayed by passions rather than by reason—the chief of these passions, vanity. In his persuasive *Discourses on Davila* John Adams analyzed the dominant drive of man's nature as desire for attention, esteem, praise, expressed in varying levels of emulation, ambition, jealousy, envy, vanity. More cautious than Hamilton in his conclusions, Adams acknowledged that reason often directs man despite the driving winds of passion. He acknowledged also that an unselfish concern for the welfare of others was present in human nature, though not of sufficient vitality to balance the selfish passions. In a few men only, thought Adams, the spirit of benevolence rises to pre-eminent authority. The science of both education and government must be founded, therefore, on the principle of regulating and controlling man's selfish passions, which are essentially the means of his self-preservation. Neither Adams nor Hamilton traced the origins of these passions to environmental effects; they believed them to be rooted ineradicably in man's nature.[5]

In *The Federalist,* as we might expect, Hamilton and Madison were less sanguine about the rational faculties of the common man than Jefferson in the Declaration. If Jefferson spoke for the potential of man, in an environment, as he always insisted, unpoisoned by the rooted evils of Europe, then Hamilton and Madison spoke for the sober actuality of the common man in past ages. One of Hamilton's first statements in *The Federalist* is that "men are ambitious, vindictive, and rapacious." In the United States the authors feared the "abuses of liberty" more than the "abuses of power"; hence their insistence on the curbing of the power of the House of Representatives by a Senate removed from the people's ballot. In popular assemblies the passions of men invariably overwhelm their reason. The larger the assembly the more likely it is to become a mere mob. Indeed, they wrote, "had every Athenian been a Socrates, every Athenian assembly would still have been a mob."[6]

The mass tyranny must at all costs be prevented; yet Madison and Hamilton wanted no class tyranny either; the Constitution protected the people against both. The benign man is not the rule but the exception; on this assumption the makers had anticipated every evil of human nature, every bypath to power that history traced. Possessing unequal faculties, wrote Madison, men invariably will acquire unequal possessions; and the opinions arising from these unequal faculties and possessions will be passionately upheld. To Madison it was axiomatic that the government's first task should be to protect the superior faculties of men, but specifically the faculty of acquiring property. In this discussion Madison assumes that the faculty of acquiring property is not acquired, but innate. Nevertheless, in a remarkable statement about the nature of man, filled with humility and insight, Madison points to the ignorance and uncertainties prevailing in the study of man, from whence arose the difficulty faced by the makers in setting up divisions of power in a constitution of permanent worth. If Hamilton and Madison distrusted the masses, and wished to remove the ultimate source of power from their hands, it cannot be said that they were therefore blind to the other side of the coin of man. If they were not democrats, they were no worshipers of the aristocratic bloodstream. Rather they had proved themselves ready to "rest all our political experiments on the capacity of mankind for self-government." If there was not yet sufficient virtue in man to justify total democracy, he ought at least to be trusted with a republic, in which government assumed a degree of confidence in man's constructive traits. "It belongs to us," wrote Hamilton, "to vindicate the honour of the human race."[7]

In *The Federalist* Hamilton and Madison did not speculate at length on what is innate and what is acquired; it was enough for them that in the record of man's past his passions and vanity had overwhelmed his reason and benevolence. Undoubtedly the more democratic views of Madison moderated the statements of Hamilton; but it is significant of Hamilton's statesmanship that in *The Federalist* he allowed no impulsive denunciations of the people to escape; all is orderly and reasoned, moderate and balanced in thought. How incisive could be Hamilton's reasoning on the nature of man appears in a passage on mechanics and manufacturers. Because of their daily habits, asserts Hamilton, they do not possess "those acquired endowments, without which, in a deliberative assembly, the greatest natural abilities are for the most part useless." Here Hamilton speculates on man's potential growth much as Jefferson himself might have done in a similar analysis. Such a statement is remote indeed from Hamilton's passionate denunciation of the people as a "great beast." Unlike Jefferson, Hamilton remained a city dweller; he never tested his concept of the bestial mass by the psychology of the American frontier.

IV

Against the extreme positions of Hamilton and Adams Jefferson projected from early years the weight of his energy and knowledge, citing examples of man's intellectual and moral plasticity, not only from the ancients, but from English, French, and Indian history, buttressing his arguments with the latest lore of biology, psychology, linguistics, mathematics. Though he did not, like Adams, write a treatise on human nature, no contemporary entered the lists of embattled democrats better armed, either with facts or with powers of leadership, than Thomas Jefferson. To the believers in man's outsweeping intelligence as irresistibly penetrating his institutions, carrying him to new frontiers of achievement in science, government, and social morality, Jefferson brought the dreams of democratic sages old and new. With the resources of these believers he joined the astuteness of a successful lawyer, the grace and charm of Virginia aristocracy, and the most facile, nimble pen that the colonists could muster. Jefferson trusted the common man's capacity to reason—to reason not only for his own interests, but for the interests of the community which might act against his own. The American experiment in self-government and, indeed, every extension of the suffrage was to him an expression of confidence in the common man's rationality. "My hope," he wrote to George Mason, "[is] that we have not laboured in vain and that our experiment will still prove that men can be governed by reason."

More sanguine than Adams and Hamilton in his estimate of man's plasticity, Jefferson often excused human failures by the accidents of circumstance, and hoped for the redemption of men through the persuasion of ideas. "Men are disposed to live honestly," he wrote, "if the means of doing so are open to them." Of the toughness of hereditary limitations he had no doubt; but he was convinced that no limitation was impervious to the modification of an awakening mind. As we cannot expect every tree to bear fruit, asserted Jefferson, so we cannot expect every man to bear virtue. You cannot make a vine out of a brier, but as the brier may be made more useful by cultivation, so the most limited of men may become happier and more useful through the benefits of education. Indeed the process of improving even the mediocre mind and personality may be carried on indefinitely by educational means.

Jefferson's estimate of man's nature was rooted in a dogged realism embracing the advanced biological and psychological researches of his age. Like his French contemporaries, Tracy and Cabanis, and like his ideological enemy, Thomas Hobbes, Jefferson sought a rational, materialistic explanation of man's intellectual equipment, denying the efficacy of intuition, revelation, and all theological assumptions. Man's intellectual machinery Jefferson looked upon as an extension of his nervous system, the central secrets of which would ultimately yield to the probings of science. At eighty-two Jefferson was still an avid follower of the latest probings. On January 8, 1825, only eighteen months before his death, he wrote with elation to John Adams recounting the researches of Flourens on the brains of vertebrate animals. When Flourens removed the cerebrum, the animal continued to live, but lost all sensation and perception. When, from another animal, Flourens removed the cerebellum, leaving the cerebrum intact, the animal retained its understanding and sensory perception, but lost control of its movements, acting like a drunken person. Jefferson concluded that the cerebrum, a part of the nervous system, is the thinking organ. He scoffingly wondered what the devotees of the spirit would say to this. Will they say that the soul leaves the body when the cerebrum is removed? "But all this," concluded Jefferson ironically, reconciled to the nearness of his own demise, "you and I shall know better when we meet again, in another place, and at no distant period." Such unswerving insistence on rational explanation of man's primary nature was rooted in Jefferson's mentality from youth to age. Milton's assumption of man's nobility and dignity derived from God's image was to Jefferson merely a noble superstition. Man's genius was rooted in the flesh-and-blood structure of his nervous system.[8]

In his emphasis on sensory reactions as the basis of all ideas and all knowledge, Jefferson represented the most advanced scientific thinking of his age. Accepting the same biological approach as Hobbes, Jefferson and his fellow-intellectuals, like Locke before them, rejected Hobbes's conviction that the drive of self-preservation would remain perpetually dominant. Hobbes assumed from his premises the necessity of an orderly authoritarian society, every man uncomplainingly in his place, preferring the security of injustice to the perpetual struggle for a higher place in the social order. But in Jefferson's day no great intellectual came forth to uphold Hobbes's banner; the great thinkers in the science spoke unhesitatingly for self-government, for progress, if not for man's perfectibility. A materialistic psychology was the basis of their democratic fervor, their unswerving confidence in man's limitless capacity to surpass his intellectual, scientific, political, and spiritual achievements.

The conception of sensations as the foundation of human development appears, with close parallels, in the French intellectuals whom Jefferson knew so well, Cabanis, Condorcet, and Tracy. A century before, Locke had stated their position succinctly in the opening chapters of his *Essay Concerning Human Understanding*. He had rejected unequivocally all possibility of innate ideas, placing the origin of all learning with the senses alone: "Let us then suppose the mind to be, as we say, white paper, void of all characters, without any ideas." From sensations "all those sublime thoughts which tower above the clouds . . . take their rise and footing." In his *Rapports du physique et du moral de l'homme*, which Jefferson denominated "the most profound of all human compositions," Cabanis was equally categorical, denying any separation of sensory and spiritual action. Even in the first sentence of his great work, *Outlines of an Historical View of the Progress of the Human Mind*, Condorcet expressed the same assumptions, compressing the conclusions of Locke and Cabanis. Indeed, wrote Condorcet, the first great advance in thinking was Aristotle's conclusion that all ideas, even the airiest abstractions and intellectual flights, originate in man's sensations.[9]

Among the English intellectuals with whose thought Jefferson's materialistic psychology had much in common was William Godwin, whose *Enquiry Concerning Political Justice* so profoundly influenced his generation. To Godwin, as to his French contemporaries, the root of all experience was sensory. In the English biologist Hartley he found the most satisfying description of sensory action, which he summarizes in the *Enquiry*. Like the strings of a musical instrument, both body and brain of the human being are sensitive to vibrations. Vibrations striking the senses are relayed instantaneously to the brain, whereupon a second set of vibrations shoots out to the various parts of the body. Unlike Godwin, Cabanis, and Hume, Jefferson made no elaborate study of the human mind; he was not a trained philosopher or psychologist. In the spirit of scientific, rational inquiry, however, he was one with them; he sought the answers to his main questions about man in the most advanced and learned thinkers, repudiating theological and philosophical traditions for the new science.

V

From this entirely rational concept of man's nature Jefferson wavered, however, on one critical issue. He was at least a partial believer in an inherent "moral sense." Man is aware of his rationality, aware of his own and others' physical needs, of the dangers he must undergo, of the choices he must make. He has a "moral sense," a recognition of relative kindness and cruelty, fair play and foul, freedom and repression. He recognizes the pleasure derived from generosity. "Nature," wrote Jefferson, "hath implanted in our breasts a love of others, a sense of duty to them, a moral instinct, in short, which prompts us irresistibly to feel and succor their distresses." The moral sense is as much a part of man as his hearing or seeing, as his legs and arms. Like an arm or a leg, it may grow strong with exercise. Was this moral sense extrasensory, or was it rooted in the nervous structure of the brain? It is apparent that Jefferson believed it to be rooted in the physical organism before birth. Experience, he felt, can modify the moral sense, but it cannot create it.

In his concept of the moral sense Jefferson assumed, as did David Hume, that man's passions lean to generosity as well as to egotism and self-preservation. Moral distinctions, wrote Hume, arise not from the reason, but from the passions. We are generous because it gives us pleasure, both physical and intellectual. We pity and sympathize with people because we see that they are like us, and it is easy to pity ourselves. To see others in distress makes us uneasy; to see others happy makes us joyful. "There is no spectacle," wrote Hume, "so fair and beautiful as a noble and generous action; nor any which gives us more abhorrence than one that is cruel and treacherous. . . . To have the sense of virtue, is nothing but to *feel* a satisfaction of a particular kind." Influenced by Hume in his analysis of human motives, William Godwin also assumed that a moral sense is rooted in spontaneous pleasure. Repeated often enough, the passion becomes habitual, especially if approved by the reason, and eventually becomes almost second nature. Jefferson made no such minute analysis of passion or the moral sense as derived from pleasure. In his conviction, however, that the moral sense had its origin in spontaneous emotion rather than in intellectual exercise, Jefferson was speaking the convictions of eminent contemporaries whose special learning he could not match. "The love of what is good and true," wrote Destutt Tracy, "is a real passion . . . and it is as energetic and more constant than any other."[10]

Though the moral sense was present in all men, its quality, thought Jefferson, was extremely variable and malleable. Not only does it vary among men of the same community at any one time; it varies also from country to country and age to age, depending on the level of refinement and culture. Experiences of individuals and societies drastically reshape the moral sense. Among savage tribes, notes Jefferson, the moral sense justified the execution of captives; but this penalty more advanced societies reduced to slavery, and still later ones to a ransom. Here Jefferson again postulates the drastic effect of environmental pressures upon the human organism; even that quality which he regarded as most deeply rooted in man's nature was sharply modifiable by sensory impressions and the resulting reflections. The accumulated thought of one society and the advances that it has made in refinements or morality make their imprint on the minds of succeeding generations.

Did he believe that a modification of the moral sense in the fathers will be inherited by their children? Jefferson did not elaborate his conception of human nature sufficiently to answer this question. In one place he writes, it is true, that "moral and physical qualities ... are transmissible in a certain degree"; but he leaned to the calculable and observable pressures of environment upon the human organism rather than to conjectures about its debts to heredity. In his thinking about human nature Jefferson was pragmatic, observing effects rather than delving for first causes. He looked to education to supply the defects of nature.

VI

To Jefferson the passions and sensations of man's nature were less malleable than the powers of his intellect. Man's capacity for expanding the use of his reason in the development of special talent and genius, in scientific researches, in the refinement of the moral sense, in the progress of self-government, was limited only by his energies and the resources of his intellectual environment. Jefferson's constant reiteration of his confidence in the people as the repository of political power was in reality an expression of his faith in the reasoning powers of the common man. He assumed with Godwin that "democracy restores to man a consciousness of his value, and teaches him, by the removal of authority and oppression, to listen only to the suggestions of reason."

VII

Jefferson's concept of man as essentially a plastic organism, changed irresistibly though not equally by the impact of ideas, accounts for his lifelong labors for the utilization of educational machinery. In his educational blueprints Jefferson did not envision a utopia of intellectual equality; he assumed that each person would yield in some degree to the forces of an intellectual atmosphere. Though every man is limited, he is also teachable. In the elementary schools he planned, Jefferson thought history was the decisive subject, the main aim being "to enable every man to judge for himself what will secure or endanger his freedom." In talents, though not in rights, men are born unequal; the "most precious gift of nature" is the man of talent and genius. The function of education is not to allow this man to be submerged by an unfavorable environment, but to uncover him to the world, to enable him to take the place in society to which his talents entitle him. Geniuses, whom nature fertilizes as frequently among the poor as among the rich, "must be raked from the rubbish" and sent to the university, there to prepare themselves to lead the cause of the people: "Worth and genius would thus have been sought out from every condition of life, and completely prepared by education for defeating the competition of wealth and birth for public trusts." Jefferson objected to the artificial inequalities imposed by family and inherited wealth, not to those decreed by the accidents of heredity. That government is best which elevates, not its *pseudo-aristoi*, as Jefferson called them, but its natural *aristoi*, to the highest offices available.

So malleable, then, is man, that even the outcropping of genius is a process to be nurtured and accelerated by the rational use of available forces. In his analysis of genius and the frequency of genius, Jefferson, like Turgot before him, sought illumination in time, circumstance, and intellectual climate, rather than in the vagaries of genetic characters. If Corneille had lived his life as a plowman or Racine had been born among the Hurons of Canada, or in a less intellectual century, their genius would not have flowered. To Buffon's and Reynal's deprecation of American achievements he replied with the delineation of historical parallels. If, as Reynal insists, America has not produced a single great poet, the deficiency is not to be explained by the partiality of nature: the Americans also will produce a great poet when their society is as old as that of Homer's Greece or Virgil's Rome, Voltaire's France or Shakespeare's England. In other fields, Jefferson contended, America, with only three million people, has been productive of genius: in war, a Washington; in physics, a Franklin; in astronomy, a Rittenhouse. France, with her twenty millions, should have six times as many geniuses, six Washingtons and Franklins; and England, with her ten million, three times as many. Though she is "but a child of yesterday," America has already shown marks of genius in many fields: war, philosophy, sculpture, art, oratory, and government. In no field of achievement is America wanting in genius, even now.[11]

In his answer to Buffon Jefferson illuminates his position on man's inherent capacities and the frequency of genius with a pertinent query: Is nature really partial to a particular race of men? Can Buffon really believe she is partial to one side of the Atlantic? If so, his reason has been seduced by his eloquence. To Jefferson races and countries were potentially equal in their capacity for the production of geniuses; the difference in productivity lay in the intensity and length of their civilization, not in gifts of nature. The American Indian was not, insisted Jefferson, inherently inferior to the white colonist; the circumstances under which the Indians lived did not encourage the production of genius. In advancement of civilized customs they should be compared to the European tribes before the extension of the Roman Empire north of the Alps. How many great inventors, poets, mathematicians, had Europe then produced? From that day Europe required sixteen centuries to produce a Newton. In such perspective, not in suppositions about nature's favoritism, should the achievements of the Indians be weighed. Even in their comparatively primitive society, insisted Jefferson, the Indians had already produced the eloquence of a Logan; already they had shown gifts in painting and sculpture; and in their treatment of the white man they had shown a magnanimity superior to his.

VIII

Notwithstanding his dominant belief in the essential equality of races and peoples in their capacity for intellectual and political advancement, Jefferson was convinced that the inferiority of the

Negroes was the indelible mark of nature. In his *Notes on the State of Virginia* he treats the topic at uneasy length. Of his moral and aesthetic objections to the Negroes remaining in America, Jefferson first brings forth the difference of color. This blackness, together with a less graceful figure and less abundant hair, makes the black man an aesthetic anomaly. Jefferson objects to the black man's odor, to his sexual ardor, to his carefree wasting of midnight hours, to his "dull and tasteless" imagination, to the predominance of his sensations over his reflections, to his failure to improve his social habits after association with the whites. In music, grants Jefferson, the Negroes are more gifted often than the whites; but who can yet say they can compose a melody of great length or a harmony of complicated structure? Even their miseries have given birth to no poet, no great painter or sculptor, no sign of native genius comparable to that of the Indians. Not slavery but nature has decreed their place in the scale of men.

Led slowly and reluctantly into his belief in the natural inferiority of Negroes, Jefferson was eager for a scientific refutation of his conclusion. In a letter to the Negro mathematician, Benjamin Banneker (August 30, 1791), Jefferson wrote as follows: "No body wishes more than I do to see such proofs as you exhibit, that nature has given to our black brethren, talents equal to those of the other colors of men, and that the appearance of a want of them is owing merely to the degraded condition of their existence." On the same day Jefferson wrote to Condorcet, praising Banneker and speaking of him as "a very worthy and respectable member of society." "I shall be delighted," he said, "to see these instances of moral eminence so multiplied as to prove that the want of talents observed in them is merely the effect of their degraded condition."[12]

Eager as always for experimentation, and unwilling to draw conclusions from the various Quaker experiments in manumission, Jefferson projected the settlement (never realized) of his own slaves on farms of fifty acres each, intermingled with imported Germans similarly provided. The children of blacks so reared, thought Jefferson, would be sound citizens; about the fathers thus transplanted from slavery to freedom he was less sanguine. Like Tracy, Godwin, and Cabanis, Jefferson thought that man's nature was shaped primarily by the numberless, varied pressures of his environment. He realized, as these statements show, that his attitude toward the Negroes, however inescapable to him, was a contradiction of his belief in the essential plasticity of human nature.

To Jefferson the only equitable solution to the slavery problem was the emancipation and deportation of the Negroes. Whatever their talents, their right to freedom was to him unequivocal. In 1784 Congress defeated by one vote his proposal to exclude slavery from the territories forever. Of this signal defeat Jefferson wrote: "The voice of a single individual . . . would have prevented this abominable crime from spreading itself over the new country. Thus we see the fate of millions unborn hanging on the tongue of one man, & heaven was silent in that awful moment!" The opponents of slavery he denominated as "friends to the rights of human nature."

On August 7, 1787, Jefferson wrote to Richard Price that the cause of emancipation "is gaining daily recruits, from the influx . . . of young men grown, and growing up." Trained for the greater part at William and Mary, these young men, Jefferson thought, would fall under the benevolent influence of his old teacher, George Wythe. To Jefferson it was incomprehensible that men should sacrifice unbelievably for their own freedom, and then keep their fellows in bondage. He exhorted himself to patience with inexplicable human nature. A God of justice would awaken to the distress of the Negroes, "our suffering brethren," conquering the oppressors with light or exterminating them with his thunder. Emancipation would come in the march of time; but near the end of his life the Missouri Compromise warned Jefferson, "like a fire-bell in the night," that the shattering of the Union might prove to be its consequence.

Jefferson's analysis of the effect of slavery on the master and his family illuminates his conception of the malleability of human nature. The positions of master and slave encouraged in the one tyrannical passions, in the other a degrading subservience. In vent-

ing his anger upon a helpless slave, the master forgot the welfare
of his children; he forgot their plastic and imitative minds:

The parent storms, the child looks on, catches the lineaments of wrath,
puts on the same airs in the circle of smaller slaves, gives a loose to his
worst of passions, and thus nursed, educated, and daily exercised in
tyranny, cannot but be stamped by it with odious peculiarities. The man
must be a prodigy who can retain his manners and morals undepraved
by such circumstances.[13]

IX

Jefferson's materialistic conception of man's nature prepared him
for stupidity, crassness, deceit, fraud, and the thousand dark depths,
profound or trivial, to which his fellow-men retreated under the
merciless rod of self-preservation. The last-minute attempts of the
Federalists to retain a portion of their power through federal judge-
ships did not destroy, as it well might have, his affection for John
Adams or his staunch kind among the opposition. Nor did the
conspiracy to place Aaron Burr in the President's chair plunge him
into cynicism or despair. In both the heroic and the trivial decisions
he knew the dire likelihood of human failure; but this likelihood
he counted as the almost impersonal opposition of storms and rough
weather to the growing of corn and the harvesting of wheat.

To effect the printing and publication of Tracy's great work,
A Treatise on Political Economy, Jefferson in his retirement toiled
with unflagging persistence. As he wrote to Du Pont de Nemours
(August 3, 1816), he first gave Tracy's manuscript to William
Duane for translation and publication. But two years passed, punc-
tuated by Jefferson's urgent letters and Duane's excuses, before he
returned the manuscript and his translation, saying he was unable
to publish it. When a printer named Ritchie said he could not print
the translation immediately, Jefferson gave it to a Mr. Milligan,
saying he would revise Duane's translation where necessary. When
Jefferson began work on the revision in June, 1815, he found the
translation very faulty, Duane having no deep comprehension of
either French or English. For two or three months he spent five

hours a day on it, sending it to Milligan April 6. Milligan wrote that he was unable to begin work until July 4, 1816; but on July 21, when Jefferson wrote him last, he had not yet begun. The volume finally appeared in 1817. In the five-year series of disappointments in editor and printers, Jefferson never for a moment wavered in his conviction of the project's worth in influencing American minds; nor was he dismayed by the failures and excuses and slipshod work of the men he trusted. In Jefferson's mind faith in the ultimate pressure of ideas always rose more powerful than his disillusionment with his fellows; and even his disillusionment was reluctant and elastic, balanced always by his awareness of the boundless reaches of ignorance.

X

Though a less systematic student of human nature, Jefferson was a more practical, realistic one than Godwin and Condorcet. Whereas Condorcet and Godwin wrote for the ages to follow, Jefferson confined his speculation to the foreseeable future. Godwin maintained that human beings are perfectible, that no individual can resist the force of truth—that error, indeed, carries in its heart the seed of its own annihilation. Similarly Condorcet rejected any limits to the improvement of man except the continued existence of the earth, basing his conclusions upon the historical march of the sciences in banishing superstition and the accompanying development of human talents and insight. This prophecy was too sanguine and enthusiastic for Jefferson's observations to sustain. If his ideas impelled him to visions, his bitter experiences with human frailty allowed him to calculate uncannily the measure of change his contemporaries would absorb. "There is a snail-paced gait," he wrote, "for the advance of new ideas on the general mind, under which we must acquiesce." Jefferson knew the tenacious resistance of minds shaped early with prejudice and superstition. The long stride in his vision he was ever ready to reduce to a short step on the solid earth.

To William Godwin the voluntary distribution of wealth would be the inevitable result of the pressure of enlightened ideas on the privileged and propertied classes. "If, in any society, wealth be estimated at its true value," he wrote, "and accumulation and monopoly be regarded as the seals of mischief, injustice and dishonour . . . inequality of conditions will be destroyed," not by regulation, or coercion, but by "a revolution of opinions." But Jefferson saw in the future no such disinterested relinquishment for the sake of the spiritual benefits inherent in the abolition of poverty. He dreaded the increase of wealth and the power of wealth in the new America. The influence of accumulation on human nature he measured with a canny realism: "I have not observed men's honesty to increase with their riches." Reluctantly he granted that rogues climb to high places with more agility and skill than honest men. In legislatures, he wrote to John Adams, men of wealth would always find their places and make their power felt. Jefferson did not anticipate the voluntary abolition of poverty by the rich or the conquest of their spirits by the power of ideas. For the immediate American future he counted on the power of the many common men to frustrate domination by the wealthy and privileged few.

With Condorcet Jefferson shared, however, the conviction that natural sciences would help break the chains of moral and political superstition. Freedom Jefferson called "the first-born daughter of science." On this point Condorcet was much more explicit than Jefferson. "All the errors in politics and morals," he wrote, "are founded upon philosophical mistakes, which themselves, are connected with physical errors." The disciplined reasoning required in mathematics and science would demolish the flimsy structure of social superstitions. How much was still unknown! How many of nature's phenomena were unwatched, unrecorded! How many practical arts, how many chemical combinations, that might enrich and sustain man's life! Like Bacon in *Novum Organum*, like Turgot in his *Notes on Universal History*, Condorcet was certain that the world trembled on the threshold of miraculous discoveries and inventions, all to enhance man's comforts and delights. What folly, he averred, to confuse existence with happiness, to believe only in "encumbering the earth with useless and wretched mortals"! Now for the first time the real happiness of man through the marvels of science would become a reality. With the march of science, moreover, would proceed the discovery of man. As yet man really knew little of himself, insisted Condorcet—of his capacity for genius, of his rights and duties, of co-operation with his fellows.

Jefferson was one with Condorcet and Godwin, moreover, in his conviction that the impact of ideas on the human mind was ultimately irresistible. He believed with Destutt Tracy that "the happiness of man, is proportionate to the mass of his intelligence, and that the one and the other does and can increase indefinitely." The corruption of wealth, the superstitions of theology, the blindness of ignorance, the degradations of poverty would inevitably yield to the dictates of reason and the pressure of the common man's power. The process of enlightenment he believes more likely to succeed in America, with men accustomed to think for themselves, "than with minds nourished in error, and vitiated and debased, as in Europe, by ignorance, indigence and oppression." Through education, through freedom of the press, through the pressure of free inquiry, civilization would emerge triumphant over barbarism. "Enlighten the people generally," he wrote in a sanguine moment, "and tyranny and oppressions of body and mind will vanish like evil spirits at the dawn of day."[14]

XI

Jefferson's belief in the beneficent reaches of human nature he grounded in part on the enormous enlargement of man's intellectual environment through the medium of the printed word. Taking no stock in eugenic transformation of man's nature, he visualized the enormous pressure that reading, discussion, and education might have on his fellow-men. For the dispersal of knowledge he counted, like his fellow-reformers, on the magic power of the printing press. Each new book, thought Condorcet, was an immortal warrior fighting in the armies of truth and freedom, ultimately invincible. The printing press alone had made the march of liberty irreversible. "Where the press is free," wrote Jefferson, "and every man able to read, all is safe."

Jefferson did not anticipate, however, the new power and concentration of wealth that the industrialization of his country would make inevitable. He did not foresee the gradual canalization of the agencies of enlightenment into the hands of the enemies he dreaded. He did not anticipate the inevitable shift of newspaper propaganda power into the hands of a propertied class more powerful than any of his day. Nor did he realize to what extent concentration of wealth would frustrate, even in his own state, the educational policies he had so ardently championed.

XII

In terms of the potentialities of a democratic society in America, however, Jefferson was the most realistic critic of human nature among his contemporaries. As Joseph Priestley had recommended in his *Lectures on History,* Jefferson sought to make facts and scientific data the basis of his conclusions about man's nature. He was eager to dispel the central myth that had emerged from centuries of aristocratic assumptions: human nature is fixed in essence before birth by the genetic patterns of one's ancestors. In its place he set forth a belief in what we might call the democratic myth of a plastic organism shaped in essence by the patterns of the world in which it is born. In testing both myths, however, Jefferson sought only the verifiable evidence that to him was the essence of the scientific method.

His close and accurate knowledge of history made him aware not only of those times and countries that had fertilized genius, but also of the reaches of human nature, both repugnant and sublime. From his long leadership in the colonies, from his experience as a practicing lawyer, from the interminable discussions, debates, and intrigues of political life, he had learned the perennial pressures of egotism and vanity. He could gauge the precise point at which the visions of a man's youth would yield to the power of his interests or the pressure of his fellows.

If to trust human nature was folly and frustration, to trust it too little was a repudiation of reason and persuasion. The times were propitious for the impact of new ideas. A new country lay formless, awaiting the hands of a thousand bold sculptors. As the aristocratic notions of Europe moved west from the coastal cities, they faced the impregnable psychology of men with a new sense of power and with land of their own under their feet. In such a new elastic land, where the meanest citizen, in Jefferson's view, was less miserable than nineteen million Frenchmen, the Revolution was daily justifying the propaganda of equality. The common man was bold, fearless, resourceful, as never before in the Western world. From the vital stuff of the common man had already emerged men of uncommon attainments: Madison, Washington, Rush, Logan, Franklin, Banneker, Jefferson himself. Not in birth, but in growth, lay the genius of man and the illimitable greatness of the American future. To the common man Jefferson therefore addressed himself; in this man, his expansive reason, his plasticity, his inevitable response to images of enlightenment, lay Jefferson's faith in the new land and the principles of his great Declaration.

The question of whether this faith was vain and hollow the years have left unanswered and some will say unanswerable. But in Jefferson it was a faith shaped slowly and surely, born of a frontier boyhood, tested in a mind devoid of superstition and steeled to utter honesty, and finally justified by the most profound knowledge of natural and humanistic science that his age could communicate.

II

The Plastic Mind:
Tocqueville and Horace Mann

We have no practical belief that the human intellect, under a course of judicious culture, can be made to grow brighter and brighter, like the rising sun, until it shall shed its light over the dark problems of humanity, and put ignorance and superstition to flight.

—Mann

In the United States society has no infancy, but it is born into man's estate.

—Tocqueville

LIKE Jefferson before them, Horace Mann and Alexis de Tocqueville sought to apply scientific means, however crude and imperfect, to their study of human nature. Unable to pierce the mystery of genetic inheritance, and dissatisfied with the concept of destiny fixed at conception, they pursued the habit of close, persistent observation of the thousand blows, rough or slight, blunt or subtle, that play upon the human organism from the world without. Whereas Tocqueville sought to measure and assess the impact of institutions, of manners and customs, of economic forces on human nature, Horace Mann labored toward a quantitative as well as a qualitative measurement of the forces of teachers, books, and ideas on the plastic minds of the young. To Tocqueville the institution of slavery had identified blackness with inferiority irretrievably in the minds of both North and South, white and black; he could not anticipate a time when its effects would be nullified and overwhelmed by enlightened action. Both Tocqueville and

44

Mann rested their scientific credo on the belief that no cause is without its effect, no word without its influence, no image of cruelty or kindness without its impact on the beholder, no institution without its grooves of force over the minds of the people it enfolds. If you believe that corn will grow under cultivation, asserted Mann, or that a stone will fall, you must also believe that the human mind is ultimately unable to resist the force of education; that indeed, if such force is accelerated and strengthened, the human mind can banish ignorance and superstition from the world.

Tocqueville, it is true, could not concur with such utopian hopes in either ends or means. He was content to observe the forces of society at work in his own time, to evaluate the depth and duration of their effect on the manners and customs of the population. In the tracing of these forces, Tocqueville labored with eye and mind miraculously detached from both democratic hopes still unfulfilled and the myths of his aristocratic forebears. This indeed was his genius, enabling him to compare with an acute, impartial judgment the social strains and upheavals, the manners and customs of aristocratic Europe with the rough democracy in America. If this was not the science of the mathematician applied to human beings, still Tocqueville's methods embodied an uncanny insight that cast a long gleam toward the science of man still struggling to be born.

"Aristocratic nations," wrote Tocqueville, "are naturally too apt to narrow the scope of human perfectibility; democratic nations, to expand it beyond reason." Such a democratic nation was the America of the 1830's; in such men as Mann, Alcott, Emerson, and Channing it roused hopes of a creative citizenry remote from realization a century later. However necessary the satisfactions of the economic man might be to creative flowering, many Americans to Tocqueville were too rudely stamped by the process of making a living for the seeds of their genius to sprout and grow. To the Americans, it is true, a full stomach was not enough. Though they hungered for the satisfactions of the flesh, they reached perennially for the waters of the spirit, driven by fresh envy and inspired by new dreams. New patterns of poetry, abundant inventions, the con-

fident extension of human reason into every field: these were the
too infrequent fruits of a turbulent democracy. The very nature of
America's restless life, its fluid economic forces, its incitement of
new hopes both social and financial, its rise and fall of rich and
poor, its lightning-like elevation and debasement of human fortunes:
all these, insisted Tocqueville, enforced an adaptability without
parallel in the history of the human organism. The imagination of
the poor was haunted by the comforts of the world, that of the rich
by the specter of sudden disaster. Wealth and movement, restlessness and equality—could they yield in time Athenian perfection
among millions of men? In the sober view of Tocqueville democratic nations expected too much perfection from the nature of
man. Yet Americans gave him pause. Never before had he visualized
the sudden mining of so much gold in human beings.

II

Of the thousands of Americans who envisaged an increased flow
of benevolence and creative talent in the American scene, Horace
Mann was the most versatile and convincing exponent of ways and
means. Like Jefferson, he asserted that the plastic free mind of
childhood can be poured into any mold; like Jefferson, he believed
that the mind of man, unlike anger, hunger, and the sexual drive,
is capable of infinite expansion, however limited by the genetic
structure. In Horace Mann we find exemplified the extension of
Jefferson's profound faith in education. To Mann the free common
school (initiated by Massachusetts in 1642) was the most influential
discovery in the history of human progress. To enfold impartially
all children in its bosom, to direct their energies toward constructive citizenship, stirring their creative powers to crystallization,
shaping their conduct to the social will, counterpoising the books
and ideals of the schoolroom against the pressures of a competitive
society—this was the purpose of the common school in the dreams
of Horace Mann. For twenty years he traced the details of his
educational blueprints, affirming the realism of his premises, point-

ing to ways and means as practical and sure, he said, as the process of manufacturing. "Our means of education," he wrote, "are the grand machinery by which the 'raw material' of human nature can be worked up into inventors and discoverers, into skilled artisans and scientific farmers, into scholars and jurists, into the founders of benevolent institutions." Under the sunlight of persistent and improved common-school teaching, the shadows of poverty, crime, and ignorance would dwindle and fade.[1]

Mann was born in Franklin, Massachusetts, May 4, 1796, the son of strongly reserved parents accustomed to long labor on the farm. Mann's childhood was not a happy one. From early years he kept his feelings to himself, never told his mother of physical sufferings. "By nature I was exceedingly elastic and buoyant," he afterward wrote, "but the poverty of my parents subjected me to continual privations. I believe in the rugged nursery of toil, but she nursed me too much."

To the Mann family, hell was a living reality pictured with Calvinistic thoroughness. When Mann was thirteen, his father died. At the funeral of his brother, who was drowned at twelve years of age, Horace Mann first began to doubt the depravity of human nature. Rejecting solace for admonition, the minister speculated on the destiny of the brother's soul, whereupon Horace's mother let forth a sob he never forgot. If his sister or his mother might go to hell, he thought, any other place would be a hell to him. Henceforth, even as a boy, Mann rejected the theory of depravity. More important, he began a serious study of the nature of man in its creative potentialities. In September, 1816, he entered the sophomore class of Brown University. Three years later, when he was graduated at the head of his class, Mann chose a subject for his valedictory address significant of his intellectual probings, "The Progressive Character of the Human Race."

Admitted to the bar in December, 1823, Mann became a member of the Massachusetts House of Representatives in 1827 and was elected to the State Senate in 1833. As a member of the Senate, Mann was responsible for the law creating the State Board of Education, the secretaryship of which appeared so important that he accepted the position at a small salary. In 1837 he began a series of twelve annual reports on education in the state of Massachusetts, reports rich and provocative in their analysis of human nature as a basis of his educational philosophy. In 1848, after initiating far-reaching reforms in common-school instructions, Mann resigned his position to take a seat in Congress made vacant by the death of John Quincy Adams. As a Whig of antislavery views, Mann criticized Webster's speech of March 7, 1850, and ultimately became a co-worker of Theodore Parker and Charles Sumner in antislavery agitation. In 1850 he was defeated as Free Soil candidate for governor of Massachusetts. Assuming the presidency of Antioch College in 1853, Mann served for six years before his death on August 2, 1859.

Mann looked upon children as pliable organisms of tremendous energy, ethically neutral at birth. To train the mind of the organism was not enough. The common school must direct its emotional and physical energy into constructive behavior. Was there one child in a hundred who could not thus be redeemed, whose energies could not be channeled into useful or creative directions? Mann doubted it. He was reluctant to admit, indeed, that the deficiencies of any child were irremediable. To document his argument of the potentialities of the common school, Mann proposed in 1847 the question that he had already answered in his own mind: "What proportion or percentage of those under your own care . . . could be turned out the blessing, and not the bane, the honor, and not the scandal, of society?" To this question, sent to a number of experienced teachers, the answers were remarkably unanimous: one teacher wrote, "substantially the whole population"; another declared that there were "scarcely one or two percent of really incorrigible members that the common school could not mold."[2]

Mann envisaged the common school, then, as the machinery of universal redemption from ignorance and antisocial action. He and his fellow-idealists were not content with nature's aristocratic off-shoots, with a few exceptional men among the lumpish mass. When

Emerson said, "I do not wish any mass at all, but honest men only, lovely, sweet, accomplished women only," he spoke the aim of Horace Mann, much as he distrusted the cramping pressures of co-operative enterprise. In the new era the common school was to be the grand machinery shaping a whole population of upright citizens as its inevitable product. Mann's logic, like that of all democratic idealists, was more accurate in tracing the effect of ideas on human nature than the thousand subtle stampings of egotism and survival.

If Mann embodied in his dream the ever-shattered and ever-renewed hopes of the democratic educationist, he spoke also for an experience pattern already deeply embedded in American life. In 1835 the free common schools of Massachusetts were already two centuries old. By that year, though one-fourth of America's population was still illiterate (compared to one-third of the men and one-half the women of England), free elementary schools, rough and imperfect as they were, played an inextinguishable role in every settlement, their power enhanced by the westward step of the pioneer and the confident new states.

IV

To Mann the raw material of the human cargo was neither bright with angelic benevolence nor dark with the familiar depravity of Calvinist imagery. In the scales of justice and injustice, sin and righteousness, the nature of the young child inclined neither left nor right; it awaited the touch of the sculpturing parents, the thoughtless friend, the word fitly spoken, the handshake of a tempting, sinister world. To both the benign and malevolent fingers of the earth it yielded as clay to the potter's wheel, now black with wild passion, like Plato's dark horse, now aglow with charity, transformed anew with the ebb and flow of the potter's moods. Children "do not come into life barbed and fanged against each other"; on meeting for the first time, they do not salute each other with blows of the fist. Yet children are not angels, either. No Platonist like Emerson or Alcott, Mann made no claims of the child's innate nobility, or recollections of perfection stamped indelibly in the prenatal chambers of his personality, wanting only freedom of expression to scatter light. Even those with the bleakest outlook on human nature will grant that the young are less hateful than the old; will admit, too, that all too soon the world poisons them. If the child has no genius for unselfish action, neither is he stamped with the horns of the goat, the leer of the miser, or the acquisitive snarl of the criminal.

The child bears in his organism, however, certain propensities and appetites that may lead in their ultimate expression to violent antisocial extremes. Necessary not only to self-preservation and race-preservation, but also to happiness, these appetites require normal satisfaction if sustenance of the mind and spirit is to be maintained. Hunger is such an appetite, and sex, and the body's demand for warmth. Then, too, continues Mann, each child has a feeling of self-importance, self-respect, a desire for possession of what pleases his fancy, and a desire for approval. These appetites are man's normal equipment; they possess a social and ethical validity. Yet each of them may be expanded to disastrous or absurd proportions, like the cupidity of Alexander and Napoleon's quest for fame. Pride built the Pyramids; avarice, the slave trade. Sex has led to excesses shocking to the most hardened detractor of human nature. These appetites and propensities, blind to all considerations except their own release, are necessary to the survival of the race and the well-being of each person. But on their uninhibited extension hang the disasters of mankind. Most human sorrows have originated in these appetites, incipient monsters that each child brings with him into the world.

Mann contended, as did Tocqueville, that a democratic society offers innumerable encouragements to these antisocial extremes. Not only hope of pecuniary gain, desire for success, love of money and comforts, but also political ambition and love of power are expanded to most dangerous lengths in a country which has broken its old restraints and has not yet established new conventions. In the Old World the pressures of tyrannical rule and rigid enforcement had built a harsh and natural barrier to human expression. In the New World, with this restraint removed, with each man free to express his vice as well as his good will, restraints of the inner man must be expanded through benevolent instruction. As in Europe, under the old tyrannies, physical education had strengthened men for warfare, so in the New World education of the mind and spirit must prepare them for the arts of peace and the duty of self-government. But the art of self-government must begin in childhood, with the training of children to direct their own moral and social destiny; otherwise it is absurd to expect self-guidance from adult citizens.

The appetites and propensities implanted by nature, however, are the stuff of virtue and unselfishness, as well as the raw materials of destructive egotism. As the hand of man may break into a safe or sculpture a statue, so may the hunger with which he is born drive him, at extreme points, either to homicide or to conviviality. "Each one has the capacity of immeasurable virtue or vice. . . . Each soul has a pinion by which it may soar to the highest empyrean, or swoop downwards to the Tartarean abyss." Whether or not a man uses the raw material of his nature to destructive or constructive ends depends inevitably upon the pressures of his environment. This is the central teaching of Horace Mann.

In educational philosophy Mann was a mechanist, altogether convinced that the child reflects in his growing years the complex and frequently contradictory influences of his home, his school, and his friends. By understanding the cause and effect reactions, the educator can bring the pressure of ideas to bear in sufficient force to overwhelm the vicious effects of contradictory pressures. To Mann, then, the triumph of enlightenment over barbarism meant only a marshaling of superior forces, of which the common school was the surest co-ordinator, the skilful teacher the most delicate instrument. Attacked with sufficient time and persistence, no set of vicious habits acquired by the child in his early years could maintain supremacy over his conduct. Within the framework of the

common school Mann would concentrate the forces of enlightenment and unselfish example. The teacher should lead by persuasion,
not compel by force. He should arouse the curiosity of his pupils,
opening their minds to noble patterns, their hearts to the tug of
benevolence.

V

The child is born alone and helpless in a world of conflicting
and interweaving pressures. The very food he eats, the daily care
of his body, sustains or retards the health of his frame. After he
enters school, the improvement or decline of his health is determined in part by the physical conditions of the classroom. No topic
of education was more vital to Mann than the opportunity of the
classroom to assist in manufacturing health, the most precious commodity in the world. As a supplement to his first annual report of
1837, he drew up at great length an indictment of unsanitary and
uncomfortable schoolhouses, revealing in minute detail the requirements of healthful lighting, seating, ventilation, heating, location
of school buildings, provisions for sanitary water supply, and even
providing at the end a sketch for a schoolhouse, the plan of which
he considered superior. In each schoolroom children and teacher
should practice cleanliness and elegance; unless the room is dusted
daily and washed often, the children cannot keep their books or
clothes clean.

To dramatize the vicious effects of unsanitary schoolrooms,
Mann quotes in his 1843 report a description of an English school
from the report of a Parliamentary committee:

In a garret, up three pair of dark, broken stairs, was a common day-
school, with *forty* children, in a compass of ten feet by nine. On a perch,
forming a triangle with a corner of the room, sat a cock and two hens;
under the stump bed, immediately beneath, was a dog-kennel, in the
occupation of three black terriers, whose barking, added to the noise of
the children and the cackling of the fowls on the approach of a stranger,
was almost deafening. There was only one small window, at which sat
the master, obstructing three-fourths of the light. There are several

schools in the same neighborhood which are in the same condition, filthy in the extreme.[3]

To magnify the importance of health as a critical environmental determinant, Mann expounded at great length the necessity for superior teaching of physiology. To Mann health was a social wealth that could be manufactured by parents, teachers, and children working together, an absolute necessity to a cheerful disposition, to physical labor, or to intellectual creativeness. His report for 1842 Mann gave over entirely to the topic of the teaching of physiology in the common schools, asserting that ignorance caused one-half of all sickness and death, reviewing in minute detail the points to be communicated and encouraged by the example of the teacher. If the school could help manufacture health in early years, this would be a greater art than the physician's task of restoration.

VI

As the physical environment of a child determines the state of his health, so the intellectual and emotional forces shape his personality. Though we have laws against infanticide, wrote Mann, we do murder our children in a refined manner by denying to them intellectual sustenance. Merely to breathe and eat is not to live. "Why," wrote Mann, echoing Condorcet, "preserve the natural life of a child, why preserve unborn embryos of life, if we do not intend to watch over and to protect them, and expand their subsequent existence into usefulness and happiness?" If the community allows life to be "a curse to its possessor," it should not hesitate to snuff out the flame at birth. A child living in the senses alone is secluded from the whole heritage of intellectual life stored up in books; the spiritual and intellectual food that the community can supply the child through the common school is his rightful property just as much as the food his parents give him. Either the child should not be permitted to live at all, or he should be permitted to gather the full fruits of his inheritance, both physical and intellectual.

Food, books, teachers, work, exercise, rest, the laws of physiology —these, then, are among the forces to be brought to bear on the plastic organism of childhood. These forces the wise educator can calculate and direct; but he knows they have scarcely been tried. Education, wrote Mann, has never yet been brought to bear with one-hundredth of its potential force upon children, and hence upon the characters of men. Mann often re-creates the concept of the intellectual surveyor analyzing and calculating the pressures which may mold a whole population. "The philosopher of humanity," he wrote,

looks at the institutions which are moulding the youthful capacities of a nation; he calculates their energy and direction; and he is then able to foresee and foretell, that, if its course be not changed, the coming generation will be blessed with the rewards of parental forecast or afflicted with the retributions of parental neglect.[4]

This reliance upon the principles of cause and effect has for Mann the reliability of mathematics. Again and again he returns to this emphasis, paralleling cause and effect in psychology and morality with cause and effect in the natural sciences.

VII

Like Condorcet, Mann was convinced that the extension of educational privileges to the whole population would tend inevitably toward the gradual abolition of want. "If education be equably diffused," he wrote, "it will draw property after it by the strongest of all attractions; for such a thing never did happen, and never can happen, as that an intelligent and practical body of men should be permanently poor." Without abundant natural resources, Massachusetts was more prosperous than other states only because her citizens had more education. To demonstrate the relation of education to earning power, Mann sent inquiries to employers, asking each which employees received the highest wages. Invariably, the replies ran, the better-educated workers were the most productive and efficient, hence the recipients of the highest wages.

Mann was not content, however, with the mere acceleration of prosperity. He asserted, as Henry George was to do after him, that poverty might be totally annihilated. (Mann defined poverty in educational terms. A poor man, he said, was anyone who could not afford to sustain all his children and send them to school from ages 4-16, ten months out of the year.) The root cause of poverty, he insisted, was ignorance, ignorance of the educated as well as the illiterate. Could any intelligent man conceive that poverty was the unalterable decree of nature? As was his habit, Mann sought to answer this question not with the platitudes of Beacon Street, but with the idealistic logic of the zealous reformer. "Poverty," he wrote, "is a public as well as a private evil. There is no physical law necessitating its existence. The earth contains abundant resources for ten times—doubtless twenty times—its present inhabitants. Cold, hunger, and nakedness are not, like death, an inevitable lot." The coal fields of Pennsylvania could for centuries provide warmth to every inhabitant of the land; the state of New York alone could supply the clothes; and any one of several states could raise food enough for the whole population. Mann observed with dismay the stratification of classes as industrialization in America superseded an agricultural economy. But he visualized machinery as a new tool in the obliteration of poverty. This obliteration only ignorance could frustrate, and ignorance must flee unresisting before a really determined onslaught of books and ideas.

VIII

In his analysis of human nature, Alexis de Tocqueville was at once more realistic and more inclusive than Horace Mann. It is plain from his *Democracy in America* that he came to the New World with a mind already stocked with the psychological concepts of the French Revolution no less than with the aristocratic beliefs of his ancestors. Ugliness and beauty, hatred and love, barbarism and enlightenment he observed with an impartial eye, his mind prepared by long reading of contradictory philosophies to interpret human behavior with unwavering precision. Unlike Mann, he did not dream of perfect citizens to come, citizens shaped by the matchless forces of enlightened educational pressure. He observed rather an imperfect dream world already in the making, with social and economic forces creating irresistible behavior patterns remote and strange in aristocratic countries. "The great object in our time," he wrote, "is to raise the faculties of men." Elsewhere he wrote, "I wish that they [the rulers] would try a little more to make great men; that they would set less value upon the work and more upon the workmen." This elevation and expansion of human faculties Tocqueville conceived as the result of the democratic manners and customs rather than the persuasive discipline of ideal schools. Not from books, but from experience, the Americans were shaping a new society, intermingling, borrowing from each other, listening, experimenting, governing and teaching themselves.[5]

Tocqueville was born in Normandy on July 29, 1805, in a family deep-rooted not only in Catholic Christianity, but also in pride of ancestry and dignity of family station. As a child he was taught to be deeply sympathetic with the French monarchy. Both his parents had been imprisoned by the Revolution, his aunt and grandfather guillotined. One evening in his early years his mother began to sing by the hearth at the family mansion in Verneuil; Tocqueville later recalled the lovely, sweet voice and the tears of the company at the end of the song, tears for the tragedy of a monarchy departed and destroyed. Tutored by the Abbé Lesueur, Tocqueville completed his studies at the *lycée* at Metz, won prizes, read widely in his father's library, and lost his religious belief at the age of sixteen. Precocious and brilliant, he developed early a capacity for critical and original thinking, subordinating his reading to intense and prolonged reflection.

Completing his studies of law at twenty, Tocqueville set out with his brother Edward on a trip to Italy and Sicily; his letters demonstrate his genius for observing institutions at first hand as opposed to theoretical framework. His visits to England, intense and fruitful, provided further comparative judgments for his great work on American life. His friendship with an English woman, Mary Mottley, whom he married on October 26, 1836, also enhanced his understanding of English society. Appointed to a judgeship in the law courts of Versailles, Tocqueville became acquainted with a nobleman of liberal interests like his own, Gustave de Beaumont, who accompanied him to America. On May 11, 1831, when Tocqueville was only twenty-five, he and Beaumont landed in New York, ostensibly to study the American penal system for the French government, but actually to explore the inner meaning of democracy in a country unencumbered by layers of aristocratic tradition.

In the months that followed, until February 20, 1832, when they sailed for France, the two young men traveled by steamer, stagecoach, and horseback through the American states west as far as Wisconsin, north to Quebec, south as far as New Orleans, visiting every state east of the Mississippi except Florida, Indiana, Illinois, New Hampshire, Maine, and Vermont. The genius of Tocqueville lay first in his detachment of observation. Emotionally, as he said, he was sympathetic with aristocratic life; intellectually he accepted as inevitable the impress of democratic ideas. As a sociologist Tocqueville was a master in visualizing concrete institutions, unhampered by bias but informed by the great classics of political theory.

Upon his return to France Tocqueville first completed his obligation to the French government in issuing *The American Penal System and Its Application in France,* with Beaumont as his collaborator. Then, after two years of labor on his great project, Tocqueville published in 1835 *Democracy in America,* which won immediate acclaim as a masterpiece in both Europe and America. In 1839 Tocqueville was elected to a place in the Chamber of Deputies, where he continued until after the Revolution of February, 1848. In 1849 he served as president of the Assembly, and for a few months acted as Minister of Foreign Affairs. During his legislative career he consistently voted against the proposals of the ultra-democratic party. As an opponent of Louis Napoleon he was arrested at the coup d'état of December 2, 1851, after which he retired from public life. In 1856 appeared Tocqueville's *L'Ancien Régime et la Révolution,* a classic of historical analysis depicting the inevitable disintegration of French aristocratic institutions. Tocqueville's untimely death occurred only a few years later, in 1859.[6]

IX

In analyzing the American democratic scene Tocqueville asked himself in effect, "What is the essence of the inner man in American life? How is this unique essence implanted in his character?" While pondering these questions, Tocqueville concluded that the decisive impact upon the American personality was made by the factor of equality inherent in the country's origin and expansion. America was settled, he wrote, neither by the noble nor by the very poor people, but by groups of men substantially equal in social position. The work of hewing out a new country from the wilderness, of setting up new societies, of breaking the conventions of the Old World, of warfare against the Indians—all these labors enhanced the substantial equality that existed among the original settlers.

In hopes for material betterment and ambition for power and leadership Americans were also roughly equal. A whole continent lay unexplored, with rich land and new opportunities available to the whole population. In the new wilderness life, river life, farm and trail life, in the new commerce of cities and towns, the artificial restraints of English society, together with pride of family and social position, faded into a dim and remote world. The new work, the new country, required strong arms and rough clothes, the endowments of the average active man rather than the superior attainments of the intellectual or the prestige of aristocratic graces. The farther west Tocqueville traveled, the rougher the people he found and the more profound the spirit of social and vocational equality. To Tocqueville no element of equality in the American scene had more profound effects than the equality of hope for the increase of the citizens' material wealth. In their expectations of greater abundance of material comforts the Americans were remarkably similar. To Tocqueville, these forces were much more powerful than political equality, which was fast becoming a reality, or the rough equality in educational advancement, which to Horace Mann was the most precious promise in American life.

In the new democracy no social position was static, no man's wealth secure, no poor man's lot unalterable. If men were unequal in their talents and attainments, they were equal in the perennial buoyancy of their hopes. Hopes filled the dreams of the social reformer, the pioneer farmer, the poet, the artist, the maker of shirts; fresh hopes stirred the heart of the laborer. "There is no permanent class of hired laborers amongst us," wrote Lincoln in 1854. "Twenty-five years ago I was a hired laborer. . . . Free labor has the inspiration of hope; slavery has no hope. The power of hope upon human exertion and happiness is wonderful."

The impact of equality on human nature, thought Tocqueville, was by no means entirely beneficent. Equality produced a restlessness, an insecurity in the American heart, a heart no longer steadied by the authority of family, or church, or static community manners that had prevailed in the Old World. The emotional security of the Englishman, sure of his rights and privileges, his economic status, however lowly, equality had banished forever from the American scene; but no democratic serenity, no self-assurance, no calm expectation of familiar patterns had taken its place. If Americans were restless, they were also envious. "I found there," wrote Tocqueville, "the democratic feeling of envy expressed under a thousand different forms." Americans were envious of each other because they knew that good fortune, wealth, honor, might also be theirs. Another weakness in human nature engendered by equality, asserted Tocqueville, was "a mixture of ignorance and presumption." Men in a state of social equality assumed an equality of mental power, an equality of knowledge, that did not, in fact, exist. Was one man's opinion as good as another's? Equality taught Americans to think so, yet they knew not the depths of their ignorance.[7]

Accustomed to the graces of the French aristocracy, Tocqueville delineated with acute penetration the shaping of American manners by the equalitarian ideal. "True dignity in manners," he wrote, "consists in always taking one's proper station, neither too high nor too low; and this is as much within the reach of a peasant as of a prince." But the equality of American democracy had produced social fluctuations so violent as to make all stations in life tenuous and impermanent. American manners were therefore untrained, undignified, arrogant, presumptuous. In America there was no aristocratic class to enforce by its example either the spirit or the social techniques of good breeding. Secure in his own worth and his good sense, each man followed his own code, acting often with bumptious pride and complacency. "In democratic countries," wrote Tocqueville, "even poor men entertain a lofty notion of their personal importance: they look upon themselves with complacency, and are apt to suppose that others are looking at them too. . . . To preserve their dignity, they think it necessary to retain their gravity."[8]

X

Like most Europeans, Tocqueville erroneously supposed that American life had not yet produced a genius of the first order. It was not possible, in his belief, for a democratic society to produce geniuses in comparable numbers to those of aristocratic nations. The very nature of the fluid, hustling life destroyed the conditions of creative endeavor. In America men lived not to create, but to enhance their comfort and security. As yet no leisure class, no aristocracy of the intellect as well as of wealth, was ready to subsidize the labors of genius. The busy Americans were not adapted, he thought, to the pursuit of knowledge for its own sake, or to long periods of solitude and meditation, which are the rich soil from which genius springs. Talented men, he thought, the American democracy would create in abundance; and in the application of scientific ideas through the common inventive genius of independent workmen they were far superior to the Europeans.

From these conclusions, it is apparent that Tocqueville under-

estimated the reaches of American creative vitality. In his estimation of the frequency of American genius he faltered and erred,
unaware that at the very time he wrote America was giving birth
to Emerson, Lincoln, Lowell, Poe, Mark Twain, Whitman. Already
New England was using its savings to send its citizens to endowed
colleges and libraries, to send its brilliant men abroad, to establish
journals for their writings. America was giving birth to a whole
brood of rare creative spirits; and the prophecy of Jefferson
fluttered on the boundaries of fulfilment.

Two elements of equality, in Tocqueville's judgment, reduced
the extent and vitality of intellectual labors in America. One was
the mere physical movement and excitement of a whole eager population engaged in "a sort of incessant jostling of men, which annoys
and disturbs the mind without exciting or elevating it." In this
bustling new society, in this relentless pursuit of gain, where opportunities for material welfare were unsurpassed, there was no time
for meditation, no incentive to a life of reflection, no aristocratic
class sure of its living and undisturbed in its intellectual pursuits.
Except in the practical contrivances of their physical and commercial labors, the Americans were too busy to think out the parts of
any problem that confronted them. Consequently, in every field of
intellectual endeavor, they generalized too much and particularized
too little. Too busy to go to the heart of the matter, whether it was
science, philosophy, or government, they jumped hastily to conclusions which they upheld with dogged pertinacity, each encouraged
by the spirit of equality to enhance the validity of his own opinion.

XI

If physical movement and practical pressures forced Americans
into shallow intellectual waters, the drive of individualism inherent
in equalitarian manners might lead to sinister dangers. Tocqueville
defined individualism as an exaggerated selfishness produced by
equality, a concentration on personal needs and satisfactions to the
exclusion of the community's welfare. The more extensive the

applications of equality, the greater the danger of extreme individualism. In an aristocracy, wrote Tocqueville, a man's actions were
restrained by his fixed place in society, by his responsibility to his
family, to his class, to his community. But in a democracy like
America, no such restrictions obtained: family, home, church, community lost their influence over a man who shifted constantly from
one community to another, leaving behind his home and friends,
meanwhile rising or falling in the scale of wealth or social position. Such a man felt responsible to no one but himself. He often
lost interest in the standards of his friends and family, the customs
of his church and his home town. He became a law unto himself,
concentrating with equalitarian assurance on the accomplishment
of his aims, oblivious of his duties to his fellow-men. "Not only,"
wrote Tocqueville, "does democracy make every man forget his
ancestors, but it hides his descendants and separates his contemporaries from him; it throws him back forever upon himself."

Much as Tocqueville deplored the insidious effects of an
equalitarian individualism, he was quick to observe those democratic forces which reduced its dangers and softened its extremes.
In each small community, wrote Tocqueville, where all the members are required to attend to public affairs, each one seeks the
good will of his neighbors. The rich man seeks the esteem of the
poor, the strong man that of the weak. The necessities of local
self-government perpetually bring men together, requiring them
to help one another make important decisions in which each has
a stake. Democratic institutions, wrote Tocqueville, remind each
citizen daily that he needs the good will of his fellow-men. If he
is proud or selfish or hateful, he may fear to reveal himself to his
neighbors. At first he engages in his social responsibilities on
account of his self-interest, but at last he acts from habit and intention. In a democracy a man may no longer respect the opinions of
his family or his church, but he is perennially aware of his neighbors' appraisal of the good or ill of his ambitions.

The influence of equality on American women stirred in Tocqueville an admiring enthusiasm. Having more freedom than in

the aristocratic countries, the American woman showed from early years a striking independence of spirit and plasticity of mind. Encouraged to comprehend the harsh realities of the world of men, she engaged freely and boldly in conversation, aloof but aware in the midst of enticing pleasures. To her nature and accomplishments, however different from his own, the American man gave daily his spontaneous respect. Though the European may flatter a woman, wrote Tocqueville, he will never admit that she is his equal. The American, on the other hand, though he seldom complimented his wife, would daily show how much he esteemed her. In her intellectual powers he had as much confidence as in his own. Not in seclusion from society, but in the development of her understanding, lay her protection against the world's seductions. In the spirit of equality, encouraged to be physically active and socially aggressive, women were granted great freedom of movement, often traveling alone over long distances. Confident, proud, elastic, they had been elevated by the impulse of equality to a loftier position than women had held in any other country. In explaining, indeed, the expanding strength of the American people and even their economic well-being, Tocqueville asserted that the key factor was the superiority of American women.

XII

Nowhere is Tocqueville's delineation of human nature more penetrating than in his analysis of the effect of slavery on the blacks and whites of the New World. In this newest offshoot of civilization, amidst the pressures of equality and universal hope, an ancient wrong had taken root and flourished mightily, a wrong destined to vanish before the onslaught of ideas or submerge the nation in suicidal strife.

The Negro, asserted Tocqueville, led a life brutalized beyond hope, withered beyond redemption. Even in the womb he was bought and sold. Passionate, servile, impetuous, knowing nothing but servitude from birth, thinking only the thoughts of an inferior, he was insensible to his own wretchedness, unresponsive to his own reason, oblivious of the hopes of a free man. His wife and children were slaves; he had no family, no home. He was ashamed of his nature, having been told from birth that his very blackness doomed him to inferiority. In the states where slavery dominated economic life, his manumission was virtually prohibited. Even the white father of a black child could not free his son. He possessed no property, not even his own person; he could not take his own life without fraudulently depriving his owner of a valuable possession. "He admires his tyrants," wrote Tocqueville, "more than he hates them, and finds his joy and his pride in the servile imitation of those who oppress him." In many states he could not legally be taught to read or write. If he entered into freedom, he was a child of passion and irresponsibility, unable, after he had broken the chains of his body, to escape the servitude of his soul.[9]

In his long passages on the Negroes and their future in America, Tocqueville leaves no hint that the differences between the blacks and whites were derived from hereditary characters; he would not grant, with Jefferson, that nature had placed upon the blacks a difference in mind as well as in color. Every one of the Negro's uncivilized customs, every one of his immature passions, his attitude of servility, and the irresponsibility that accompanied his freedom—all these were the direct and inevitable effects of his degraded condition. To convince the whites that they were not morally and intellectually inferior, the Negroes must raise themselves from the muck of their degradation. But this very conviction on the part of the whites prohibited opportunities for the transformation of Negro habits and customs. To Tocqueville the natural inequality of the Negroes was purely imaginary. Given free birth, equality of opportunity, political and educational equality, it was inevitable that they should attain success in every field equal to that of their former masters. In this inference, like Horace Mann, Tocqueville was in actuality a mechanist, a believer in the inevitability of environmental pressures. More shrewdly than Mann, however, he evaluated the dominant nature, the all-powerful pressure of manners and customs, as opposed to the fleeting touch of books and ideas.

XIII

To the casual reader the ideas of Horace Mann and Alexis de Tocqueville arrange themselves at remote ideological poles. A French aristocrat sent here to investigate American prisons, Tocqueville showed little interest in the growth of America's free common schools. With an almost incredible precision and insight, however, intensified by his understanding of European societies, he observed manners, read American laws, studied the Americans' concepts of equality, analyzed their hopes and fears. Horace Mann, on the contrary, immersed himself in educational reform, anticipating the perfect citizens of the future rather than attending to the imperfect realities of the present. The common school Horace Mann visualized too often as a constructive, benevolent influence, little realizing that in school a boy or a girl learned also the tawdry colors, the repressive cruelty, and the ugliness of temperament perennially visible in a world of children. Both men were hopeful of the success of American democracy, but Tocqueville's imagination played on the realities of crushing forces, whereas to Horace Mann America's dream could come true only in the ideal schools of America's future.

In their ideological premises, however, Horace Mann and Tocqueville were of one persistent pattern, the pattern to be delineated in countless minds of American spokesmen for the nature of man. They believed wholeheartedly in the plasticity of the human organism. They believed in the creation of constructive pressures, in the inevitable effects of beneficent forces—Mann in the forces of education, Tocqueville in the tonic force of equality. Nowhere is Tocqueville's environmentalism more illuminating than in his analysis of the effects of slavery on blacks and whites. In the whole of his great work he never deviates from his environmentalist position. He takes no thought of an inherent criminal tendency, of the innate depravity of the black slave, or of the superior ancestry of the southern planter or the Boston aristocrat. To neither Mann nor Tocqueville, then, was the explanation of man's destiny to be found in the chemistry of his blood or the chance characters of his biological inheritance, but rather in the countless interweaving pressures that pounded against him from the day of his birth.

In such an approach to the nature of man, Mann and Tocqueville boldly disregarded the assumptions of the philosophers and theologians for a dependence on evidence of the eye and ear. True, they did not reduce this evidence to the statistics of the economist or the case studies of the sociologist, trusting rather to the superiority of their general intellectual perspective—a perspective that prohibited in the main extrasensory conclusions about the nature of man. If their evidence could not be final or complete, it pointed the way to more exact and sustained studies by the scholars of psychology and anthropology yet to come. If American hopes were still a promise unfulfilled, a myth yet to be tested, the method of Tocqueville and Mann, like that of Jefferson, posed a reliance on observable phenomena as the main resource for a science of man.

1835
Year of Seedtime and Doubt

In the year 1835, though Tocqueville deplored democracy's dearth of great men, genius lay heavy and quivering in the womb of American life. On the frontier American life was pregnant, pregnant with the lonely great, to be borne aloft and forward by the perennial hopes, the rich promises, of an unfilled continent. In 1835 on a farm near New Salem Ann Rutledge died; and Abraham Lincoln, twenty-six years old, told his friend William Greene that the thought "that snows and rains fall upon her grave" filled him with despair.

In 1835 aristocratic Boston stirred with genius—genius fertilized by generations of educated men, nourished by European scholarship, sustained by Puritan savings. In that year Bronson Alcott labored at the Temple School to unfold from little children the patterns of divinity. On January 4 he wrote: "He who kindles the fire of genius on the altar of the young heart unites his own prayers for humanity with every ascending flame." In 1835 Ralph Waldo Emerson walked through the woods of Concord in early morning: "Saw the morn rise from the hilltop, but could not wait for the sun. Those long slender bars of cloud swim like fishes in a sea of crimson light." On February 2 he wrote: "Let Christianity ever speak for the poor and the low... if by opposing slavery I go to undermine institutions, I confess I do not wish to live in a nation where slavery exists."

In 1835 Nathaniel Hawthorne still lived in solitude at Salem (where his family left his meals beside his chamber door), his heart low with doubts, his wings still unready for full flight. "Often," he

67

wrote, "a delicious stream of thought would gush out upon the page at once, like water sparkling up suddenly in the desert; and when it passed, I gnawed my pen hopelessly, or blundered on, with cold and miserable toil." Or again he would rejoice: "I walked along a hilly road on a starlight October evening; in the pure and bracing air, I became all soul, and felt as if I could climb the sky, and run a race along the Milky Way."

In 1835 Herman Melville, a youth of sixteen, was a clerk in an Albany cap and fur store, a part-time student, dreaming of the sea at night, among his father's books.

In 1835 Walt Whitman walked the streets of Manhattan, a boy careless and slouching, now a carpenter, now an apprentice printer, his ambitions loose and hazy.

In 1835 Mark Twain was born.

In 1835 Edgar Allan Poe, obscure and penniless, lived with Virginia Clemm and her mother on Amity Street, Baltimore. The degradation of his poverty smote him with despair. On March 15 he wrote to Kennedy: "Your kind invitation to dinner today has wounded me to the quick. I cannot come—and for reasons of the most humiliating nature in my personal appearance ... if you will be my friend so far as to loan me $20, I will call on you tomorrow —otherwise it will be impossible."

Year of seedtime and doubt, when the harvest was planted but its riches were remote and unpredictable. Year of promise, year of gropings and soundings, year of a thousand westward marches ... the pioneer with his ax on his shoulder, the black man brooding in his hut, the writer by his lamp, the boatman singing at the helm, the philosopher musing among his books, all uneasy, restless, expectant.

Whence came the genius of Melville and Hawthorne and Walt Whitman, now rooted if not flowering in American life? In 1835 no one could tell, nor could anyone trace certainly the origin of genius twelve decades later. Jefferson, it is true, had believed that genius was a product of minds stirred to fertility in an atmosphere of association. Tocqueville assumed that a serene leisure was neces-

sary to a work of genius—a leisure cherished and practiced in aristocratic countries, but rare in a turbulent democracy. Yet none of the geniuses awakening in American life possessed the leisure of aristocratic tradition, Lincoln least of all. If not a settled leisure, what elements in American life combined to awaken their vision of themselves as great men, their solitude of purpose, their agony of creative action in the years before the critics awakened to their worth? To this question also there was no answer in 1835, and no decisive answer has yet appeared in the age of atomic energy.

If the examination of American life brought no certain clues to the emergence of genius, the search of nature's genetic mysteries led only to the impenetrable dark. Was the birth of genius simultaneous with conception? Did nature have a way of giving a favorite child genetic resources of talent that no poverty could quench or discouragement wither? As hereditary characters were the measure of nature's constancy, the response of the brain to all life was the measure of human plasticity. From which source or from what mingling of sources were to come the flow of talent, the uniqueness of Poe's melodies, the sad autumnal beauty of Hawthorne's prose, the electric brightness of Melville's images, the relentless logic of Lincoln's thought? To such a question many scholars brought guesses: none as yet could bring the indisputable proof.

III
Perfection A Priori:
Ralph Waldo Emerson

> *What is a man born for but to be a Reformer, a Remaker of what man has made; a renouncer of lies; a restorer of good and truth, imitating that great Nature which embosoms us all, and which sleeps no moment on an old past, but every hour repairs herself, yielding us every morning a new day, and with every pulsation a new life?*
>
> —Emerson

IN the American search for a science of man, as in every such quest, the insight of the poet or the philosopher often anticipates the findings of the laboratory. We search then in Emerson and Whitman, no less than in the realists Jefferson and Lincoln, for those glimmerings of light that the scientists of a later century may reduce to the certainty of mathematical measurement. What is fixed and certain and immutable in the nature of man? To this question Horace Mann has given one answer, a physician like Holmes another, and a novelist like Dreiser still another. Our task is to select and assess those ideas from the stream of American thought that point most usefully and most exactly to the potential of certainty to come.

In so capacious a mind as Emerson's, it is not surprising to find contradictory approaches to the nature of man, like the two sides of his face, one the mirror of Yankee shrewdness, the other the embodiment of mystic vision and Platonic perfection. From both Emersons, the Yankee observer and the disciple of Plato, we may draw inferences useful to the gradual emergence of a science of man.

In his essential early doctrine, no critic of man could have stood more remote from the realism of Jefferson, Tocqueville, and Lincoln than Ralph Waldo Emerson. While they calculated discernible if not always measurable forces, looking to the acorn, the village store, the struggle for bread, the persuasion of bookish visions, Emerson boldly announced an invisible, measureless infinity of light radiating from the bosom of God into the souls of men: a light irresistible and perpetual, radiant and magnificent, dispersing with lightning shafts the horrible pressures of environmental malevolence. To this divine reason every man has open access; at will he may gather perfection to his heart, transform his life, his world, scattering his accumulated errors as rain scatters the summer dust. This light, this Universal Soul, Emerson had never seen or touched; yet from youth to death it was as real to him as the leaves he trod in the Concord woods or the fire crackling on his hearth. Upon this belief rested his most profound beliefs in man, in democracy, and in himself.

In the market place Emerson was transformed into the canny Yankee, a disciple of Montaigne, an acute watcher of lips and eyes, a prober of earthy motives. In the woods his senses were alive as an Indian's. But like his master Plato Emerson distrusted the senses; they could not show the ultimate truth. His transcendentalism was a fusion of Greek and Christian, a mingling of Plato, Jesus, Swedenborg, and Kant. In "The Over-Soul" he describes the doctrine of the Idealist with a charm and persuasion unmatched in Kant or Coleridge, though pale and weak indeed beside the glowing parables of the *Phaedo*. Surrounding the earth, he thought, throbbing through all life, is a divine energy striving for perfection, an energy accessible to all minds and spirits, however humble, degraded, or unintelligent. This is the Over-Soul, the Universal Soul, the Supreme Critic of ideas, the endless heavenly screen shadowing forth knowledge, perfect conduct, the wisdom of nature, the secrets of science:

The Supreme Critic on the errors of the past and the present, and the only prophet of that which must be, is that great nature in which we rest as the earth lies in the soft arms of the atmosphere; that Unity, that Over-Soul, within which every man's particular being is contained and made one with all other; that common heart . . . that overpowering reality which confutes our tricks and talents, and constrains everyone . . . to speak from his character, and not from his tongue, and which evermore tends to pass into our thought and hand, and become wisdom and virtue and power and beauty.[1]

In the spirit of God, then, in this exhaustless energy, all men are united and indivisible; they are both inlets and outlets of an incomparable radiance. If man will permit himself to commune with the Over-Soul, of which he is a part, he can not only discover for himself that wisdom conducive to the greatest happiness; he will also find his whole intelligence intensified, and his perceptions, even his practical talents will be immeasurably heightened and expanded: "When it breathes through his intellect, it is genius; when it breathes through his will, it is virtue; when it flows through his affection, it is love."

In their access to the infinite riches of the Over-Soul, all men are equal. On this conviction Emerson rested his belief in the potential spiritual and intellectual power of the humblest people. On the same premise he based his stand for the democratic ideal. "Democracy, Freedom," he wrote, "has its root in the sacred truth that *every man hath in him the Divine Reason. . . .* This is the equality, and the only equality of all men." An illiterate man may be the mouthpiece of God, projecting the realities of a just world yet unborn.

To be profound, to express his genius, to grasp the bottom truths of the universe, the humblest man has only to "watch that gleam of light which flashes across the mind from within." Not on books nor people nor the opinion of the crowd, but on the unheralded, the half-worded thoughts of expectant searchers do God's messages ride into the world. Thus Emerson's reiteration of self-reliance as the first duty of man in seeking the truth. "The root and the seed of democracy," he wrote, "is the doctrine, Judge for yourself.

Reverence thyself." To revere one's thoughts is to listen to the echoes of perfection.

Emerson continually defined the nature of man in terms of his central Platonic conviction: "Man is a stream whose source is hidden. . . . Every man is a channel through which Heaven floweth. . . . A man is a god in ruins." Steeped and shrouded in Plato's doctrine of recollection (a doctrine to Jefferson absurd and fanciful), Emerson visualized man's soul as the repository of perfect behavior patterns, the mirror of ultimate justice and beauty, the transmitter of God's dreams for perfectible man and perfectible earth. Not that Emerson neglected the conclusions of science; he merely incorporated the scientific advances of his day into his vision of God's plan for man. "Civilization," he wrote later, "is the result of highly complex organization. In the snake, all the organs are sheathed; no hands, no feet, no fins, no wings. In bird and beast the organs are released and begin to play. In man they are all unbound and full of joyful action."[2]

The activity of the Over-Soul is beclouded, not enhanced, by the pressure of daily experience. It is true, thought Emerson, that in one's heart-to-heart communication with one's fellow-men the sublimity of the Over-Soul flashes forth; it is true also that in the presence of nature, the same mystical communication often illumines the searcher. But Emerson did not count so much upon these stimuli as upon the solitary, exclusive concentration of the lonely watch. Not from books, not from observation, should a man speak, but from the intuitions of his silent moments. The great poets, the great seers and sages, are those who have thus searched and thus spoken: Jesus, Herbert, Spinoza, Kant. Those to be distrusted are Locke, Macintosh, and Stewart, who look for evidence from the sensory record outside themselves. "Jesus," wrote Emerson, "speaks always from within, and in a degree that transcends all others. In that is the miracle." Shakespeare also spoke from within, unburdening himself of but a fraction of the golden wisdom that the Over-Soul spilled into the infinite recesses of his mind.

Though all men have equal access to the Over-Soul, and though

all are capable, therefore, of sudden and apparently effortless perfectibility (such as in art, ethics, or social vision), Emerson concluded that few men in the history of the world have opened their
minds to the ultimate wisdom. A few only have used the divine
reason; those who have not have been the pieces, the *fractions* of
men, transformed into wholes at scattered moments, but in the
perspective of a lifetime deficient in the same sense as the deluded
or the insane. Emerson did not claim, therefore, that one man's
opinion was as valid as another's. Men are equal in the sense that
the source of truth is open to all. Why do some men use the divine
reason more fully than others, placing themselves under the guidance and illumination of the supreme wisdom? This is a question
that Emerson answers only by implication: It is man's own choice
that determines whether he open his life fully to a flood of illumination or open it only a chink. "There is imparted to every man," he
wrote, "the Divine light of reason, sufficient not only to grind corn
and plant wheat by, but also to illuminate all his life, his social,
religious, political actions. Sufficient . . . *If used*." This significant
passage reduces to man's choice the illuminations, the inventions,
the moments of revelation and intuition that Emerson regarded as
communications from the Universal Spirit.[3]

The charm of this persuasive concept of man cannot blind us
to the searching questions of an Aristotle, a Bacon, a Lincoln. Was
Shakespeare then, or Jesus, only an extension of the Universal
Spirit, not in any critical sense the product of the environmental
forces under which he lived? Could Shakespeare have flowered in
the age of Boswell, the age of Victoria, the age of Pope? Could
Jesus have arisen in the Babylonian captivity? To Emerson every
man was an unrecorded genius; but he does not explain why so
many millions of geniuses die without the recognition of their
powers. Assuming momentarily that a man has only to speak from
within to discover the ultimate truth, what proportion of his destiny
is traced by the Over-Soul, and what proportion by the accidents
of family, wealth, education, time, country, friends, community?
Emerson never attempts to unravel this mystery. The rational mind

insists on tracing the relative force and power of the Over-Soul because he is accustomed to tracing if not measuring the effects of a great teacher, a Mermaid tavern, a London expectant and confident, an illiterate people eager for play-making, new wealth and leisure and confidence among the trading classes.

"Man is a dwarf of himself," wrote Emerson, but enlargement to his normal sublimity waits only upon his will. The conditions that created the will to open one's soul to intuitions Emerson did not describe; he visioned a heavenly world opening to every man by the touch of his hand on the latchstring. Without reading, without education or suggestions from wiser men, every man was a harp sensitive to the winds of heavenly perfection. Before such a doctrine the rational critic stands humbly, remembering the demon of Socrates, the miraculous sayings of Jesus, the visions of Blake, the genius of St. John; but he turns away at the end incredulous. He cannot record perfection a priori; he cannot trace the subtle forces or the sudden transformations radiating through man's flesh from the dynamo of an unknowable power. He remembers Gerrard Winstanley and his utopian ministry, prohibited from imagining a God beyond the earth and its meaning. In earth knowable and in man knowable Winstanley, like every rational critic, places hopes for man's salvation; not in the forces he cannot trace or the voices he cannot hear.

Every reformer would like to universalize his media of salvation. Though Emerson rounded out no doctrine and set up no cult, he preached the gospel of intuition, revelation, self-reverence. In his own life he exemplified his creed, attuning himself soon and late to the strains of the divine music. From the patterns of his existence we may reconstruct the psychological milieu of the searching and listening transcendentalist. He made himself as serene as possible, often avoiding the obligations of clubs and societies, walking in the woods alone, communing with Alcott and Thoreau, drinking deeply of the Bhagavad Gita, Plato, Swedenborg. Boldly he questioned, bluntly he challenged, restless, eager, expectant, testing on the anvil of the Universal Spirit the social superstitions of his day. He came to cherish the hours of reflection, to hoard them against the evil hour when he would be thrust again into the cross fire of his friends' ideas or the superficial alertness of fireside and table. When Ellen Tucker died, leaving him twenty thousand dollars, she freed him partially from labor, assuring him year after year of golden, lonely hours, each one pregnant with irradiations from the Over-Soul.

Of such to Emerson was the gold of life; no one except Thoreau and Hawthorne sought more zealously than he the solitude indispensable to creative endeavor. Solitude and serenity he sought and possessed, freedom from worry and the harassing pressures of making a living, precious hours in which he might hear the subtle whispering of ultimate wisdom.

How to universalize these patterns, how to sow the seed of a thousand Emersons, of half-Emersons, bringing millions within the verge of the unerring Voice? By taking thought any man may hear; by looking within any man may find. Thus Emerson; but his own life exemplified the absurdity of his answer. The pressures of his environment were uniquely beneficent. Not choice, but the patterns of childhood and the books of the masters fashioned the structure of his world view. Few men of the Western world have had or could now have, by taking thought, Emerson's companionship with the Universal Spirit. Generations of intellectuals, the stinging atmosphere of Harvard, the friendship of Mary Moody Emerson, Margaret Fuller, Alcott, Carlyle, the beneficent cradling of his genius, and many other influences in the sharp currents of the New England renaissance—all these stamped and shaped his dreams. How few Americans lived within the magic circle of forces that gave birth to Emerson, Margaret Fuller, Thoreau! Of those who lived in the golden glow, how many were as free from the labor of getting a living as Emerson? To have years of precious solitude from other men's sweat, as Milton said, to steep one's mind in Plato and Plotinus and Coleridge's *Aids to Reflection*, this was the way to the riches of intuition. This education, these friends, this freedom were the way to the Over-Soul, not the process of a free choice, the sudden opening of an unprepared mind to the radiance of revelation. And to universalize this process was a dream more remote from American life than the most utopian vagaries of Brook Farm or its hundred sister settlements.

The main riches, moreover, that Emerson claimed as the unburdening of the Over-Soul were in reality the ideas of Plato impregnated in a mind richly stocked with the literature of idealism and salted with the unique flavors of the New World. The concepts of Plato Emerson synthesized with his strong faith in American intelligence and American progress. In "The American Scholar" his declaration of intellectual independence is but an offshoot of the Platonic confidence in supersensory recollection. It was a much-needed message to New Englanders doubtful of their powers in the presence of European genius; but the soil from which it grew was wholly derived from the books and followers of Emerson's master. In "The Senses and the Soul," when he writes of "The deep sleep of the higher faculties of man"; in his analyses of the creative process in "The Poet," when he again declares the superiority of the intuitional principle, denominating most people as mutes or minors, but the poet as the complete man; in "Intellect," when he writes that "God enters by a private door into every individual"; in "Politics," when he declares again that men have equal access to reason and "what the tender poetic youth dreams ... today ... shall presently be the resolutions of public bodies"; in these seminal essays, as well as in "Experience," "Nominalist and Realist," "Illusions," *Representative Men*, the central ideas are always sparks from Plato's anvil. Though Emerson extolled intellectual self-reliance, no American thinker was more derivative in his main concepts than the sage of Concord. Like Jesus, who spoke, he said, a priori, Emerson sought diligently to "watch that gleam of light which flashes across his mind from within." But he was too immersed in great books to follow the example of the unlearned Galilean. When Emerson snatched a thought from the Over-Soul, more often than not, however felicitously phrased, its descent may be traced from the pages of the *Phaedo* or *The Republic*.

I have said that the Over-Soul concept occupied only one shelf of Emerson's mind. His evaluation of great men lies in a separate category, his uncanny perception of human motives in still another. To turn from Emerson's essays to his letters is to meet a man startlingly worldly and practical. Especially in his letters to his brother William we find little mention of ideas, much tart talk of family finances and obligations: "Can you send me 500 or 400 or 300 or 200 dollars now, and fix a day when you can send more?" When William wished to borrow money, Emerson wrote, "Tell me what is the utmost you wish from me? What is the least? and then I will try the farthest that quiddling will do." He tactfully refused to entrust to William any substantial portion of his capital. His letter to Ripley refusing to engage in the Brook Farm project reveals a shrewd weighing of personal benefits financial and creative, rather than a generous acceptance of his obligation to a venture he describes as "noble and humane." "It seems to me," he wrote, "that it would not be worth my while to make the difficult exchange of my property in Concord for a share in the new Household." A week later he wrote to William that he wanted him to know "how much and how little we are bitten by this madness of G. R.'s Socialism."[4]

Emerson's confidence in the Over-Soul as the source of highest truth produced an irreconcilable contradiction in his analyses of education. Like Wordsworth and Alcott he distrusted education as the shackling of man's natural genius. After hearing Horace Mann, whom both he and Alcott regarded with disparagement, he wrote the following contemptuous note on the education of his time: "We are shut up in schools and college recitation rooms for ten or fifteen years, and come out at last with a bellyful of words and do not know a thing." To Emerson the best education was not books or schools at all, but the opening of one's mind to the currents of the Universal Being. Yet, as he grew older, Emerson placed education on a pinnacle without elaborating the kind of training he would establish. "The highest end of government," he wrote in "Politics," "is the culture of men; and if men can be educated, the institutions will share their improvement, and the moral sentiment will write

the law of the land." Even more extravagant is his statement, in
the same essay: "To educate the wise man, the State exists; and
with the appearance of the wise man, the State expires." In his
essay on "Books" Emerson reviewed the ideal reading program,
but nowhere does he set down, as did Horace Mann and Henry
Barnard, the forces he would have brought to bear in the schoolroom on the growing child. How to educate the wise man? Emerson
does not say. To have crystallized patterns of educational reform
would have been to assume the formative power of those worldly
forces which he thought subtracted from rather than added to the
natural genius of the uncultivated man. Nowhere in Emerson's
thinking does he reveal more clearly, more emphatically, the essentially flimsy foundation of his idealism than in his contradictory
estimates of the value of education. Horace Mann's plan of using
available forces, however humble, assumes a remarkable magnitude
beside Emerson's hazy generalities about the superiority of the
voice of nature.

As Emerson grew older, he gave hints to the world that he was
himself dissatisfied with the transcendental roots of his *Weltan-
schauung*. In his written works the world of the Over-Soul gradually
yielded to the world of the solid earth. His first book, *Nature* (1836),
draws more fully than any other upon supersensory assumptions,
assumptions that persisted in his *Essays* (1841 and 1844). In
Representative Men (1850) and *English Traits* (1856), however,
he veered sharply away from transcendentalism, grounding his
premises solidly in experience, meanwhile injecting part of his
energies into the antislavery campaign. In *Conduct of Life* (1860)
Emerson is more empiric than ever before. Though it is true that
through the rich sensory evidence of "Beauty" and "Illusions" we
still hear the old transcendental overtones, Emerson's growing
realism strikes home on every page. His lecture on "Behavior,"
especially such a remarkable sally as the passage on eyes, was
evidently too earthy for his listeners. "Eyes," he wrote,

are bold as lions,—roving, running, leaping, here and there, far and near.

They speak all languages. . . . When the eyes say one thing, and the
tongue another, a practiced man relies on the language of the first. . . .
There are asking eyes, asserting eyes, prowling eyes; and eyes full of
fate—some of good and some of sinister omen. . . . 'Tis very certain that
each man carries in his eye the exact indication of his rank in the
immense scale of men, and we are always learning to read it.[5]

In response to his friends' complaints that he had discussed
fate, power, and wealth on "too low a platform," Emerson returned
in "Worship" to a few passages of his old idealism. But in the next,
"Considerations by the Way," he is more realistic than ever. In
Letters and Social Aims (1876) Emerson returned to the strain of
his early years, but this, as we know, was under the compulsion of
publishing demands for a volume of his old essays. Not his newer
realism, therefore, but his older transcendental philosophy is the
substance of the last volume published before his death. The later
essays and addresses written before the decline of his powers, such
as "American Civilization" (1862), "Solitude and Society" (1870),
"Farming," and "Perpetual Forces" (1877), reveal Emerson's reliance upon the certitude of external forces and movements sustained
in the last address he made, "The Fortune of the Republic" (March
30, 1878).

Where, then, if not in his Platonism, shall we look for Emerson's
genius? Scarce a random page can we read that does not, with an
unerring phrase, surprise the heart or illumine a shadowy image.
Emerson sharpens and completes our images of experience, our
impressions of times and men, of movements and ideas. The Over-
Soul occupied only one shelf of his capacious intelligence. Though
he called genius "a child of the old eternal soul," we discover
Emerson's own genius not in his intuitions but in his acute reporting and evaluation of the world he lived in. He was the best educated, imaginatively and intellectually the most versatile, of the
great of his times. His evaluation of the living and the dead
was equally profound and exact. The overflowing sexuality of
Leaves of Grass may have revolted and dismayed him; but his
mind gave to the author his rightful place in American literature,

his imagination triumphing over his prejudices and the very coldness of his nature. Can one imagine Alcott or Whittier, Longfellow
or Hawthorne, hobnobbing from youth to death with Montaigne,
turning from Montaigne to Swedenborg to Whitman with fresh
delight? Of Shakespeare no one has written more justly: "What
king has he not taught state, as Talma taught Napoleon? What
maiden has not found him finer than her delicacy? What lover has
he not outloved?" Thoreau, Napoleon, Tennyson, Wordsworth,
Carlyle, Alcott, Webster, Newton, Plutarch, Plato, the quick and
the dead, rascal and saint, warrior and statesman, poet and scientist, he sketched with the sure touch of a faultless painter. "I count
him a great man," he wrote, "who inhabits a higher sphere of
thought, into which other men rise with labor and difficulty; he has
but to open his eyes to see things in a true light." Thus it was with
Emerson. But behind his eyes lay the demigods of Plutarch, the
images and words of Socrates and Plato, the canny insight of
Montaigne; by the gifts and words of choice spirits, by a whole
galaxy of perfect patterns, he measured the worth of men and
books. Tracing the patterns of perfection, evaluating men and
moments by history's parallels, is a process solidly empiric. In this
process no American is Emerson's superior.

Time after time Emerson reveals a canny insight into those
elementary democratic forces that were tracing new patterns in
the American scene. The American educational process he called
the "most radical of revolutions," a revolution accepted in the early
years of Massachusetts,

namely, that the poor man, whom the law does not allow to take an ear
of corn when starving ... is allowed to put his hand into the pocket of
the rich, and say, "You shall educate me, not as you will, but as I will;
not alone in the elements, but, by further provision, in the languages,
in sciences, in the useful and in elegant arts."[6]

In "Politics," long before, he had written that people, not property,
must be the primary concern of the state. The far-reaching rights
of man in a democracy he summarized thus: "A man has a right

to be employed, to be trusted, to be loved, to be revered." The poor man, he wrote, must have access to the material wealth of America. "The state must consider the poor man, and all voices must speak for him. Every child that is born must have a just chance for his bread." On this issue he praised the teachings of the social- ists, who had set men to thinking "how certain civilizing benefits, now only enjoyed by the opulent, can be enjoyed by all." Though he deplored the impracticality of Owen, Fourier, and St. Simon, he understood that a democratic culture was impossible without a broad access to wealth and leisure. "To be rich," he wrote, "is to have a ticket of admission to the master-works and chief men of each race." Though wealth did not necessarily pull culture after it, there could be no culture, Emerson thought, without the purchas- ing of leisure, education, and travel.

Emerson's lofty conception of man, however suspect may be its origins among rational critics, has been an electric force in the stream of American thought. In page after page he has dramatized for us the fragmentary extension of man's personality resources. With unfinished men, with men who had explored only fractions of their creative powers, he was perpetually unreconciled. Even the humblest man deserved to be measured for his fullest reach. If man was limited and stunted by his quadruped ancestors, he possessed an individuality that society should seek and cherish. As Emerson hated the word *masses,* so he was expectant of a unique vein of hidden greatness in each personality. But for mining this greatness Emerson has left no machinery. He was no believer, like Mann, in the efficacy of education; he pictured no utopia, nor, in an age of experimental communities on the American scene, did he live in one. Emerson taught his countrymen to treasure the eye of expectancy in viewing themselves, to concentrate each man his resources, if only for one moment, in a harmony of original thought or action; thus from America there might rise up many uncommon men.

"Opinion in good men," wrote Milton, "is but knowledge in the making." Should a science of man ultimately emerge from the collective illumination of searchers in many fields, it will trace some beginnings and hypotheses to Emerson's uncanny perceptions. Though lacking the rigorous scientific outlook of Jefferson, and the sociological insight of Mann and Tocqueville, Emerson sensed more accurately than they the vast potential of originality in the Americans of his time.

1855
The Black Man in the Scales

In 1855 the population of the United States was over 23,000,000, of whom 4,000,000 were slaves and 434,000 free Negroes. One-third of the population fell between the ages of one and ten, another third between sixteen and twenty-six. In New York City lived 675,000 people. In New England one in four hundred could not read or write, in the slave states one in twelve, in the non-slave states one in forty, in the nation one in twenty-two. Free high schools were yet a rarity; New York had eighty-eight free grammar schools and one free academy. In 1855 a free laborer in Alabama received forty-nine cents a day and meals, in North Carolina forty-two cents, in California and Oregon four dollars. A carpenter in Alabama received $1.76 a day without board, in California $7.60, in Oregon $10.00. Sailors on Dr. E. K. Kane's expedition to northern Greenland, which returned on the Advance *to New York harbor October 11, received fifteen dollars a month. A ten-hour day for factory workers was under discussion in Congress.*

II

In 1855 Uncle Tom's Cabin was three years old. Still people read and sighed, unable to resist its spell, unable to forget the dying Eva in Uncle Tom's arms, Tom's staunch manhood, or St. Claire's words after Eva's death, "O Tom, my boy, the whole world is as empty as an eggshell." The Cabin *scattered doubts and complexities, stirred endless hatred against Legree:* "This yer fist has got as hard as iron knocking down niggers."

In 1855 Illinois refused Abraham Lincoln a seat in the United

States Senate. Though he thought himself a Whig, he wrote to Speed, people called him an Abolitionist. The Know-Nothings he berated with bitter scorn: "As a nation we began by declaring 'All men are created equal.' We now practically read it, 'All men are created equal, except negroes.' When the Know-Nothings get control, it will read, 'All men are created equal except negroes, foreigners and Catholics.'"

In 1855 John Brown and his four sons were serving in the Fifth Regiment, First Brigade of Kansas Volunteers, resolved "to defend the City of Lawrence ... from threatened demolition by foreign invaders." They were reconciled uneasily to a treaty of peace between Kansas and Missouri, finally convinced in December that "Missourians will give up all further hope of making Kansas a Slave State." In October Graham's Magazine *asserted that a clash between North and South was inconceivable. How could a busy, diverse people afford to concentrate its energies on such an issue?*

In 1855 Henry Thoreau was immersed in nature's secrets, remote from slavery and reform, unstirred as yet by the fierce message of John Brown. What was a man's right in property, in land? To this question he returned Locke's answer: No more than he can use. On November 9 he wrote in his Journal: *"The Irishman moves into town, sets up a shanty on the railroad land, and then gleans the dead wood from the neighboring forest, which would never get to market. But the so-called owner forbids it and calls him a trespasser. The highest law gives a thing to him who can use it."[1]*

In 1855 Oliver Wendell Holmes, Jr., was fourteen, reading Uncle Tom's Cabin *and James Fenimore Cooper, listening to his father's quips at the dinner table or his stories of his struggles with puerperal fever in the hospital wards of Boston's Fruit Street. Was Parker right that war was coming? Dr. Holmes thought not.*

III

In 1855 George Fitzhugh's Sociology for the South *was still the book of the hour. Without slavery, that is, without an oppressed*

*class, asserted Fitzhugh, no society can endure. The law of Aristotle
can never be abrogated: some men are born to be slaves, others
to be masters and creators. The Negro is a slave to the manner
born. In four thousand years of opportunity, he has preferred his
barbarous habits to the superior culture of the white. He is but a
child grown tall. Circumstance, however manipulated, can only
accentuate nature's division between slaves and masters. The durable aspects of life are the raw materials of human nature, its
selfishness, passions, greed, timeless and ineradicable qualities
that project themselves invariably in a society of stratification. To
understand human nature is to confess the failure of equality and
the necessity of slavery, whether black or white. Can anyone point
to a durable free society? In every state "every man has property
in his fellow man." Wherever there exists a labor surplus, in Fitzhugh's opinion, in that country somebody has to work for slave
wages.*[2]

*To the insecurity and oppression of free labor Fitzhugh con-
trasted the benefits of a slave society. Were not one-half of the
population of the North common laborers or servants, poor, oppressed, insecure? In the South, on the contrary, the "slave is never
without a master to maintain him." The institution of slavery, he
insisted, "gives full development and full play to the affections.
Free society chills, stints, and eradicates them." In a less dogmatic
vein the* Southern Literary Messenger *in March traced the inequalities of society to "the joint operation of the imperfection of human
nature and of the inevitable varying conditions of human life."
Whatever the offenses of the wealthy, insisted the editor, the poor,
if placed in power, would act with infinitely less wisdom. The division of man into classes is dictated not by evil institutions, but by
the nature of man himself and the unchanging order of the universe.*

*But even in the South voices were not wanting for a more
sanguine estimate of Negro nature. In January, the urbane, temperate* Messenger *carried William Archer Cocke's hostile review of*
Types of Mankind; *unlike the authors, Cocke asserted the spiritual
unity of men, black or white, rich or poor. In a more emphatic*

vein the Southern Quarterly Review *pointed to the countless links that bind into one family the genius and the savage, Milton and the Hottentots. Is not the rational faculty the possession of all men? Is it not this very faculty that makes government possible and responsibility a reality? The author is struck by the employment of Negroes, both slave and free, that requires diligence, judgment, and rational choice of action, all of which "speak favorably of their position in the wide range of humanity." Since genius varies with circumstance, not color, it is unfair to demand genius in races long degraded. The emotional oneness of man is everywhere apparent; tears, laughter, delight, grief know no distinction of race or color.*

In February and March the Western Journal and Civilian, *advocating the colonization of 200,000 Negroes annually as the most humane solution of the common problem, struck an even bolder note as to the Negro potential: "No candid man will deny to the African," asserted the author, "powers which, if unfolded, would raise him to an equality with other men." But what chance has he in America? Here his powers can never be realized; the doors of the professions, law, theology, medicine, are locked and barred against him. If the black man remains, he must intermarry with the whites and become their social equal. How could he be happy otherwise, to know blackness the badge of his inferiority, whatever his talents? Late in the year* Putnam's Monthly *echoed the sentiment of its southern contemporary. In a half-daring, half-facetious article titled "About Niggers," the author bemoaned the waste of human tissue in the black man's struggle, and hoped for his colonization in Africa where he could flourish without hindrance and yet prove the nobility of human fiber.*

IV

On January 6, 1855, the People's Organ *protested local brutality toward servants. On a bitterly cold night a family in Clinton Township, New Jersey, had required their servant to do the family wash in a shed exposed to the elements, refusing her permission to stop working long enough to warm her body by the fire.* So badly were the girl's feet frostbitten that amputation, reported the People's Organ, *was found to be necessary, and the girl "is doomed to spend an embittered life at the expense of the public authority."*

In March, 1855, the Christian Examiner, *in reviewing James Paxton's Biography of Horace Greeley, recalled with pride Greeley's astounding success. On August 18, 1831, he had landed in New York with one suit of clothes (the rest of his belongings tied in a bundle on the end of a stick), with ten dollars in his pocket, and not a friend in the city. Twenty years later he was the editor-in-chief of the persuasive* Tribune, *with many thousands of daily readers.*

In September, 1855, the Living Age *reprinted from the* New York Times *an essay castigating the free-love thought of Byron, Shelley, Bulwer, Sand, Eugène Sue, Robert Owens, and Fannie Wright, all heretical also as Fourierists or Socialists. Not casual or incidental, insisted the author, the movement for free love is now advanced in America and Europe by persistent and reputable authors; not by novelists only, but by scientists and social planners.*

V

In 1855 Orestes Brownson and Parke Godwin dealt telling blows *at the Know-Nothing enthusiasts and dominant Protestant prejudices. In his* Quarterly Review *for January Brownson wrote feelingly of the place of Irish immigrants: "A man is run over. 'O, it is only an Irishman.' A man has fallen from a house and broken his back. He is a foreigner, and we 'pass to the order of the day.' Need we be surprised if the immigrants do not fall in love with us,— if they do not readily fraternize with us?" The poverty of the Irish, like their Catholic faith, he continued, is a byword of ridicule. Not only our charity but our vaunted religious liberty we deny to the Catholic conscience, as we may deny them tomorrow to the Congregationalists, the Baptists, the Methodists. But the real American character, asserted Brownson, is concealed by a coat of changing colors in the fluid changes and habits of American life; its real outlines are yet unborn: "In order to study the real American character, we must study as in the child, what we are becoming, rather than what we are. Like children we live in the future . . . We have hope, but no memory."*

In his essay, "America for the Americans," written in May, Parke Godwin struck with Brownson the note of democratic welcome to Europe's oppressed. *We must reject the immigrant utterly, asserted Godwin, or receive him in full brotherhood; no middle way avails. Good citizens are not born, but made. Let us inject the foreigner, stunted though he may be by social wrongs, into our democratic processes; then only will he rise to the full stature of his manhood.*

VI

In 1855 the subsidization of genius was a high calling in New England, however feeble in proportion to the fallow fields of unplowed man. In this year Emerson wrote to Frederick Beck and others urging contributions to an annuity for Alcott *"that may at least secure him a philosophic loaf every day."* To this cause Longfellow would give a poem, Lowell money, Whipple, Parker, and King each a lecture. But on the subject of slavery in this year Emerson was almost mute. His letter to Parker on November 11 was full of caution and reserve.[3]

In 1855 Henry Adams, sitting in Lowell's study at Harvard, found a new world opening before him, with Goethe equal to Shakespeare, Kant superior to Plato, in the hierarchy of the masters of thought.

In 1855 Nathaniel Hawthorne expressed dissatisfaction with the Briton, writing that *"an intellectual and refined American is a higher man than he—a higher and finer one."*

In July, 1855, Walt Whitman sent forth Leaves of Grass *from the print shop of Tom and James Rome, his Brooklyn friends. In July came Emerson's letter: "I am not blind to the worth of the wonderful gift of* Leaves of Grass . . . *the most extraordinary piece of wit and wisdom that America has yet contributed."* When Whitman received this letter, said his brother George, he was much elated. In the September United States Review *appeared high but accurate praise of* Leaves of Grass, *by Walt himself:* "An American bard at last! One of the roughs, large, proud, affectionate . . . his voice bringing hope and prophecy to the generous races of young and old."

In 1855 prophets other than Walt Whitman looked to the future American with buoyancy and hope. In this year Margaret Fuller's brother sent forth a new edition of her Woman in the 19th Century. "Were every path laid open to Woman," she had written, "as freely as to Man . . . the divine energy would pervade nature to a degree unknown in the history of former ages." In an essay titled "The New Civilization," the United States Review *insisted that only democracy could support a rich individualism in the common man. In a similar vein* Harper's *rejoiced in the immense vitality of America's common strain.* "One of the people!" *it exclaimed.* "Was not Luther such? One of the people! Was not Washington such?" *From the people,* "that great central fire," *have leaped the flames of timeless books and patterns. In America the people will yet project the noblest outlines of the Divine Plan. The nation is happier, kindlier, more tolerant, than ever before. Here labor has acquired a new dignity; it needs only the long blossoming time in the soil and sun of equality.*[4]

In 1855 George Bancroft's oration to the New York Historical Society was eagerly sought and read again. Unlike the workmen of Plato's day, asserted Bancroft, labor in America is elevated and free. A new era looms. Is man evil by nature? Democracy cannot grant it: "The love for others and for the race is as much a part of human nature as the love of self; it is a common instinct that man is responsible for man." We live now only at the dawn of man's dreams. Still we are haunted by needless inequalities; still we hear "the heartless jargon of over-production in the midst of want." How-

ever true it may be that no science of distribution has yet emerged, it is irrational to assume that none can be invented. Meanwhile the common man must be his own champion of a fuller existence. To educate him is not only to give him a richer life but to equip him with the machinery of his own elevation. Thus Bancroft's vision of the new brotherhood, the democracy to come, with every workman a creator and everyone enclosed by society's enfolding arms.[5]

IV

A Contrast in Democratic Temper:
Lincoln and Emerson

For he is the rich man in whom the people are rich, and he is the poor man in whom the people are poor; and how to give all access to the masterpieces of art and culture, is the problem of civilization.

—Emerson

He liked to tell of the strict judge of whom it was said: "He would hang a man for blowing his nose in the street, but he would quash the indictment if it failed to specify which hand he blew it with."

—Sandburg, *Abraham Lincoln*

EVERY man seeks for a body of certainties about the nature of the human animal, the human mind. Even the child must of necessity trace for himself an expectation of the stranger's normal behavior: with one child, it may be a cuff or a frown; with another a smile and a warm voice. From such immature tracings of human nature, the grown man advances to more complex judgments; yet often even these judgments are only extensions of his boyhood musings. So it was with Lincoln and Emerson; the conclusions of each man were rooted in boyhood experience. In Emerson's mind the deepest reality of human nature was its vast potential of unused spiritual and creative energy, a view of man rooted in the religious teaching and examples of his youth. To Lincoln the least changeable reality of human nature was its plastic response to forces, malign or beneficent, a view of man gradually evolved from his canny analysis of frontier life. Though neither of these views of man is yet subject to proof or disproof in the laboratory, both are pregnant with ideas to the searcher for a science of man yet to come.

Of the choice spirits emerging from the womb of American life in the 1840's, no two strike the critic as more strange and dissimilar than Abraham Lincoln and Ralph Waldo Emerson. It is inconceivable that the same mother could have borne them, the same school nurtured them, the same community stamped their faces with its manners and customs. Lincoln shaped by the silences of the forest, the rollicking story-telling of the frontier, the clasp of the wrestler, the slash and bite of the ax, the drifting snow upon the cabin floor, the stalking of the bear, the grunting of the hogs, the ignominy of illegitimacy in his family. Emerson pressed from the mold of a diluted Puritanism, reared in Brahmin gentility, correct manners, tolling of church bells, clean linen, noble friends, the shadow of Harvard College, the gracious order, the expectations of a New England pregnant with intellectual life, rich in creative fervor. Emerson, like Dickens, complained of the American "fury of expectoration," a fury common enough in Illinois but unthinkable in the drawing rooms of Concord. Mary Todd complained that Lincoln disliked soap, a grievance inconceivable in the mouth of Ellen Tucker or Lydia Jackson. Lincoln and Emerson were democrats both, living and thinking at remote poles and strange contradictions of the New World, one emerging from the milieu of frontier equality and frontier crudity, the other from the cumulative intellectual riches of New England's Golden Age. As we read the pages of Tocqueville, it is easy to imagine the lanky, awkward form of Abraham Lincoln and a thousand of the same breed, if of lesser genius. From the pages of Horace Mann, on the contrary, we catch a vision of men like Emerson shaped by great books and famous friends and visions of sages into highly organized and creative human beings.

The face and frame of Abraham Lincoln bore mute testimony to the rough school of his boyhood, of a frontier life the delicate Emerson could not have survived more than a few winters. Lincoln's leathery face showed the sting of wind and rain, sun and snow; the long arms and thick shoulders, the years of labor as child and man, the swing of oar and ax and spade. At eleven a gangling, curious boy, tirelessly inquisitive, knocked to the ground by a father impatient of his questionings; at seventeen a man as tall as the tallest axman, his prowess the coin of neighborly esteem, his mind slow but tenacious. Until he reached the White House, he was a stranger to fatigue of mind or muscle. In him worked the pride and confidence of the frontier, a confidence evoked in spontaneous respect of his fellows, a confidence grown with his great height, his long arms, with the strong steady movements of the determined laborer. In his face were the long silent nights of his youth, the bed of cornhusks and leaves, the sputtering of the pine logs, the long thoughts in the forest silences.

Shaped by contradictory forces, Emerson's mind was early filled with visions, Lincoln's with the harsh realities of a crude existence. Emerson borrowed his main thought currents from the masters; but Lincoln distilled his own convictions in the deep recesses of his mind, trusting to life and a few great documents for the raw materials of his meditations. Books, a rarity to Lincoln, were to Emerson the breath of life; and while Emerson resolved the main riddles of life in "the honied head of Plato," Lincoln thrust them one by one into the slow, sure mill of his daily reflections, superbly certain of its grindings, trusting no mind so profoundly as his own. If Lincoln ever read "Self-Reliance," or drank of Emerson's effervescent wine more than a single cup, he has left no record for his biographers; yet no man in American life was intellectually more self-reliant than the crude Abraham Lincoln. To the "iron string" of self-trust his heart vibrated from youth to death. "He was a close, persistent, continuous, and terrible thinker," wrote Herndon; "he was self-reliant, self-helpful, self-trustful, never once doubting his own ability or power ... Mr. Lincoln thought, at least he so acted, that there were no limitations to the endurance of his mental and vital forces." At his death, insisted Herndon, he had by no means expanded the reaches of his intellectual powers. As a close critic of intellectual processes, Lincoln was constantly aware of his own superior gifts, an awareness he could not help but reveal. "It was his intellectual arrogance and unconscious assumption of superiority," wrote John Hay, "that men like Chase and Sumner never could forgive."[1]

In his pursuit of ultimate truth Emerson vaulted to the skies in one long leap, listening for the whisperings of the Universal Spirit; but Lincoln hugged the earth, his search cautious and skeptical, rooted to the sweep of the eye and the touch of the hand. "In order to believe," wrote Herndon, "he must see and feel, and thrust his hand into the place. He must taste, smell, and handle before he had faith or even belief." Unlike Emerson, Plato, and Coleridge, Lincoln arrived slowly and laboriously at generalizations, trusting, like Aristotle and Bacon, to the multitudinous and verifiable evidence of the sensory man. Emerson and Lincoln exemplify the difference between the theologian and the lawyer, the philosopher and the scientist, each gifted with occasional insight into a country far from his own—Lincoln into the ideal, Emerson into the sharp realities of dollars, faces, and the mighty arms of a new machine age. On the essential contrast between the two natures, no one has spoken more fittingly than Herndon: "Emerson had the genius of the spiritual and ideal; Lincoln had the genius of the real and the practical. Emerson lived high among the stars; Lincoln lived low among men. Emerson dreamed; Lincoln acted. Emerson was intuitional; Lincoln reflective."[2] To Emerson the electrical messages of the Over-Soul bombarded men's minds from the earliest infancy; to Lincoln truth was a trickle of light in the gloaming, a bright spurt of flame from a pine log after supper, after a long day of labor, hunger, and the thousand trivial tasks of a rough, primitive frontier.

In their search for the true nature of man, Lincoln observed the senses, Emerson the working of the spirit. From boyhood, when he ascended tree stumps to repeat the preacher's sermon to his brothers and sisters, Lincoln studied the faces before him. At a sally of humor they relaxed into grins; in the sweep of a story, their

eyes never wavered. Their hearts unlocked; their minds opened.
Like him, they hated vagueness, generalities, heavy abstractions.
"When a mere child," he wrote, "I used to get irritated when anybody talked to me in a way that I could not understand." Hearing
the neighbors chat with his father, he would ponder over their
words half the night, resolving their mysteries "in language plain
enough, as I thought, for any boy I knew to comprehend." To the
end of his life Lincoln spoke unerringly to the ignorant, the sloth-
ful, the axman, the worker, the charwoman, pointing his idea with
his anecdotal magic, perennially aware of the sensory man. Who
can forget his images of the slain whites of the Black Hawk War?

The red light of the morning sun was streaming upon them as they lay
heads toward us on the ground. And every man had a round red spot
on the top of his head about as big as a dollar where the redskins had
taken his scalp. It was frightful, but it was grotesque; and the red sunlight seemed to paint everything all over.[3]

Unlike Lincoln in this passage, Emerson seldom descended to the
imagery of realism; for the most part he blithely bypassed the
psychology of the senses for the airy geography of ideas. His
hearers loved his serene, noble countenance; but his transcendental
shafts struck rafters and roof, not the minds and hearts of the average listener. What did Lincoln himself remember from Emerson's
lecture, apparently the only one he ever attended? Here is the
record from the *Journals:* "Oh, Mr. Emerson, I once heard you say
in a lecture, that a Kentuckian seems to say by his air and manners,
'Here am I; if you don't like me, the worse for you.'"

Fragile and sickly from his youth, his presence stamped with
the reticence of Puritan gentility, Emerson absorbed an attitude
toward women remote and strange to most frontiersmen of Lincoln's
breed. In the contradictory notions of the two great democrats
about love and marriage, one may trace the many conflicts to come;
one projecting the shadow of Puritan repressions to be magnificently
delineated in *The Scarlet Letter;* the other anticipating the icono-
clasm of Whitman, Stephen Crane, and Theodore Dreiser. To

Emerson the sexual passions of man represented a distasteful remnant of his animal ancestry; to Lincoln, on the other hand, the same passions assumed in his mind a place of normality and inevitability. In his discussions of passion he accepted not the condemnations of the moralist, but the tacit approbation of the crude and vigorous frontiersman.

If Lincoln's robustness issued naturally from the rough strength of his body and the boisterous habits of the frontier, Emerson's physical coldness was created inevitably enough by his weak constitution and the Puritan climate of his boyhood. In quoting Elizabeth Hoar's description of Thoreau, he delineated his own weakness: "I love Henry," she said, "but I cannot like him; and as for taking his arm, I should as soon think of taking the arm of an elm tree." As Ludwig Lewisohn aptly observes, Emerson early lamented his own coldness. He was "born cold." He lacked a "warm heart," "animal spirits," "the kind affections of a pigeon." In a crowd he was uneasy, restless, aloof, shut out from the warm glow of the comradely circle. If in his youth Emerson himself had been "a watcher of windows, and studious of a glove, a veil, a ribbon, or the wheels of a carriage," if he had been "all eye when one was present and all memory when one was gone," he rejected as unwaveringly as Cotton Mather the sensual delights of love. The pleasures of physical love, he wrote in his condemnation of Boccaccio, can be intense "only a few times in a lifetime." He acknowledged passion to be a "powerful spring," though a "bad regulator." This passion Emerson felt was a part of the chimpanzee in man, sure to disappear with the advance of evolution; he bewailed the "deep sleep of the higher faculties of man." If Emerson ever felt the harsh passion Lincoln describes so frankly, he has left no accessible record; the conclusion is inescapable that if he did feel it, it brought a surge of shame to his bosom; whereas to Lincoln, as to the average man of the frontier, the rough, almost impersonal, physical hunger fell upon him as normally and inevitably as the rain.

Lincoln's physical robustness, curbed as it was by a monotonous diet and deficient elimination, found expression in channels that to

Emerson were crude and vulgar. Many of his stories were shockingly frank and coarse; until the end of his life he was curiously insensitive to the inhibitions of refinement, his conceptions shaped by the rough manners of the frontier, the humor of the stagecoach, the village store, the hotel lobby, the courtroom intermission. To his friends, according to Herndon, he did not hesitate to relieve his feelings by telling them ridiculous stories about himself, such as the night at the Cottenbarger home when, aroused by the daughter's feet on his pillow, he caressed her legs and awakened her. The girl in turn aroused her mother and Lincoln, infinitely mortified by what the *devil in him* had done, hastened away the next morning while Cottenbarger was out of the house. When he was thirty years old, Lincoln asked Speed, in the vernacular of the day, where he could buy sexual release. With satisfaction imminent, however, Lincoln found he did not have enough money and gently refused the prostitute's offer of credit for her services. "I have seen women make advances and I have seen Lincoln refuse or reject them," wrote Herndon. "Lincoln had terribly strong passions for women, could scarcely keep his hands off them, and yet he had honor and a strong will, and these enabled him to put out the fires of his terrible passion."[4]

All this to Herndon was merely a matter of honest record, like the movements of Lincoln's arms, the position of his feet on the platform, the high, thin pitch of his voice as he opened a speech. To Herndon the stature of Lincoln was irrevocably shaped by his genius for concentration, his unerring gauging of national forces, his infinite compassion, his timely utterance of the nation's spiritual strivings. No stain of illegitimacy, thought Herndon, no coarseness, no uncouthness, could diminish the shadow of his hero over the long reaches of history. He was the greatest of all men since the Galilean himself had walked the earth. Let all be told, nothing be hidden: let all men know the stains, the misery, the shrewdness, the sadness, the stormy passions of a great man's soul. In the long reaches of history a man's blunt hunger for flesh may slip into insignificance; but the address at Gettysburg rings on forever, telling with every phrase the magic of language and the premises, wise or foolish, of the American dream.

Emerson's impressions of Lincoln reveal at once his unerring grasp of essential superiority in a personality alien to his own. How alien he felt to one of Lincoln's stamp, and how keenly he deplored traits unbecoming, as he thought, to the President's office, one reads in the *Journals*. In 1860 Emerson, like most liberal New Englanders, was distressed when Lincoln won the nomination over Seward. In February, 1862, however, when Emerson met Lincoln at the White House, he swiftly revised his original estimate. "The President impressed me more favourably than I had hoped," he wrote.

A frank, sincere, well-meaning man, with a lawyer's habit of mind, good clear statement of his fact; correct enough, not vulgar, as described, but with a sort of boyish cheerfulness, or that kind of sincerity and jolly good meaning that our class meetings on Commencement Days show, in telling our old stories over. When he has made his remark, he looks up at you with great satisfaction, and shows all his white teeth, and laughs.[5]

Thus, in a face-to-face appraisal, some of Emerson's doubts dissolved. Though he did not recognize a great statesman, he liked the solid, salty man. But still he could not accustom himself to Lincoln's lack of polish, whatever his talents. In 1863 he wrote, "We must accept the results of universal suffrage, and not try to make it appear that we can elect fine gentlemen. We shall have coarse men, with a fair chance of worth and manly ability, but not polite men." Emerson deplored Lincoln's lack of dignity. "You cannot refine Mr. Lincoln's taste," he wrote, "extend his horizon, or clear his judgment." Why should a President cheapen himself by making a speech at every railroad station, getting into arguments with little men, writing letters to Horace Greeley, or running around town in a cab to frustrate the execution of a deserter? Such trivial actions Emerson thought unworthy of the President's office. With his unfailing fairness, however, Emerson later qualified these impressions also. A man of mighty decisions cannot pause for the niceties of charm and culture. In such a man, meeting a crisis every hour, do not manners and appearance fall into insignificance? "*He* cannot palter, he cannot but carry a grace beyond his own, a dignity, by means of what he drops . . . all his pretension and trick, and arrives, of course, at a simplicity, which is the perfection of manners."

Though he at times deplored Lincoln's polemic and like most New Englanders condemned Lincoln's delay in issuing the Emancipation Proclamation, Emerson was full of praise for Lincoln when it was at last promulgated in September, 1862. He commended Lincoln as possessing "so fair a mind that none ever listened so patiently to such extreme varieties of opinion." The Proclamation Emerson denominated as one of the great milestones of human liberty, along with the Declaration of Independence, the English Republic of 1648, and the passage of the English Reform Bill. By this time, two years after Lincoln's election, Emerson was prepared to admit that "we have underestimated the capacity and virtue which the Divine Providence has made an instrument of benefit so vast." Lincoln, he added, "has been permitted to do more for America than any other American man. He is well entitled to the most indulgent construction. Forget all that we thought shortcomings, every mistake, every delay." Three years later, in his address at Lincoln's funeral services, held at Concord on April 19, 1865, Emerson rendered a judgment of Lincoln filled with unerring tribute. His ill manners, his undignified comings and goings, were now forgotten. In his years at the White House, said Emerson, Lincoln's overflowing good will had become a "noble humanity." His humor and jocularity endeared him to men and helped him bear the racking strain of daily conference. If in manners he was deficient, in intelligence, and in co-ordination of talents and energy, he was superior. "In four years," declared Emerson, "four years of battle days,—his endurance, his fertility of resources, his magnanimity, were sorely tried and never found wanting. There, by his courage, his justice, his even temper, his fertile counsel, his humanity, he stood a heroic figure in the centre of a heroic epoch."[6]

If one task of the future science of man will be the mining of greatness and the secrets of greatness, it must go to Emerson and Lincoln for examples as well as assumptions. The greatness of Emerson, excluding the mysteries of genetics, is more traceable than that of Lincoln. Behind Emerson, essentially a contemplative man, we see hovering the great sages and poets and thinkers of his past. Behind Lincoln, whom Sandburg has called "the baffling Hamlet of democracy," we sense no ancestry of greatness except the magic of a few great documents and a great hope born mysteriously somewhere in his early years. Whereas Emerson has left us no workable process by which a science of man can help bring great men to being, his words about the average man's untapped resources are a mass of incandescent guesses, each of which merits a scientific appraisal. Though Emerson names the way to greatness, he cannot show us the steps by which one reaches the path. Lincoln, on the other hand, will teach the searcher to apply the first test of science to human behavior: let man try his powers in action. Give the Negro the soldier's test on the battlefield. Give the frontier man his chance to speak, to persuade his fellows that he should sit in the White House. Nothing makes man great more than great hope, and in a true democracy great hope is no delusion.

V

Lincoln: Human Nature in America's Crucible

> *I think the authors of that notable instrument intended to include all men, but they did not intend to declare all men equal in all respects. They did not mean to say that all were equal in colour, size, intellect, moral developments, or social capacity.*
>
> —Lincoln

ON the nature of man Lincoln was a slow and cautious thinker, limiting himself to a few seminal beliefs, content with an incomplete picture of man's personality, reluctant to hazard either guesses about his origins or prophecies about his future. He possessed neither the amazing scope of Holmes's knowledge of man nor the broad learning of Jefferson in history, philosophy, and psychology. Nor would he venture, like Emerson, into theological speculation on man's divine nature. Unlike Horace Mann, he did not visualize the illimitable pressures of education on the plastic minds of youth. He knew fewer books, and fewer classrooms, than any of his great contemporaries; yet from examining himself, his frontier world, and a few great documents, he slowly and confidently shaped the foundation of his intellectual structure, a foundation grounded in a few unshakable convictions about the nature and the rights of man.

To expect a worthy reward for one's labor, to want opportunities for self-advancement, to struggle mightily before the prospect of material improvement, to possess a sense of relative justice and injustice, these to Lincoln were the primary patterns of human nature. Whether these patterns were innate or acquired he did not attempt to determine; he was certain only that they were created by forces over which the individual man has no control whatever. Man has no free choice; but his nature is plastic and responsive. Lincoln believed in taking a *chance* on human intelligence and integrity; the American experiment was itself to him a sally in this direction, a *chance* on the responsiveness of the common man to opportunities hitherto undreamed of. Thus he was willing to risk a broadening of the suffrage, not excluding women; he did not know that Negroes would make resourceful soldiers, but he wanted them given the chance to prove themselves; he wanted human nature tested in the crucible of social experiment, not in the towers of speculative thought.

Lincoln's faith in democratic government was rooted, like that of Jefferson, in his profound reliance on the constructive conditioning of the human organism. The Declaration of Independence was the touchstone of his faith in the nature of man, in the illimitable response to the spirit of equal rights:

Most governments have been based, practically, on the denial of the equal rights of men . . . ours began by affirming those rights. They said, some men are too ignorant and vicious to share in government. Possibly so, said we; and, by your system, you would always keep them ignorant and vicious.

Here Lincoln asserts the impact of two governmental *systems* on the nature of man: the one to keep him vicious and ignorant; the other to stir him with hope and the magical spectacle of continuous human betterment. In no American had the spirit of equality that Tocqueville observed struck a clearer flame than in Abraham Lincoln. At forty-five, he spoke of his own debt to the spirit of the Declaration of Independence:

There is no permanent class of hired laborers amongst us. Twenty-five years ago I was a hired laborer. The hired laborer of yesterday labors on his own account to-day, and will hire others to labor for him to-morrow. Advancement—improvement in condition—is the order of things in a society of equals . . . The power of hope upon human exertion and happiness is wonderful.[1]

In these words Lincoln the statesman looked upon Lincoln the symbol, symbol of the living truth of the Declaration, the electricity of hope and the right of the humblest man to self-realization.

When he faced and wrestled with arguments for slavery, Lincoln returned again and again to the Declaration's exaltation of the nature of man and the rights of the humble. Between slavery and the Declaration stood an irreconcilable contradiction; the nation would either return to the principles of the Declaration or bow its face before the shadow of tyranny and despair. As he spoke, his great frame shook with passion; his hearers marveled at his eloquence when he touched on the Declaration. At Beardstown, in 1858, he spoke again of the great manifesto of Jefferson and his fellows:

This was their majestic interpretation of the economy of the universe. This was their lofty, and wise, and noble understanding of the justice of the Creator to his creatures—yes, gentlemen, to all his creatures, to the whole great family of men. In their enlightened belief, nothing stamped with the divine image and likeness was sent into the world to be trodden on and degraded and imbruted by its fellows. They grasped not only the whole race of man then living, but they reached forward and seized upon the farthest posterity. They erected a beacon to guide their children, and their children's children, and the countless myriads who should inhabit the earth in other ages. . . . They established these great self-evident truths, that when in the distant future some man, some faction, some interest, should set up the doctrine that none but rich men, none but white men, or none but Anglo-Saxon white men were entitled to life, liberty, and the pursuit of happiness, their posterity might look up again to the Declaration of Independence and take courage to renew the battle which their fathers began.[2]

No words exemplify more aptly than these Lincoln's faith in the right of the humblest man to circumstances favorable to his growth; no words more decisively depict his conviction that the nature of the humblest man is so plastic and rich as to justify the optimism of the democratic impetus. If the principle of slavery sold human nature short and the Declaration sold it long, he would stand steadfastly with the men of the Revolution. Nor would he allow a discriminating division of human nature by race, by creed, or by color: the poor, the humble, the oppressed stood under one banner.

When Lincoln voiced his belief that all men are created equal, he did not conclude that Negroes and whites are born equal in gifts or intelligence. He affirmed not the equality of human nature, but, like Jefferson, the equality of privileges and opportunities that the nation should provide. Less philosophical and acute than Jefferson, Lincoln did not attempt to divide the shaping of man's nature into hereditary and environmental forces. Less learned and less theoretical than Tocqueville, he did not attempt a minute analysis of the psychology of servitude or the environmental roots of Negro habits and customs. Though the evidence is fragmentary, Lincoln appeared to believe that the Negro (whether from pressures inherent or environmental) was inferior to the white man. In his debates with Douglas Lincoln guardedly conceded the inferiority of the Negro, affirming meanwhile equal economic rights for unequal persons: "I agree with Judge Douglas he [the Negro] is not my equal in many respects, certainly not in color, perhaps not in intellectual nor moral endowment. But in the right to eat the bread . . . which his own hand earns, he is my equal . . . and the equal of any living man."

Though at the end of his life he expressed himself as willing to give the suffrage to the more intelligent Negroes, Lincoln was on the whole opposed to suffrage for the black man; each state should decide, he said, on one occasion; but as for himself he was against giving the Negro either political or social equality. On the other hand he believed Negroes should have the privilege of fighting for their freedom in the armies of the North; his trust in the adaptability of the Negroes to the rigors of war, a trust often expressed against the opinions of his advisers, exemplifies his disposition to let the Negro, like every humble person, have his talents tested in the fires of performance rather than in the prejudgments of philosophers and statesmen.

Though Lincoln leaned, then, to the belief that the black man is stamped with inferiority, he was not ready to pronounce a final judgment. Meanwhile he took a middle position on Negro rights: "I do not understand," he said, "that because I do not want a Negro woman for a slave I must necessarily want her for a wife. My understanding is that I can just let her alone. I am now in my fiftieth year, and I certainly never have had a black woman for either a slave or a wife." He would not allow the Negro political and social equality. But assuming his inferiority, did he have no economic rights? Did his blackness condemn him to servitude? On this point Lincoln was vehement and decisive:

You say A is white and B is black. It is color, then; the lighter having the right to enslave the darker? Take care. By this rule you are to be slave to the first man you meet with a fairer skin than your own. You do not mean color exactly? You mean the whites are intellectually superior to the blacks, and therefore have the right to enslave them? Take care again. By this rule you are to be slave to the first man you meet with an intellect superior to your own.[3]

Whatever his limitations, the Negro is not a hog, not a bear or a wild buffalo, but a human being. If the Negro is not a man, we can enslave him as easily as we would a horse. If the Negro is a man, "is it not . . . a total destruction of self-government to say that he, too, shall not govern himself?"

Nothing in Lincoln's estimate of man's nature is more searching than his description of the impact of property on motives and opinion. Speaking at Hartford, Connecticut, on March 5, 1860, he reminded his northern audience that in finding motives to keep its property human nature North and South is equally resourceful. The cash value of the slaves of the South was two billion dollars. "This amount of property value," he asserted, "has a vast influence on the minds of its owners, very naturally. The same amount of property would have an equal influence upon us if owned in the North." Even the theology of the South was influenced by the pull of property. As he searches the Bible, the Rev. Dr. Ross concludes that for some men to be slaves is the will of God. But how to judge a particular slave, the case of his own slave Sambo? Dr. Ross is puzzled. The Bible does not answer categorically. He does not think of consulting Sambo. "So at last it comes to this, that Dr. Ross is to decide the question; and while he considers it, he sits in the shade, with gloves on his hands, and subsists on the bread that Sambo is earning in the burning sun." Dr. Ross's answer is an inevitable extension of his circumstances; his economic interests make it impossible for him to render an impartial decision. This story, like many others, shows Lincoln's realistic awareness of man's response to the dynamics of self-preservation.

But the humble man, the propertyless man, also strives to preserve himself. With the labor of his hands he seeks to get his bread. Centuries ago, before the invention of printing, the great masses of common men had no thought of equality, no thought of rising in the social scale, or of acquiring property like their masters. They considered themselves inferior by nature. But in the minds of these men, oppressed by an unbelievably strong conviction of their inferiority, the invention of the printed word worked a gradual miracle. Previous to that miracle they had been "utterly unconscious that their condition or their minds were capable of improvement." But now the printed word was emancipating the mind "from this false estimate of itself." In the vast new America the emancipation of men's minds proceeds apace. Here, moreover, a man can labor for himself. He can become an inventor and discoverer. He can become a man of property. On no other point was Lincoln so insistent as on the right of the humble man to gather the fruits of his labor. In a country established in the spirit of aiming "at the elevation of men," of endeavoring to achieve "the progressive improvement of all men, everywhere," it was abhorrent to Lincoln that any human being, black or white, should be denied the right to eat the bread he had worked for. "Every man," he asserted, "black, white, or yellow, has a mouth to be fed, and two hands with which to feed it—and bread should be allowed to go to that mouth without controversy." To Lincoln, then, the cause of the Negro slave was indivisible from the cause of the poor man, the propertyless man, all over the world. He regarded their human wants as natural and satiable. Their right to improvement, their right to labor for property, was inherent not only in the Declaration, but in the very nature of man. In America why should any man stand in servitude? "I say there is room enough for all of us to be free."

In the long struggle between poor man and propertied man, slave and master, subject and king, Lincoln placed himself solidly on the side of the weak. The cause of the weak was the cause of justice. The tyranny of the powerful in the long struggle he reduced and simplified to the theft of the common man's labor. "They [right and wrong] are the two principles," he declared,

that have stood face to face from the beginning of time, and will ever continue to struggle. The one is the common right of humanity, and the other the divine right of kings. It is the same principle in whatever shape it develops itself. It is the same spirit that says, "You toil and work and earn bread, and I'll eat it."[4]

Though the poor man is driven by his need for bread, and the rich by the impulse to preserve his ownership, property is not the only force that shapes motives and opinions. Each man has a sense of right and wrong that at times overweighs material necessities. In each man's breast a war is waged between selfishness and justice, kindness and cruelty, interest and generosity. Lincoln had often pointed to the generous spirit of many southerners in freeing their own slaves or alleviating the miseries of servitude.

In 1841, when Lincoln and Speed had traveled by steamboat from Louisville to St. Louis, they had seen daily a dozen Negroes shackled together. The sight caused Lincoln continual suffering. Though he was constantly delving for primary causes, Lincoln did not trace the forces that shaped his suffering; he was certain only of an outraged sense of justice. Whence came his sense of justice? Was it inherited with the color of his eyes? Lincoln did not say it was inherited; nor did he trace it to the teachings of great books and the exemplary conduct of his heroes, Clay and Jefferson. But somehow in all men it was there; he believed, like Tocqueville, in the "singular principle of relative justice implanted in the human heart," a principle in frequent clash with the economic motive. "The love of property," he said, "and a consciousness of right or wrong have conflicting places in our organization, which often makes a man's course seem crooked, his conduct a riddle."

To Lincoln the nature of man was rooted in the forces of heredity and circumstance: man therefore through his sensory mechanism responds mechanically and inevitably to the world in which he is born, a world set in motion in the infinitely remote past. "There are no accidents," said Lincoln, "in my philosophy. Every effect must have its cause. The past is the cause of the present, and the present will be the cause of the future." Every choice man makes, every idea he conceives, is dictated by a chain of causes and effects over which he has no control. Except in a limited degree man is not free in will or mind; his actions are merely the projections of the pressures of his environment. According to Herndon, Lincoln often said, "I always was a fatalist"; he was fond of quoting Shakespeare's lines:

> There's a divinity that shapes our ends,
> Rough-hew them how we will.

To press home his point, Lincoln argued with Herndon that the assassination of Caesar was the inevitable outcome of conditions and causes which Brutus and Caesar were powerless to change. "What is man?" he asked. "He is a mere child moved and governed by this vast world machine, forever working in grooves, and moving in deep-cut channels; and now what is man? He is a simple tool, a cog, a part and parcel of this vast iron machine that strikes and cuts, grinds and mashes."[5]

This interpretation of Lincoln's belief Herndon documented too well to suffer demolition by a whole series of religionist attackers. The implications of Lincoln's assertion are profound and revolutionary; they deny that any human being is responsible for his conduct. No organized society can accept this denial of human responsibility: for the lawbreaker there must be a jail, for the irresponsible man the condemnation of his community, for the sinner the threat of spiritual damnation. Yet the practical necessity of human responsibility does not of itself invalidate Lincoln's thesis —a thesis that has a distinguished ancestry among the great thinkers. When Socrates argued, as in the *Protagoras*, that virtue is knowledge and evil ignorance, he denied free will; when Jesus pleaded for forgiveness seventy times seven, and prayed, at the end, "Father, forgive them, for they know not what they do," he placed the blame for the actions of his enemies upon the spiritual poverty of their environment. When Shelley and Godwin proclaimed that man is infinitely perfectible, they placed the burden of his perfection upon the community, not upon man himself. When Robert Owen wrote, "Man's character is made for him and not by him," he also denied free choice, bringing upon his head the wrath of Victorian England. To respectable Americans of 1886, when Herndon's biography appeared, it was inconceivable that the martyred Lincoln, who so often in the war years had appealed to a just God, could deny man's freedom of choice. But Herndon had fully anticipated the exclamations of horror from the learned and the pious; he had even secured from Nicolay a statement that to Nicolay's knowledge Lincoln had not changed his beliefs after leaving Springfield for the White House. From the mass of subsequent evidence, Herndon's interpretation of Lincoln's limited determinism remains to this day incontrovertible.

To the orthodox Christian Lincoln's denial of free will was a denial of the faith; but to Herndon, as to many democratic thinkers, a denial of free will was the indispensable prerequisite to the attainment of that uttermost compassion which to Paul was the heart of the Christian message. Lincoln's deep compassion, in Herndon's judgment, sprang inevitably from his outlook. He would neither condemn nor praise, neither eulogize nor berate. As a good man deserved no credit for the pressures that made him a high-principled citizen, an evil man deserved no harsh words, no jail, no gallows for the forces that harried his soul. Only a few days before his death in 1891, Herndon gave his last testimony on this point:

"His whole philosophy made him free from hate, free from love ... free from malice. No man was responsible for what he was, thought, or did ... he was a child of conditions. ... Hence Lincoln could well exclaim: 'With malice toward none and charity for all.'"

Abundant evidence exists to corroborate Herndon's analysis of the origin of Lincoln's charity. In 1854, as often afterward, Lincoln spoke his good will for the slave owners of the South; he hated slavery, not its advocates: "Let me say that I think I have no prejudice against the Southern people. They are just what we would be *in their situation.* [Italics mine.] If slavery did not now exist among them, they would not introduce it. If it did now exist among us, we should not instantly give it up." In this persistent belittlement of human differences and concurrent emphasis on circumstance, Lincoln did not waver. His pardoning of deserters, his forbearance for Stanton and Seward, his patience with Mary Todd Lincoln, his last words to his Cabinet, all point to the same unrelenting belief. "I hope there will be no persecution, no bloody work after the war is over," he said. "None need expect me to take any part in hanging or killing them. Frighten them out of the country, let down the bars, scare them off. Enough lives have been sacrificed. We must extinguish our resentment if we expect harmony and union." On the day of his assassination, he countermanded the arrest of a Confederate spy, began "a new pile of pardons," and endorsed General Van Alen's recommendation of "a Union of hearts and hands as well as States."

Lincoln's compassion for people was rooted, then, in his sober, sustained reflections on the nature of man and his world. Skeptical, realistic, rational, rejecting the theological assertion of human responsibility, Lincoln embodied in his concept a compassion for man and a conviction of his potentialities unique in American annals. Man is a creature of forces, of forces both benign and malevolent, forces material and intellectual, forces social and biological. To Lincoln the corollary of such a deterministic outlook was not despair but infinite hope. The invention of printing had unleashed into the world forces of infinite promise; it had banished from millions of minds the superstition of fixed and unalterable inequalities; and now, for the first time in the history of man, a new country had established equality as its way of life, opening its vast treasures and precious privileges to the humble people of all lands, opposing before the eyes of all men the forces of democratic opportunity to the restrictions of aristocratic authority. And was not he himself, born in a log cabin, reared on the frontier, for many years a manual laborer, at last elevated to the nation's highest office, a symbol of the new era of democratic pressures, the justification of democratic hopes?

To many Americans Lincoln became the exultant proof that the Declaration's sally of faith in the common man was not abortive. He symbolized the vigorous and sturdy growth of human nature in a new soil of equality and a new climate of opportunity. The country rejoiced that its martyred President had risen to the White House from the humblest ranks of frontier life. American masters of language were proud that a simple man, born in a log cabin, could speak the immortal words of Gettysburg, ringing proof of the long-submerged genius of the common man.

In his eulogy of Lincoln to Congress on February 12, 1866, George Bancroft compared the humble origins of Lincoln with the aristocratic ancestry of Lord Palmerston. The early teachers of Lincoln were the stars, the forest, the prairie; those of Palmerston, the best minds of Harrow and Cambridge. Whereas Palmerston spoke for the best blood of England, tracing his lineage to the Conqueror, Lincoln spoke for the family of man, careless of his forebears; a grandfather was good enough for him. Whereas Palmerston cherished the approval of the Commons, Lincoln "thought always of mankind, as well as his own country, and served human nature itself." Whatever the source of his mysterious genius, Lincoln became a symbol to the world of the vast potential of growth in America's common men. How many common men among ten thousand could rise to greatness? To this question no experiments had yet provided even a partial answer.

Lincoln's central conception about human responsibility was

never better posed than in his statement, "A man can no more help being a coward than he can help being a hunchback." Only a science of man, as rigorously rationalistic as the method of the physicist, can prove or disprove Lincoln's statement. Even the criminal law does not see free choice as a matter of black-and-white clarity; upon occasion it acknowledges the influence of temporary insanity and reduces the guilt of the criminal. The church, too, makes allowance for degrees of guilt in the granting of absolution. Even the military code is now finding the words *courage* and *cowardice* more and more difficult to define in terms of free choice. In claiming that there is "no such thing as a bad boy," Father Flanagan pointed to conditions, not free choice, as the root of delinquency. Many a social worker has said, "I was just lucky I wasn't born on the same street as my clients." To function at all, society must *assume* free choice on the part of its citizens. But this is far from the acceptance of freedom of choice as a reality in a scientific sense. For a future science of man to answer such a question will require infinite patience and experiment; even so, there are those who will say that this question is unanswerable. Perhaps that is true. But if the solution to the riddle posed by Lincoln is ever crystallized, it will come only when a future science of man has amassed evidence as incontrovertible as mathematics to minds of every race and creed.

1865
Year of Victory, Year of Gloom

In 1865 the long struggle drew to a close, a struggle that to Henry George ended chattel slavery, not slavery itself. Nor could it end the slavery of mutual hate. With each slow death, starving prisoner, amputated leg, burning home, the black magic of hatred wrought its phantasms anew in American breasts. Of the 3,000,000 men engaged for the North and 1,300,000 for the South, over 600,000 lost their lives. In the northern ranks alone there were thirty thousand amputations, almost twice as many as American amputations in World War II. Yet in the minds of some, such as Moncure Conway, the war had been far from inevitable. Lincoln and Davis had forced the issue to needless crisis. Over two-thirds of the southerners and almost all the northerners, in Conway's extreme view, had preferred secession to war. Now the South lay in ruins, many of her ablest men ill or wounded, her fields desolate, her commerce withered, her cities gutted. The Nation for July estimated that five-sixths of the property of Georgia, not counting slaves and land, had been destroyed by war. Gloom and bitterness hung like a pall over the prostrate South. In some immature minds hatred turned against the helpless blacks, cause of all their misery.

In the first week of April Abraham Lincoln walked the streets of Richmond, his mien humble and sad at the distress of his enemies. As he paused to rest, reported the Atlantic, an old Negro cried out, "May de good Lord bless you, President Linkum." Then, continued the witness, Lincoln "removed his own hat, and bowed in silence; but it was a bow that upset the forms, laws, customs, and ceremonies of centuries." Thus did the Atlantic place Lincoln's act

114

in its historic setting: a bow, a bared head, challenging the ancient assumption that nature bestows talents upon the white and the rich which she denies to the poor and the black.

On April 9, about eleven in the evening, New York newspapers had received the news of Lee's surrender at Appomattox Courthouse. The next day, Monday, April 10, the Tribune carried the correspondence of Lee and Grant, with Greeley exultant: "The new birth of the Nation is accomplished; the revolution, begun a hundred years ago, is fulfilled." On the same day Greeley revolved anew his conception of human nature, denying the validity of race as a criterion of intelligence, asserting that the freed Negroes would show as good a record of progress as unlettered immigrants. To believe otherwise was "a slander on Human Nature."

April 14, 1865. Ford's Theatre, crowded and gay. A muffled shot, a wild shout, a man jumping to the stage and stumbling off. The President slumped over, already unconscious, carried across the street to his deathbed, too short for his long frame. In its issue of April 15, each column enclosed in heavy black lines, the Tribune printed eleven dispatches about the President's assassination, the last of which read, "The President is slowly dying. The brain is slowly oozing through the ball-hole in his forehead. He is of course insensible. There is an occasional lifting of his hand, and heavy stentorious breathing; that's all."

Amid the shock and gloom that followed the President's death, his detractors were silent, or damned him with faint praise. Honest and unbending, Henry Adams showed no horror at the crime or grief for the fallen man; in Rome with his father when the news came, as he tells us in his autobiography, Adams thought only that that city, "the nursery of murderers and murdered," was a most appropriate setting in which Henry Adams should have received the news. History records no more contemptuous farewell to an American President. Adams regarded Lincoln, as indeed did Justice Holmes, as "a man out of the primitive ooze." But what gifts, what ingredients, came from this ooze that Henry Adams' ancestors and education could not bestow upon him?

To the Times, *however, as to many millions of Americans, Lincoln was a symbol of hope not to the slaves only, but to oppressed men everywhere: "The tears of the forgotten and outcast and oppressed slave, now redeemed to his manhood, will be the sincerest tears that fall on the grave of the President. From the cottages of the poor and the downtrodden will come his truest requiem." On April 19, all his doubts about Lincoln now resolved, Emerson asserted: "Old as history is, and manifold as are its tragedies, I doubt if any death has caused so much pain to mankind." Lincoln might prove a more powerful benefactor in death than in life. To the* London Review *the assassination seemed likely to call forth a frenzy of insane fury in the North; but no such mass frenzy made itself felt from Lincoln's death; that was to come later, concentrated in the fanaticism of Thaddeus Stevens. To George W. Bancroft the assassination of the President symbolized the stern necessity of democratic success; now, as never before, the course of the Republic should run firm and smooth. Popular liberty throughout the world waited upon America's example. Beneath American affirmations seethed a new pride in the capacity of the common soil of humanity to yield consummate intelligence amid the storms of national upheaval and dismay. In the life of Abraham Lincoln the common man felt himself vindicated—his intelligence, his burning ambitions, his roving hopes.*

II

In 1865 the black man stood forth anew in the national consciousness as the focus of the perennial argument over the nature of man. Did nature's color, notwithstanding the Negro's freedom, doom him forever to menial labor, forbid his entrance into creative manhood? "He is free of a chain," wrote Greeley, "but oppressed with a prejudice." On the issue of the Negro, the rhetoric of the North was florid and eloquent, its deeds few. On April 14, speaking at the raising of the flag at Fort Sumter, Henry Ward Beecher cried, "Ye homeless and houseless slaves, look and ye are free. At length you, *too, have part and lot in this glorious ensign." Yet in 1865 only six northern states allowed the Negro to vote. Indeed, in 1865 Connecticut voted to deny him the suffrage. In Philadelphia he did not yet ride on the white man's streetcars. Tocqueville's conclusion that to the American blackness was the symbol of the inferiority of slavehood was confirmed anew in millions of northern minds.*

On August 3 the Nation *reviewed the progress of the Negroes in organizing their numbers for political and educational action, noting with pride the decorum of their conventions, one in Michigan, another in Virginia, still another in Tennessee. In October the* North American Review, *in an article titled "Education of the Freedmen," reviewed the progress of education of blacks in the slave states, under the guidance of the Federal army of occupation. To many blacks the magic of reading was more real than the notion of freedom itself. Forty-four thousand Negro children were already in school—about a tenth of the goal—in addition to those attending night schools. As farmers of their own land the Negroes were proving themselves equal to the whites; one had raised fifty bales of cotton from eighty acres, the best record of any local farmer, black or white.*

III

Notwithstanding northern jubilation at the downfall of slavery, thoughtful critics pointed anew to the growth of poverty in the industrial cities, the ravages of ugliness and want on the nature of man. In the Tribune Greeley *denounced high prices and slum dwellings with colorful rhetoric. On March 9, in an editorial called "The Dwelling-Caves of New York City," he deplored the blighting of twenty-five thousand lives by dark, damp cellars, where even at midday one could not read the print of a newspaper. In one month, according to the health inspector, 1,773 children had died in New York City; 1,606 the sons and daughters of immigrants, and many of them dwellers in the cellar caves. On April 11 Greeley* *denounced the evictions of thousands of tenants (to make way for higher rents) as the "temporary insanity of capital." In 1860 only 1 per cent of the income receivers of New York City had been paid $842 or more per year (equal to about $2,000 in 1929). The workingman spent at least half his money for food, a fourth or more for shelter; in 1860 unskilled laborers in New York had received about $1.00 a day.* The Atlantic Monthly *for June reported that during the war an old woman had made forty-six buttonholes and twenty eyelet holes in tents and sewed on forty-six buttons, all for sixteen cents, often going a whole day without tasting food. A soldier's wife had bought coal all winter by the bucketful, at sixteen dollars a ton. In America's greatest city there were more starving women, more women beggars, more prostitutes than ever before. To Henry George the full flowering of man could come only with the banishment of want throughout the land. In his biased view the victory of the North left the main national enemy yet to be destroyed.*

VI

Of Crime and Responsibility:
Oliver Wendell Holmes

> *The attitude of modern Science is erect,*
> *her aspect serene, her determination in-*
> *exorable, her onward movement unflinching.*
> *... She has reclaimed astronomy and cos-*
> *mogony, and is already laying a firm hand*
> *on anthropology, over which another battle*
> *must be fought.*
>
> . . . .
>
> *We must study the lines of direction of*
> *all the forces that traverse our human na-*
> *ture. We must study man as we have*
> *studied stars and rocks.*
>
> —Holmes

OF America's literary masters, Holmes was the first to attempt a scientific study of the nature of man; for this task his medical knowledge gave him a pre-eminent advantage over all his great contemporaries—over Emerson, Hawthorne, Lowell, Mark Twain. His intellectual method, though it did not lead him to the environmentalist conclusions of Lincoln, Steffens, or Henry George, was rigorously scientific; like Huxley in "The Physical Basis of Life," which Holmes knew and admired, he wished to exclude both the suppositions of logic and the traditions of theology for a full reliance upon the sensory evidence of experimentation. In this approach he was not altogether successful; he could not divorce himself completely from the Brahmin teachings of his youth on the potency of blood. But his learning, crisscrossing history, philosophy, theology, literature, geology, and biology, was so broad and catholic, his intellectual humility so sincere, that his picture

119

of man's nature is a vital tributary to the stream of American thought.

Like Bacon in *Novum Organum*, Holmes classifies the types of superstition that interpose between man and his grasp of the scientific fact. In man's appraisal of criminals Holmes cites three types of superstition: the spirit of unthinking community revenge, the judgments of the courts, and the conclusions of the clergy. "The idols of the market, of the bench, and of the pulpit," he asserted, "must be treated as so many stocks and stones by the naturalist who comes to the study of man as Huber gave himself to the study of bees, or Agassiz to that of tortoises."[1] Though Holmes had no doubt about the ultimate victory of the scientific method, he knew also the clifflike inertia of accepted beliefs; not only in his papers, "Mechanism on Thought and Morals" and "Crime and Automatism," but also in *Elsie Venner* he attempted to combat the idols and clear the way toward a rational examination of the nature of man.

To Holmes a study of brain structure and brain tissue, as one would study the stomach, was a first necessity in explaining man's nature. To understand the processes of thought, one must observe and record the chemical actions of the blood on brain tissue, the speed of sensory reactions, the response of hunger to mental activity, the effects of chemicals on thought acceleration and of thought acceleration on the chemical composition of the blood. Holmes quotes with approval Huxley's contention that thought is "the expression of molecular changes." Food, like intoxicants, has an effect upon thought that has not been adequately observed: "The brain must be fed in order to work; and according to the amount of waste of material will be that of the food required to repair losses. So much logic, so much beef; so much poetry, so much pudding."[2] The study of the brain is, suggests Holmes, in reality still unattempted by rigorous scientific method: The brain must be approached "microscopically, chemically, experimentally, on the lower animals, in individuals and races, in health and in disease, in every aspect of external observation, as well as by internal consciousness."[3] Thus did Holmes set forth his confident dependence on the method of science to unlock the secrets of man's thought processes.[4]

Holmes himself did not attempt such a rigorous study of brain structure and brain chemistry; but from his mastery of anatomy and his curious sallies into psychology, he was certain that many more patterns of thought and action than hitherto supposed are rooted in interlocking brain mechanisms independent of the will. The work of the memory itself is in the main mechanical, coloring every waking moment, mixing its images with the sensations of the passing milieu, impelling by obscure processes curious shifts in speech, mood, and action. "What happens," asks Holmes, "when one idea brings up another?" His answer: "Some internal movement, of which we are wholly unconscious, and which we only know by its effect."[5]

The association of ideas, then, Holmes concluded, was an automatic process, whether it crystallized in the voices of Socrates' inner oracle, the image of Michelangelo's Moses, or Bunyan's cry of "Sell him! Sell him!" Into the conscious reflections of the poet, the philosopher, the musician, will creep unawares the words, the wisdom, the melodies of another, so deep-rooted in his memory that the thinker steals them thoughtlessly, as though from his own treasure. Beneath the level of conscious thought the brain plants ideas, often stolen ideas, bringing its fruit to light after long diligence, while the body sleeps or the thinker grapples with the tasks of daily toil. Through such a process, which Holmes calls "the spontaneous evolution of thought," Sir William Hamilton made a long stride toward his discovery of quaternions, recalling with utter clarity the particular moment on October 15, 1843, when he suddenly "felt the galvanic circle of thought close"; the subconscious mechanisms of the brain had mysteriously completed their work.[6] Whether in conscious or subconscious action, however, whether accelerated by chemicals or retarded by disease, the brain of the poet, the scientist, or the mathematician depends, in Holmes's view, upon the automatic functioning of certain mechanisms remote from the human will and as yet untraceable by the human mind.

Holmes's analysis of the brain's mechanical processes—processes leading to creative moments, moments of love and hatred, forgiveness and murder, and the infinite range of human action—impelled him to shattering attacks on the freedom of the human will. He stopped short, it is true, of accepting Godwin's doctrine of necessity as a workable faith; but he claimed the right of science to eliminate from the area of human responsibility all those mechanisms of body and mind that function automatically. Such an intellectual position led Holmes to revolutionary outbursts against the theological and legal maxims of his day, outbursts that extend the convictions of Lincoln and anticipate the outlook of Clarence Darrow, Lincoln Steffens, and Justice Holmes on the doctrine of responsibility. If men's actions are voluntary, wrote Dr. Holmes, why is it that the statistician can anticipate the number of suicides in a given area, the number of men and women, young and old, even the methods of self-destruction? "The will, like the wind," he insisted, "is anything but free; it is so largely governed by organic conditions and surrounding circumstances that we calculate upon it as on sunrise."[7] Moral choices, then, are in reality the inexorable grinding of pressures. "Automatic action in the moral world," wrote Holmes in *Elsie Venner,*

the *reflex movement* which *seems* to be self-determination ... until somebody shall study this as Marshall Hall has studied reflex nervous action in the bodily system, I would not give much for men's judgments of each others' characters. Shut up the robber and the defaulter, we must. But what if your oldest boy had been stolen from his cradle and bred in a North-Street cellar?[8]

Many men are perverted from birth by parents they did not choose and schools they did not create. When men live thus under the heel of merciless conditioning, how can we maintain that they are free and responsible agents?

However emphatically law and theology may condemn the criminal or the mob yell for his hanging, science discovers in him merely the repository of compulsions and the expression of organic defects. The law in Holmes's view barely scratches the surface of man's motives, leaning on the verbiage of theology, oblivious of the researches of the physician and the psychologist. Theology is even more barbarous and cruel, asserting often the fantastic and mechanical notion of transmissible sin, setting man apart from the world that molded his habits, posing with sublime assurance the judgment of an unknown God on mortal man. Toward a murderer science alone demonstrates the compassion of true knowledge:

To the lamppost, shouts lynch-law; Full term of imprisonment, pronounces the Chief Justice; Bound for perdition, exclaims the Priest. A moral idiot, says M. Despine; take him up tenderly (to the constable); treat him gently, for he is an unfortunate brother entitled to a double share of pity as suffering under the gravest of inherited calamities.[9]

Now what are the causes of moral idiocy? Though Holmes finds these causes in intoxication, hysteria induced by sex, anger, hatred, insanity, or poison, he leans to Despine's belief, set forth in *Psychologie Naturelle* (1868), that "crime can be shown to run in the blood." To this belief in the inheritance of criminal traits Holmes returns again and again; it is one of the few convictions he held about the nature of man that his beloved science has since discredited. Yet Holmes, like Despine, was constantly aware of the pressures of exterior circumstance. "It is so easy," he wrote in *Elsie Venner*, "to hang a troublesome fellow! It is so much simpler to consign a soul to perdition, or say masses, for money, to save it, than to take the blame on ourselves for letting it grow up in neglect and run to ruin for want of humanizing influences!"[10]

It is inevitable that criminals conditioned by merciless misery and ugliness should show no compunction, no sense of guilt, no horror before the bar of society's condemnation. What such a moral idiot needs is not the gallows, a symbol of society's absurd vengeance, and not the prison, where his nature further deteriorates, but a moral hospital in which society can exert on him those humanizing pressures it blithely overlooked in the prisoner's youth. *"Treat bad men,"* wrote Holmes, *"exactly as if they were insane.*

They are *in-sane,* out of health, morally."[11] To advance such a scientific treatment of crime, the scientist will be forced, however, to struggle against the vested rights of law and theology in the interpretation of *crime* and *sin.*

To the question of human responsibility, Holmes did not answer alone in the language of criminology; from early manhood until old age he turned the problem over and over under the brilliant lights of his many-faceted mind. "Do you want an image of the human will," he wrote in *The Autocrat,* "or the self-determining principle, as compared with its pre-arranged and impassable restrictions? A drop of water, imprisoned in a crystal."[12] Already he is absorbed with the automatic activities of creative minds, with the harsh pressures of "that larger Inquisition which we call civilization." The forces limiting the human will, asserted Holmes, were the physical organization imposed by heredity, the nature of formal schooling, and the conditioning imposed by home and community. If heredity makes a human being an idiot, we do not look upon him as a responsible person. But does he have greater freedom of choice when he is shaped irretrievably by circumstance? Nine-tenths of man's wickedness, he asserts in *Elsie Venner,* springs from "outside influences, drunken ancestors, abuse in childhood, bad company," conditions from which good people have been preserved through no merit of their own. It was this reasoning that led Holmes to assert that "the limitations of human responsibility have never been properly studied."[13]

Nowhere did Holmes give more reign to his thoughts on responsibility than in *Elsie Venner;* in this novel he was free to voice, through the mouth of the village physician, opinions that the pious world could not then condemn as his own. The purpose of the novel, he wrote to Harriet Beecher Stowe, was "to *stir* that mighty question of automatic agency in relation to self-determination."[14] Some months before the birth of Elsie Venner, the heroine, her mother was bitten by a rattlesnake; to the entrance of the poison into the child's blood stream Holmes traced "the animalizing of her nature," which manifested itself in curious glittering eyes, unnatural biting instincts, and moments of venomous passion, ultimately inducing death itself in their conflict with the warm humanizing pressures of Dudley Venner, old Sophia, and Bernard Langdon.

Fortunately for credibility, Holmes makes no attempt to provide a scientific justification for Elsie's reptilian tendencies. His main concern is to undermine the theological dogma of free will with the realism of the physician; the effect not only of the peculiar and unnatural circumstances surrounding Elsie, but of *any* circumstances is to circumscribe the will almost to annihilation. "Ministers talk about the human will," asserts the doctor, "as if it stood on a high look-out, with plenty of light, and elbow-room reaching to the horizon. Doctors are constantly noticing how it is tied up and darkened by inferior organization, by disease, and all sorts of crowding interferences."[15] Where the theologian sees depravity, the physician sees a need for iron and an outdoor life; where the theologian often sees a sinful child, the physician sees a self-preservative necessity imposed by nature; where the minister looks for wilfulness, the doctor looks for moral invalidism. If a man has a bad temper or a tendency toward drunkenness, he may be no more responsible for them than for gout or asthma; all may have been imbedded in his organization. Human beings, in the physician's view, are "a kind of self-conscious blood-clocks with very limited power of self-determination."[16]

In *Elsie Venner* Holmes hacks away mercilessly at the theological insistence on responsibility; he is rigorously materialistic in explaining man's nature. Is it not true that the rise or fall of the barometer affects man's outlook? "A permanent depression of one inch in the mercurial column would affect the whole theology of Christendom."[17] The true understanding of man is to be sought not in assumed depravity, but in detached observation and recording of the chemical, physical, and social forces that shape his body and mold his thoughts. Thus with Elsie Venner. Her personality, her strange tendencies, required the understanding of the scientist, not the dogmas of the theologian. In her brief life, a maelstrom of forces benevolent and malign, Elsie made no choice of any consequence; she was guided by automatic agencies beyond her power to divert or control.

In neither *The Guardian Angel* (the least "medicated" of his novels) nor *A Mortal Antipathy*[18] does Holmes elaborate, as in *Elsie Venner*, his convictions about human responsibility. As always, however, he is pursuing the secrets of man's internal rhythms, secrets which he conceives to be grounded in the beneficent processes of nature. In *The Guardian Angel* Holmes traces with many a sharp, acid stroke the poisonous forces of Myrtle Hazard's childhood: the mournful hymns; the doleful accent of daily speech; the solemn faces; the religious mania of the highly-sexed person who "loved all the forms of non-alcoholic drunkenness." Against the images of damnation, against the sour faces of her aunts, Myrtle Hazard finally revolts. "You can't scare me into being good with your cruel hymn-book," she cries. And again, after her escape and rescue from death: *"Was it wicked in me to live?"*[19]

In his passages describing the beauty of a June night and Myrtle's joyous acceptance, Holmes symbolizes the essential soundness of man's constitution. Man is born for joy and delight. It is the wickedness of his environment—too often the monstrosities of the theologians—that destroys his faith in himself and generates fierce emotional conflicts perpetually unresolved. To Holmes the resistance and escape of Myrtle Hazard represent the triumphant revolt of man against the bitter repressions of Calvinism and its twin corollaries of responsibility and condemnation.

In the pages of Holmes we search in vain for a political and social outlook consistent with his rational examination of the nature of man. In the former he was guided by tradition, in the latter by the impact of scientific experimentation. Enmeshed in the milieu of aristocratic Brahminism, Holmes carried on his face a serene and unperturbed indifference to militant reform. Not even against slavery did he raise an impetuous or a passionate voice. Abraham Lincoln was not his hero, nor John Brown, nor Horace Mann, nor William Lloyd Garrison. This does not mean, it is true, that Holmes was blithely unaware of the onrushing streams of democratic agitation. "If to be a conservative," he wrote in *The Professor at the Breakfast-Table*,

is . . . to shut out the sun from the east and the wind from the west,—to let the rats run free in the cellar . . . and the spiders weave their lace before the mirrors, till the soul's typhus is bred out of our neglect . . . I, Sir, am a *bonnet-rouge*, a red cap of the barricades, my friends, rather than a conservative.[20]

Only against the barricades of theology, however, did the red cap Holmes charge again and again with undiminished fervor.

From his study of medicine and physiological psychology Holmes was led to a deepening distrust of theology's interpretation of man. This distrust in turn was finally resolved not only in the rejection of theology's claims to an understanding of human nature, but also in a renunciation of the philosophical doctrine of free will. Though he was not an environmentalist, Holmes's rejection of free will identifies him indisputably with Lincoln, Tocqueville, Howells, Bellamy, and Steffens. Like them he evolved from his study of man's nature a compassionate attitude toward all frailties as the essence not only of the Christian spirit, but also of scientific rationalism.

Unlike Lincoln, Tocqueville, Steffens, and Bellamy, however, Holmes possessed tools not accessible to his contemporaries—a knowledge of the latest science, not only in medicine, but also in physics, psychology, and anthropology. With these weapons he carried on his attacks mercilessly in essay after essay, novel after novel, on the doctrine of human responsibility. This is not to say that Holmes was unaware of the limitations of science. In his essay, "Border Lines of Medical Science," he defines science as the "topography of ignorance." In *A Mortal Antipathy* he speaks of the history of medicine as in large part "a record of self-delusion." The science of Holmes's day, however, had already pointed the way to a rational examination of man. It revealed to him the absurd pretensions of traditional explanations. Though anthropology was yet

in its infancy, its promises were bright and dazzling for the banishment of superstition.

With truer insight than any of his contemporaries, even those
militant workers for the extension of the democratic process, Holmes
visualized in the infinite expansion of scientific observation the
great hope for unlocking the secrets of human nature. This scientific
approach to man's nature he conceived to be enormously difficult;
scholars were first required to overleap the centuries-old assumptions
of theology and philosophy. Nowhere is Holmes more explicit on
this point than in *The Poet at the Breakfast-Table*. "The scientific
study of man," he wrote,

is the most difficult of all branches of knowledge. It requires, in the first
place, an entire new terminology to get rid of that enormous load of
prejudices with which every term applied to the malformations, the
functional disturbances, and the organic diseases of the moral nature is
at present burdened. Take that one word *Sin*, for instance: all those who
have studied the subject from nature and not from books know perfectly
well that a certain fraction of what is so called is nothing more or less
than a symptom of hysteria; that another fraction is the index of a
limited degree of insanity; that still another is the result of a congenital
tendency which removes the act we sit in judgment upon from the
sphere of self-determination, if not entirely, at least to such an extent
that the subject of the tendency cannot be judged by any normal
standard.[21]

In such awareness of a science of man struggling for birth, of the
hindrances of superstitions that only science can obliterate, of the
need of applied anthropology as the most decisive science in human
destiny, Holmes was unique among his contemporaries. While
Emerson tuned himself to the messages of the Over-Soul, Thoreau
sought to simplify life at Walden Pond, Whitman studied the faces
of men and dreamed of the Giant Bards to come, and Henry George
wrestled with the stamp of poverty on the human spirit, Holmes
applied himself steadily to man's internal structure, probing for the
secrets of the automatic life, exultant over the approaching science.

1875
Tensions and Contradictions

In 1875 America lay still prostrate in the grip of depression. In June Scribner's complained of too many railroads, of too much manufacturing, of mills lying idle or running at a loss, of the great shrinkage in values, of businesses on Broadway forced into side streets. In the midst of depression dwellers of the slums labored desperately for food and shelter, "whole families," asserted Scribner's, "compelled to work sixteen or eighteen hours every day." Not only that: thousands worked at trades that poisoned their bodies. In New York City alone fourteen thousand men and women were engaged in making cigars. Two thousand boys and girls absorbed arsenic in the manufacture of artificial flowers and wallpaper. "They breathe death," asserted the author, "that they may live." Poor Italians and poor Jews poisoned themselves in the silvering of mirrors. America was beginning to count its poorest citizens. The North American Review reported that "pauperism is becoming a fixed condition in our large towns." In England one in 25 was a pauper, in Ireland one in 74, in Boston one in 325. In February Harper's Weekly deplored the sight of crowds of homeless children roaming the streets of New York, surrounded by civilization but isolated from its beneficent touch.

In 1875 a mighty Chicago had risen anew from its ruins, succored by gifts of millions from home and abroad, its people housed again, its brick and stone buildings rising with magical speed— a raw city, violent, hopeful; its poor desperate and courageous, its leaders young and venturesome; city of Altgelds, Debses, Darrows, and Dreisers to come. In 1837 its people numbered 4,170; in 1865,

178,000; in 1875, 420,000. Of these, in 1875 only 31,000 were pupils in the city's 51 schools. The first circulating library, established in 1873, had 23,000 borrowers two years later. Chicago was the focus of forces: the new industrialism, the easy flow of capital, the raw courage of workers, the agitation of restless leaders, the churning of democratic culture. In this vortex the nature of man expanded to sharp extremes: the cynicism of Swift and Field, the gray human wrecks on the waterfront, the dreams of the westward march.

In 1875 Harper's Weekly complained that six million Americans were illiterate, "as uncultivated as the brutes around them." In many issues Harper's carried editorials of agitation against public support of parochial schools, declaring on February 6 that "political Romanism is the chief peril that hangs over our future progress," advocating an expanded system of free secular education. As the truest support of republican government, asserted Eugene Lawrence, schools should occupy the chief attention of both people and rulers. In contrast to Lawrence, who expected a plastic response from the humblest citizen, Charles W. Eliot in the June Atlantic favored a concentration on the talented few. The country would lose nothing from allowing the many to stop at the compulsory limit, the end of elementary school. "One splendid genius," he asserted, "may well be worth more to humanity than multitudes of common men." But Americans, for good or ill, were fast rejecting Eliot's assumptions about the infertile lumpiness of the mass. In 1875 President Grant urged an amendment to the Constitution providing for mandatory state support of free public schools, schools divorced from all religious influence or control.

Though the first free high school had not been established until 1821, by 1860 there were 321 free high schools, 78 in Massachusetts alone. The Supreme Court's decision, in 1872, upholding Kalamazoo's right to establish a free high school was decisive in the expansion of the high-school system in other states. In tracing the development of state universities Charles Adams, echoing Emerson's "Politics," wrote in the North American Review, *"The State, therefore, says to the rich: You shall contribute of your abundance for the education of your poor neighbors' children." In August Scribner's quoted Mills with high approval: "The power of education is almost boundless; there is not one natural inclination which it is not strong enough to coerce, and, if needful, to destroy by disuse." Witness the American dream, ancient as man's hopes: the reaches of the common man are unexplored. Let us hasten. Let us stretch him to his uttermost powers.*

On the response of Negroes to the educational process, a few northern voices were still persistent. In the New Orleans schools for blacks, insisted Eugene Lawrence in Harper's Weekly, *Negroes had already proved not only their intelligence but their humanity, a humanity often superior to that of their former masters. Lawrence violently opposed segregation; for the hatred of the Jew, he insisted, the whole Christian tradition may be held responsible; but for the hatred of the blacks Americans alone must take the blame.*

II

In 1875 Charles Ingersoll examined afresh the conflict of interests in American life, posing again Hamilton's contempt and Jefferson's hopes for the common man. Whatever their defects, asserted Ingersoll, the people at last have a voice; in America the die is cast for the democratic interpretation of the human potential. Already America's democracy has been extended beyond the fearful boundaries reluctantly traced by the Founding Fathers. The dangers to democracy are not the people, who never knowingly commit atrocities or initiate cruelty. Not in them, but in their ignorance and the weakness of their leaders, lurks danger. In 1860 New York had rejected Negro suffrage; in 1862, Illinois; in 1865, Connecticut; in 1867, Ohio. To Ingersoll this was not malice, but ignorance. In some centuries, he thought, the world slumbers, progress slows; but with the advent of democracy the world had awakened again, leaping forward in the exhilaration of a larger freedom. Democracy might err and falter; it could not fail. To Ingersoll the common man was the plastic, responsive creator of his children's destiny.

Unlike Ingersoll, in 1875 many American intellectuals, in their reflections on universal suffrage, voiced persistent doubts of the capacity of the common man. Not insight at critical moments, as Emerson had insisted, but blindness, was their common expectation. In a temperate and thoughtful article in the June Atlantic, *Robert Dale Owen expressed concern about Negro suffrage initiated without a trial period and against the will of the South. Milton's old assertion that universal suffrage would bring into office "the vilest miscreants of our taverns and brothels" found an echo even in Mark Twain's "The Curious Republic of Gondour," where every man possessed at least one vote, but educated men eight or ten, in proportion to their years in school. No longer, asserted Mark Twain, was a hod-carrier elected because he was a hod-carrier. In the April* North American Review *Gryzanowski quoted Comte's conclusion on the suffrage with high approval: "It is absurd that inferiors should elect their superiors." Did vile men, then, or ignorant men, elect their like to office? Had democracy sent to its presidency men inferior to the leaders of aristocratic nations? Emerson himself had felt some such uneasy fears before Lincoln won his reluctant approbation; in the supreme crisis neither the learning of Seward and Sumner nor the gifts of Palmerston could match the mysterious wisdom of the forest-bred man. But in 1875 the issue could not be resolved: American experience was yet too brief, the suffrage too narrow.*

III

Who can measure the stoppage of genius by the fingers of disease, the whine of the bullet, the clasp of the dungeon, the stab of worry, the clutch of poverty? In 1875 Sidney Lanier was thirty-three, with six years left of precious creative hours, the burden of his music pressing hard for escape, the Atlantic's *pages closed to him, and Howells cold. Upon him, too, weighed the burden of new sorrows, the darkness of mines and factories, the blackening skies and grimy skylights over pale faces, the grinding of gears, the encirclement of young hearts in relentless walls. The old slavery wrought its bitterness under the sun, the new in dens and caves.*

*How to give voice to a deep love for stricken man? His new poem,
"The Symphony," would not let him rest; it "racks all the bones of
my spirit." In "The Symphony" he told the burden of his fears for
the poor, the new poor of mills and factories, their lives drained
by toil as was his by consumption. How could they ever love their
brothers, or lose themselves in the green of nature's secrets, or
distil in their hearts the harmony of mighty sound? Not music for
them, not "love in search of a word"—nor could the tender poet
gather them in his arms, however clear in his ears sounded their
sad lament:*

> *. . . Ever love hears the poor-folks' crying,
> And ever Love hears the women's sighing,
> And ever sweet knighthood's death defying,
> And ever wise childhood's deep implying,
> But never a trader's glozing and lying.*

*In 1875 George W. Cable's "Madame Delicieuse" appeared in
the August Scribner's. Frank R. Stockton's The Girl at Rudder
Grange was appearing in serial form. In the April Atlantic Howells
ran Holmes's memorable essay, "Crime and Automatism." Life on
the Mississippi was being serialized, with Howells also awaiting the
birth of Tom Sawyer. On November 21 he wrote to Clemens:
"I finished reading Tom Sawyer a week ago, sitting up till one A.M.,
to get to the end. . . . It's altogether the best boys' story I ever read."
In 1875 appeared William Dean Howells' A Foregone Conclusion,
with flashes of insight that kept him readable: "For a long time
after their marriage, she seemed to have no other desire than to
lose her outwearied will in his . . . there was a kind of bewilderment
in her gentleness." In 1875 Henry James achieved a promising eminence with Roderick Hudson. In 1875 Bret Harte's Gabriel Conway
was appearing in Scribner's. In 1875 Edward Bellamy sent forth his
story, "The Cold Snap," with a curious analysis of the impact of
cold on the human organism: "Other forms of nature have in them
something that the spirit of man can sympathize with, as the wind,*

the waves, the sun; but there is something terribly inhuman about the cold."

In his journal for April 10, 1875, Bronson Alcott remembered a Phi Beta Kappa procession at Harvard long ago. When Alcott had doubted whether he belonged with the procession, Emerson had caught him by the arm, saying, "We will not mince matters. You are a member by right of genius." Now, in 1875, Alcott was seventy-six, Emerson seventy-two. Which of them, Alcott wondered, would withdraw first into the shades?

In 1875 critics sensitive to European standards studied with misgivings the faces and postures, the manners and reflections of American manhood. Whereas in Europe the possession of money and culture assumed no incongruities, in America the vulgar man was often rich. As America grew richer and more confident, were her leaders losing depth, forgetting their origins, becoming contemptuous of European values in an isolationist smugness? "Certain it is," exclaimed the Atlantic Monthly in May, "that with the two foreign nations who see most of us, our women have become a byword for lightness, our men for blasphemy and coarseness. . . . Are we rotten before we are ripe? . . . What is the name of America now in Europe? A synonym for low rascality." In his A Foregone Conclusion Howells had lamented the sickliness of American women; in the January Atlantic Holmes asserted: "We must recognize a strong tendency in American families to run down and run out." In his Forty Years of American Life, Dr. T. L. Nichols deplored the unhappiness of American faces: "In no country are the faces of the people furrowed with harder lines of care." Not lack of intelligence, but lack of honesty, asserted Dr. Nichols, was the pre-eminent American deficiency.

Thus the American critic, sensitive to the smugness, the simplicity, the crudities of our tourist classes; anticipating the barbs of Henry James in The American; unaware, like James, of the crude gold in the American farmer, lumberman, preacher, in mothers who traveled from Columbus to Red River County, Nebraska, measuring off the new homestead. Was Whitman's faith a truer index to Ameri-

can manhood than the gloom of James? They observed different men, Whitman the crude beginnings of the many, James the vulgar end of the few. If The Gilded Age *was true, so also were the tough honesty and the magic phrase of Mark Twain himself, rough and crude enough to curl the lips of Henry James.*

In 1875 the trial of Henry Ward Beecher directed the thoughts of philosophical Americans toward the magic power of sex behind the façade of Puritan conformity. When Theodore Tilton charged Beecher with committing adultery with his wife, Beecher was at the height of his fame and influence, preaching to huge throngs at Plymouth Church, exhibiting that masterful eloquence, that self-possession, that even the ordeal of his trial could not ruffle. For five months the Tribune, *for once detached and uneasy, reported almost daily the verbatim testimony. On April 10 the* Tribune *reprinted an editorial comment by the* St. Louis Democrat: *"Either he [Beecher] is swearing to falsehoods by the score, or he is inno-cent, and Tilton, Moulton, and Mrs. Moulton are the basest falsifiers the world ever saw." Still Beecher preached, and hushed audiences heard and marveled at his depths.*

In 1875 the ancient concepts of inborn laziness, inborn selfish-ness, inborn genius, were offered again in endless assurance as central explanations of life. In the Overland Monthly *for October, J. W. Gally asserted that "certain people are born with a suscepti-bility to certain impressions—not necessarily to a* belief *in those impressions. . . . With Shakespeare the susceptibility was the mim-icry of man." In 1875, attacking communism for its misconceptions of man's inmost self, W. W. Crane asserted that "human nature will hardly ever, and never long, submit to such galling restraints as these dreamers would impose upon it." Was not the principle of competition (i.e., economic competition) necessary to man's richest development? Human nature must change before communism is practical. To Charles Nordhoff, however, who recorded his impres-sions in* The Communistic Societies of the United States *(listing seventy-seven communes as active in 1875), men worked more happily and imaginatively in communism than out. "I conclude," he wrote, "that men are not naturally idle." Even the shiftless visitors, who came to the communes when winter fell and often left with the coming of warm weather—even these fell into the habit of daily work and liked it well.*

In 1875 John Fiske sent forth his Outlines of Cosmic Philosophy, *borrowing heavily from Sir William Hamilton, Mill, and Lewes, but illuminating afresh the dark tunnels of cause and effect, rejecting, like Mill in his* Outlines of Logic, *all extrasensory explanations of human action. Every action or condition has a tangible cause, that is, a force. But what is a force? Fiske explains as follows: "The falling of a stone, the union of two gases, the vibration of a cord, the expansion of a heated body, the sprouting of a seed, the circulation of blood . . . the thinking of a thought, the excitement of an emotion." Every such force has a cause and a result; it receives and transmits energy. In terms of the human will, as Mill had shown, such a concept poses the elimination of free choice for human action. A man may weigh alternatives, may talk himself into an enlightened choice; but this talking to himself, this wrestling with his conscience, itself had a cause—the reading of a book, the glance of a friend, the image of faces long forgotten. No such wrestling takes place without the use and transmission of energy; thus Fiske, and thus, in essence, John Stuart Mill and Oliver Wendell Holmes.*

VII
Whitman and the Ideal Man

> Shut not your doors to me, proud
>   libraries,
> For that which was lacking on all your
>   well-fill'd shelves, yet needed most,
>   I bring;
> Forth from the army, the war emerging—a
>   book I have made. . . .
> The entrance of Man I sing.
>
> —Whitman

LIKE his teacher Emerson, Whitman envisioned the fashioning of superior men and women as the chief function of the American experiment. "Democracy, in silence, biding its time," he wrote, "ponders its own ideals, not of literature and art only—not of men only, but of women."[1] If the first task of the Republic was the establishment of its credo in the Declaration and the Constitution, and the second the accumulation of wealth, inventions, and conveniences, the third would be the growth of a unique and unparalleled creativeness in man. From its boundless energy had not yet emerged the Republic's supreme and perfect patterns in men or forms. Much as Whitman exulted in American life, its men and women were yet crude and inharmonious when measured by the distant ideal that he painted inevitably in part from the image of himself. In the perspective of time the democratic man, like the ideal society, was still a promise, not a reality; America had yet "originated nothing." As Bellamy and Howells were to set forth the ideal social blueprint, so Whitman sought to leave an image of the ideal man as a lasting legacy to the American future. Less realistic than Bellamy and Howells in appraisal of economic forces, Whitman envisioned neither the future concomitants of industrial

137

poverty nor their institutional correctives; but he observed often with uncanny accuracy those personality traits in American life which, extended and strengthened, might give rise to "a copious race of superb . . . men and women."[2]

Whitman was no blithe optimist about the human fiber thus far created in the stormy processes of American life; he was painfully aware of the raw and ugly souls about him: Democracy could degrade as well as ennoble. "The People!" he exclaimed. "Like our huge earth itself . . . man, viewed in the lump, displeases."[3] The common run of mankind Whitman found "full of perverse maleficence," "crude defective streaks," and "vulgar contradictions." The leaders of business and politics he found more depraved than the mass of their followers. Recalling the constitutional conventions that nominated Buchanan and his predecessors, he denounced seven-eighths of them as

the meanest kind of bawling and blowing office-holders, office-seekers, pimps, malignants, conspirators, murderers, fancy men . . . spaniels well-train'd to carry and fetch, jobbers, infidels, disunionists, mail-riflers, slave-catchers, pushers of slavery . . . spies, bribers, compromisers, lobbyers, sponges, ruin'd sports, expell'd gamblers.[4]

When he thought of these men as the leaders and guides of farmers and mechanics, infinitely more honest, Whitman shuddered. As yet America had produced no "crops of fine youths, and majestic old persons."[5] Her manners were crude, her faces pasty, her morality shallow. In 1857 Whitman estimated that nineteen of every twenty American young men of the mass were clients of houses of prostitution. If such habits continued, the result would be "dropsies, feebleness, premature deaths, suffering infancy."[6] The savagery of war Whitman knew and recorded: had not the northern troops killed the crawling wounded of the enemy? During his hospital years, Whitman witnessed the hideous descent of man into the abyss of cruelty and greed: the dead unburied, the wounded unattended and victimized, money stolen even from the pillows of the sick and dying. The attendant, the official, the superior officer he found less courteous and less honest than the common soldier and the lowly clerk.

II

In the womb of American life, nevertheless, sired by the father-stuff of democratic fertility, Whitman felt the stirring of perfect man, a "hundred millions of superb persons." Until the "divine average" of man has risen to heights yet dark and remote, the supreme poets and dreamers of the American era cannot emerge. In *Democratic Vistas* Whitman traces "a basic model or portrait of personality for general use for the manliness of the states,"[7] and in this portrait we may discern many features of Whitman's ideal citizen. As one would guess from *Leaves of Grass*, Whitman's ideal man, "exercised proportionately in body, mind, and spirit," is from youth earthy and muscular; without the vitality of heart and blood and bone, he would be but an invalid in the race. "To our model," writes Whitman, "a clear-blooded, strong-fibered physique is indispensable; the questions of food, drink, air, exercise, assimilation, digestion, can never be intermitted."[8] On this foundation of exuberant health the citizen builds

a well-begotten selfhood,—in youth, fresh, ardent, emotional, aspiring, full of adventure; at maturity, brave, perceptive, under control, neither too talkative nor too reticent, neither flippant nor somber; of the bodily figure, the movements easy, the complexion showing the best blood, somewhat flush'd, breast expanded, and erect attitude, a voice whose sound outvies music, eyes of calm and steady gaze, yet capable also of flashing—and a general presence that holds its own in the company of the highest.[9]

If Whitman traced this ideal in his own image, he knew also thousands of Americans who symbolized his concept of robust, exuberant men, confident, hopeful, expectant, like the Athenians of Pericles' day or the English of Sidney's and Raleigh's. "A man, a sure man," Whitman said to Traubel, "must have guts . . . Burroughs, you see, has guts: and oh! there is so much in that—to have the grit of the body first of all."[10]

No youthful civilization had flowered without the substructure Whitman describes, without the elasticity and exuberant confidence of health. In his emphasis on perfect health, Whitman incorporated an Athenian, an Elizabethan standard for the first time in the projection of a democratic ideal. Not restraint, not shame for one's body, but ease, poise, grace, pride in every muscle, every sense, this was the Whitman expectation of the physical American. It was an expectation foreign, perhaps repellent, to New England restraint, to the genius of Emerson, Lowell, Holmes, Longfellow, whose vitality had been dissipated by generations of bookishness and the encroachments of the Puritan milieu.

III

To Whitman the concomitant of vibrant health, health reinforced and renewed by the intimacy of sunshine, earth, water, and animal life, was abundant sexual energy. The ideal American would be a highly-sexed animal, rejoicing in his fertility, unashamed of his wide-ranging urges. In the release of sexual energy a joyful freedom was more important to Whitman (at least until he was forty-five) than monogamous love or Greek moderation in the expenditure of sexual energy. He was the first American poet to justify as a way of life the roving outpourings of the fornicator and the adulterer; these epithets of society were meaningless to him beside the joyous acceptance of nature's uninhibited mating. "Die for adultery?" asks Lear, as judge of his mock court. "No. The wren goes to't, and the small gilded fly does lecher in my sight. Let copulation thrive."[11] This is the spirit of both "Children of Adam" and "Calamus."

Whitman set his face directly against the values of Puritan monogamy, repudiating all social channelings of the sexual drive, rejecting by implication the institution of marriage itself, making no attempt to reconcile his justifications of promiscuity with the needs of men and women for a stable family relationship. To Whitman the family as an institution was apparently less important than the full, free expression of the sexual man and woman. He did not pause to examine the conflict between his doctrine of sexual freedom, if accepted as a component of democracy, and the conventions of marriage, however latitudinarian. To Santayana, as he reveals in the essay, "The Poetry of Barbarism," the sexual freedom advocated by Whitman represents a rejection of civilized restraint, a rejection indeed of the whole Greek concept of moderation, of Plato's aristocratic man. But this is of less significance perhaps than Whitman's apparent unawareness of the dichotomy between sexual freedom and the socially-imposed traditions of monogamous marriage, and the resulting psychological hazards. His own sexual freedom, as well as his ethical poise and assurance, Whitman retained by remaining outside of marriage; but what would have been his advice to the millions of future readers of *Leaves of Grass?*

In American society with each passing decade the automatic promiscuous sexual response has become a more commonplace expectation under stimulation by feminine dress, posture, nakedness (pictured or actual); yet the convention of marriage, essentially unloved by Whitman, loses no tenacity with age in the public mind. Whatever the normality of promiscuous sexual impulse, it is in constant friction with the rooted dreams of home and family, the fireside refuge, the freshness of child life, of all that marriage yet symbolizes not only to adolescent youth, but also to the millions of parents whose sexual turbulence has diminished, whose hopes for enhanced happiness are now centered on the marriages of their children. Society grooms every unwed girl to invite universal sexual response; the more inviting the girl, the more promising the husband; yet the act of marriage by implication forbids henceforth not only response but invitation. Thus the promiscuity imposed by nature, celebrated by Whitman, lives uneasily with an institution forbidding its existence. In his depiction of sexual compulsions Whitman embodied a rugged honesty unparalleled in America before his day. With his successors, Dreiser and Anderson, Whitman has forced an open recognition of nature's wide-ranging forces; but he did not attempt to delineate the institution (if it was not to be monogamous marriage) that society would create to rear the perfect children of which he dreamed.

It is a fatal error in judging Whitman, however, to suppose that for him the physical exuberance of life and the joyous release of sex are ends in themselves superior to intellectual and spiritual creativeness. Plato's attack on the democratic man in *The Republic,* as placing on an equality the pleasures of the body, the passions, and the reason, finds no justification in Walt Whitman. To Whitman, as to Plato and Milton, the sublimation of sexual energy, of all physical vitality, is the true gold of man. *Leaves of Grass,* which "radiates physiology alone," was only the foundation to Whitman of his unwritten book of the soul. But without vitality there is no sublimation, no beauty, no comradeship, no unfolding brotherhood, no race of great bards. In the Preface of 1872 he called for "boundless products for feeding, clothing, sheltering everybody . . . then the esthetic and mental business will take care of itself."[12] All beauty springs from the flesh and the earth. "How shall the eye separate the beauty of the blossoming buckwheat field," he wrote, "from the stalks and heads of tangible matter?"[13] Flesh and earth are the energy and the machinery of man's spiritual ascent. In *Goodbye, My Fancy,* Whitman left a final reminder of his position: "The Highest said: Don't let us begin too low—isn't our range too coarse—too gross? . . . The Soul answer'd: No, not when we consider what it is all for—the end involved in Time and Space."[14] The end involved is the harmonious development and expression of the full, complete man, with a ripeness of the spirit as the supreme, triumphant flowering from the soil of the flesh.

Whatever the creative uses of sexual energy, the ideal American, in Whitman's view, would be filled with an intense, quick sympathy for men and women, a warmth and vibrancy overflowing from abundant health and sexual exuberance. The recipients of Whitman's sexual love, whether men or women, or both, have never been identified; but whatever his own sexual relations, he rejected in an emphatic letter to Symonds the homosexual implications[15] of the

Calamus poems, "which are disavowed by me and seem damnable."[16] Nevertheless, Whitman did not reject whatever sexuality is at the root of the attachment of man to man, even manly love, which excludes physical manifestations. "It is to the development, identification, and general prevalence of that fervid comradeship," he wrote, "(the adhesive love, at least rivaling the amative love hitherto possessing imaginative literature, if not going beyond it) that I look for the counterbalance and offset of our materialistic and vulgar American democracy, and for the spiritualization thereof."[17] To Whitman it was inevitable that "intense and loving comradeship, the personal and passionate attachment of man to man," should be a normal experience for any vitally healthy person; he did not see how any warmhearted, healthy man could fail to embrace emotionally a great many men; he would become acquainted easily, exude a friendly aura, respond quickly and warmly to people in distress, conceive quickly a strong desire to befriend, to help, to relieve distress.[18]

But the warmth of the ideal American would project itself far beyond the people he meets to the oppressed, the hungry, the friendless of distant states and distant lands; the love energy of the ideal man passes "in compassion around the whole earth," rejecting none—the criminal, the slave, the hunted. "Love," he said, tracing to that power the sadness of Lincoln's face, "is never wrong."[19] The vitality of Whitman's ideal American, while it is directed at particular moments to amative or adhesive love, embraces the stranger, the foreigner, the weak and suffering of every land.

IV

Though he prescribed no detailed educational pattern, Whitman denominated the reading of seminal books as indispensable to the ideal American of the future; indeed the burden of *Democratic Vistas* is anticipation of great democratic classics yet unborn, with *Leaves of Grass* as his own token of the new era. A disciplined, purposive reading Whitman apparently distrusted, preferring, like

Emerson, the chance impact of great minds on free, unfettered youth. The seminal books Whitman compares to little ships sent forth from distant lands "over wide, century-stretching seas," preserved miraculously for future man, "all the best experiences of humanity, folded, saved, freighted for us here."[20] Homer, Aeschylus, the Old and New Testaments, Plato, Dante, Shakespeare, the last "luxuriant as the sun, artist and singer of feudalism in its sunset, with all the gorgeous colors, owner thereof, and using them at will,"[21] these were Whitman's "precious minims" for the ideal American, speaking in glorious accent for the bygone eras, preserving the rich heritage democracy must digest into its own. German philosophy—Leibnitz, Kant, Fichte, Hegel—the young man must eagerly enfold; it is "the most important emanation of the mind of modern ages and of all ages," more vital than science itself, answering, "as far as they can be answered, the deepest questions of the soul," incorporating "the conception of a divine purpose in the cosmical world and in history."[22] The prophecies of India and Judea, the image of the peaceful, brooding Christ, the "eternal [Athenian] shapes of physical and esthetic proportion," the genius of Michelangelo—all these the democratic man must infuse into his intellectual structure, gleaning and preserving the gold of the past, mindful always that they must be the servants, not the masters, of the democratic future. To Whitman there was always a danger that culture would destroy a man's original flavor. In "the sweet democratic despots of the west," he believed the gold of the past would enrich but not dominate the bright shining metal of democratic vitality.

V

But to Whitman the supreme achievement in the ideal man's ethos was religious idealism, an idealism in no sense inconsistent with the exuberance of sexual and emotional expression. The source and strength of Whitman's idealism was a sense of cosmic purpose, an infiltration of divinity into man's personality, a perennial awareness of divine function in oneself. How deep this conviction lay in Whitman's mind no one can doubt who accepts such a poem as "Song of the Universal" as a seminal utterance:

> In this broad earth of ours,
> Amid the measureless grossness and the slag,
> Enclosed and safe within its central heart,
> Nestles the seed perfection . . .
>
> In spiral routes by long detours
> (As a much-tacking ship upon the sea),
> For it the partial to the permanent flowing,
> For it the real to the ideal tends . . .
>
> Out of the bulk, the morbid and the shallow,
> Out of the bad majority, the varied countless frauds
>   of men and states,
> Electric, antiseptic yet, cleaving, suffering all,
> Only the good is universal . . .
>
> Thou too surroundest all,
> Embracing, carrying, welcoming all, thou too by
>   pathways broad and new,
> To the ideal tendest . . .
>
> Give me, O God, to sing that thought,
> Give me, give him or her I love this quenchless faith,
> In Thy ensemble, whatever else withheld withhold not
>   from us,
> Belief in plan of Thee enclosed in Time and Space,
> Health, peace, salvation universal . . .

Such religious awareness, which in the end sustained Whitman's confident old age and invoked his many welcomes of imminent death, he believed yet to be a rare element in American personality. In American life he found "a hideous depletion, almost absence, of such moral nature"[23] as he found in Elias Hicks. In recalling his impressions of Hicks, Whitman denominated his intense religious fervor as his most admirable trait: "In the making of a full man," he concluded, "all the other consciences (the mental, courageous, intellectual, esthetic, &c.) are to be crown'd and effused by the religious conscience."[24] For George Fox's religious conscience alone

Whitman would prefer him to Shakespeare. To Whitman there was
no conflict between the advance of science and the unerring messages of the inner light. The inner light anticipated in lightning
flashes what science laboriously unearthed. Thus in his emphasis on
religious nature Whitman runs contrary to the rationalistic emphasis
in American democratic thought. Implementing as he does the
religious tradition of John Woolman, Emerson, Thoreau, and Whittier, he clashes with the vehement or tacit renunciation of the super-
natural inherent in the philosophies of Abraham Lincoln, Clarence
Darrow, Theodore Dreiser, and Thorstein Veblen. The later democratic thinkers who have based their hopes on science alone would
find in Whitman's cosmic idealism a deluded enthusiasm; yet Whitman would gladly accept their science without renouncing Emerson's great Over-Soul and its bombardments of divine messages.

Another face to Whitman's religious idealism, however, is the
practical social gospel which to him is always an essential dignity
of the ideal man. In such a social gospel all sects can concur. Does
not the brotherhood of man lie at the heart of all religious faith?
"I say at the core of democracy, finally, is the religious element. All
the religions, old and new, are there. Nor may the scheme step
forth clothed in resplendent beauty and command, till these, bearing
the best, the latest fruit, the spiritual, shall fully appear."[25] Not
Christ the Divine, but Christ the brother and healer, is Whitman's
image of perfection. As Christ embodied the spiritual dignity of
man, so the democracy of the future must embody the social, economic, and educational dignity of man, affording to each person a
recognition of his unique needs and his unique promise. "The noble
soul," asserted Whitman, "rejects any liberty or privilege or wealth
that is not open to every other man and every other woman on the
face of the earth."[26] His concept of the brotherhood gospel he
expresses nowhere more memorably than in the 1855 Preface to
Leaves of Grass:

This is what you shall do: Love the earth and sun and the animals . . .
give alms to everyone that asks, stand up for the stupid and crazy, devote

your income and labor to others, hate tyrants, argue not concerning God
. . . re-examine all you have been told at school or church or in any
book, and dismiss whatever insults your own soul; and your very flesh
shall be a great poem . . .[27]

In dozens of his *Leaves* Whitman sets forth the same doctrine of
practical Christianity as the essence of his democratic faith.

VI

Whitman's ideal American, then, embodies the religious enthusiasm that Emerson believed to be the central impetus to democratic
reform; the image of Jesus recurs again and again. The new
American is the disciple of Jesus, disciple also of Socrates, Plato,
Hegel, Jefferson. He rejects none of the models of the past. With
his democratic fervor he incorporates the aristocratic genius of the
Greeks and the feudal perfection of the Elizabethans.

To these traits the ideal man adds another: the persistent search
for his uniqueness among his superior fellows: Every man bears
within him the seeds of a differentiated distinction. The ideal man
is not deceived; he knows that the materialistic forces of democratic
civilization, left unresisted, force men into cultural molds, "like uniform iron castings." But the ideal man will strive for variety, for
expression of uniqueness, as the apex of personal growth. In *Leaves
of Grass* Whitman's main aim was to leave no segment of his own
personality, no impression, unexplored and unrecorded. So the ideal
American will seek to express his sharpest deviations from accepted
patterns, prospecting always for his own uniqueness, rejecting no
thought, no impulse, by the cultural index alone. This was the lesson
of Emerson, as Whitman said, to make each man his own guide, his
final critic: "The best part of Emersonianism is, it breeds the giant
that destroys itself. Who wants to be any man's mere follower? lurks
behind every page."[28] Not uniformity, then, but infinite variety of
uniqueness in men, is the aim of the ideal American for the realization of democratic freedom. This is the meaning of Whitman's
personalism: an awareness and expression of one's uniqueness.

VII

No American poet has grown old more gracefully than Whitman; in his life of later years as well as in his words, he embodied the harmonious aristocratic man that few classicists have emulated. On this point the testimony of Burroughs in 1877 is decisive:

After the test of time nothing goes home like the test of actual intimacy, and to tell me that Whitman is not a large, fine, fresh magnetic personality, making you love him, and want always to be with him, were to tell me that my whole past life is a deception, and all the perception of my impressions a fraud.[29]

Nor can the evidence of Bucke, Traubel, and O'Connor be dismissed as hero worship only. The point is indisputable that Whitman's old age was full of fruit, sunshine, buoyancy, whatever the lapses into pettiness, distrust, and occasional stinginess, the by-products of organic deterioration. Now such an old age is incompatible with Santayana's image of the barbarous democrat whose life ends with the fading of his sexual steam. The passions of hate, envy, and greed persist, moreover, after the passions of the flesh have ceased to excite. Was Whitman a victim of hate and envy, or did he believe in expressing them indiscriminately? In Whitman's mind, on the contrary, ranged a hierarchy of virtues, with love, kindness, and brotherhood at the top; and even in his old age he proved that they were not a vision only. Old age, he asserted, should be the culminating beauty of a harmonious life:

The bud of the rose or the half-blown flower is beautiful, but only the perfected bloom or apple or finish'd wheat-head is beyond the rest. Completed fruitage like this comes (in my opinion) to a grand age, in man or woman, through an essentially sound continuated physiology and psychology (both important) and is the culminating glorious aureole of all and several preceding.[30]

What Whitman really wanted, then, was the aristocratic man of Plato, Aristotle, Milton, and Santayana (infused, however, with democratic fervor) created in millions of molds, not a few hundred.

When Santayana asserted, long ago, that Whitman's "perfect man of the future, the prolific begetter of other perfect men, is to work with his hands, chanting the poems of some future Walt,"[31] he voiced a profound misconception of Whitman's vision, a Platonic misconception shared by many modern scholars who believe that the normal democratic man must be an intellectual and spiritual mediocrity. To Santayana Whitman—and Whitman's hero—is a barbarian, "a man who regards his passions as their own excuse for being; who does not domesticate them either by understanding their cause or by conceiving their ideal goal."[32] Now it is true that in *Leaves of Grass* Whitman rejoices in sexuality and regards it as a legitimate end in itself; it is clear, too, that as a young man he felt, like all vigorous youth, that his sexual energy was inexhaustible; it did not require either conservation or domestication. But it is not true that he did not conceive the end or ideal of passion; he saw clearly enough that sexual energy was the powering of a rich emotional and intellectual life. From this energy, from his enormous physical vitality, came his warmth for the stranger, his delight in crowds, his kindness to his family, and his poems themselves. Whether or not Whitman achieved his ideal of personality is of small moment in the end compared to the ideal itself, which preferred, it is true, vitality to decorum, order, and restraint; but Whitman would have denied as readily as Milton and Plato the superiority of sexual joys to the creative passion in which the *Iliad* was born, or *Paradise Lost,* or *Leaves of Grass.*

VIII

For the formation of his ideal man, erect, strong, confident, full of warmth and tenderness, Whitman projects no complete educational formula; though distrusting schools less than Emerson, he provides no machinery after the manner of Plato, Comenius, Mann, or Owen, whereby his ideal man rises to health and harmony. Four years in a printshop, he said to Traubel, "[are] better than so many years in a university."[33] He hated "the castrated goodness of schools and churches."[34] Did Whitman expect his ideal man to grow, as he had grown, without social plan, with only the chance impressions of crowds, ferries, beaches, books, hospitals, wounded men, trees, and ocean? Whitman learned early to harmonize and synchronize his impressions, to admit them effortlessly into the rounding of his philosophy of life, his very carriage and manner, later into his *Leaves;* but important as this synchronization is, we have no record of its working in Whitman's mind, and still less a hint of the means by which the superb persons of the future could possess such a wonderful faculty. The finished product we behold in Whitman himself, the unfailing courage, cheerfulness, and radiance; an exuberant hope superior to internal conflicts, wounds, insanity, or death itself; ideas digested, harmonized, flowing at ease into speech and countenance. But how was Whitman's harmony shaped and rounded? We do not know. To create many such superb men, the state, as Aristotle well knew, must provide calculated pressures, open doors, invitations, personality models in early youth. A mass of superb men, a hundred millions, if we take Whitman seriously, do not appear by the chance, spasmodic operation of social forces.

Though Whitman did not, like Horace Mann, visualize the schools of the future as the incubators of greatness, he was convinced that one birth-source of democratic man lay in the classrooms of early youth. He denied vigorously that the child absorbs hateful attitudes more quickly than beneficent ones: "It is this wicked world—it is the corruption which accumulates in the habits and thoughts of society—that make the young, as they grow up become more and more deficient in virtue."[35]

The classroom world should above all be healthful and pleasant; no whipping should ever mar the good will between teacher and pupils. The teacher should gain his ends only by "treating them gently" and appealing to them as "rational creatures." In the minds of youth the energies of genius lie rich and fallow, awaiting only the seeds of suggestion and the gentle guiding hand of an understanding spirit, the plower of human nature. To plow human nature,

Thomas Jefferson's intense belief in the great potential of the common man permeates the Declaration of Independence, which he wrote when he was only thirty-three years old. (*Portrait by Thomas Sully—American Philosophical Society*)

Jefferson founded the University of Virginia, where he put his educational theories into practice. In this 1826 engraving Benjamin Tanner shows a front view of the university with the sun shining on the rotunda. (*Library of Congress*)

Alexis de Tocqueville, French thinker and historian, came to America in 1831 to find the inner meaning of democracy. After an impartial study of American manners and laws, he returned to Europe extremely hopeful of the success of the American democratic system.

Horace Mann played a major role in educational reform and in the development of the free common school. (*Massachusetts Department of Education*)

Ralph Waldo Emerson defined the nature of man in terms of a central Platonic conviction that "a man is a god in ruins." (*Emerson Collection, Harvard University Library*)

Drawing of a slave auction, from *Uncle Tom's Cabin* by Harriet Beecher Stowe. *Uncle Tom's Cabin* was first published in book form in 1852; its fame soon spread.

In this 1860 Currier & Ives cartoon, Abraham Lincoln scores a home run using the bat of Equal Rights and Free Territory. Lincoln's defeated opponents are John Bell, Stephen A. Douglas, and John C. Breckinridge. (*American Antiquarian Society*)

Lincoln reads the Emancipation Proclamation to his Cabinet on July 22, 1862. (*Library of Congress*)

A dead Confederate soldier lies in the trenches of Fort Mahone at Petersburg, Virginia. (*Brady Collection, Library of Congress*)

A group of free Negroes rest by a canal in Richmond, Virginia, in April of 1865. (*Brady Collection, Library of Congress*)

Ulysses S. Grant demonstrated a genius for leadership during the Civil War—but this genius failed him when he came to lead a nation at peace. (*Brady Collection, Library of Congress*)

In his poetry Walt Whitman set forth an image of the ideal man which he based largely on himself. Whitman sought to leave this image as his legacy for future Americans. (*Brady Collection, National Archives*)

Owing to its strategic position along lines of transportation, the frontier settlement of Leavenworth developed rapidly to become the first incorporated town (1855) in the Territory of Kansas. (*The Kansas State Historical Society, Topeka*)

A frontier family poses in front of a sod hut in Nebraska, 1887. (*Library of Congress*)

The American Indian once roamed the continent hunting buffalo. As the national frontier expanded, the Indians were forced to abandon their lands and move farther westward. (*Library of Congress*)

Painting of an Indian medicine man working in his tepee. (*Library of Congress*)

watching for the beauty of man to open and flower, that is the art
of the teacher and the parent and all watchers of the young. If a
school is hated as a prison, its end is lost and frustrate: "It is
evidently then a great object gained when the school is loved and
sought, not hated and shunned."[36] In these lines we may read not
only Whitman's advice, but also his own practice as a teacher. In
his story, "Death in the School Room," Whitman depicts a sadistic
teacher ("I would that he were an isolated instance in his profession") advancing, after school, to flog the sick lad Barker, who sits
with his head on his arms, apparently asleep. Though Lugare flogs
and flogs, the lad does not awaken. At last a comrade lifts Barker's
head and looks at his face: immobile in death. "Death was in the
school room," concludes Whitman, "and Lugare had been flogging
a corpse."[37] Thus Whitman's memorable protest. In an age when
whipping was a daily necessity, even in the schools of the metrop-
olis, he spoke for the pervasive power of a democratic classroom,
with the teacher watchful, loving, expectant of the greatness, the
beneficence to come.

IX

As the ideal spiritual man can emerge only from hardy flesh,
so the American geniuses of the future can emerge only from the
elevated, robust mass. Already, asserted Whitman, America had
produced *masses* of men superior to any in the world's history:
America "presents a magnificent mass of material, never before
equal'd on earth."[38] Here in America "we have the sound heart, the
uncorrupted core of primal fresher soul."[39] He praises the rank and
file of the Civil War; it was the study of the common soldier that
gave him hints of the well-hung men of the future. The average
Americans he found full of "good nature, decorum and intelligence,"
full of buoyancy and electric response. But the present "divine
average" of Americans, superior as it is to the social products of
feudal Europe, is as yet only a promise, a trickle of the "hundred
millions of superb persons" to come. In America, though man has

"burst forth," he has not yet flowered. The ideal man Whitman believed was as yet not a familiar offshoot of American society, but a rare and unusual one. He presaged the day, many decades to come, when his ideal man would walk in every village on every street. These ideal men, however rich in expression of their uniqueness, would in turn be the rich soil from which thousands of authentic geniuses would grow and fructify. In such an era thousands of geniuses could flourish for every handful that had emerged from the barren ground of feudal life or the sporadic fertility of American democracy.

Like Thomas Gray, Jefferson, and Henry George, Whitman believed that genius was planted thick in the common soil of humanity; but it is genius that rots in the ground without feeling the heat of the sun. A genuine democracy "breaks up the limitless fallows of humankind, and plants the seed, and gives fair play."[40] For what is genius but the unique self free to be itself, to speak, to sing, to sculpture, to seek the channel of its energy? Writing of Robert Burns in *November Boughs*, Whitman exclaimed, "How clear it is to me that the common soil has always been, and is now, thickly strewn with such gems."[41] When a man finds his purpose, and can concentrate his power, he has grasped the main secret of genius. "All men are not born with genius," asserted Bulwer-Lytton, quoted approvingly by Whitman in his *Notes on Oratory*, "but every man can acquire purpose, and purpose is the marrow and backbone of genius."[42] For a man to see his own worth, to become aware of his divinity, his dignity, his personalism, that is the uncovering of genius. In a society of superior men and women, the genius will find not only a universal tolerance of his idiosyncrasies, even a positive encouragement of strange behavior, but also the warmth of comradeship and a subsidy commensurate with his creative fervor.

Such was Whitman's image of genius, the fruitage of an ideal society planted thick with superior men. As the fruitage of prosperity is a hardy mass of vital men and women, so the fruitage of the mass is to be the forming of millions of ideal citizens from whom in turn thick-planted genius will emerge. To Whitman it was clear that ideal men and genius are social products rather than genetic accidents. America must act decisively to shape its ideal men. The impact of so-called imponderables, of music and poetry, on the human material must be traced and measured. "I should demand a programme of culture," he wrote in *Democratic Vistas*, ". . . generous enough to include the widest human area . . . its spinal meaning the formation of a typical personality of character."[43]

No American thinker has been more certain than Whitman of the resistless impact of social forces. When he said, "Produce great persons, the rest follows," he meant *produce* in an active, literal sense. Even as he speaks of himself as the product of his time, the focus of patterns and currents pulsating in American life, so the social currents of the future would form irresistibly the ideal millions. As in Shakespeare culminated the genius of feudalism, so in Whitman himself and in his ideal man, Lincoln, culminated in his mind the genius of democratic forces. Presaging the emergence of Lincoln in *The Eighteenth Presidency*, Whitman wrote, "I would be much pleased to see some heroic, shrewd, fully-informed, healthy-bodied, middle-aged, beard-faced American blacksmith or boatman come down from the West across the Alleghenies and walk into the Presidency."[44]

As in this image, Whitman invariably traced the link between man and the soil from which he sprang. "What real Americans can be made out of slaves?" he asked. "What real Americans can be made out of the masters of slaves?"[45] When Traubel asked him if he expected the same physical perfection in the tenements as elsewhere, he answered, "No—I do not. The tenements are hot-beds of disease . . . I think I now see better what you mean when you speak of economic conditions as coming before all the rest."[46] Again he wrote, "Did you ever stop to think . . . how so many young men full of the stuff to make the noblest heroes of the earth really live—pass their lives, year after year, so till death? Constant toil . . . no rational pleasure . . . never knowing once in their whole lives real affection . . . always kept down?"[47] The function of the poet is to see in man smitten and man crushed by social forces the materials of spiritual ascent: "Where others see a slave, a pariah, an emptier of privies, the poet beholds what, when the days of the soul are accomplished, shall be the peer of God."[48]

Among his contemporaries Whitman spoke most often of William Douglas O'Connor as his ideal; a man incorporating not only the physical and emotional vitality Whitman so coveted, but also vast intellectual power, even genius. Whitman never tired of praising O'Connor's virtues to his friends, especially to Traubel. Whitman first met O'Connor in Boston in 1860. "As I saw and knew him then," wrote Whitman in *Goodbye, My Fancy,*

in his 29th year, and for twenty-five years further along, he was a gallant, handsome, gay-hearted, fine-voiced, glowing-eyed man; lithe-moving on his feet, of healthy, magnetic atmosphere and presence, and the most welcome company in the world . . . personally and intellectually the most attractive man I had ever met.[49]

O'Connor's voice, full of sad music, cast a spell over Whitman. As a debater, a persuader, as a presence among men, as a defender of Sand, Hugo, Rabelais, Byron, as a critic of insight and power, O'Connor was supreme, in Whitman's view, among all his contemporaries. Reading *The Good Gray Poet* today, the scholar finds, despite fulsome tones, surprising justification of Whitman's evaluation: a mind more richly stocked than Whitman's own with the heritage of "precious minims"; a supple, pointed style, rigorous in logic; his defense of *Leaves of Grass* Areopagitican in range and fervor. Beyond his magnetism, his capacity for friendship, his power as speaker and thinker, Whitman sensed in O'Connor the genius thwarted by circumstance from making a timely record of himself. "William has a world all his own," he said to Traubel, "—a political world: I used to think that he would some day give it birth: but the days pass, bye and bye William will pass, I am afraid, with the work undone. That damned job at Washington ties him down to a few feet of grass."[50] Whitman's prophecy was fulfilled: O'Connor died unbequeathed. In him we may trace Whitman's image of the ideal man, full of life's juices, enthusiasm, buoyancy, humor, warmth, his personality crowned with intellectual range and daring: a mind lost that might have been bequeathed, recorded, transmuted to the immortality, however obscure, of the printed page. O'Connor lacked the purposefulness of genius; in Whitman's view his job was the grave of his highest talents.

To Whitman no genius of the future would wield such magic over the souls of men as the poet himself. He and his fellows, offspring of democratic plasticity, "a race of giant bards," would crystallize for future eyes the perfect patterns and ideal men of the democratic era, even as the Greek poets had preserved for us the perfection of Athenian fruitage. Whatever the magic of shape and color and sound, the magic of words is the supreme permanency: "Over all arts, literature dominates, serves beyond all."[51] The poets of the past have stood aloof from the people, feeling themselves a superior race; but the democratic geniuses will embrace the masses, feeling for the heart of their needs, certain of the gold to come from the lumpy ore; submerged in the people, they know "the measureless wealth of their latent power and capacity."[52] Against sectional hatreds[53] the giant bards will sing their songs, rejecting no race or creed, embracing all in the fervor of faith, defying injustice, unifying and harmonizing with irresistible magic, setting a new star in the firmament to beckon "the flag of man." In the democratic era new woes and new sufferings will descend. Not poets only, then, but prophets, "larger than Judea's, and more passionate—to meet and penetrate those woes, as shafts of light the darkness."[54] But the giant bards have not yet come, he thought, himself excepted. They lie restless and stirring in the deep unmined riches of the American mass.

X

Among American thinkers on the nature of man Whitman embodies concepts repeated again and again among the classic formulas of democratic faith. Like William Godwin, Thomas Paine,

Henry George, and Franz Boas, he conceives man as the mirror of his environment rather than as the index of genetic determinance. Thus man is endlessly plastic, projected by circumstance toward the ripeness of a complete man or compressed to fractions and splinters. In one of his early editorials Whitman exclaimed, "What a Devil art thou, Poverty!" Of an unfortunate victim, McDonald Clarke, he wrote, "Through the chilliness of destitution this man . . . was prevented the chance of becoming an ornament to the world."[55] Not man's perverseness, but the pressures of poverty, drove him to crime: "Poverty stalks unchecked, dragging by the hand his brother, Crime."[56] Temperance advocate that he was, Whitman looked beyond man's choice to the play of forces: drinking man was bored or weary. "Routine," he wrote, "baffles the powers of thought."[57] Again: "Had men more play, they would be too full from within of animal spirits ever to feel the need of external excitement."[58] In Europe the bitter outward influence had marred the happiness of the masses: "Kingcraft and priestcraft [were] dwindling down humanity there to a lower and lower average."[59] In America a new play of beneficent forces, he hoped, would enhance man's happiness and increase his stature. In these intellectual positions Whitman is at one with his great predecessors, Jefferson, Tocqueville, Horace Mann, and Abraham Lincoln. He anticipates, too, the convictions of Howells, Steffens, Darrow, Dreiser, and Boas.

If Whitman was less aware than Henry George and Edward Bellamy of the pressures of the economic struggle, he was a closer observer than they of the end product. Every man, asserted Scott Nearing in a later era, "bears upon his face the stamp of the economic society in which he lives." Whitman's analysis of faces was as unerring as that of Emerson himself. He began to fear that the United States would breed, like the countries of Europe, "vast crops of poor, desperate, dissatisfied, nomadic, miserably-waged populations,"[60] a portent to Whitman of social quicksands to come. Without understanding the marching patterns of industrialism, he sensed in men the effects of the coming era. In February, 1879, he wrote, "I saw to-day a sight I had never seen before—and it amazed, and made me serious; three quite good-looking American men, of respectable personal appearance, two of them young, carrying chiffonier-bags on their shoulders, and the usual long iron hooks in their hands, plodding along, their eyes cast down, spying for scraps, rags, bones, &c."[61]

If the responsibility for man's stature, puny or gigantic, is rooted in social forces rather than in individual choice, the poet can have only infinite compassion for his erring brethren. Hence Whitman, like Clarence Darrow, embraces the prostitute, the thief, the murderer, not alone by the Christian justification of infinite forgiveness, but also by an intellectual probing of the scientific fact. Like Clarence Darrow, Dreiser, and Oliver Wendell Holmes, Whitman rejected the concept of free will as incompatible with both scientific evidence and the efficacy of compassion. To Whitman, therefore, as to Heywood Broun and Edward Bellamy, Jesus never appears in the robes of justice, but only as the brother of the criminal and the prostitute. "My spirit to yours, dear brother," he wrote. "Do not mind because many, sounding your name, do not understand you; I do not sound your name, but I understand you. . . ." To many critics of American life, as to D. H. Lawrence, this attempt to fuse Christianity with the scientific truth is only a sentimental lie; but in this fusion we may trace the confident march of democratic ideas from Jefferson and Lincoln and Emerson to Whitman, John Dewey, and Franklin Roosevelt.

Whitman was a less systematic thinker on the nature of man than Thomas Jefferson, less detached than Tocqueville or Dewey, less experienced in human depravity than Mark Twain. On man's historical interactions with society, he was less well informed, less profound and searching, than Henry George. He possessed neither the scientific knowledge of Holmes nor the relentless intellectual rigor of Abraham Lincoln. Though the range and accuracy of Whitman's intellectual background have been generally underrated, he was not in this field the equal of either Emerson or Jefferson.

More profoundly than any of these thinkers, however, Whitman conceived and portrayed the ideal human product of America's social machinery. If in himself he saw embodied a shadowing of his ideal, none of the great thinkers, we must grant, was as complete in a Greek or Elizabethan sense as Whitman. Unlike Emerson, Lincoln, even Jefferson, he found in life a buoyancy, a joyousness in the play, the freshness of man and nature, rejoicing in physical perfection. Without discounting prolonged intellectual labor, Whitman did not permit the strains of intellectual life to sap his emotional warmth. With superior insight he labored the necessity for the harmonious sustenance of body, emotions, and mind; to the Greek star, the aristocratic man, he would hitch millions of democratic wagons. Of this harmonious man Whitman has projected in his prose alone a sharper, more complete delineation than any of his great contemporaries. The fascination of an ideal American, his basic personality patterns repeated in millions of citizens, his genius unique and differentiated, his spirits warm and fresh, his temperament buoyant— this image no other American has so fully or persistently embodied in his life or in his books. "Ideal Americanism," Whitman asserted, "would take the Greek spirit and law, and democratize and scientize and (thence) truly Christianize them for the whole, the globe, all history and ranks and lands."[62] In this ideal lay the superiority of the democratic credo, that it asserted for all men the same right of growth to full stature—to vitality, brotherhood, genius—that Athens had bestowed on the chosen few.

XI

It remains to ask: "What traits peculiar to Whitman convinced him of the noble American potential?" The American is yet, he asserted, only half made; "much of him is yet in a state of dough."[63] Notwithstanding his incompleteness, the average American farmer or mechanic is "just as eligible to the highest ideal of perfection as any." Of the origins of Whitman's seminal convictions, traced in detail by his biographers, we can for our purposes mention only a few; but certainly among these was his own early growth to relatively full stature from humble origins. The son of ordinary farmer folk, with no college training or tradition of professional prestige in his family, Whitman advanced from printer and teacher to editor before he was twenty-one. From nature, and the impact of nature on himself, he learned much, as he said Burroughs learned, of the gentleness and harmony in man. The texture of his early religious training was radically equalitarian. Then his reading of great books had inspired him to noble images of man's destiny; and before him, in Brooklyn, in New York, he saw every day the growth of man from obscurity to success.

Then came Emerson, who required Whitman to believe more fully in himself than he had ever dared hope: the result was *Leaves of Grass*, a record of himself, complete, shameless, buoyant. In himself he had endless proof of the plasticity of human personality—of depravity, elevation, dreams, ambitions crude and noble. As he looked about him he saw the infinite fluidity in American life; he sensed the potential in man that he had uncovered in himself. With the images of the Greeks before him, Whitman began to study American life; he studied faces as searchingly and unerringly as Emerson himself.

But what scope and breadth there was in his study of faces! What copious, variegated settings! Whitman aspired to feel the very pulse of the mass man, his thousand tones and shades, the worker, soldier, farmer, mechanic, testing and appraising them as he had appraised himself, their warmth, bearing, intelligence, their capacity for elevation and genius. His search was endless: on buses, trains, ferries, streets, wharves, in hospitals, trains, hotels, wherever the faces of humanity were molded not in one cast, but in many, he plumbed the reaches and channels of American vitality. Without images of perfect men, without Homer, Plutarch, Epictetus, Shakespeare, without Lincoln ("if the old Greeks had had this man!"),[64] without a historical sense of social creativeness in man, Whitman's search would have gone awry; but to the study of men he brought "a long foreground," a mingling of life and theory forbidden by circumstances to his caustic detractors, Henry James and Santayana.

Such were, in brief, the gifts Whitman brought to the study of human fiber. No other American poet studied the faces of men with such skill and insight and expectant compassion as Walt Whitman, and none transmitted more accurately the whole scale of American manhood. Endlessly plastic, of limitless potential, the nature of man justified, in Whitman's belief (and this is the sum of his search), the most extreme assertions of the great Declaration. This is not to say America might not fail; she might go down, asserted Whitman, as the most colossal failure in history, even as Mark Twain was to believe in his last gloomy years; the "high universal noon of Democracy" might never appear. But to Whitman, as to Henry George, that failure would not be an index of human nature, but rather of the repudiation and reversal of democratic patterns in the American scene.

1885
The Death of Ulysses Grant

On June 16, 1885, Ulysses Grant, near death from cancer of the throat, was taken by his family from New York to a cottage on Mount McGregor, near Saratoga. Day after day Grant sat on the porch, gasping for breath, his face drawn, his hands shrunken and wrinkled, writing or dictating the last of his memoirs, or visiting briefly with a friend. For many months he had found it impossible to rest except in a sitting position; but on July 22 he wrote a note asking to be placed in bed. Once in bed he fell asleep; his hands and feet grew icy cold. When one of his sons said, "Father, is there anything you want?" Grant whispered, "Water," but he could not drink except from a sponge. A little after eight in the morning of July 23, his breathing stopped. One of his physicians listened to his heart and crossed his thin hands upon his breast. The dead man was sixty-three.[1]

On Wednesday, August 5, the body of Grant was carried by train to New York, where it lay in state until the morning of August 8; thousands of people hourly passed Grant's coffin at City Hall, perhaps in all over a quarter of a million. In the funeral procession on August 8 to Riverside Park, some forty thousand soldiers and veterans marched: others in the procession were President Cleveland and his cabinet; former Presidents Arthur and Hayes; the justices of the Supreme Court; and governors from many states.

Thus Ulysses Grant came to the end of a career full of strength and weakness, insight and blindness—a man infinitely inferior to Washington in the arts of peace, if superior in the tasks of war.

"War hath made many great," wrote Milton of Cromwell, "whom peace makes small." Few generals came to military power in American life better fitted than Grant to the command of men; but perhaps few men have sought to enter the White House less prepared than he to practice the arts of peace or to cope with the limitless forms of chicanery possible in the use of governmental machinery for private gain.

The events of Grant's life, especially of the last two years, and the curious blend of sagacity and blindness in his outlook are full of instruction to the searcher of unanswered questions for the science of man to come. When he entered the White House, Grant acted as a military commander, not as the agent of a democracy; he had little knowledge of his own limitations, especially in making crucial appointments. His appointment of Orville F. Babcock as his private secretary; of William W. Bellknap (a conspicuously brave and resourceful officer) as Secretary of War; of Adolph E. Borie as Secretary of the Navy; of Elihu B. Washburne as Secretary of State; of Alexander T. Stewart as Secretary of the Treasury; his abrupt dismissal of John Lothrop Motley (from the Court of St. James), of Judge E. Rockwood Hoar, of Benjamin H. Bristow (who uncovered the Whiskey Ring); his associations with James Fisk, Jay Gould, Roscoe Conkling, and Zachariah Chandler—all these actions displayed in Grant an appalling lack of perception. Unwittingly he allowed his friends and relatives to use his name and influence for the enhancement of their private fortunes through federal agencies. The man who had taken Vicksburg and forced Lee's surrender had an almost superstitious reverence for the mysteries of money-getting, though no one claimed that this led him to a single dishonest act. The Nation called him "an ignorant soldier, coarse in his taste and blunt in his perceptions, fond of money and of material enjoyment and low company." This was too harsh an estimate; but it cannot be denied that Grant's very humility and his trust in men who had proved their mettle on the field of battle unfitted him to some degree in the selection of his colleagues for government service.

II

At the end of his two terms in the White House, and after a triumphal European tour, Grant returned to New York with savings of $100,000, part of a fund raised by his friends to assure him a comfortable living in later years. Meanwhile his son Ulysses had joined the firm of Grant and Ward in Wall Street, with which firm he believed he had amassed a fortune of $400,000. General Grant invested his savings of $100,000 with Grant and Ward. Apparently he did hope to make money as his son had done, perhaps to prove to himself that a man who could be both general and President could also amass a small fortune in the years of active life that seemed to lie ahead of him. But again he trusted men too easily, as had his son Ulysses, who knew nothing about the firm's business, but left everything to his partner Ferdinand Ward and his silent partner James D. Fish, president of the Marine Bank.

For two or three years everything went smoothly. The firm of Grant and Ward proved so prosperous that friends and relatives of the Grant family invested in it also. Then the first blow fell. On Sunday morning, May 4, 1884, Ferdinand Ward called at the Grant house on East Sixty-sixth Street, and asked the general to borrow $150,000 to prevent the possible closing of the Marine Bank, in which the funds of Grant and Ward were on deposit. Grant was persuaded. He went to the house of W. K. Vanderbilt, who gave him a check for the amount asked, not to help the bank or firm, he insisted, but to be of service to General Grant. The next day young Grant took a check of Grant and Ward, drawn on the Marine Bank, to Mr. Vanderbilt, thinking he was paying the loan in full. On Monday the general was asked to borrow more money to help Grant and Ward; he applied to Jay Gould, who refused him assistance. On Tuesday the Marine Bank failed, meanwhile refusing to honor checks by Grant and Ward.

When, on the same day, May 6, General Grant went to the office of Grant and Ward, Ulysses said to him, "Grant and Ward have failed, and Ward has fled." Grant was overcome. His first *thought was of his trust in Ward, and in Spencer, who had kept two sets of books for his employer. "I made it a rule of my life," he said, "to trust a man long after other people gave him up; but I don't see how I can ever trust any human being again." Now all was lost, and he was in debt $150,000 to Vanderbilt; his friends and relatives had been swindled as well. Ward, like his earlier counterparts in federal service, had skilfully used Grant's name to induce many other investors to place their money in his care. Grant and his family were without sufficient funds for more than a few days of household expenses. As one of his generals wrote, "He was penniless in the house that was crowded with his trophies."* These gifts and trophies, as well as all his possessions, he and his wife now assigned to Vanderbilt. Friends gave him emergency aid. A stranger, Mr. Charles Wood, sent him a loan of $1,000, renewable without interest; Mr. Romero, the Mexican minister, long a personal friend, brought a check for $1,000 and left it lying on the living room table.*

But Grant was never more resourceful than on the brink of disaster. His energies, after a lapse of lethargic despair, grasped for solutions. When the Century renewed its request for a series of articles on the crucial battles of the war, he consented at once and went to work. The success of his first article and the extra remuneration he received for it inspired him to continue. Finally, out of his experience in writing emerged his determination to write his memoirs, which publishers told him would bring him a substantial income. With the help of one of his generals, Adam Badeau, he set to work, writing, dictating, writing again.

III

Grant's first article, "The Battle of Shiloh," is a revelation of a few ideas he held about war and the nature of man. Two Union colonels, he wrote, led their troops from the field of battle at the first burst of enemy bullets. These colonels Grant calls "constitutional cowards." Whether he meant by this term that they were cowards by genetic nature or cowards from the impact of childhood* experience does not appear; nor does it appear that he thought constitutional cowards could, by taking thought, make themselves into brave men. The suggestion is that, whatever its root, the cowardice of these men was permanent and unalterable.

But to Grant the ordinary kind of cowardice in battle was the result of inexperience, not the lack of innate fortitude. In later engagements, he points out, the very men led off the field by the cowardly colonels proved themselves to be brave and resourceful soldiers—so brave, in fact, that "better troops never went upon a battle-field." At the Battle of Shiloh there were thousands of deserters from the Union cause. As many as four or five thousand of these men were lying demoralized under the bluff along the river bank in the Union rear, "most of whom," wrote Grant, "would have been shot where they lay, without resistance, before they would have taken muskets and marched to the front to protect themselves." General Buell, who was with Grant at the time, attempted to rouse the stragglers to action, exhorting them in derisive language, even threatening them with fire from the gunboats. But to Grant such an attitude was naïve. Among men unused to battle he expected such action, except under the inspired leadership of a man like Sherman, who did command untested troops at the Battle of Shiloh. Most of the five thousand, Grant believed, would with more experience turn into gallant soldiers. Nevertheless, in dealing with fleeing troops, Grant imposed a counter fear; at Shiloh he posted cavalry, which could not be used in the forefront of that battle, in the rear of the line to halt deserting soldiers. Shiloh was a bloody holocaust; on one field, when the carnage ceased, wrote Grant, one could have walked on bodies the whole way across, not touching a foot to the ground. It was a part of soldier courage to get used to sights like this. Grant himself, however, was not indifferent to suffering; once the guns of battle ceased he could not stand the sights and sounds within a hospital hut, where arms and legs were amputated during the night; he returned to the rain-swept tree that had been his first shelter.[4]

Such were Grant's impressions of the nature of man in the face

*of death. Part of his own genius for war lay in his dogged resolution
to force himself and his men to face death, to kill or be killed. In
a war between Americans, in which if the Confederates were more
dashing the Federals were more persistent, it was masses that
counted; and the North could afford more deaths than the South.*

IV

*The acceptance by Century of his article on Shiloh encouraged
Grant to continue his writing, which was a distraction from his
worries, though he was still lame from a bad fall on Christmas Eve,
1883, and could not get about except on crutches. Often he worked
from five to seven hours a day. In October, 1884, however, while
living at Long Branch, New Jersey, he began to complain of pains
in his throat. Within a few weeks he was advised by Dr. Costa, of
Philadelphia, to consult a specialist in New York. His throat condition was pronounced cancerous, though it was claimed his strong
constitution might keep the disease arrested for some years. By
December he could not swallow except in agony. Finally he could
take nothing but liquid food; he would rise from the table before
the end of the meal and walk up and down in the hall or a
near-by room.*

*At first he had been so stunned by the dread news that he did not
care to write; he sat gazing into space or at the wall of his room,
"like a man gazing into his open grave."⁵ But he soon recovered his
enthusiasm and set to work again, and in the evening would often
read aloud what he had written to the family. Every day his grand-
children would come in to romp and play with him. He still had a
trust in his children that was simple and absolute, the kind of trust
that endeared him to his friends and had made it easy for unfaithful
ones to use his renowned name for private ends.*

*Through the winter of 1884-85 the disease grew steadily worse;
on March 31 it was thought that the end would come within
forty-eight hours. In April the family was on two occasions called
to his bedside. He gave them his blessing and said goodbye. But
his energies rallied. Gradually the many messages from North and*

South revived his spirits, as did his restored status of lieutenant general, passed by special act of Congress; he was at last convinced that his countrymen as a whole valued him as a human being of deep personal honesty and greatness of spirit, whatever their regrets for his lapses of judgment. Thousands of letters encouraged him— from comrades-at-arms, Confederate generals, old friends. A contract signed in March assured his family of a substantial income from his memoirs. On April 27 he was able to join his family for a part of his own birthday dinner. By May 1 he was able to dictate passages for his memoirs, an activity he continued until June. He experienced a revival of his faculties and enthusiasms; now and then he would take a ride in the open air. But intermittently the cancer would strike again at his vital energies. On June 16, to escape the heat of New York, Grant was moved to the cottage on Mount McGregor.

The personality of Grant poses several enigmas to the future scientist of measurable data on the nature of man. His Memoirs *call to our attention, first, that no definitions of the words* courage *and* cowardice *have yet been formulated upon which rational analyses would agree. Such definitions are increasingly important in an age when military service is universal and when confessions are induced by torture and brainwashings, confessions which society needs to assess by both military and civil codes of justice. Grant believed that courage, at least in battle, is the result of experience and leadership, rather than the gift of nature. What is the difference between cowardice and battle fatigue? Does every man have a breaking point at which he might be called a coward by one of his officers? Such a definition of* courage *or of* cowardice *would have to cope also with the riddle of responsibility. The very word* courage *implies a freedom of choice to act or not to act. On the other hand, a statement such as, "No one knows another man well enough to call him a coward," assumes that each personality is beset by forces too complex and mysterious to be assessed in terms of human responsibility.*

Another riddle for the science of man posed by Grant's career is this: Is there a necessary contradiction between a rigorous training for military command and enlightened preparation for statesmanship in a democratic society? As a man Grant was modest and humble with his colleagues and subordinates, though decisive and self-possessed as a commander. But as a professional soldier he did not know much of American history or the forces acting in the society of which he was too little a civil part. Like every candidate for office, he came to see that it was necessary to deal with political bosses and the financial powers which supplied them with campaign capital. What seemed to many people bad taste in his associations was perhaps just a more direct way of acknowledging his debts to people who supplied him with funds to attain high office. But for these associations he had no theoretical preparation, no deep comprehension of either democratic aspirations or political astuteness, such as that possessed by Andrew Jackson. Can generals in a democratic country be trained in the arts of democratic citizenship and of world responsibility? This is one of the questions in American life the answer to which must await the emergence of more certainties about man than we now possess.

VIII

Utopian Dissent and Affirmation: Howells, Bellamy, and George

> *A child no more inherits his father's knowledge than he inherits his father's glass eye or artificial leg; the child of the most ignorant parents may become a pioneer of science or a leader of thought.*
>
> —George

IN ANTICIPATING a science of man to come, the searcher examines all conditions of men and theories about human fiber; but in testing either theories or conditions, each of us is guided by his experience to assumptions he often finds impossible to hold in abeyance. If one has known repeated disillusionment in close friends or dishonesty in business dealings, it is natural to paint human nature in the image of treachery and deceit. The most acute intellectual is not immune to this conditioning, which his reading reinforces with countless instances in fiction, history, sociology, or medicine. In a competitive society even the most altruistic thinker may see that suspicion is more pervasive than trust, belligerence than kindness, greed than generosity. A whole society, then, conditions the average searcher to believe that his view of human nature is factual and realistic. True, he may have known utopias in private homes, perhaps in his own, and perhaps also a utopia or two in the classrooms of his youth, or in the stories of Jesus, St. Francis, Father Damien, Abraham Lincoln. But these are aberrations; he has not seen a whole society seething with uncommon men and women.

Looking to time and the science of man to verify or reject his assumptions, the utopian presents a picture of the mass man stretched, in Whitman's phrase, to a new "divine average." The utopia a man such as William Dean Howells knew in his own home he covets for all men. When he was a boy in Martin's Ferry, tired out from barefoot play, Howells' mother would follow him to bed and wash his feet; he never forgot the music of her voice at these moments, or the touch of her hands.[1] Of such was his utopia. The idealism of his minister father was to Edward Bellamy a reality that made him reject Marx's concept of violence in the revolution to come; and to Henry George the strains of his mother's voice repeating the poems she loved echoed not only in the rhythms of his prose but also in his view of man's potential compassion.

It is easy to laugh at the utopian; the world he pictures has not yet come to pass except in scattered golden splinters: a home where food and love and shelter are held in common; the lines of Whittier's poem, "I hate to go above you"; the image of Jesus feeding the five thousand, symbol of the perennial plea for the priority of bread over ideas in the order of time. It is easy to laugh at the utopian when the methods of Marx have won a third of the world's people to their cause. To the utopian no feeling is so creative and revolutionary as love, none so destructive as hatred, whether of capitalists or fellow-workers. But the utopian is not content with the pervasive triumph of love; he wants also masses of extraordinary men, men uniquely creative in mind as well as in actions of love. Thus far, like the sharing of love and shelter and goods, genius has flowered only in splinters of society and splinters of time. The utopian believes, with Jefferson, that genius is an environmental product, not the spasmodic gift of nature. If love and genius are the fruits of social habit, how can we change society to make them more pervasive? Thus the utopian's reasoning. The heavy weight of custom, dragging each generation to its predecessor's level, he evaluates less realistically than the creativeness of love and the contagion of genius. Moreover, his premises are still unproved: environment, not heredity, determines both the pervasiveness of love and the density of genius. How can his premise he disproved? What experiments need to be made before society can prove his dream a delusion? A science of man, the data of which are as indisputable as the engineering certainties of Boulder Dam, is needed to answer.

II

In the 1880's the picture of human nature as predatory and depraved found abundant confirmation in the advance of industrialization. The march of the machine had wrought its magical if still slight extension of man's energies; but it also created a new breed of skilled businessmen, as Grant and Clemens found to their sorrow, who knew how to unite the machinery of government with the new opportunities in industry and finance. Industry in turn was breeding the slums dreaded by Thomas Jefferson. Soon one-tenth of the people would possess nine-tenths of the wealth; though only three men were millionaires in 1861, about 3,800 would reach that august state by the end of the century. If Jay Gould and William Tweed symbolized the successful financial and political methods of the day, the new slums of Pittsburgh spoke for the industrial genius of Andrew Carnegie and Henry Clay Frick. The steelworkers, who toiled twelve hours daily, and twenty-four hours once in two weeks, at the change of shifts, lived an existence of perpetual fatigue, brightened only by the magical escape of saloon or bottle or the joyful intermissions of family life. If the workers in the main were debauched and ignorant, the men in high business places were often described by the pessimistic as unscrupulous villains. The extremes of wealth and poverty, pictured by Thomas Paine in *Agrarian Justice*, had come to pass. Even Walt Whitman, incurable hopeful of *Leaves of Grass*, sensed the deepening trend; in its promises of social, moral, and aesthetic grandeur, America was still a barren failure.

Friends and foes of the democratic experiment were projected by the sweep of events into prophecies stern or sad. They clashed, not on the alarming symptoms of American failure, but on the causes of the disease. To critics like Henry Adams life had become too complex ever to be unraveled; in his novel, *Democracy*, he voiced his despair of the adaptability of the human organism to a democratic framework. The doubters of democracy saw in the passing scene a proof that human nature could not sustain the experiment so nobly begun; and Mark Twain was bitterly certain that the evil roots of human character would spell the doom of the American republic. A letter to Howells shows a part of his feeling in contrast to that of his friend: "I suspect that to you there is still dignity in human life, & that man is not a joke—a poor joke—the poorest one that was ever contrived."

In 1886 strikes and riots in and around Chicago had resulted in a number of deaths. By May 1 over fifty thousand workers were on strike for the eight-hour day at the McCormick reaper works, the Pullman plant, and other factories. Anarchists were agitating among the unemployed, especially against alleged police brutality. On the evening of May 4 a meeting of eight hundred to a thousand people was held at Haymarket Square, Chicago. By late in the evening some two hundred remained. The mayor, who had been present, left the scene in the belief that the meeting would continue to be peaceful.

At this juncture some 186 policemen arrived to disperse the crowd. A bomb was thrown, killing seven policemen and wounding a number variously estimated at from twenty-seven to sixty-seven. The police fired a number of volleys into the mob, wounding as many as fifty or sixty people, "who were carried to the rear," the *Nation* wrote, "and into many dark alleyways by their friends." The thrower of the bomb could not be identified; Rudolph Schnaubelt was twice arrested on suspicion and twice released. A number of the anarchists, however, were arrested, arraigned as accomplices to the throwing, and convicted. On August 20, 1887, seven were condemned to death: they were August Spies, Albert R. Parsons, Louis Lingg, Michael Schwab, Samuel Fielden, George Engel, and Adolph Fischer. Governor Oglesby commuted the sentences of Fielden and Schwab to life imprisonment. Oscar Neebe was sentenced to fifteen years. The convictions were upheld by the Supreme Court. Louis Lingg committed suicide in prison.

As the time approached for the execution, public opinion diminished in violence; and Governor Oglesby sent word secretly to leading Chicago businessmen that he would commute the sentences of the convicted men if they approved. When Marshall Field opposed the action, however, the business leaders felt reluctant to approve such a move, and the governor did not take action. The four anarchists were hanged on November 11, 1887. Six years later, on June 26, 1893, Governor John P. Altgeld granted an unconditional pardon to Fielden, Schwab, and Neebe.[2]

When the bomb exploded at Haymarket Square, William Dean Howells was forty-nine years old, a friend of the literary great, an editor of *Harper's Magazine*, a respected novelist who, despite his realism, permitted few divorces among his fictional characters. When a child of twelve, Howells tells us in *Years of My Youth*, he worked long and rebellious hours in his father's printshop, getting out of bed between four and five in the morning to deliver papers. At that time he treated with righteous cruelty a young unwed mother who lived and worked with the Howells family. At the age of twenty-three, watching the pale factory girls coming from their ten-hour shift in Lowell, Massachusetts, he felt no stab of social concern. Later Howells voted the straight Republican ticket, and supported Grant in two elections, saying: "Many of us who will vote for General Grant are not sensible of being animated by any higher motive than the desire of self-preservation."

But the Haymarket riot and its consequences were a turning point in Howells' life; he felt the convictions and executions to be an utter violation of the most elementary justice. Under the shocked excoriations of his fellow-citizens, some of whom considered him almost a dynamiter himself, he did not flinch or qualify or retreat. When he appealed on behalf of the anarchists to John Greenleaf Whittier, Whittier refused to help and published the correspondence. Howells then appealed to Governor Oglesby to commute the sentences. Two days before the execution, Howells wrote to the *Tribune*, "The worst is still for a few days reparable; the men sentenced to death are still alive"; he urged all to join with him in petitioning the governor for commutation. On the day of the executions, Howells wrote to Francis Browne that the impending deed was "forever damnable before God and abominable to civilized man." Two days later Howells wrote his father that "this free Republic has killed five men for their opinions."[3]

Few men at fifty begin to form a new philosophy of the nature of man and the impact of social forces. But the Haymarket riot and its boiling aftermath instilled in Howells a new purpose: he would unite fiction of profound psychological insight with the philosophy of social awakening. Howells began to read Leo Tolstoy, Laurence Gronlund, and William Morris. In 1888, the year of Bellamy's *Looking Backward*, he sent forth his first novel of economic protest, *Annie Kilburn;* in 1891, *A Hazard of New Fortunes;* in 1892, *The Quality of Mercy*. Of these *A Hazard* contains the most explicit statements of Howells' new philosophy in the words of Basil March: "But conditions make character; and people are greedy and foolish, or wish to have and to shine, because having and shining are held up to them by civilization as the chief end of life." Among utopians, Howells is one of the few to emphasize the several types of men existing simultaneously in the same personality: "There's the making of several characters in each of us; we *are* each several characters, and sometimes this character has the lead in us, and sometimes that." At the end of *The Quality of Mercy*, when Putney analyzes the deficiencies of Northwick, he speaks also Howells' new philosophy of human nature: "His environment made him rich, and his environment made him a rogue. Sometimes I think there *was* nothing to Northwick, except what happened to him." Here Howells represents the same environmentalist philosophy which was to appear in *A Traveller from Altruria*, a philosophy shared by Bellamy and George.[4]

At no point does Howells consider the mysterious strength of hereditary uniqueness. A mother knows that two babies are different from each other by their very actions in the womb. From the first day of birth one baby is restless and fretful, another quiet and content, and so two such children may continue through six or seven decades. What are the mysterious genetic forces that shape personality? The endocrine glands act, no one knows exactly how, or in what certain ways modifiable by the chemistry of medicine. From the first day of birth the eyes of one child are bright, those of another dull and listless, tokens of the mind's life to come. These are data the utopians neglect for a persistent emphasis on environmental forces.

But in *A Traveller from Altruria,* Howells keeps his reader in the realistic world of the 1880's, contrasting it with a perfect but remote society. The setting of the romance is a summer colony in New England. After some subdued and colorless opening chapters, Howells sketches skilfully the intellectual milieu of the leisure class and through this milieu the cancerous growths afflicting the democracy of the gilded age. With a deft, unsparing hand he outlines the gulf between Mrs. Makely's pretensions of social equality and her exclusion of workers and servants from the charmed circle; the colony's horror at the Altrurian's help to the servants in shining shoes and carrying trays; the minister's uneasy rejection of the "kingdom come on earth" by the enduring token of human nature. Mrs. Makely's definition of a lady, in which she repudiates all useful labor as unbecoming her station, is a revelation of leisure-class psychology anticipating some of the ironic strokes of Thorstein Veblen's classic. If the colony gives lip service to social equality, its men make no pretense of democratic ideals in the field of industrial methods. The manufacturer declares that the first principle of business is the first principle of nature: "We are not talking of morality; we are talking of business." When the workers destroy property and interfere with business, the businessmen call out the militia and kill a few workers, whereupon the strike is broken. "It is perfectly simple." Business has no use for college; it gives people too many ideas alien to the mechanics of acquisition.

Thus does Howells depict the bankruptcy of democratic dogma in the minds of American economic leaders; and their concepts of human nature are a curious shadowing of the exigencies of business. The egotism of survival is not only fixed and invincible in man's nature, but also natural and just. The novelist (sponge of business values) considers the principles of class subordination so firmly planted as to be an offshoot of the divine wisdom. To the question, "What is greatness? What is the loftiest reach of human nature on the American scene?" the banker has given long reflection. In the decades after the Revolution, he admits, Americans looked to the statesman as their ideal of greatness; then came the flowering of intellectual life and the rise of the poet ideal, embodied in such as Longfellow. With the whirlwind of the Civil War, the soldier stood forth as the epitome of distinction; but the eminence of soldierly greatness has now given way to that of the millionaire; on any platform the millionaire will be the cynosure of all eyes, not the statesman or the poet or the soldier.

III

Howells no doubt intended his images of business realism in *A Traveller* to make more believable his own concept of the nature of man as represented by the Altrurian's picture of his own country: a land without money, without buying and selling, without idleness, without exhaustion. A man could own nothing except what he could use. With the fading of poverty and want, no man robbed to fill his stomach or to command the world's luxuries. Throughout *Altruria* Howells calls up the usual utopian patterns: each citizen works three hours a day at manual labor, his aim beauty and quality of workmanship; the mills and shops are as beautiful as temples, not crowded together in cities as in the old days, but dispersed throughout the country and blended into the landscape, like the homes of the citizens themselves. These patterns of life inevitably produce in Altrurian citizens the virtues now present in the fortunate few.

The human nature of *Altruria* is a product of the same mechanistic forces described in *What Is Man?* It does not trouble Howells, as it had troubled Melville in *Pierre*, that virtue is not virtue when all forces are in its favor. The Altrurian is a generous man, a lover of beauty, a gentleman, thoughtful of others' needs, only because he is removed from the struggle for survival. In this Christian com-

munism every Altrurian is part of a vast family, a symbol of community to which Howells constantly returns: "Have you ever seen
sweeter compassion . . . than that shown in the family where all
are economically one and no one can want while any other has
to give?" But these are the same human beings who in the old
society would have unleashed a savage selfishness: "Conditions *compelled* every man to think first of himself." As the banker puts it:
"A man sells his vote, as a woman sells her person, for money, when
neither can turn virtue into cash." Thus does Howells clarify his
picture of human nature, adding stroke after stroke, now from the
gilded age, now from Altruria. In its essentials it contains little that
is original; Howells has applied the principles of his great predecessors, More, Campanella, Comenius, Bacon, to the American
scene; he has repeated with variations the beliefs about human
nature set forth by Mann, Tocqueville, Lincoln, George, Bellamy,
and Clemens. Like other American utopians, he makes no mention
of some two hundred American communistic communities which
had already attempted to put these principles of human nature to
the crucial test; in Howells' time most of them had already withered
and expired.

In his emphasis on the cultivation of genius, however, Howells
shows more imagination than Bellamy or Henry George. The development of creative men was the main aim of the Altrurian common-
wealth; and the industrial order, like a gigantic orchestra, was tuned
and played toward this end. After three hours of obligatory labor,
drudgery or not, each Altrurian was free to follow the creative bent
of his temperament; thus, in Howells' view, any nation could multiply its genius beyond all precedent by a series of constructive
conditions and privileges never before extended to a whole population, though in all countries accorded the exceptional and fortunate few. To Howells, as to William Morris, man is normally creative
if left with his own tools to his own means. The Altrurians entered
with joy into the task of beautifying a whole continent; but each
stone laid, each rose planted, each ax handle turned on the lathe
fused the skill of the workman with the joy of the artist.

Howells, like all modern utopians, fails to evaluate the necessity of drudgery and the absence of art in the mere tending of great machines. But in Howells' view whatever is drudgery, or whatever is exchange and transportation, is mere preliminary to each day's creative life: "The artist, the man of genius, who worked from the love of his work, became the normal man." As no man escaped the necessary drudgery, so no man was denied an opportunity for unique creative expression; the artist, indeed, was to the Altrurians the nearest reach to the divine. Even Howells' conception of genius, then, is in the main an extension of his mechanist beliefs; it is the national responsibility to nourish unique creative expression, from the humblest piece of craftsmanship to the masterpiece of art or music; to surround men with images of greatness; to enliven with example, fertilize with leisure, then watch, expectant, for the creative moment that will add to the ripened record of the unique man.

Like all his fellow-utopians, Howells lacked, as do we his descendants, a knowledge of genetics sufficient to account for exceptional men. Is genius in the main the gift of heredity alone, as Sir Francis Galton believed? Whereas Howells believed that each man is normally creative, and that every generation can bring to birth a thousand geniuses for every one now ripened, Galton assumed that genius is the fruit of the family tree. What vast experiments are necessary to prove or disprove the contradictory assumptions of Galton and Howells? Only a science of man comprehending many disciplines can answer this question, which every utopia reiterates down the centuries.

Though scorned as a visionary, the utopian must appraise human nature realistically if his book is to hold its place among the tenacious fascinations of utopian lore. Few would deny the sober realism of William Dean Howells; if, accepting Howells' premise of mechanism, one rejects the enlightened nature of the Altrurians, he must perforce repudiate as untruthful the traditional beliefs of Mrs. Makely and Mr. Bullion. This at least is beautiful theory, which the eye of the realist is slow to trace. Edward Bellamy was likewise realistic according to his lights; for he also denied that human nature had changed from 1887 to the year 2000; in his utopia men were merely subjected to pressures never before applied on a national scale. If the new world were suddenly transformed into the old, both the men of Altruria and the men of the new America would revert inexorably to the mental and spiritual framework of the older order.

IV

Edward Bellamy was born in Chicopee Falls, Massachusetts, March 26, 1850, the son of a Baptist minister. After attending local schools and failing to be admitted to West Point, Bellamy for one year attended Union College with his brother, reading literature of his own choice; he was extremely reticent and made few friends. When he was eighteen, Bellamy spent part of the year in Europe with his cousin, William Packer, living with a German family at Dresden and attending lectures there. In Europe Bellamy sensed for the first time the gulf between rich and poor; he remembered the huts of the peasants more intensely than the palaces of the great. Always a solitary and self-reverent moralist, Bellamy began to brood over "the inferno of poverty beneath our civilization." He saw Chicopee Falls in a new light; within the relatively prosperous town was an ugly core of poverty. In the first issue of his own *Penny News* he later wrote of "A School House for the Poor—Wading Through Mud to Their Lessons—More Sickness Than in Any School in City."

Bellamy studied law and was admitted to the bar, opened a law office, and represented only one client before closing his doors. Going to New York, he worked for seven months for the *New York Evening Post*. Later he became an editor for the *Springfield Union*, and still later owned, with his brother Charles, his own newspaper. But this, too, he finally gave up. He turned to fiction, beginning an account of Shay's Rebellion in *The Duke of Stockbridge*, which he never completed. With the encouragement of Howells and the *Atlantic Monthly*, a literary career seemed open to him, especially after the publication of *Dr. Heidenhoff's Process* in 1880. But rightly he sensed himself a reformer rather than a novelist. In one account of the writing of *Looking Backward,* which he began in 1880, he asserted that his first purpose was merely to write "a fairy tale of social felicity." But halfway through the first draft the idea of the industrial army as the central social structure struck him and he rewrote the novel with great care as a vehicle of social reform.

Upon its publication in 1888, *Looking Backward* became overwhelmingly popular. Over the country Bellamy clubs were formed, a newspaper called the *New Nation* was founded, and Bellamy himself took an active part in the propaganda, speaking throughout the land, apparently convinced that a peaceful revolution as he had visioned it was actually possible by the early years of the twentieth century. In Bellamy's second utopia, *Equality,* he attempted to answer some of the persistent criticism of *Looking Backward,* especially the charge that the peaceful revolution in his romance was too sudden to be credible. When *Equality* was published in 1897, Bellamy was already near death from tuberculosis. He died in Chicopee Falls, May 22, 1898.[5]

Though essentially a mechanist, Bellamy in *Looking Backward* speaks, as Milton had spoken, for the natural goodness of man. The evil of the world is a perversion, not a reflection, of the order of nature:

Human nature in its essential qualities is good, not bad . . . men by their natural intention and structure are generous, not selfish, pitiful, not cruel, sympathetic, not arrogant, godlike in aspirations, instinct with divinest impulses of tenderness and self-sacrifice, images of God indeed, not the travesties upon Him they had seemed.

For such optimism as this critics have derided Bellamy as a charming dreamer, or consigned him to the limbo of utopian fools. But the natural goodness of man, Bellamy continues, is not invincible. For countless generations it has been subjected to "conditions of life which might have perverted angels." Humanity has been pounded by so many intolerable pressures that the resilience of its natural goodness, visualized now and then in singular personalities, proved of tougher fiber than anyone had a right to expect. It was no wonder, then, that in the new society, when the evil externals of the old society vanished, human nature "like a bent tree" sprang "back to its normal uprightness." The origin of man's evil actions is not his sound heart, but the grinding forces of his rotten world.

To press home his concept of a noble nature debauched by circumstance, Bellamy compares mankind to "a rosebush planted in a swamp, watered with black bog-water, breathing miasmic fogs by day, and chilled with poison dews at night." Without avail thousands of gardeners had tried to make it bloom, though now and then a wormy bud appeared on its branches, for the moment beautiful, but soon to perish. About the nature of this rosebush and its disease the gardeners were divided among themselves. Some asserted it was not a rosebush at all, but a poisonous growth. Without condemning it thus to annihilation, other gardeners, the most numerous group, insisted that that rosebush's very fiber was so tainted that it could never bloom. A few gardeners, it is true, were disposed not to blame the rosebush at all, but only the bog. But these men, so few as to be insignificant, and indeed not professionally trained, were looked upon by most gardeners as idle visionaries. Some philosophers, conceding momentarily that the bush might improve in another setting, argued that the few feeble buds that did bloom represented such a moral victory that a richer soil was undesirable. Finally, after long and unsuccessful experimentation with various treatments, a change of soils was reluctantly decreed:

So . . . the rosebush of humanity was transplanted, and set in sweet, warm, dry earth, where the sun bathed it, the stars wooed it, and the south wind caressed it. Then it appeared that it was indeed a rosebush. The vermin and the mildew disappeared, and the bush was covered with the most beautiful red roses, whose fragrance filled the world.[6]

In the parable of the rosebush Bellamy rejected utterly the

dominance of heredity for a deep faith in the plasticity of man's organism. For centuries the philosophers of man had accepted in the main the determinism imposed by heredity. Even Plato, who shaped the character of his young philosophers through a drastic education, had assumed the dominance of genetic characters. From golden men, he thought, would spring only a few brass and iron children; from brass and iron men only a few golden children. It was the revered justification of mankind's unyielding inequalities of wealth and talent. When Robert Owen had said, "Man's character is formed for him and not by him," he had struggled in vain against the belief in blood that stamped the British mind from nobleman to peasant. In 1878, when Sir Francis Galton sent forth his remarkable *Heredity and Genius*, he stamped anew the old beliefs, justifying a creed rooted deep in the centuries, apparently oblivious of the amazing environmental pressures exerted on children in remarkable families. Against this creed, which rationalism had still only dented, Edward Bellamy set the whole argument of his utopia. Upon drastic environmental impressions he placed his whole reliance for the transformation of corrupted men into the enlightened citizens of the year 2000.

Although *A Traveller* contains more realism than *Looking Backward*, Bellamy's imagination had pierced deep into the abyss of man's hatred and cruelties. It is true that neither he nor Howells had witnessed the violence or degradation familiar to Mark Twain; true also that their optimism about human nature, like that of all utopians, was a projection of theory rather than images of men they had known. But Bellamy, like Howells, understood the forces that drive men to baser cruelties than any other animals are capable of. In Reverend Barton's sermon he repeats the story of the Black Hole of Calcutta, in which gallant soldiers lost all humanity and became raging beasts, tearing each other to pieces to reach the precious air that spelled survival. If this was an extreme debasement of human nature, it was only a minute flame in the fires that engulfed the world, not because men were evil at heart, but because the smoke of poverty or insecurity or hatred was always pressing into their throats and lungs. Men of the nineteenth century he called "beasts of prey." In describing Boston's South Cove slums, Bellamy again pointed to the degradation imposed by circumstance:

From the black doorways and windows of the rookeries on every side came gusts of fetid air. The streets and alleys reeked with the effluvia of a slave ship's between-decks. As I passed I had glimpses within of pale babies gasping out their lives amid sultry stenches, of hopeless-faced women deformed by hardship, retaining of womanhood no trait save weakness, while from the windows leered girls with brows of brass. . . . Swarms of half-clad brutalized children filled the air with shrieks and curses as they fought and tumbled among the garbage that littered the court-yards.[7]

In this description is no sure touch of Mark Twain or Charles Dickens or Stephen Crane; but it shows that Bellamy was realistically aware of the extremities of mankind's degradation. To him this degradation was rooted in impersonal socially-imposed forces, not in the genetic determinism that impelled one woman to become Crane's Maggie, and another a Margaret Fuller.

In the America of 2000 A.D., according to *Looking Backward*, transformed conditions of life have acted automatically to transform the habits of man. Everyone who works possesses not only security, but also the luxuries of life in the same degree as his neighbor. Fear of want afflicts only those who refuse to work. No dollars that can be hoarded, but only credit stamps that must be spent, are the medium of exchange. By equalizing income at approximately $4,000 per family, the Americans of the future have eliminated not only the fear of want, but also the desire to surpass one's neighbor in earning power and material prosperity. Competition for a living, by fair means or criminal, has disappeared; but competition for approval, for relative distinction and merit, for professional and creative reputation, is infinitely stronger than in 1887.

Private initiative for private profit has likewise vanished, though everyone must work to have his credit stamps; but private initiative for attending college, for exploring a new world, for inventing a

beautiful bridge, for writing a great book, for using one's leisure
time creatively—this kind of initiative, surprisingly energetic in the
old order, has been enormously expanded. The hours of labor vary
with the collective desires of volunteer workers; a miner may work
two hours, a teacher eight; a writer may prefer a sewer cleaner's
job to a forester's in order to have more leisure for himself. A
country in which harsh incentives have withered and noble ones
bloomed; a country without want, virtually without crime, lawyers,
insanity, suicide; a land without ugliness—this is Bellamy's utopia,
realized not through any change in man's nature, but through a
transformation of the conditions under which he lives. Bellamy
denies, however, that the America of 2000 A.D. represents the ultimate in human happiness; its magnificent achievements are a
symbol only of the collective conquest of poverty and fear. The
"unbounded possibilities of human nature" are in reality still
unexplored.

Nowhere does Bellamy depend more confidently upon the
mechanistic play of forces than in his conception of the new
education of American youth. Though he did not develop a system
of psychology, his beliefs reflect the same convictions that had
agitated Horace Mann: no one, however weak in natural endowment, is immune to the educative process; no one can resist
altogether the benevolent blows of an enlightened classroom. The
structure of Bellamy's educational dream is merely an upward
extension of the established school system to the college level, a
process now familiar to hundreds of American communities. To all
youth a college education under Bellamy's plan is obligatory, college to mean not training for jobs but training for life: humanistic
studies, social responsibilities, the enjoyment of leisure. Such a
cultural program, while permitting the free play of natural endowment, raises to the highest pitch possible the intellectual capacities
of the masses of men: "One generation of the world today represents a greater volume of intellectual life than any five centuries
ever did before." Such benefits the nation has a right to insist upon,
not only for the self-enjoyment of the citizens, but also for the

well-being of their neighbors and the welfare of the unborn children whose parents they will become. Upon this program the resources of the nation are poured out without stint; nothing is so important to Bellamy's Americans as the impact of the people they meet, "whose voices are always in our ears, whose behavior in innumerable ways affects our enjoyment,—who are, in fact, as much conditions of our lives as the air we breathe." The planting of men, then, as in Howells' utopia, is the main aim of *Looking Backward;* and Bellamy believed insistently that in this process the material resources of the nation could be transmuted into the gold of a more abundant spiritual and intellectual life.

In the perspective of American thought, Bellamy is one of the most optimistic observers of human nature. Like the writer of Genesis, he seriously believed that man was made in the image of his Creator. In the framework of Bellamy's wider belief, however, the original nature of man is of little moment; for Bellamy, like his great predecessors of the American scene, visualized the human organism as incredibly plastic and changeable, an organism capable of infinite debasement or infinite nobility. In man's *conditioning*, not in his original nature, lies his social destiny, his success as a father, a friend, a citizen. In this conditioning lies also the destiny of the democratic experiment. Like the tempering of steel or the smelting of ore, like the application of energy to inorganic matter, the conditioning of man is the application of energy to personality. An intricate and difficult process, irreducible for the most part to mathematical terms, the conditioning of man has a practical validity exemplified in every parental admonition, every church, every school, every hour of military training, every hour spent in reading a book. Though all the complexities of the process escape us, its essentials express themselves in almost every spoken sentence. Now Bellamy, like Howells and Henry George, wanted the conditioning process applied to men on a scale hitherto undreamed of. It is easy and perhaps irrational to say that it would or would not work; certainly in the past few centuries no such a priori rejection of the application of energy to inorganic matter, or even to human beings in the field of medicine and surgery, has been considered scientifically valid. What Bellamy stands for, then, may be considered a tough realism in the field of sociology: no one can say positively whether a great social idea will succeed or not. The proof or disproof of its soundness is in the *actual trial*, not in the pronouncements of the philosophers, whether amateur or professional.

Bellamy predicted that the final consolidation of industry and ensuing nationalization would take place "early in the last century," that is, in the early 1900's. His prophecy, then, of the time when the people of America would achieve a scientific attitude toward social theories and say, "Let us try it," has proved far too sanguine. Indeed, despite the vast experimentation of the New Deal, the probability of any such widespread view of social action appears extremely remote. Upon the application of scientific reasoning to sociology, however, and its ultimate acceptance by the nation, depends the reconcilement of democratic aims with the vastly accelerated pace of industrial mechanization. In this emphasis also, then, Bellamy was a realistic critic of both the nature of man and the nature of the machine age.

V

Henry George knew the bitter realism of American life more intimately than did his great contemporaries, Howells and Bellamy. As a boy of fifteen, hot-blooded and curious, he had sailed before the mast for fourteen months, hardening himself to the rough discipline of the forecastle, the cruel accidents of sailor life, the miseries of Calcutta, and the dead bodies of the Ganges, picked to pieces by the crows. Before nineteen he had sailed through the Straits of Magellan, watched a comrade buried at sea, and seen the strange customs of many ports. In 1858 he landed in San Francisco, three years before Mark Twain; in the ensuing years he was typesetter, gold miner, tramp, rice mill worker, farm hand, reporter, peddler, and editor—meanwhile sharpening and seasoning

his capacious intellect. By the age of thirty, overwhelmed by the
extremes of New York's wealth and poverty, he had crystallized his
life purpose in a solemn vow:

Years ago I came to this city from the West, unknown, knowing nobody,
and I saw and recognized for the first time the shocking contrast between
monstrous wealth and debasing want. And here I made a vow from
which I have never faltered, to seek out, and remedy, if I could, the
cause that condemned little children to lead such a life . . . in the squalid
districts.[8]

Ten years later George sent forth his masterpiece, *Progress and
Poverty*, a book fortified by harsh experience, illumined by rich
gleanings from the world's great books, instinct with logic and
eloquence, bitterness and hope.

Henry George's acute awareness of American misery filled him
with despair. "Where the value of land is highest," he wrote,
"civilisation exhibits the greatest luxury side by side with the most
piteous destitution." Every daily newspaper brought him a new
awakening to the horrors of civilization. At the Vanderbilt ball
wine flowed like water, diamonds sparkled, and each beautiful rose
was more expensive than a day of the laborer's time; but near by,
on the same night, thirty-nine men and women sought shelter at
the police station; the next morning they were marched off to prison
for six months, the women weeping and screaming bitterly on the
way. Or there was Margaret Hickey, of Boston, sentenced to six
months on the Island for deserting her baby on Forty-third Street,
after a fruitless search for work. "Better for them," lamented George,
"and better for society were they drowned outright, as we would
drown a useless and mangy kitten." Short items, not nearly so
important as the society notes: A mother of two days in a Brooklyn
tenement, with no medical help, her child dead, her husband
slumped over in a drunken daze. Paupers and criminals alone in
New York would populate a street twenty-two miles long. Women
of New York, working from fourteen to sixteen hours a day, stitch-
ing shirts at thirty-five cents a dozen, earn three or four dollars a
week! According to one judge's testimony, two extra children in

many poor families meant "a boy for the penitentiary and a girl for the brothel." These accusations, taken from *Social Problems*, George denies are the "blackest shadows." They but reflect the nauseous by-products of civilization; they reflect, not the inherent evil of man's nature, but society's criminal neglect. "In every civilised country," he had written in *Progress and Poverty*,

pauperism, crime, insanity, and suicides are increasing. In every civilised country the diseases are increasing which come from overstrained nerves, from insufficient nourishment, from squalid lodgings, from unwholesome and monotonous occupations, from premature labour of children, from the tasks and crimes which poverty imposes upon women.[9]

Not content with these gloomy pictures, George vehemently asserted that slavery still held sway over the lives of American workers. Chattel slavery we had abolished, yes; but this was only a coarser form of slavery that the plantation owners themselves would not want reinstated. Chattel slavery was only "a rude and primitive mode of property in man." The newer slavery, the more subtle and insidious slavery, kept men nominally free but actually in bondage. When a workingman's wages would not support his family, but had to be supplemented by the earnings of his wife and children; when thousands would gladly work for board and clothes, and other thousands would sell themselves into slavery for the necessities of life; when many men and women were driven in despair to a life by crime or a death by suicide; then slavery still existed, with the iron impersonal master Necessity wielding the whip and dictating the terms of survival or extinction. "The man who gives me employment," wrote George, "which I must have or suffer, that man is my master, let me call him what I will." To such profound pessimism was Henry George led by the misery and degradation of American workers. If chattel slavery were once more introduced to American life, the employers themselves would reject it: For "who would buy men when men can be hired so cheaply?"

Like Howells and Mark Twain, though by dissimilar logic,

Henry George bemoaned the advancing disintegration of the American Republic. In every new country, he asserted, where land is cheap, wages are high and economic equality is real; but the older the country, the lower the wages, the higher the land values, the richer the few: "Wages and interest tend constantly to fall, rent to rise, the rich to become very much richer, the poor to become more helpless and hopeless, and the middle class to be swept away." This was America, like the republic of ancient Rome. Without the restraints of aristocracy or a conservative middle class of political breadth and honesty, a democracy can by gradual revolutionary technique be transformed into a dictatorship. To establish such a tyranny, it is not necessary to alter its constitution or forbid elections. It is too easy to buy courts and legislatures to be concerned with elections; the despotism, moreover, will be advanced in the name of the people, a people already debased: "A corrupt democratic government must finally corrupt the people, and when a people become corrupt there is no resurrection."

To the Americans success had become synonymous with virtue; they did not pause to examine the means of triumph; evidence of its reality was sufficient to rally their support and command their admiration. The corruption of legislators, the careless, egotistic power of the rich, the indifference of the multitude, all these joined with signs of economic breakdown to discourage the clear-sighted patriot: "Industrial depressions, which cause as much waste and suffering as famines or wars, are like the twinges and shocks which precede paralysis." Henry George's prediction of a fascist America, written sixty-five years ago, has proved thus far wide of the mark. But the twentieth-century advent of fascism in four nominally democratic European countries—fascism established in each case in the name of the masses—gives both his prediction and his diagnosis a relevance none can deny.

The material blessings of the richest land in the world were, then, being utilized in a manner utterly contradictory to the democratic premises of its founders. Without economic opportunity political equality was a hollow mockery: with the advance of mechanization and the centralization of land ownership, economic inequalities were imposing a penalty upon the masses prohibitive of a decent existence. Thus ran the argument of Henry George, from his first important articles to his last book, from his first speech to that fatal night in 1897, five days before the New York mayoralty election, when apoplexy suddenly struck him down. On the Sunday following, as his body lay in state at Grand Central Palace, a hundred thousand people filed past the coffin of their spokesman.

George subjected human nature to a closer scrutiny than either Howells or Bellamy, and with more scientific precision than Mark Twain. His conclusion was similar to theirs, that human nature is the effect of a conditioning process; and that men's actions, good or evil, are but their unconscious and automatic reactions to the people and places and ideas which surround them. But unlike his contemporaries, George devotes long passages to the relative influence of heredity and environment, a topic pregnant with suggestion to the student of human nature. As we should expect, he rejects all assumptions of original sin or evil propensities; and though he leans slightly to Bellamy's conception of man's original nobility, he lays before the reader what he believes is overwhelming evidence of the plasticity and malleability of the human personality.

"The influence of heredity," wrote George, "which it is now the fashion to rate so highly, is as nothing compared with the influences which mould the man after he comes into the world." Language, morals, religion, parents, food, books, ideas—all these are inherent in his world, not in the stuff of his original nature. A white child captured in infancy by the Indians will grow up with no trace save color of the white man's world upon his face or in his heart. A white baby placed in the heart of China will grow up a thorough Chinaman, "using the same speech, thinking the same thoughts, exhibiting the same tastes." The dilemma of *Pudd'nhead Wilson* Henry George resolved in the manner of Mark Twain: "Change Lady Vere de Vere in her cradle with an infant of the slums, and will the blood of a hundred earls give you a refined and cultured woman?"

George would not admit any innate difference in the intelligence of whites and Negroes; in school the Negroes, according to Bishop Hillery, did equally well with the whites in the early grades; but as soon as the Negro boys and girls realized the vast ramifications of inequality, and knew themselves destined to be no more than menial workers, they lost their ambition. This realization, coupled with their discouraging home environment, Henry George believed to be the true explanation of white superiority in educational competition. Thus did Henry George anticipate the findings of Otto Klineberg and twentieth-century anthropology. Not in heredity, not in color, but in the environmental transmission of accumulated ideas lies the productive mental power of mankind.

Henry George, like James Harvey Robinson half a century later, believed that all men are born completely uncivilized. He devotes many pages in *Progress and Poverty* to Herbert Spencer's thesis, based on the researches of Darwin, that man's nature, subjected generation after generation to the pressures of civilization, undergoes a permanent change; that is, the impact of civilized practices becomes fixed in the brain structure and is transmitted genetically from parents to children. The exigencies of war, famine, and pestilence gradually eliminate the unfit; genetically improved men and races assume their rightful leadership, and civilization advances at a slow but inexorable pace. Against this theory of man's nature Henry George arrayed some arresting evidence. He pointed to the majestic civilizations that vanished, decayed, or retrogressed:

The Hindoos and the Chinese were civilised when we were savages. They had great cities, highly organised and powerful governments, literatures, philosophies, polished manners ... when our ancestors were wandering barbarians. ... While we have progressed from this savage state to nineteenth-century civilisation, they have stood still. If progress be the result of fixed [hereditary] laws, inevitable and eternal, which impel men forward, how shall we account for this?[10]

Progress is not continuous, and "the earth is the tomb of dead empires, no less than of dead men." These facts alone, in George's belief, demolished the evolutionary theory of progress. The explanation of the great eras had to be sought, not in genetic change, but in the combinations of social circumstance. There was no difference at birth between the savages of the jungle and citizens of Beacon Street or Park Avenue. We were all born uncivilized.

"Man is an animal," wrote Henry George; "but he is an animal plus something else. He is the mythic earth tree, whose roots are in the ground, but whose topmost branches may blossom in the heavens!" This passage is the key to Henry George's conception of the nature of man. Man is driven by a hierarchy of desires. As an animal he wants food, shelter, sex, the necessities of survival; but no sooner are these wants satisfied, than man has new desires: to sail the sea, to trace the stars in their orbits, at last perhaps to aid "in making life better and brighter, in destroying want and sin, sorrow and shame." This is the master passion, the supreme desire. But as manure and black earth presage the blooming of the rose, so the needs of the animal must find satisfaction before the desires of the mind can take root and grow and bloom in beautiful patterns. "Out upon nature, in upon himself, back through the mists that shroud the past, forward into the darkness that overhangs the future, turns the restless desire that arises when the animal wants slumber in satisfaction."

So Henry George answers those who would denounce as ignoble schemes for gratifying man's material needs. These needs must first be met, not because they are pre-eminent, but because the man cannot act until the animal is no longer tormented by hunger, weakness, worry. Would a general deploy his forces without food, or an architect build a façade without a foundation? Man does not live by bread alone, but by bread first. A gnawing stomach pulls to the earth the soaring spirit. To be a creative person, to desire a creative life, one must first live, breathe, have the strength to work, be free from hunger and cold.

The secret of civilization, then, asserted Henry George, was to release, not a few thousands, but many millions of men, eventually all men, from the struggle for bread; then only can they apply their mental energies to the satisfaction of those desires that would elevate both themselves and their fellow-men. Only when free or partially free from want are men inspired through their associations to travel, to learn, to create, to relieve the miseries of mankind. The extension of political liberties, the growth of law, the opening of economic opportunity, the knittings of communication and commerce, all these have given opportunities, especially in America, to classes of people who never before had a surplus with which to expand and apply their mental powers. The wider and more realistic the extensions of equality, *the more abundant the mental power applied to social gains.*

To Henry George the decline and death of civilizations may be traced to the denial of equality, hence to the disuse of available mental energy; and civilization flourishes when equality advances: "Mental power is, therefore, the motor of progress, and men tend to advance in proportion to the mental power expended in progression—the mental power which is devoted to the extension of knowledge, the improvement of methods, and the betterment of social conditions."

Not as isolated individuals, however, but as members of society, where associations are most intense and ramified, and when co-operation reduces the labor of necessity, do men expend their mental labor with most beneficent rewards: "Men tend to progress as they come closer together, and by co-operation with each other increase the mental power that may be devoted to improvement." If, on the other hand, association results in war, class struggle, slavery, or inequality, too much mental power is expended on destructive purposes or the labors of necessity; the processes of progress slacken, halt, and finally retreat.

The picture of mankind released from want, obsessed with new and ever ranging desires, pouring out its energies for common betterment, of whole peoples infused with creative fervor, this was the utopia of Henry George. If critics have derided it as useless and visionary, it may be said with justice that the experience of the world thus far weighs heavily for their sober judgment. But Henry George also pointed to experience as the justification of his utopia: to the thousands of men in the past who, wholly or partially removed from want, had devoted their mental energies to the enlightenment and elevation of mankind. What he proposed was to universalize the favored condition of the few who had been mentally productive, like Humboldt, Franklin, Michelangelo, Herbert Spencer, all of whom were released for long periods from the necessity of making a living. "To remove want and the fear of want,"

to give to all classes leisure, and comfort, and independence, the decencies and refinements of life, the opportunities of mental and moral development, would be like turning water into a desert. The sterile waste would clothe itself with verdure, and the barren places where life seemed banned would ere long be dappled with the shade of trees and musical with the song of birds. Talents now hidden, virtues unsuspected, would come forth to make life richer, fuller, nobler, happier.[11]

Not every man, of course, would be a genuine creator; but society's crime of poverty would be annihilated; then only would the relative genius of men and the collective power of intellect shine forth in true perspective.

But if men with slight exertion were released from want, would they not cease to labor beyond this minimum? To this timeless query Henry George shaped a reply in terms of the fundamental nature of man. Beyond the needs of the body man's desires are infinite, desires taking root as he observes the wonders of other men, other manners, other countries. Ascending in the hierarchy of desires, man works as never before; not under the lash of necessity, but driven by fascination, curiosity, new hopes and dreams. "Each step that he takes opens new vistas and kindles new desires. He is a constructive animal; he builds, he invents, and puts together, and the greater the thing he does, the greater the thing he wants to do." The poet at his desk, the inventor toiling into the night, the painter forgetting the world for days in the fascination of his task, the men who advance civilization and permanently enrich the race, do not toil merely for a living: "It is not the work of slaves, driven to their task either by the lash of a master or by animal necessities. It is the work of men who perform it for its own sake. . . . In a state of society where want was abolished, work of this sort would be enormously increased." This kind of labor is not drudgery but delight: it is work with a goal, a reward, an impact on a wider life. Not a shirking, then, not laziness, but an infinite outpouring of men's energies, in Henry George's view, would follow the banishment of poverty.

But even if men were not lazy and shiftless under the spell of prosperity, would they still not be greedy and avaricious after the rooted ways of human nature? This perennial and searching question Henry George had also foreseen. He does not deny that men are greedy; but the root of greed lies not in the man but in the exterior impetus that shapes his motives. A man is greedy from one of two reasons: either he does not have enough of the necessities and luxuries of life, or he is afraid of losing what he already has. If a table groans with food, and everyone knows there is plenty, no one is greedy; but where there is not enough food, or enough wealth, to make each secure, then the response of greed is instantaneous, because then greed is necessary to survival. In some restaurants of London and Paris the knives and forks are chained to the table. Is this a symbol of human nature? If so, what of men and women eating together in a courteous manner, no one hurrying, no one fearful? In George's view, greed is made by society, not born in man. "Did you ever see a pail of swill given to a pen of hungry hogs?" he wrote, in *Social Problems*. "That is human society as it is. Did you ever see a company of well-bred men and women sitting down to a good dinner, without scrambling, or jostling, or gluttony, each knowing that his own appetite will be satisfied, deferring to and helping the other? That is human society as it might be."

The waste of mental energies inherent in the history of man weighed heavily upon the imagination of Henry George. Convinced as he was that the gnawing need for food and clothes and shelter was synonymous with the waste of sleeping intellect, he visualized man as a fertile, creative animal, born to vistas of achievement but living among thorns and barren wastes. Like Gray in his "Elegy," musing among the obscure dead, Henry George also bemoaned the loss of potentially great souls in the heedless mill of ignorance and want. "Chill Penury repress'd their noble rage,/And froze the genial current of the soul." Thus Gray had posed the role of circumstance in the frustration of genius; and Henry George, fourteen decades later, echoed his belief in many a brilliant passage. "Turn to the lives of great men," he wrote,

and see how easily they might never have been heard of. Had Caesar come of a proletarian family; had Napoleon entered the world a few years earlier; had Columbus gone into the Church instead of going to sea; had Shakespeare been apprenticed to a cobbler or chimney sweep; had Sir Isaac Newton been assigned by fate the education and the toil of an agricultural laborer; had Dr. Adam Smith been born in the coal hews, or Herbert Spencer forced to get his living as a factory operative, what would their talents have availed? But there would have been, it will be said, other Caesars or Napoleons, Columbuses or Shakespeares, Newtons, Smiths, or Spencers. This is true. And it shows how prolific is our human nature.[12]

Human nature is prolific, but circumstance is niggardly and capricious. For every one who stretches to the zenith of his talents, an untold number starve and wither, their intellectual energies untapped, their dreams unfertilized, their eyes still dark with the veil of ignorance.

Though Henry George, like Howells and Bellamy, accepted circumstance as the inexorable determinant of man's motives, hopes, and dreams, his picture of human nature is sketched with a surer hand than theirs, and with more patience for the dark and shadowy corners. The doubts and questions that Bellamy failed to grapple with thoroughly in *Looking Backward* George had already met in *Progress and Poverty* with more complete and incisive reasoning than any of his contemporaries, with the exception of Herbert Spencer, could muster. If in *A Traveller* Howells was skilful in sketching the psychology of American leadership, George endeavored, like Mark Twain, to pierce to the common root of human action in his interpretation of men's desires. More concretely than Howells or Bellamy, George defined civilization in terms of the expenditure of mental power, buttressing his argument with a deep awareness of history and biography that neither of his fellow-utopians could command. His knowledge was as prodigious as his logic was powerful. Though *Looking Backward* is an infinitely more appealing book than *Progress and Poverty,* and shows a much more practical understanding of the average human mind, bringing into focus in broad strokes the essential (and still unsolved) problems of civilization, George's great book clashed more solidly and scientifically than Bellamy's with the accepted theories of human nature and economic life. Like every gifted thinker, he knew the worth of his creation. In inscribing a copy to his father, he wrote, "It will not be recognized at first—maybe not for some time—but it will ultimately be considered a great book, will be published in both hemispheres, and be translated into different languages."

The three men, however, deposited in the full-flowing stream of American thought ideas and concepts of a common acceptance among their great fellow-spokesmen on the nature of man. All three, though Howells mainly by implication, rejected hereditary forces as potent in even slight degree in the shaping of man's motives. Though none of the three denied hereditary differences, each placed the main responsibility for life differences on environment. The innate intellectual differences among men, contended George, are no greater than physical differences; but chance elevates and improves one man's mind, whereas another's lies fallow all his life. If men were only animals, breeding would serve to improve the stock; but men are more than animals; they are infinitely responsive in mind as well as in body. To change the man, change the life around him. To transform a whole nation of people, to elevate their motives, infuse them with new ambitions, and release their creative energies, transform from dark to bright the circumstances that made them. To work such a transformation, to extend to each man the conditions of happiness, whatever his response, is a goal inherent in the Declaration of Independence; without a new and realistic extension of the American ideal of equality into economic life, political liberty and the Declaration itself can be but a hollow dream. Thus spoke the three utopians, Howells, Bellamy, and George; and each subscribed to the saying of Tocqueville: "A new and fair division of the goods and rights of this world should be the main object of those who conduct human affairs." Whether their concepts of economics and human nature are truth or illusion only a science of man, endowed with unlimited funds and committed to decades of experimentation, will be able to tell.

IX

Mark Twain: On the Bitter Root
of the Human Tree

> *From the cradle to the grave, during all
> his waking hours, the human being is under
> training. . . . He is a chameleon; by the law
> of his nature he takes the color of his place
> of resort.*
>
> — Mark Twain

No AMERICAN has explored more relentlessly than
Mark Twain the deep caverns of human frailty. Into man's hypocrisies he probed, into his persecuting fervor, his cowardice, his
cruelty and corruption. No walled recess of human nature escaped
the keen searchlight of his mind; no behavior except the sexual
escaped the acid of his published scorn. Nor did the great souls
that he had known, living or dead, diminish in perspective the
range of his pessimism. They were to him but a handful of the
wicked multitude, a multitude from birth liars and hypocrites,
doomed one and all to misery and despair. To the intelligent death
was a benefit, life an unending sorrow. From his inspection of man
Mark Twain drew back forlorn and disillusioned; from the study
of himself he knew only doubt and sadness. As fully as any man
of his age he knew the gulf between democratic pretensions and
oligarchic actuality. No faith in the impulse of good will, no faith
in schools, in a benevolent God, in evolution, in the social assumptions of a democracy, softened the despair of his later years. The
acceleration of centralized control, both economic and political,
would hasten, he thought, the downfall of the Republic. By 1935
the shadow of dictatorship would fall like a blight upon the land,
a blight inherent in the lord-loving nature of man.

One need not exaggerate the bleakness of Mark's outlook. In his early years he was not a pessimist. Looking back at seventy, he wrote that life at twenty-seven had been a "fairy tale." His pessimism was in the main inconsistent with *What Is Man?*, the only extended and disciplined effort he ever made to pierce to the roots of man's nature. Mark Twain's mechanistic outlook, filled as it was with hope for the human race, did not dissipate his pessimism: the one was intellectual, the other emotional. Nor did he project his mechanism fully, as Lincoln did, into an image of the power of democratic institutions to elevate men's motives.

If mechanism qualified Mark Twain's pessimism, so did his joy in being alive, a joy he felt from youth to age despite the incongruities of the human comedy. He would skip up and down the stairs, convulse his guests with gales of laughter, stride at sunup through the halls of his great home yelling gleefully for Howells to come down. To the end he was a child in his little fancies and impulses of delight; he had the child's trust in the pledged word of a man he liked; his animal spirits, like those of a child, embraced new friends and clasped tight the old. But in the deep recesses of his mind Mark was seldom joyful in the last bitter years; his personal sorrows, his systematization of despair, his image of mankind blind and bestial to the end, blotted out of his mind—except in rare moments—that great hope for human nature set forth by inference in *What Is Man?*

Throughout Mark Twain runs a profound insight into motives destructive to the democratic assumptions of Jefferson and Lincoln. Like the prophets of fascism, like Hobbes and Nietzsche, Mark Twain forces us to examine the fears and hatreds that lie beneath the veneer of civilized habits and customs. When Melville wrote in *Pierre*, "Philosophy is air; but events are brass," he spoke the mind of Mark Twain. Before the drive of self-preservation ideals fall shattered and helpless.

This realism he spoke from a richer, more varied experience than that of any other American writer; he had observed human nature as printer, miner, pilot, and journalist, as confidante of the

humble and the mighty, the ignorant and the learned, the ribald
and the pious, the defeated and the successful; he had supped with
kings and presidents, and found them wanting; he had lived with
Buck Fanshaw, Colonel Sellers, Laura Hawkins, Huckleberry Finn,
Nigger Jim, Andrew Carnegie, John D. Rockefeller, Ulysses Grant,
Orion Clemens, Olivia Langdon, William Dean Howells, Mark
Twain. As fully as any American writer, he had witnessed and
recorded, in Browning's phrase, "the stages of all life," high and
low, profound and superficial, violent and serene, bitter and generous, serious and burlesque. No American more than he had to
sweeten life with laughter while despair at the vagaries of human
nature hung heavy in the heart.

II

To Mark Twain man's evil nature had been dominant and unalterable since the birth of the race. Though he would have scoffed
at the theological notion of original sin, he did believe in original
and continuous evil as a dominant element in man's nature. "The
first man," says the admirable Satan in *The Mysterious Stranger,*
"was a hypocrite and a coward, qualities that have not failed in
his line; it is the foundation upon which all civilizations have been
built."[1] In Satan's panorama of history Twain visualizes murder,
rape, war, massacres, and Christian refinements of ancient unspeakable cruelties, all as the inevitable extensions of man's nature. Mark
Twain's stories of his later life abound in epithets of contempt:
we are "a shabby, poor, worthless lot," "a paltry race," "only poor,
dumb beasts groping about," "liars from the cradle onward." All
men are dishonest in so many ways they can't help but be honest
in a few. "Even I am dishonest," he wrote to Twitchell. "Not in
many ways, but in some. Forty-one, I think it is." Man is unalter-
ably selfish; the fitting symbol of the race would be a man carrying
an ax concealed for timely grinding. Of all the animals he is the
only one who is senselessly cruel. If God created man because He
was disappointed in the monkey, the result, in terms of intelligence,

was doubtful indeed to Mark Twain. When a Presbyterian journal spoke of man as "the chief love and delight of God," Mark unloosed one of his bitterest diatribes on the race of man:

I watch him progressing and progressing—always progressing—always mounting higher and higher . . . sometimes by means of the Terror . . . sometimes by help of a St. Bartholomew's, sometimes by spreading hell and civilization in China, sometimes by preserving and elevating the same at home by a million soldiers and a thousand battleships; and when he gets down to today I still look at him spread out over a whole page of the morning paper, grabbing in Congress, grabbing in Albany, grabbing in New York and St. Louis and all around, lynching the innocent, slobbering hypocrisies, reeking, dripping, unsavory, but always recognizable as the same old Most Sublime Existence in all the range of Non-Divine Being, the Chief Love and Delight of God.[2]

Whatever moral sense man possesses Mark Twain denounced as a sham and a delusion. The morality of the animals is far superior to that of man: their morality is inherent in the animal mechanism; his is the whim of circumstance, lighting fagots under child witches, manufacturing wars against helpless people, inventing a thousand cruelties in the name of God or country. "There is one thing that always puzzles me," he wrote:

As inheritors of the mentality of our reptile ancestors we have improved the inheritance by a thousand grades; but in the matter of morals which they have left us we have gone backward as many grades. *That evolution* is strange & to me accountable & unnatural. Necessarily we started equipped with perfect and blemishless morals; now we are wholly destitute; we have no *real* morals, but only artificial ones—morals created and preserved by the forced suppression of natural & healthy instincts. Yes, we are a sufficiently comical invention, we humans.[3]

Time after time Mark Twain hammers home the same conviction: the inherent evil of man is a permanent possession beside which his enlightenment is a flimsy and fleeting artifice. The people of Hadleyburg, being only artificially honest, were easily corrupted. If man does not err, it is only because he has not been tempted. There was the clergyman, for instance, who discovered in the home of a farmer a first-edition Shakespeare (with an autograph) worth in the rare-book market about $67,000. How did he reward the poor farmer, who knew nothing of the value of his first edition? "The generous clergyman did not forget the poor farmer," wrote Mark Twain, "but sent him an encyclopedia and $800." This was typical of human nature. In the first rush of generosity, Mark himself would have sent the farmer the whole amount, but after his feelings had cooled, he would have sent the farmer only nine-tenths of the money; on still further reflection he would have kept even more than 10 per cent, finally grabbing all the money and reimbursing the farmer with a single encyclopedia. "For this would be the way of the human race, and I am the human race compacted and crammed into a single suit of clothes but quite able to represent its entire massed multitude in all its moods and inspirations."

In *The Mysterious Stranger* the hideous cruelties of childhood easily master the torturing of conscience. Who can forget the sad story of Nicky's apple? As a boy of nine he had earned it by going on a long errand for the fruit dealer. "I met him," said Theodor,

and he let me look at the apple, not thinking of treachery, and I ran off with it, eating it as I ran, he following me and begging; and when he overtook me I offered him the core, which was all that was left; and I laughed. Then he turned away crying, and said he had meant to give it to his little sister. That smote me, for she was slowly getting well of a sickness, and it would have been a proud moment for him, to see her joy and surprise and have her caresses. But I was ashamed to say I was ashamed, and only said something rude and mean, to pretend I did not care.[4]

And now, when Nicky had only a few days to live, did this and other cruelties rise up to torture Theodor. But this is a man's cruel nature, as old as the race itself. He realizes too late his pride and meanness toward those he loves most deeply.

Nothing runs deeper in man's nature than the necessity for self-preservation. "Morals are not the important thing," Mark Twain wrote, "nor enlightenment—nor civilization. A man can do absolutely well without them, but he can't do without *something to eat*. The supremest thing is the needs of the body, not of the mind &

spirit." The choice between hunger and honesty is always resolved in favor of hunger. But even if a man is well fed, like the Richards family in *The Man Who Corrupted Hadleyburg,* the opportunity for material gain always dissolves even a long habit of upright dealing. Hadleyburg was honest only for lack of swindling opportunities. When the opportunity came in the form of a bag of gold, nineteen of her leading citizens threw away their honesty to claim it as their own. "O Edward," sobbed Mrs. Richards, "we are so poor!" This was the justification of their dishonesty, though there was no threat of hunger in the offing.

Mark Twain's realistic and often cynical appraisal of the dominance of the economic motive found expression even in *Extracts from Adam's Diary,* when Adam exclaims, "I find that principles have no force except when one is well fed." The triumphs of the human spirit over circumstance, as in the life of Joan of Arc, or in the steamboat explosion in *The Gilded Age,* when the little French boy faces death with utter resolution, calmly directing the doctor to save lives not already forfeit—such triumphs to Mark Twain were an insignificant rarity in human experience.

Man's capacity for lying, not only to others but also to himself, called forth from Mark Twain more scathing scorn than any other trait. "All people are liars from the cradle onward, without exception," he wrote. ". . . They begin to lie as soon as they wake in the morning, and keep it up, without rest or refreshment, until they go to bed at night." People lie by their silences, by their expressions, by their actions, a thousand times more frequently than by their words: "I find that the proportion of the spoken lie to the other varieties is as 1 to 22,894." Whole communities lie, even whole nations—as did the people of the North, when in the face of slavery they ignored for years the cries of the abolitionists, silently asserting that all was well with their consciences, editors and preachers as determinedly as the common man. The whole of France lied when all but a handful of her people averted their faces from the persecution of the innocent Dreyfus. Most Englishmen lied when they silently watched Chamberlain light the fagots of war against the

Boers. An Englishman will not tell a spoken lie; he "will not even tell a lie for the fun of it"; but as a participant in a gigantic national lie he has no conscience at all. In the midst of persecution, witch-burning, inquisitions, war fever, men stand silently by, afraid to speak the truth burning in their breasts. Their mute lies, like their polite white lies, are a symbol of human nature; the one rooted in cowardice, the other in reluctance to wound a fellow-heart.

At the farthest verge of his pessimism Mark Twain touched the depth of human depravity, that depth which Adolf Hitler and his followers were to sow with a million dragon teeth in the far years to come. "Cannibalism in the Cars," shocking as it is, especially in the warm, satisfied feelings the starved passengers have after the first repast, is only a short reach of human degradation when visualized beside the extensions of Nazi persecution. These lowest reaches Mark Twain anticipated in *The Mysterious Stranger.* "The vast majority of the race," he wrote,

whether savage or civilized, are secretly kind-hearted and shrink from inflicting pain, but in the presence of the *aggressive and pitiless minority* [italics mine] they don't dare to assert themselves. Think of it! One kind-hearted creature spies upon another, and sees to it that he loyally helps in iniquities which revolt both of them.[5]

Mark Twain now and then admitted that his scornful condemnations of the human race were unwarranted and inconsistent with his philosophy of mechanism. If men were evil, they should not be hated; if they were good, they should not be praised. "I wish I could learn," he wrote to Twitchell, in 1904, "to remember that it is unjust and dishonorable to put blame upon the human race for any of its acts. For it did not make itself, it did not make its nature . . . its performance is wholly automatic. . . . I wish I could learn to pity the human race instead of censuring it and laughing at it." To hate Theodore Roosevelt the politician was a vexing, useless business, unprofitable and unfair: "I know that neither praise nor blame is due to him for any thought or word or deed of his, he being merely a helpless and irresponsible coffee-mill ground by the

hand of God." Here Mark Twain reveals the war within himself.
Intellectually, having arrived at a thorough belief in man's mechanical responses, in the absurdity of free will, he wanted to feel compassion for erring man, for man pushed and pulled automatically
by a thousand strings. But his old habits of condemnation, his
feelings of revulsion and hatred of hypocrisy and greed and superstition, dissipated his rational diagnosis. He *could* pity the human
race if "the outside influences of old habit were not so strong upon
my machine."

III

Mark Twain was deadly serious when he asserted that the tragic
flaws in man's nature would bring an end to democratic America.
Men were too selfish to co-operate for the common good. In *The
Gilded Age* he had painted their follies from the life he knew: the
persistent overriding of public benefit for private gain, the buying
of congressmen, senators, judges, the money lust, the savage tactics
of the cynical rich and the envious poor. In the decades since the
Civil War the virus of corruption had spread and deepened. The
Republican party, in Twain's view, had welded its forces into a
dictatorship through the power of concentrated wealth used to
corrupt the voters. Theodore Roosevelt, "the worst President we
have ever had," had allowed his election to be bought by the very
corporations he affected to cudgel. Senator Clark of Montana
unloosed Mark Twain's supreme contempt: "He is said to have
bought legislatures and judges as other men buy food and raiment
... He is as rotten a human being as can be found anywhere under
the flag; he is a shame to the American nation." Like leaders, like
people: the Americans allowed their votes to be bought, their liberties to be prostituted by unscrupulous leaders. "Vote bribes . . .
have taken away the pride of thousands of tempted men and turned
them into willing alms receivers and unashamed." To Twain it was
the story of Rome all over again, the massing of great wealth and
the buying of votes. A republic of such rottenness could not endure.

Not only man's corruptible heart, but also his need of an earthly superior, will hasten the crumbling of democracy. By nature we are all king-worshipers, or aristocrat-worshipers, or leader-worshipers. "In our blood and bone, and ineradicably," he wrote, "we carry the seeds out of which monarchies and aristocracies have grown: worship of gauds, titles, distinctions, power. We have to worship these things and their possessors, we are all born so and cannot help it." As each man would be the master of an inferior, so would he also worship and envy a lord, rich or blooded, decent or rotten. "This is his nature," concluded Mark Twain,

... unchangeable, indestructible; therefore republics and democracies are not for such as he; they cannot satisfy the requirements of his nature. The inspirations of his character will always breed circumstances and conditions which must in time furnish him a king and an aristocracy to look up to and worship. In a democracy he will try—and honestly—to keep the crown away, but Circumstance is a powerful master and will eventually defeat him.[6]

How repugnant and absurd such a national decision would have been to him no reader of Mark Twain can for a moment doubt. In *A Connecticut Yankee* he had dramatized unforgettably all his biting hatred of kingship. That the English would need a royal house, Clarence and the Yankee admitted; but a royal family of cats would satisfy the people's longing with equal efficacy, the character of the cat being much superior to that of the average king. The worship of a king, asserts Mark, in one of his sober outbursts, is rooted in irrationality; "It is enough to make a body ashamed of his race." But Mark's beliefs and his expectations ran in opposite directions; the older he became the more irrational the world loomed, and the deeper appeared the unalterable superstitions of humankind.

IV

In the extremity of his despair about human nature, Mark Twain felt the heavy burden of explaining the origin of man's wickedness. If man was just a machine, as he asserted in *What Is Man?*, if he was not responsible for his tragic shortcomings, then how to account for man's vile and hateful nature? To answer this query, Mark Twain veered away from his scientific outlook; he was driven to that kind of theological reasoning that he had so often denounced as specious nonsense. He was driven to postulating an original Creator, an all-intelligent, but vicious and malign Maker. Upon this God Mark Twain heaped his wrath, upon the Maker of earthquakes, typhus germs, rattlesnakes, the Great Flood, the Plagues of Egypt, along with constellations, rivers, trees, and the marvels of muscle and brain. "God, the limitless God, manufactured these things, for no man could ever have done it. The man never lived who could create the humblest of God's creatures." But this God cares nothing for the destiny of man, about his comfort or happiness; He is not a God of pity and tenderness. It is this Maker who is responsible for man: "Why, even poor little ungodlike man holds himself responsible for the welfare of his child to the extent of his ability. It is all that we require of God." Upon this God of indifference to man's happiness, the God who had allowed hypocrisy and cowardice to consume, as he thought, the soul of man from Adam onward, Mark Twain uttered that terrible malediction in *The Mysterious Stranger:*

A God who could make good children as easily as bad, yet preferred to make bad ones; who could have made every one of them happy, yet never made a single happy one; who made them prize their bitter life, yet stingily cut it short; who gave his angels eternal happiness unearned, yet required his other children to earn it . . . who mouths justice and invented hell—mouths mercy and invented hell—mouths Golden Rules, and forgiveness multiplied seventy times seven, and invented hell; who mouths morals to other people and has none himself; who frowns upon crimes, yet commits them all; who created man without invitation, then tries to shuffle the responsibility for man's acts upon man, instead of honorably placing it where it belongs, upon himself.[7]

In these lines, the most eloquent and terrible an American has ever uttered against the anthropomorphic God, we may hear the tolling of Mark Twain's ultimate despair. They toll with a personal, emotional despair, rooted in a deep unhappiness still inexplicable; but the intellectual despair is complete, a despair resulting from Mark

Twain's failure to explain the roots of man's evil personality in the rational terms so deeply ingrained in his intellectual creed.

V

It is a refreshing experience to turn from the Mark Twain of *The Mysterious Stranger* to the Mark Twain of *What Is Man?* The two men found strangely different answers to the enigma of human frailties. Mark Twain the pessimist, the God-hater, the scorner of the human race, was at war with Mark Twain the mechanist. In *The Mysterious Stranger* Mark Twain's bitterness overflows from the realities of his experience; in *What Is Man?* he is mellow, urbane, wholly rational, with no scornful diatribes, no Satans, no angry God. If *The Mysterious Stranger* reflects the tragedies of actuality, *What Is Man?* demonstrates that they were not inevitable. As a work of art, as an image of man's illimitable capacity for evil, the novel will undoubtedly survive the dialogue; but as a balanced description of man's nature, *What Is Man?* has more illumination in one page than *The Mysterious Stranger* in many a long bitter chapter. *The Mysterious Stranger* is an indictment of man in the midst of his failures. But man's nature, as Mark Twain knew, requires a more scientific and humanistic analysis, a more thoroughly logical medium than the short story or the novel.

Van Wyck Brooks has spoken of *What Is Man?* as "quite worthless except for the light it throws on Mark Twain." To many critics the annihilation of free will is the gospel of slavery, not the gospel of hope. Bernard DeVoto blandly dismisses *What Is Man?* as behaviorism "perfectly accommodated to the minds of sophomores," thus condemning Mark Twain for that utter clarity so rare in philosophical utterances. But Mark Twain's purpose was deadly serious; he wanted to synthesize his philosophy of human nature in terms the world could not misinterpret. The result is an amazing document without parallel in American literature; no other creative writer in America, Holmes not excepted, has even attempted a systematization of such profound illumination of man's depths. The accumu-

lated reflections of thirty years, the intellectual retreats and gropings, the slow and laborious shaping of premises, the slow push
forward, are all mirrored here and set in order. Had Abraham Lincoln possessed Mark Twain's genius for creative expression, it is
the kind of book he would have written: it speaks point by point
his own philosophy of man. *What Is Man?* is one more proof that
Mark Twain's creative intellectual energy could not play over any
topic without leaving behind a fresh and indelible clarification
of life.

In his bitter invective against the human race Mark Twain
assumed, as we have shown, a tendency toward evil as inherent
in man as the cast of his face or the bones of his feet. But in
What Is Man? he retreats from this supposition toward a premise
that tinges his maledictions with superstition. The dominant motive
of man's existence, asserts Mark Twain, is to secure his own praise
and approval, *"to content his own spirit."* Every human, then, is
selfish, from the most hateful persecutor to the most exalted saint,
from the villain Slade to Joan of Arc: "Both the noblest impulses
and the basest proceed from that one source." The mother who
suffers hunger, cold, nakedness, torture, even death, for the sake
of her child, seeks the reward of self-approval first and her child's
welfare second. "She would do it for your child," concludes Mark,
"if she could get the same pay."[8] A soldier often goes to war not
because he wants to fight, but because his spirit can only be contented by having the approval of his neighbors. Because public
opinion was more precious to him than his hatred of dueling and
his love of family, Alexander Hamilton fought a duel and sacrificed
his life. A man never performs a generous action without the fulfilment of self-approval. Mark Twain calls for the elevation of
selfishness to the level of beneficent social effect. A selfishness that
tortures a soldier to death by pouring ice water over his face, as
an American lieutenant did to one of his own men in the Philippines,
is at a remote pole from the compulsion of Arnold Winkelried, who
gathered the sheaf of spears into his arms to break the phalanx of
the tyrant. Mark Twain was eager only to clarify the dominance of

the motive of self-approval; as much as any man he rejoiced in brave and honorable deeds.

But what shapes the quality of one's self-approval, what force transmutes hatred into satisfaction on one plane and enlightened action into contentment on another? To Mark Twain in *What Is Man?* neither one is inborn. Men have inborn temperaments, he believed, some of them so fixed that, as in the case of Henry Adams, no accident of favorable circumstances can make them happy people. In most men, however, such a mingling of temperaments obtains that environment is the decisive molder of spirit-contentment. Man is an impersonal machine, made of original metals neither good nor bad; into this machine pour the fuels and the lubrication of his environment. Man originates no thought; everything that he thinks or believes originates from his environment. A million "outside influences" press upon him from birth to death: "It is his human environment which influences his mind and his feelings, furnishes him his ideals, and sets him on his road and keeps him in it." His reaction is the automatic result of the million collisions and coalescences between his temperament and the pressure of influence, with influence usually decisive. His environment shapes his politics, his religion, his moral and aesthetic concepts. None of these ideals is his own; they are the creations of circumstance. Neither God nor free choice, but circumstances, associations, create an honest man: "God makes a man with honest and dishonest *possibilities* in him and stops there. The man's *associations* develop the possibilities—the one set or the other." Since man is not the creator of his honesty, he deserves no praise for possessing it.

Thus does Mark Twain renounce in *What Is Man?* that inborn hypocrisy, cruelty, hatred, that he had so often castigated as the bone and structure of man's nature. These traits are often in man, it is true; but *associations placed them there after his birth.* God did not create a contemptible being after all, but a neutral machine of infinite complexity and plasticity, a machine responsive to a million impersonal fingers, benign or evil. To symbolize the plasticity of man's nature, Mark Twain used the word *chameleon.* Like a chameleon, man changes color when he shifts his habitat from one scene to another. The coloring of one place may make him kind; of another, hateful. Far from being a curse to man, this plasticity, this *chameleonship,* is his most valuable asset: by shifting to a more constructive environment, he changes similarly the tone of his personality. It is true that the impulse to change one's habitat must originate from *outside* the man himself, often germinating from an apparently incongruous accident, such as the broken leg of the wicked Ignatius Loyola, which forced him under religious influences, or the cutting words of a young woman, " I hear that you are a coward."[9]

The most fortunate accident in Mark Twain's own life, according to Paine, was that day in Hannibal (Mark was only twelve) when he picked up from the street a leaf from a book picturing the Maid of Orleans in her prison cage. His compassion was stirred to the depths; his fascination with history was from then on an unceasing goad: "The chance reading of a paragraph in a newspaper can start a man on a new track and make him renounce his old associations and seek new ones that are in *sympathy with his new ideal."*

Many people wisely or unwisely try to take advantage of man's plasticity to help him progress—people such as the missionary and the distributor of tracts. Such attempts Mark Twain called "the laying of traps for people," traps baited with *"Initiatory impulses toward high ideals."* The government itself ought to do this very work, but it does not often succeed. If this kind of mechanism is the gospel of slavery, Americans who exhort the young to go to college have made the most of it. Mark Twain only echoes the teachings of Aristotle's *Ethics,* that it is the duty of the state to mold the virtuous citizen.

What Is Man? places Mark Twain incontestably in the ranks of the environmentalists. It is true that he insists upon temperament; but he does not attempt to define such an elusive term; nor does he attempt to evaluate the relative weight of environment and inheritance in the scales of human destiny. Each man bears a temperamental limitation of his plasticity. "There are gold men, and tin men, and copper men, and leaden men," he writes. ". . . You can build engines out of each of these metals, and they will all perform, but you must not require the weak ones to do equal work with the strong ones." In his brilliant article, "The Turning Point of My Life," written only a few months before his death, Mark Twain retraces the main trails of *What Is Man?*, devoting much space to circumstance, little to temperament. The main element of temperament, indeed, is man's plasticity. God placed in Adam a temperament which said, "Be weak, be water, be characterless, be easily persuadable."

Mark Twain reviews the accidents of circumstance by which he became a writer. He tells of the epidemic of measles in Hannibal, when he became so obsessed with the indecision of catastrophe that he jumped into bed with a playmate and caught the measles to be rid of the suspense; of his quitting school; of his forced travels about, seeking work as a printer; of his projected boat trip to Para; of his chance acquaintanceship with a pilot and his adoption of that profession; of the Civil War and the stopping of the boats—all those and others were links in the chain of accidents that shaped his life and made him eventually a writer. Had he been of a different temperament, he admits, the story might have ended differently: "A circumstance that will coerce one man will have no effect upon a man of a different temperament." But circumstance has a million hands; much of its work it performs silently, pressing and rounding and molding the characters of the human race. "I see no great difference," concludes Mark Twain, "between a man and a watch except that the man is conscious and the watch isn't, and the man tries to plan things and the watch doesn't. . . . Outside influences, outside circumstances, wind the *man* and regulate him."

VI

Nowhere has Mark Twain so dramatically belittled the power of inheritance and exalted the pressure of circumstance as in *Pudd'nhead Wilson*. Not, of course, that the book was written for

this purpose, or even that Mark Twain was conscious of the implications he had drawn in this remarkable story. But no writer, least
of all one of Mark Twain's preoccupation with the roots of human
nature, could construct such a tale without betraying his convictions
between the lines. Tom Driscoll is one-thirty-second Negro; but
nowhere in the story does Mark Twain suggest that from his Negro
blood Tom had inherited his laziness, his cowardice, his cruelty, his
thieving talents, or his willingness in extremity to sell his mother
down the river and murder his benefactor. Roxy, it is true, in
berating her son, speaks the aristocratic notion of "blood will tell":
"Thirty-one parts o' you is white, en on'y one part nigger, en dat
po' little part is yo' *soul*. 'Tain't wuth savin'; 'tain't wuth totin' out
on a shovel en throwin' in de gutter. . . . Whatever has come o' yo'
Essex blood?" But this is not Mark Twain, who so often, as in
Captain Stormfield's Visit to Heaven, showed his contempt for
assumptions of racial superiority. In *Pudd'nhead Wilson* Mark
Twain accounts for Tom's laziness and cowardice only on the basis
of childhood circumstance: he was a spoiled child; he never had
to work with his hands or play rough games; he was never taught
to stand up and fight for himself. Chambers, on the contrary, lived
a rough and ready life among Negroes, ate coarse food, worked
hard, was always required to pummel even white boys to protect
his little master. Chambers, pure white, is a Negro by habit only.
At the end of the story, when he finds that he is son and heir of
Percy Driscoll, not of the Negro Roxy, he finds it impossible to feel
or act his part:

The real heir suddenly found himself rich and free, but in a most
embarrassing situation. He could neither read nor write, and his speech
was the basest dialect of the negro quarter. His gait, his attitudes, his
gestures, his bearing, his laugh—all were vulgar and uncouth; his manners
were the manners of a slave.[10]

Thus does Mark Twain explain the Negro nature of Chambers; the
words might have been written by Alexis de Tocqueville, Emile Zola,
John Dewey, or a latter-day anthropologist such as Franz Boas or

Ruth Benedict. They are completely consistent with Mark Twain's "gospel," *What Is Man?*, and his last remarkable treatment of circumstance, "The Turning Point of My Life."

VII

Mark Twain left to the world, then, contradictory solutions to the riddle of human nature: the rooted, ineradicable evil of *The Mysterious Stranger* and the neutral plasticity of *What Is Man?* The former is the sour fruit of experience, the latter the slow accumulation of rational theory. *The Mysterious Stranger* is bitterly pessimistic: man's nature is evil beyond any redemption. But *What Is Man?* is filled with a great hope, a hope perhaps unintentional and only partially spoken: Limited by each man's temperament, *human nature can soar as high as favorable circumstances require it to.* Man's *chameleonship* is the great glory of his nature, the most marvelous asset a benevolent God could have bequeathed. As the Old Man says to the Young: *"Diligently train your ideals upward and still upward toward a summit where you will find your chiefest pleasure in conduct which, while contenting you, will be sure to confer benefits upon your neighbor and the community."* This is Mark Twain's ideal of citizenship, an ideal he believed could be achieved mechanically by the creation of environmental pressures. Man's climb upward depends upon the number and effectiveness of *"Initiatory impulses toward high ideals."* The creation of such impulses, now in the main accidental, should be the business of the government.

In 1906 Mark Twain felt compelled to publish *What Is Man?* under an assumed name. Was it revolutionary in 1906 to publish a philosophy of man believed by Abraham Lincoln, the philosophy that gave birth to his charity and his patience with human frailties? To many it may have appeared blasphemous to portray man as an unreasoning, irresponsible machine; to others it added dignity to man's stature and infinite hope for the expansion of his faculties. Certainly *What Is Man?* may be considered part of the gospel of democracy, possessing a proud place with the essays of Jefferson, the speeches of Lincoln, the educational treatises of Horace Mann. For only by such a gospel may the humblest man appear worthy of a vast number of *Initiatory impulses toward high ideals,* impulses that the state can provide in a quality and quantity corresponding to its material resources, and hitherto undreamed of. For America has never seriously attempted the building of men as the worthiest aim of national existence. "If you would plan for a year," says the old Chinese proverb, "plant grain. If you would plan for ten years, plant trees. If you would plan for fifty years, plant men."

VIII

But upon the structure of his gospel Mark Twain did not build a dream for an America busy at the *training upward* of human nature. His prophecy of an American dictatorship was induced by his distrust of human nature rather than by the mechanist philosophy of *What Is Man?* His castigations of the race, as he wrote to Twitchell, were unreasonable and unfair; yet he ended his days not in hope for the emergence of an intelligent world, but in despair. Whatever the roots of his pessimism, it spoke out bitterly in his last years, demolishing his objectivity, scattering the hopeful implications of his gospel, calling up the tragedies and violence of his life, driving deep into the recesses of his spirit. "His books," writes Bernard DeVoto, "contain a judgment of the collision between democratic ideal and democratic reality. . . . The vision was democracy; the acknowledgment was the human race." America's social failures, as he saw them, were a spring of bitter waters; but the wells of his personal life may have been more bitter still. Mark Twain abhorred dishonesty; yet he found it impossible to be wholly honest; his creative sallies were always running against walls of friendship or love or deference to the Mark Twain image in the minds of his readers. As Van Wyck Brooks has demonstrated, Mark Twain was infinitely more mature than his America, and he could not write for the "fit audience, though few."

Another strain of Mark Twain's sadness was his realization that fame and fortune showed him only the hollowness and tinsel of the world, no happiness at all. Finally, one by one, his loved ones died. At seventy he wrote: "When I was 43 and John Hay 41 he said life was a tragedy after 40, and I disputed it. Three years ago he asked me to testify again: I counted my graves, and there was nothing for me to say." Two years before, when Mrs. Clemens had died, he had written to Howells: "How thankful I am that her persecutions are ended. I would not call her back if I could. . . . I am tired and old; I wish I were with Livy."[11]

Those are not all the streams that fed the deep springs of Mark Twain's pessimism; all of them cannot be traced until the documents now withheld are accessible to many searchers and lovers of Mark Twain. But these streams alone show why he could not render in his last years a judgment of human nature consistent with *What Is Man?* His agony was too intense to allow him to extend to its logical conclusions his reasoning on man's plasticity. At times his despair was irrational by the beacons he had lighted in his own books: "Anybody who knows anything," he said to Paine, "knows that there was not a single life that was ever lived that was worth living. Not a single child ever begotten that the begetting of it was not a crime." In his sober moments, when he thought of Joan of Arc and Nigger Jim and Anson Burlingame and Olivia Clemens and William Dean Howells, this was a despair he could not wholly have felt without instantly dispatching himself. Whatever the proportion of irrationality in his despair, it was the dominant coloring of Mark Twain's reflections at the end of his life. His own tenderness and compassion, the world-wide glow of affection for his spirit, his priceless friends, could not dispel the agony of his soul or his contempt for Mark Twain and the human race.

In tracing the follies and superficialities of his age, Mark Twain rendered a service to the impetus of a mature and democratic life. He was a serious moralist waging unending war against sham and humbug and pretense. His soul writhed with anger at injustice; his agile, capacious mind darted to the roots of every incongruity of his

time. Several times, when he tried to write about the American
lieutenant in the Philippines who had tortured one of his men to
death, he was so unnerved by anger he could not go on. His essay,
"Concerning the Jews," is still a classic treatment of the irrationality
of race prejudice. Born in the South, accustomed in childhood to
the psychology of slavery, he exhibited in story after story the
superficial assumptions of white supremacy, both North and South.
The yellow race he knew, as well as the white and the black; and
he had no superstitions about color. The hypocrisy of churches he
knew, and the blinkers of superstition they had fastened on whole
peoples; the savagery of oppression of mind and body heaped upon
the helpless, centuries deep. Of the French Revolution he wrote:

There were two "Reigns of Terror," if we would but remember it and
consider it; the one wrought murder in hot passion, the other in heartless
cold blood; the one lasted mere months, the other had lasted a thousand
years; the one inflicted death upon ten thousand persons, the other upon
a hundred millions; but our shudders are all for the "horrors" of the
minor Terror, the momentary Terror, so to speak; whereas, what is the
horror of swift death by the ax compared with lifelong death from
hunger, cold, insult, cruelty, and heartbreak?[12]

And Mark Twain knew the vagaries of the human heart. He
knew the impenetrable stubbornness of ideas fixed in childhood and
sanctified by the halo of public approval. He knew the gulf between
the love of people and the love of truth. For love of Livy he could
not speak the whole truth. Even with Howells he could not be
wholly frank. The American public would not stand the serious
thinker, Mark Twain. From his youth onward he knew that no
solemn admonition could really demolish the superstitions and
cupidities that beset his countrymen. Other great reformers—
Milton, Jefferson, Godwin, Horace Mann, Bellamy—were too sanguine of man's response to intelligent persuasion. Not so Mark
Twain. Before the mind acts, he thought, the belly must tremble.
His weapon, then, would be laughter; with this bright blade he
would open unaware the hearts of the ignorant and then trap them
with an impulse to a more intelligent outlook upon the world.

"Your race," says Satan, in *The Mysterious Stranger*, ". . . has one really effective weapon—laughter. Power, money, persuasion, supplication, persecution—these can lift at a colossal humbug—push it a little—weaken it a little, century by century; but only laughter can blow it to rags and atoms at a blast."[13]

Born in a sleepy village on the American frontier, out of school at twelve, learning early the magic of laughter to dissolve the distance between two hearts, or one heart and the world, gaining fame and fortune as a wit while the world's wrongs rankled in his breast and a pity possessed him for the weak and lowly and despised ones of the earth—Mark Twain came in sorrow and sadness and humility to his death, his heart troubled with self-accusations and the spiritual poverty of the human race, and the wrongs of the world pressing down more heavily than ever upon the weak and the starved and the heartbroken. "It is in vain," wrote Howells in *My Mark Twain*,

that I try to give a notion of the intensity with which he pierced to the heart of life, and the breadth of vision with which he compassed the whole world, and tried for the reason of things and then left trying. . . . Emerson, Longfellow, Lowell, Holmes—I know them all and all the rest of our sages, poets, seers, critics, humorists; they were like one another and like other literary men; but Clemens was sole, incomparable, the Lincoln of our literature.[14]

The very fiber of Mark Twain—his compassion, his unflinching honesty, his remarkable capacity for learning the great lessons of civilization and transmuting them into the gold of literature—is in itself a heroic denial of his gloomy prophecies of American failure. No other country than America could have borne him, or shaped him, or made him aware of the worth of his genius.

1895

Obscure Births of the Uncommon Man

In 1895 the world held out its hands to Mark Twain, fifty-nine years old, fellow to kings and statesmen and great men around the globe. Yet, half a century before, who could have placed his hand on the shoulder of the boy Samuel Clemens and predicted his magical talent? Who could guess the forces that drive one man to creative fruition, another to the harbor of obscurity? A science of man was needed to measure and harvest the crop of greatness. "Be an artist," wrote John Burroughs in 1895, "or prepare for oblivion." In 1895 Mark Twain was writing Joan, *sure of his immortality, and writing to Rogers, "Possibly the book may sell, but that is nothing—it was written for love." He was lecturing to pay his debts: "I intend the lectures as well as the property for the creditors. The law recognizes no mortgage on a man's brain. . . . But I am not a business man, and honor is a harder master than the law."[1]*

Does one man create a great work when he is financially secure, another when he is penniless? What are the conditions of creative flowering, when a man's energy flows in an electric stream, when he has daily leisure, or exchanges energy for leisure in the midnight hours, when life has not yet shattered his dreams of a new creation or the color of his uniqueness? No uncommon man but appeared common to someone in his youth, to his friends, his teachers, his family. What happy concert of forces is indispensable to the birth of talent? Society has yet to inquire what circumstances it might create to increase the yield of its genius born or made.

In 1895 Theodore Dreiser was twenty-four years old, awkward and hesitant in his search for a reporter's job, a man with no confi-

dence in his destiny, walking the streets of New York, appalled at
the misery of the poor and the icy stares of the mighty. In April,
1894, Dreiser had come across Mark Twain standing before a nov-
elty window on Doyers Street in Chinatown. Who was he to speak
to Mark Twain, one of the great ones, along with Howells and
Warner? But at last the words tumbled out: "Are you—you're not
Mark Twain, the author?" Mark was friendly but not responsive.
The Webster bankruptcy had burst upon him like a thunderbolt
only the day before. "Now see here, young man, I know what you're
thinking. But you can't interview me. I'm not to be interviewed this
way." Dreiser fumbling and awkward, his words slow, his manner
apologetic: "I was reduced and ashamed." The birth of the uncommon man in Dreiser had not yet come. To walk with the great, to
dream that one day he might write a memorable novel such as
An American Tragedy, was as remote to him as the days of hunger
in the Sullivan winters.[2]

In 1895 Willa Cather, twenty-one years old, lofty and mannish
to her classmates, was a senior at the University of Nebraska, writing
for the Lincoln Courier, letting her wings grow, dreaming of no
middle flight in the world of literature. Who could have predicted
her obscure creative birth, still years away? Certainly not Stephen
Crane. In February of 1895, penniless and discouraged, though
The Red Badge of Courage was already in proof, Crane stopped
over in Lincoln, waiting for money that would take him to Mexico.
His shoes were worn and dirty, his clothes shabby, his spirit low.
"I cut my classes to lie in wait for him," wrote Cather later.
Listening to Crane as he talked about the life of the artist, Cather
found him relentlessly bitter. When she said to him that ten years
from now he might regard his discouragement as a passing mood,
he replied, "I can't wait ten years, I haven't time." In early 1895
Willa Cather heard the young Bryan speak at Red Cloud, Nebraska,
six months before the Chicago convention, to an audience of
farmers. His eloquence held a magic comparable to the sweep of
the sea. Afterward she wrote, "I saw those rugged, ragged men of
the soil weep like children."[3]

In 1895 John Burroughs, fifty-seven years old, pondered the perennial question of inherited and acquired talent. To Burroughs Stevenson was not a great artist: "His literary equipment surpasses his more solid native human equipment, as with so many of the late school of writers. He was not a man of mass and power, any more than I am." *Yet, unlike Howells, Stevenson inspired love:* "The thought of him, gone from life, and sleeping there in far-off Samoa on a mountain peak, fills me with sadness." *Henrik Ibsen was not a born artist either; to Burroughs he was* "not a sky-shaker—shakes the doors and windows a little, that is all." *Nor was William Dean Howells a writer of first rank. He was a man with a wonderful talent, yes,* "so fine that it is almost genius," *but not a man to make us love his places or his people.*[4]

In 1895, on December 28, Robert Frost, twenty years old, married Elinor Miriam White. Five years earlier, his first published poem had appeared in the Lawrence, Massachusetts, High School Bulletin. *One year before, when Frost was nineteen,* "My Butterfly, An Elegy," *had been accepted by* The Independent. *Who would have guessed his capacity for a growth of talent that led to* A Boy's Will, *published in his thirty-eighth year? In Frost a kernel of an uncommon man lay long sleeping. Who knows what forces crush such a kernel underfoot in less resolute men? A science of man was needed to tally the signs of talent, the fanatical decisions that surmounted all obstacles, the first groping lines, the single burning image on a page of pale prose. A search was needed to show the incandescent moments when genius sloughed off the traces of the common man and struck the vein of his uniqueness on every page.*

In 1895 Carl Sandburg, seventeen years old, rode freights from Chicago west, working in Kansas wheat fields, washing dishes in hotels, working as a carpenter's helper, painting stoves for handouts of food. In Sandburg a strong man kept coming on, grown out of American hopes and chemicals as yet unknown, the gradual miracle of an uncommon man in him still far off.

In October, 1895, Scribner's Magazine *published* "The Lamp of Psyche," *a story by Edith Wharton, thirty-three years old. Could a rich woman reared in Brahmin gentility search out the deep dilemmas of her life and fuse them into art? Though she had yet written no novel, Edith Wharton in "The Lamp of Psyche" set down the delicate tracery of her structure and characterization to come. The story opens with the sentences, "Delia Corbett was too happy. Her happiness frightened her." For two months Delia has been married to the man she loved desperately long before her first husband's death. One day Delia's Aunt Mary casually asks if her new husband had enlisted many years before in the Union Army. The question hangs gnawingly in Delia's throat. All the men she has known among her family and friends had fought for the Union cause. The question, "Why weren't you in the war?" Edith Wharton writes, "rose up and lay down with her. It mocked her from the eyes of strangers." One day her husband brings her a beautiful miniature of a cavalry officer killed at Chancellorsville. When, then, Delia asks the question and her husband shows no recognition of her ideal of warrior duty, her image of him is shattered. No more was her husband "like an unexplored country, full of bewitching surprises"; now "she had measured and mapped him," her ideal "slivered like the crystal above the miniature of the warrior at Chancellorsville." What energy of artistic conscience preserved in Edith Wharton the merciless self-inspection she pictures in Lily Bart? A curious alchemy worked in Wharton that the literary critic alone cannot explain, though his insight is indispensable in the gradual forging of the science of man.*

In 1895 Edna St. Vincent Millay and Archibald MacLeish were three years old, each emerging from a family of creative and intellectual distinction. In 1895 Sherwood Anderson was nineteen years old, making his living by odd jobs, having left school at fourteen when his mother died. A quarter-century was to pass before Sherwood Anderson could create his Winesburg, Ohio. Who could explain the emergence of his talent? From MacLeish and Millay as children one might expect a flowering of creative zeal. But what talent, what spark of genius, could one expect from Windy McPherson's son? To some critics the origins of talent are mysterious and unsearchable. But the mind of man probes restlessly for the origins of genius, for the glimmerings of a science, a new tool, that could detect the hidden talent or the match that kindles it into a blaze.

In 1895 Ellen Glasgow, twenty-two years old, came to New York and trusted her first novel to grave, silent Mr. Patton of the University Publishing Company. The next morning Mr. Patton said to her, "I read the manuscript last night without putting it down until I finished it at dawn. Don't worry, my child. That book shall be published if I have to build a publishing house in order to publish it." That night Ellen Glasgow could not sleep. Afterward she wrote, "Until a glimmer of day extinguished the white glare in the street, and splashed like water over the bulging clothes on the fire escapes, I lay awake and tried to imagine what the world would be like when one had published a first book." Was Ellen Glasgow, as she asserted, really "born a novelist"? She wrote, "Always I have had to learn for myself, from within." Did no one touch a match to her shavings of genius? Whence came the will, strong as her father's, which "plunged its claws into the earth"?[5]

X

Henry Adams and the Direction of Human Energies

> *A child could find his way in a river-valley, and a boy could float on the waters of Holland; but science alone could sound the depths of the ocean, measure its currents, foretell its storms, or fix its relations to the system of Nature. In a democratic ocean science could see something ultimate.*
>
> —Adams

IN 1858, when Henry Adams was graduating from Harvard College, he included in a brief class autobiography mention of the published records of his Brooks and Adams ancestry. All his life Henry Adams, descendant of two American Presidents, pondered the significance of the ancestry he could not escape or alter. Proud as he was of the achievements of his forebears, Adams never ceased to ponder the gifts of heredity as contrasted with the environmental forces at work in his own life and on the American scene. Though he would not have agreed with Thucydides' statement that "one man is much like another, except as he is the product of the more severe school," Adams was acutely conscious of the unprecedented social forces at work in America on the nature of man. No historian has portrayed these forces with a more unerring eye or impartial mind, despite his gradual retreat into the habit of ironic depreciation as his early confidence in the fiber of American manhood withered into despair. Whether full of hope for human nature, as in 1870-77, or touched with icy skepticism, as in 1890, when the last volume of his great *History* lay under his pen, Adams held steadfast to his foremost principle: to write with as much detach-

225

226 THE IMAGE OF MAN IN AMERICA

ment as if he were studying "the formation of a crystal." Adams'
habit of self-inspection kept him intellectually fresh and youthful:
and with all his arrogance he coveted nothing so profoundly as yet
another step into those mysteries he hoped still to resolve.[1]

How aware Adams was of those forces in American life remote
from his own aristocratic upbringing appears nowhere more strikingly than in his kaleidoscopic pictures of American life in the year
1800. Already Adams gauged the forces of society as the release
of energies. What happened to the humble man from Maine to
Georgia as he saw opening around him a chance to exchange his
toil for goods and privileges undreamed of in the Old World? "Few
human beings, however sluggish," wrote Adams,

could long resist the temptation to acquire power; and the elements of
power were to be had in America almost for the asking. Reversing the
old world system, the American stimulant increased in energy as it
reached the lowest and most ignorant class, dragging and whirling them
upward as in the blast of a furnace. The penniless and homeless Scotch
or Irish immigrant was caught and consumed by it; for every stroke of
the axe and the hoe made him a capitalist, and made gentlemen of his
children.[2]

At no point does Adams attempt to define the desire for power as
a fixed element in human nature; but this inferential glance at
human nature is less arresting than his picture of an almost automatic response to the clear beckoning of a chance for economic
betterment. "Gentlemen of his children"! Here as at many other
points of his *History of the United States During the Administrations of Jefferson and Madison,* Adams shows a sense of the steps
he had already witnessed throughout America, of the march upward
in the social scale. Such a mind, alien to the main stream of American beginnings, could not fail to leave behind him searching questions for the science of man to come.

The release of unparalleled quantities of energy never before
tapped in humble people was to Adams the most remarkable phenomenon of American civilization. In this release of energies, the
prospect of economic gain was the "strongest agent for moving the

mass of mankind." But beyond economic gain, in Adams' mind loomed another mechanism for the release of energies, the prospect of political control of society's resources. The release of energies in the capture of economic and political gains and in the capture of a gentlemanly future for one's children was in Adams' mind, as in Tocqueville's, an inevitable process. Indeed, wrote Adams, "The instinct of activity, once created, seemed heritable and permanent in the race." In his sanguine moods Adams could not imagine that the average American would not then struggle also for those intellectual and cultural gains denied to the mass of his ancestors. In America, six hundred years after Magna Charta, apprentices and herdsmen could "write and read with an ease such as few kings could then command, and reason with better logic than any university could then practise."

But this was not enough for the cauldron of democratic energies. In a few places in his great *History* Adams allowed himself the luxury of impressionistic prophecy he might have looked back upon as vulgar in the decline of his optimism. Five centuries hence, among a population of five hundred millions, the gradual concentration of energies on cultural and creative life might yet yield a greatness Athenian and Florentine in its range, might yet produce a time when the lowly plowboy might whistle Beethoven and calculate "in quaternions the relations of his furrows." Only such a fruition in uncommon men as produced the Parthenon and the masterpieces of Titian and Michelangelo would satisfy, in Adams' prophecy, the vast ambitions of the American mind nourished by centuries of impassioned quest for bread, literacy, knowledge, and the beauty of line and color and sound.[3]

The transmission of human energy, then, on the American scene could not possibly remain fixed alone on the satisfactions of the economic man. Instead of the degradation of energy to the mere necessities of either survival or display, Adams pictured a gradual elevation of energy to those ends nourishing the most valuable and permanent achievements in art, religion, and science. To Adams only a society of cultivated men could in turn give birth to creative

men of the first rank. Adams summarized the problems for the vast
America of his prophecy:

Could it transmute its social power into the higher forms of thought?
. . . Could it create and maintain in the mass of mankind those habits
of mind which had hitherto belonged to men of science alone? Could
it physically develop the convolutions of the human brain? Could it
produce, or was it compatible with, the differentiation of a higher variety
of the human race? Nothing less than this was necessary for its complete
success.[4]

Thus wrote the Adams of 1870-77 on the use and direction of democratic energies. Even in the disillusionment recorded in *Democracy—An American Novel* (1880), Adams spoke through the historian Gore his faith in the potential uses of American energies:
"Democracy asserts . . . the masses are now raised to a higher intelligence than formerly. All our civilization aims at this mark. We
want to do what we can to help it. I grant it is an experiment, but
it is the only direction society can take that is worth its taking." That
this statement represented a strong current in Adams' outlook even
in the midst of Washingtonian corruption is plain from a letter to
Gaskell in late 1877. In a prophetic mood, Adams wrote: "I enjoy
the expectation of the coming day, and try to imagine that I am
myself, with my fellow *gelehrte* here, the first faint rays of that
great light which is to dazzle and set the world on fire hereafter."
Thus Adams prophesies the greatness of Athens, Florence, and
Elizabethan London as a fruit of the American garden to come. In
his mind at such moments a mass of uncommon men was the inevitable product of the gradual redirection of human energy to cultural
and creative ends.[5]

At the end of his *History* Adams turns again to a study of American character, but chastened and subdued now in his expectations
of American genius in the centuries to come. No longer does the
bright vision of an American Athens, or a hundred American Ath-
enses, dazzle his eyes. He has not lost his fascination, it is true,
with the pursuit of history as a department of science. The historian of the future must cross the democratic ocean with his eyes

on the far horizon and a calculator under his hand. No longer, as in the past, can the historian concern himself with the rounded portrait of the unique man, whatever his impact on the course of events. Thus far the Americans, as a type of citizenry new in the world, had proved themselves superior to their contemporaries in the mother country. They had built better ships than England, guns with more power and accuracy. In politics they had shown a speed of decision and advance without parallel in the West: "The American people between 1787 and 1817 accepted greater changes than had been known in England since 1688." But these changes, in Adams' judgment, need a new kind of historian to record them. "The greatest democratic evolution the world could know" must be traced not by the artist, but by the scientist who could reduce to mathematics the achievements of the New World and even the emerging adaptations of human nature.[6]

One searches in vain, however, in Adams' pages, for a quantitative evaluation of American superiority in ideas, men, or institutions. The historian is not yet ready to apply to the writing of history the rigorous methods of the scientist. As he began his great work, Adams had looked forward to the production of great men on the American scene. He had recorded in a masterly way the genius of Jefferson, Madison, and Adams. What forces were at work in American life to produce the great men living and working in the crucial years 1800-1815? How many great men had America produced, great men by Adams' own definition? He does not say. Adams supposed himself to be the equal of any man of his time in the ability to define comparative greatness as applied to the men of Athens, Florence, London, and Boston. Yet at no point does he compare America's crop of great men, with her five millions of people and her brief history of a few decades, with the fruit of greatness in England or France.

In Adams' own life his entire energies had been directed to cultural and creative ends, his leisure supplied out of the sweat of other men. One of the necessities of greatness was to him the diversion of energy from the earning of a living to the growth of a mind and the gradual fertilization of ideas. Yet somehow, though he felt as a youth that residence at the White House was his almost as a matter of right, the greatness he coveted as a man of action had passed him by. In his years at Harvard he had found himself growing contemptuous of a southerner he had thought admirable, the son of Robert E. Lee. But as he describes the young Lee in *The Education of Henry Adams,* one feels in Adams a sense of failure in his own quest for greatness. The young Lee was "tall, largely built, handsome, genial, with liberal Virginian openness towards all he liked"; he also "had the Virginian habit of command and took leadership as his natural habit." But Lee was "simple beyond analysis." He had not mind enough to analyze the simplest abstraction. Adams records with contempt that the young Lee asked him to write for him a letter accepting a commission under General Winfield Scott to fight against the Mormons. Lee possessed, how-ever, an easy habit of leadership, a temperament that assured him of instantaneous respect by men of all ranks.

"Dozens of eminent statesmen" whom Adams came to know later were of the same type. Lincoln, Grant, Theodore Roosevelt, all were men of action, in Adams' view, lacking in greatness because they lacked the intellectual subtlety he found in himself. Of Lincoln, even at the end of his life, Adams never wrote except with veiled or studied contempt. His first sight of Lincoln gave him the impres-sion of a man with "a lack of apparent force," extremely uncom-fortable in white gloves. In December, 1860, Adams wrote to his brother, Charles, "The President divides his time between crying and praying."[7]

What was greatness? Adams had prepared for greatness of mind and coveted greatness of action; yet one feels in him a desperate unhappiness that each had escaped him. In action he was never more than a "stable-companion to statesmen." And in mind, though he aspired to be one of the first "rays of that great light which is to dazzle and set the world on fire hereafter," he could offer the minds of the future only the prospect of mankind's annihilation.

How was one to measure greatness? Leisure was required, the

diversion of energy from hand to brain, physical hardihood to sustain prolonged labor—but something more than these, too. Adams wrote that the young Lee, like all Virginians, had temperament. But how could the scientist measure temperament? Greatness in a statesman or a general was perhaps less easy to measure than greatness in a painter or a musician or an astronomer. Though it is plain that Adams at one time coveted for his future America a whole galaxy of great men in many fields, he did not attempt a rounded definition of greatness or chart society's use of human energy to that end. Pericles had accounted for Athens' greatness in part by the democratic ferment that excluded not even the slaves from the aspirations of Greek society. But if the genesis of greatness in Athens was difficult to trace, how much more baffling would be the search for the origins of genius in the unplumbed democratic ocean!

Certainly a great man is a focus of energy, of the energy transmitted by heredity and the energy pounding against him from birth, energy in chemicals, love, words, sunlight, ideas. A man becomes great partly by the choice he makes in the direction and concentration of his energies. But can a democratic society encourage those commitments of energy that lead to greatness? To answer this crucial question, a science of man was a national asset more needed than any other. It is the question one might rightfully expect Henry Adams to consider at the end of his *History*. Great men of the creative or contemplative type could not emerge in large numbers until the energies of society were consciously diverted to that end. But greatness was mysterious. Perhaps not even a science of man or a science of history could ultimately explain the emergence of Thucydides or Raphael or Galileo. Yet none of these could have created without a diversion of energy from the tasks of winning bread or fighting a battle to the priceless shaping of a unique mind. What was genius? How could energy be diverted to the creation of genius? These were questions for the science of man to come. And not until a science of man emerged could Adams' coveted science of history become a reality.

II

Adams' quest for a science of history is the expression of a temperament rather than the disciplined application of physics and mathematics to the problem at hand. Had Adams taken to heart one of the main lessons of Bacon's *Novum Organum,* he would have discovered in many places in "The Rule of Phase" alone great gaps of documentation in which he needed dozens of minute steps to support his generalization. His fundamental thesis is that energy, contrary to the first law of thermodynamics, is not being fully conserved at all; it is being slowly dissipated because the sun is growing cold. Some millions of years hence, as the sun grows cold, life on earth will become extinct. In all nature, as energy changes form it loses some of its original heat content. Thus, when ice changes to water and water to steam, the energy of the steam is never quite equivalent to the energy of the original ice.

Why this change of form is called *degradation of energy* never becomes quite clear. For instance, when Adams applies his idea of degradation of energy to human beings, he calls man a "thermodynamic mechanism" in which chemical energy is changed into instinct, "vital energy," the will to act, and finally into thought. At no point does Adams define these terms. The only one fully comprehensible is the word *thought.* It is clear to the layman that thought is a form of energy sustained by the interplay of the bloodstream with brain tissue. To use Adams' analogy, one would suppose that thought is an *elevation* of energy, not the end step of a process of degradation. But not so. To Adams thought was degraded energy; he asserts that superior mental endowment is a "sign of degeneration," and that man as a thermodynamic mechanism is infinitely inferior to his animal and vegetable ancestors. How can one claim, suggests Adams, that superior mental power is a superior form of energy when it is often accompanied by loss of hair and teeth and the inability to suckle children?

In his treatment of human energy Adams unhesitatingly attempts to apply his concept of degradation to Darwinian evolution. May it not be true, he suggests, that man is descended from a higher order of species, now lost to the inspection of science? But even assuming his ape ancestry, Adams continues, the energy of the ape was far greater than the energy of man. Man must pay in the loss of physical energy for every gain in the energy of thought, and this means not only degradation of energy but also a quantitative loss. Every day of man's life, as he approaches the grave, he is losing energy. Death itself is merely the result of the laws of physics in the degradation of energies within the organism, until finally chemicals remaining are returned to the earth in another form.

While making the process of aging a part of his theory of degradation, Adams does not mention the sexual energy by which nature perpetuates life energies, bringing into the world new masses of chemico-physical organisms.[8] How sexual energy makes possible the renewal of life energies on such a scale in man alone as to enlarge his numbers despite the depletions of war, famine, disease, and catastrophe Adams fails to say. His most difficult task is to make the Darwinian assumption of the rise of man's intelligence fit into his scheme of the degradation of energy. Indeed, he does not attempt at any point to show how changes in the form of energy in the transformation of ice to water to steam bear any correspondence to the steps in the evolutionary scale from vegetation to animal life to man.

A key to the science of history, in Adams' view, was the correlation between the discovery of new sources of energy in the physical world and the expansion of the energy of thought. In his essay, "The Rule of Phase Applied to History," Adams defined *phase* as an era of equilibrium during which the sources of energy derived from scientific discoveries remained constant. To Adams one phase of history was the centuries before 1600, during which religion, not science, was the dominating force; the next phase, from 1600 to 1900, brought into being new sources of mechanical energy; the third, from 1900 to 1917, brought electrical energy; and the fourth, from 1917 to 1921, would bring forth "ethereal" energy. Each phase, asserted Adams, was in length of time a square root of the pre-

ceding phase, but in its production of energy a square of its predecessor. Thus the mechanical phase of history, 300 years, provided
an acceleration in the production of energy the square of that possible in the preceding 900,000 years; the electrical phase which
followed, from 1900 to 1917, would provide production of energy
the square of that possible from 1600 to 1900; and the energy of the
period from 1917 to 1921 would have to be calculated as a square
of that of the electrical phase. This hypothesis Adams unhesitatingly
applied to the acceleration of mental energy also. With each new
phase mental power expanded with the same velocity and volume
as that of steam or electricity. By 1921, the last year of the "ethereal"
energy phase of science, thought would be accelerated "to the lfmits
of its possibilities."[9]

In this analysis Adams made no pretense of proving mathe-
matically any actual correlation between the acceleration in mental
power and that in the energy of machines or electricity. He asserts
the correlation, moreover, without for a moment showing how his
thesis relates to his main postulate of the degradation of energy.
Here is energy, both mental and physical, pouring forth at astonishing acceleration. Notwithstanding this enormous expansion, is
energy on the whole being dissipated with the cooling of the sun?
Adams does not say. This is not to deny his broad thesis that the
discovery of new sources of energy has in turn released new mental
energies in the field of science and its applications in society. But
that any mathematical progression exists in the rate of acceleration
of either kind of energy, much less any correlation between the
rates of acceleration of the two, is a point no scientist would grant,
in Adams' day or ours.

Thus Henry Adams sought in a mathematical formula, rather
than in the democratic agitation of the nature of man, the secret of
the release of human energies. In the electrical era, in a population
of a hundred millions, how could the energies of man expand?
Certainly the birth of new inventions stimulated more and more
men to commit their energy of thought to the further unlocking of
nature's secrets. As science expanded, society and individuals set

up great schools for the training of scientists. Can society, by making a master plan, increase the number of great scientists? Can society increase the volume of thought going to art, music, sculpture, the making of books of literature? Can society help to unlock the energy of poets? Before the creators must appear the citizens aware of man's potential as it has revealed itself in other civilizations. How can society raise its level of criticism, its knowledge of greatness, and divert more and more of the common man's energy to the contemplation of superb men in all fields? These are questions that Adams does not consider. If it is assumed that the number of talented men in any age is limited by genetic determinants, then society cannot work for an expansion of greatness. But Henry Adams did not assume a genetic determinant; he assumed that the growth of thought depended upon the growth of science.

At one point in *A Letter to American Teachers of History* Adams touches significantly on the term *social energy*. As he is now attempting to reduce energy to measurements of the chemist and the physicist, Adams denies that "social energy is energy at all." In one of his statements of paradox (which seldom fail to make him intellectually exciting, however inconsistent he may be), Adams then asks, "Yet how could he [Adams] deny that social energy was a true form of energy when he had no reason for existence, as professor, except to describe and discuss his acts?" This was a candid admission of the historian's central task, with or without conformity to the laws of physics. No one had pictured the direction of social energies more aptly than had Adams himself in his statement that "the American stimulant increased in energy as it reached the lowest and most ignorant class, dragging and whirling them upward as in the blast of a furnace." The social energy thus described was but the sum of human energies, which Adams believed it possible to measure. A part of "the American stimulant" was to incite people to political and cultural as well as economic attainments. How could this stimulant be expanded in progressively greater degree decade by decade, thus insuring the expansion of human energy directed to creative and intellectual ends? One might suppose Adams, from the great beginning of his *History*, as a scientific historian would have been more concerned with this problem than with the death of the sun some millions of years away.

When he used the term *social energy*, Henry Adams was apparently oblivious to the one thinker in American life who like himself sought an explanation of history in terms of human energy. That man was Henry George. No civilization could fail, asserted George, which progressively enlarged the proportion of mental energy applied to "the extension of knowledge, the improvement of methods, and the betterment of social conditions." Where men were increasingly free to associate with each other on a basis of equality, the proportion of energy needed for sustenance declined, and the proportion available for cultural and intellectual advancement expanded. To George, civilization was the sum of human energies given to the growth of scientific, artistic, and social intelligence, with social planning whereby more and more minds in the community could divert their energies in the same direction. "Men tend to progress," wrote George, "as they come closer together, and by co-operation with each other increase the mental power that may be devoted to improvement, but just as conflict is provoked, or association develops inequality of condition and power, this tendency to progression is lessened, checked, and finally reversed." Thus does Henry George account for the fall of ancient nations. In his *Law of Civilization and Decay*, Brooks Adams seems to have given no thought whatever to the analysis of Henry George; nor did his brother Henry. Yet the three men had much in common in that each believed a quantitative evaluation of human energy was the key to historical analysis.

To the physicist, wrote Henry Adams in his quest for a science of history, "man has no function except that of dissipating or degrading energy." But in his more sanguine years Adams had professed a vision of a future America in which the social energy of five hundred million people might contribute to the world crops of great men surpassing those of Athens and Florence. This social energy was a consequence of opportunities unparalleled in the world's his-

tory for men of humble station unused to sufficient bread, much
less to books and ideas, music and sculpture, art and history and
creative media of their own. Adams did not think it worth while to
pursue this vision of a future America, or calculate the mechanical
or thermal energy that would assure vast numbers leisure for creative action. But to Henry George such a society was possible by
the planned redirection of human energy on a scale undreamed of
in past ages. To George it was imperative to measure energy, not
merely for the satisfaction of mathematical exactness, but also for
assuring the continuing life of a civilization. An American civilization of this kind had the advantage of unprecedented material
resources awaiting the workers of hand and brain who could
exchange coal and oil and electricity for the creative leisure of
millions of citizens.

In formulating a science of history, Henry Adams never really
incorporated even the social energy of love and devotion he had
recorded in *Mont-Saint-Michel and Chartres.* So capacious a mind as
that of Adams could not be blind to the inspiration of the Virgin
to the humblest artisan as well as to the inspired artists of medieval
Christianity. What American historian could have written more
justly of a religion of love lacking in himself? The great cathedrals
were made for crowds, "for the whole human race, on its knees,
hungry for pardon and love." "In essence, religion was love; in no
case was it logic. Reason can reach nothing except through the
senses; God, by essence, cannot be reached through the senses."
The Virgin "was also poetry and art. In the bankruptcy of reason,
she alone was real." Only in the presence of the inexplicable art
fashioned by hands of love did life for Henry Adams become
incandescent with meaning; yet the ecstasy of the illiterate believer
was denied him to the end. He could not chronicle the social energy
of love. Despite his reverence for the Virgin, herself a Jewess
(as he points out), Adams persistently reviled the Jews of his own
time. Could the historian measure the volume of love for one's
fellow-man that might transform whole communities? Could he
measure the hate that would destroy millions by the command of

a Hitler or a Stalin? In his analysis of history as science, Adams passed over the social energy of both hate and love, even though at Chartres he had glimpsed an integration of life's meaning his later years could not sustain.

Americans of various specialized learnings are not yet united in any conscious search for a science of man. We have not yet visualized the possible correlations of sciences and humanistic resources necessary to that end, much less the particular problem each discipline might set itself to solve. A description, for example, of the conditions that have helped to produce uncommon men, such as Burckhardt set forth in *Civilization of the Renaissance in Italy*, has thus far no parallel on the American scene. But in his great *History* Adams sought, like Tocqueville, to delineate those elements of American life that in 1801-15 made it unique among the nations of the world. Adams did not concentrate on the social fertilization of the superior man, as in the lives of Jefferson, Franklin, John Adams, Benjamin Rush, and Alexander Hamilton. But he did describe the conditions that released the energies of the average man hitherto caught and held in the severe stratification of more aristocratic societies. Adams foresaw the time when these energies would in part find their way into extraordinary achievement. But the process by which the energies of men are redirected toward an accomplishment of permanent worth, as Whitman was directed from editing a newspaper to the writing of poetry, as Brooks Adams was deflected from the law to the writing of history, thus far has no minute and suggestive record in American history. At the beginning of his career Henry Adams was fascinated by the social impetus to the vast release of human energies, and in this fascination he will remain perenially instructive to the historians of the future. Nor can the future science of man disregard his concept of the accumulation of technological energy, which, by the very acceleration of its growth, makes demands upon the human organism never before visualized.

XI

Brooks Adams: Human Nature in the Decay of Civilization

> *Perhaps Caesar's army was the best an ancient general ever put in the field, and yet it was filled with barbarians. All his legions were raised north of the Po, and most of them, including the tenth, north of the Alps.*
> —Adams

T HE HISTORIAN, like the novelist and the economist, scatters through his pages colors and forms of his portrait of the nature of man, a portrait often painted in the image of himself. The more complex and many-sided the historian, the more contradictory his image of human nature. In his *History*, Henry Adams pictured man more as an energy-using and energy-producing organism than as one fixed and limited by heredity. When Charles Beard defined history as "the interplay of *ideas* and *interests* in the time-stream," he suggested the power of the human mind to absorb and act upon ideas even when they are in conflict with economic self-interest. At the end of Beard's life, his image of man was more complex than in his earliest books, when economic self-interest was to him always dominant over the dreams and visions of youth. In a search for the realities of human nature, none of us is without his myths; for myths and poetry must precede any science, and as yet we have only glimmerings of a science of man.

Like his brother Henry, Brooks Adams grew up with many high hopes for the race of man in a democratic society. But in 1880, at the age of thirty-two, Brooks suffered a nervous breakdown "which only good fortune prevented from turning out tragically for me." From this time forth, Brooks Adams believed man to be a pure automaton, who is moved along the paths of least resistance by forces over which he has no control . . . I reverted to the pure Calvinistic philosophy. As I perceived that the strongest of human passions are fear and greed, I inferred that so much and no more might be expected . . . from any automaton so actuated.[1]

By the word "forces" in the statement above, Adams means environmental forces in the main. But when he speaks of fear and greed, he considers them to be the products of heredity. Hence, though Adams is deterministic, his image of man is confused and contradictory. To him the social principle of competition arises from the inborn passions of "greed, avarice, and cruelty"; these passions do not emerge from the necessities of competition. Indeed, from the time of his nervous breakdown onward, Adams thought of every civilization as embodying two principles in conflict: "the law, or the moral principle, and the flesh, or the evil principle," the latter exemplified in the practices of competition. As he grew older, Adams leaned more and more heavily upon Rom. 7:14-24 as the central explanation of human nature. Like St. Paul he would say, "I delight in the law of God after the inward man: But I see another law in my members, warring against the law of my mind." The union of mind and flesh is necessary to life, yet perpetually a chaos. As no equilibrium can ever emerge between mind and flesh in the nature of man, so no harmony can fix itself permanently in a social organism. In a democracy, moreover, the greed and avarice of human nature are released at an accelerated pace in the ceaselessly grinding mills of heightened competition.[2]

This view of man is pervasive and persistent in Adams' works, though not always dominant. However diligently Adams aspired to view the world through the eyes of science, he succeeded least when he was formulating his image of the nature of man. Had he kept his image of man in focus, Brooks Adams could not have written his classics of social analysis. In the midst of his evidence his theory of human nature collapses and disappears. But when he writes his prefaces, his theory of man magically comes whole again. In one of his earliest works, *The Emancipation of Massachusetts*

(1886), he makes no mention of St. Paul; but many years later (1919), in a revised edition, he makes St. Paul the center of his theory, with no changes in the work itself. In *Degradation,* which also appeared in 1919, he again quotes St. Paul to the Romans on man's inner chaos. In *The New Empire* (1903) and *The Theory of Social Revolutions* (1913), Adams' view of human nature appears only obliquely. But the essentials of his portrait had already appeared with startling fulness in his preface to *The Law of Civilization and Decay* (1895), which Adams wrote "to show how strong hereditary personal characteristics are." This work we must examine closely for the strokes and shadings it added to his portrait of the nature of man.

II

Whereas Henry Adams sought to make history conform to a mathematical formula, Brooks searched for the constants of social change from the appearance of a strong agricultural economy to its disintegration. In his classic, *The Law of Civilization and Decay,* he describes a cycle of events which he believes to be inevitable. The original strength of every country, according to Adams, lies with its farming population. It was only by means of the farming population that Rome could recruit soldiers to expand its empire. As long as the population of free farmers was prosperous and sufficient, Rome could fill its legions with first-rate soldiers. Then, as the wealth of Rome increased, her rich men bought huge tracts of land on which they planted slaves taken in the wars. The free farmers, unable to compete with slave labor, were forced to mortgage their farms at exorbitant interest and finally lost their property to the usurers and bankers of the city. Then, as the free farmers forsook the land, Rome's strength declined, and the legions which were victorious, like those of Julius Caesar, were recruited from the barbarians of the empire's frontiers.

With the destruction of the free farmer, Rome's military power declined and her art decayed. Riches, not victory, usury, not oratory, became the central quest of Rome's young men. With the decline of the farming population, the family also disintegrated. As the free farmer was the bulwark of the army, so was he also the main support of the family as a stabilizing institution. To Brooks Adams a free farming population, a martial spirit, a religious fervor, an instinct for art, and family solidarity are the main props of a strong society. When these elements disappear, the civilization inevitably decays. This cycle of strength and decay Brooks Adams traces in Rome, England, and India, drawing conclusions also from the France of the nineteenth century and the America of the twentieth.

In praising *The Law of Civilization and Decay*, Henry Adams wrote, "It is the first time that serious history has ever been written. He has done for it what only the greatest men do; he has created a startling generalisation which reduces all history to a scientific formula." A cycle of events, however often repeated, cannot, however, be called a scientific formula. One may ask, for example, in Brooks Adams' law, why was it that Rome allowed its free farmers to be destroyed by its rich men? Was it inevitable that Rome should make no laws for the protection of its free farmers? In fact, Adams himself describes a period of revolt against the moneyed oligarchy in which the dictator Camillus was forced to agree to the passage of the Licinian Laws, which provided for a redistribution of the public land to the debtor class—land which had been seized in war and appropriated by the patricians. In Adams' words,

Licinius obtained a statute by which back payments of interest should be applied to extinguishing the principal of debts, and balances then remaining due should be liquidated in three annual installments. He also limited the quantity of the public domain which could be held by any individual, and directed that the residue which remained after the reduction of all estates to that standard should be distributed in five-acre lots.[3]

The impact of the Licinian Laws was, according to Brooks Adams, so revolutionary as to justify describing it as "the conquest of Italy." It was only after the passage of the Licinian Laws that

Rome gained sufficient strength to conquer Carthage and Macedon.

Just how this revolutionary era in which the free farmer and the debtor class were favored by new laws is a part of the predictable law of civilization and decay Brooks Adams fails to explain. A cycle of history may be repeated a number of times without justifying an appraisal of its events as a law. One might as well say that wherever land is denuded of trees or washed by water, erosion takes place. It is true that an effect follows from a given cause, but it is not true that the cause is inevitably repeated. Indeed Brooks Adams' own illustration of the Licinian Laws shows that the reversal of the so-called law of civilization and decay was precisely the action which permitted Rome's greatest expansion. Hence for Henry Adams to call the tracing of such a cycle of events a science of history is like calling war an inevitable extension of belligerent human nature. Henry, indeed, afterward recognized the fallacy of his own high praise when he wrote to Brooks: "You with your lawyer's method, only state sequence of fact, and explain no causes?"

III

In *The Law of Civilization and Decay,* one of Brooks Adams' crucial generalizations about the nature of man runs as follows:

Like other personal characteristics, the peculiarities of the mind are apparently strongly hereditary, and, if these instincts be transmitted from generation to generation, it is plain that, as the external world changes, those who receive this heritage must rise or fall in the social scale, according as their nervous system is well or ill adapted to the conditions to which they are born.[4]

What Adams means by the term "peculiarities of mind" he does not elaborate, but throughout his masterpiece one may find such terms as "the imaginative type," "essentially martial race," "imaginative blood," and "Latin mind." If these are the peculiarities of mind to which Adams refers, most psychologists and all anthropologists today would call his assumption an utter myth, though it is true that we do not yet possess either quantitative or qualitative proof that such a thing as "the Latin mind" does not exist.

Another generalization upon which Adams bases his conclusions is this:

Thought is one of the manifestations of human energy, and among the earlier and simpler phases of thought, two stand conspicuous—Fear and Greed. Fear, which, by stimulating the imagination, creates a belief in an invisible world, and ultimately develops a priesthood; and Greed, which dissipates energy in war and trade.[5]

Though Adams does not claim in this passage that fear and greed are inherited traits, we know from later statements that he accepted them as such. From fear comes imagination, which in turn produces mental casts that are not only religious, but military and artistic. As long as fear dominates society, the family, the army, and the church are strong. But when greed dominates, and commerce thrives, a new type of man appears whose main interests are economic and scientific; then art and religion decay, and the family declines.

According to Adams, when a nation has disintegrated through the concentration of capital in a few hands, through the growth of the population unfitted for war or art, and through depletion of its farming manhood, the only possible remedy is an invasion which supplies "fresh energetic material by the infusion of barbarian blood." This crucial statement shows that Adams regarded involuntary eugenics, not a redistribution of wealth and opportunity, as the only hope for the strengthening of race. The cycle Adams describes he was certain is irreversible by the growth of social intelligence or an economic revolution such as that set in motion by the Licinian Laws. A population in which families grow smaller and smaller and manhood less martial cannot, in Adams' opinion, rejuvenate itself. If Adams had read Henry George's explanation of the decline of civilizations as proportionate to the progressive denial of equality, he gives no evidence in The Law. To Adams society was an organism, with a birth, growth, and decline; to George society had no fixed life cycle; it was a group-

ing of social forces in which the amenities and creativity of civilization would inevitably expand with the extension of economic
opportunity to larger and larger numbers. Adams, however, always
returns to his central thesis that barbarian blood rejuvenates a
people.

Since Adams regarded England and America as far advanced
economic societies, he expected a breakdown in Western civilization by 1985. The dark races, he asserted, were gaining on us.
England was a bankers' civilization in which, to Adams, the London
Jew was a symbol of the dominance of the economic mind. In
1896 he wrote, "England is as much governed by the Jews of Berlin,
Paris, and New York as she is by her native growth. It is in the
nature of a vast syndicate, and by control of London, they control
the world." It was in vain that Theodore Roosevelt reminded Adams
that America and England were still producing a vast number of
first-rate fighting men despite the centralization of wealth and the
concentration of American civilization in larger and larger cities.

IV

In his analysis of the dispersion of human energy, Brooks Adams,
like Henry, begins with the assumption that all energy is derived
from the sun and that human life is one form of animal life by
which solar energy is released. From this statement one might
assume that Brooks believed those societies most exposed to the
sun or eating foods grown by its warmth would have the greatest
energy. On the contrary, however, Adams' thesis is that societies
have differing reservoirs of energy "in proportion as nature has
endowed them, more or less abundantly, with energetic material."
What energetic material consists of Adams does not explain; but
it is apparent that to him human energies derive from genetic
determinants rather than from proper foods or a hardy outdoor life.

In neither Adams' day nor our own do we have any scientific
data on the transmission of energy by genetic means, except for
sexual energy, the quantitative potential of which, on the basis of
the Kinsey analysis, appears to be hereditary. But a great mass of

evidence exists to show that human energies depend primarily upon work habits and the quality and quantity of food to which one is accustomed. In one brilliant study alone, Josué de Castro's *The Geography of Hunger,* we have ample proof that the energies of two-thirds of the world's people are depleted daily for lack of food. To what extent psychological forces deplete or replenish human energies no one yet knows, though William James has explored the topic with brilliant insight in "The Energies of Men." Brooks Adams does not touch this thorny problem; he is content with the inheritance of "energetic material" and the assumption that an exhausted and decaying society can be rejuvenated only through the "infusion of barbarian blood."

Brooks Adams' picture of human nature is filled, then, with grotesque inaccuracies unchallenged in the main by his contemporaries and undiluted by decades of ruthless self-inspection. To correct his image of man in a less mythical direction, Brooks needed the medical training of Oliver Wendell Holmes or William James or the earthy realism of John Dewey. Even the crude Abraham Lincoln, with no access to the wealth of Boston's learning, produced a more consistent and realistic picture of man than did Brooks Adams. If Lincoln was a determinist, he recognized, as Brooks did not, causes and effects as distinguished from patterns; whereas Lincoln was rationalistic in his determinism, Brooks put his faith in the inner chaos of flesh and spirit. To Lincoln's mind, the energies of men expanded with the conviction that their hopes had a realistic basis in the conditions of society; that too was determinism. But to Brooks Adams the expansion of democracy could only mean the expansion of greed and fear and the victories of the flesh, whatever the small triumphs of benevolence along the way.

Even Henry Adams held a more dispassionate view of the nature of man than his brother Brooks. In the writing of history, Henry achieved a detachment from himself that was not possible for Brooks; as Ed Howe said, Henry could "sit on the fence and watch himself go by." Whereas, in his study of the Licinian Laws, Brooks shows no realization whatever that Rome's success thereafter was due to the expansion of opportunity for the small farmer, and the corresponding release of energies hitherto imprisoned by despair, Henry Adams shows an acute awareness of the torrents of American energy, "like the blast of a furnace," when men understood that economic and political betterment waited only upon their labor. In a sense his history of America represented to Henry Adams and his readers the plasticity and variability of the nature of man; whereas to Brooks *The Law of Civilization and Decay* embodied his belief that greed and fear are so fixed in human nature as to prevail ultimately over all hostile forces. But whereas Henry's picture of man in his masterpiece represents a kind of dispassionate agnosticism about man's nature, Brooks's *Law* is a doleful repetition of the failure of man to achieve emancipation from his innate greed and fear.

Fortunately, however, the most significant aspects of *The Law* do not derive from the crude anthropology of its author. Nothing that Henry Adams wrote is a more brilliant synthesis of social forces than *The Law;* indeed, Brooks's masterpiece abounds with facts, insights, and parallels unique in their coherence and force among American historians. Brooks's analysis of the concentration of wealth and power as concurrent with the decline of the farming population is always informed and pithy: "For many years farming land has fallen throughout the West, as it fell in Italy in the time of Pliny. Everywhere, as under Trajan, the peasantry are distressed; everywhere they migrate to the cities, as they did when Rome repudiated the denarius." No American historian has used statistics with more dramatic timeliness: "In 1789 the average French family consisted of 4.2 children. In 1891 it had fallen to 2.1, and since 1890, the deaths seem to have equalled the births." On some problems, it is true, Brooks has a blindness hardly comprehensible: art to him is an expression of the imaginative and martial age, not the commercial. Hence he is forced to omit the glories of Florence in the time of Michelangelo and the art of

Amsterdam in the time of Rembrandt. But no historian can see the world whole, and Brooks was catholic and brilliant in his use of diverse original sources. To write his classic, Brooks was forced to detach himself from the limitations of his training as an Adams, a lawyer, a member of the privileged rich. From his image of man, however, Brooks could not escape; indeed, he never doubted the accuracy of his portrait.

XII
On the Genesis of Great Men:
William James

> *Sporadic great men come everywhere.*
> *But for a community to get vibrating*
> *through and through with intensely active*
> *life, many geniuses coming together and in*
> *rapid succession are required.*
>
> —James

ONE OF THE GREAT HOPES raised by the prospect of a science of man is for a tracing of the origins of genius. To Henry George great men were born in plenty; conditions snuffed out the flame, sometimes in one sweep of death, at other times in years of grinding poverty. But to Francis Galton, whose book *Hereditary Genius* was in the 1870's and 1880's a compelling thesis to Americans as well as Britons, genius was the gift, as the very word suggests, of genetic transmission. Despite compelling rhetoric for each argument, no facts yet existed to explain the sudden outcropping of great men in the times of Pericles, Elizabeth, and Victoria. William James and Henry James were themselves a part of the late flowering of New England, younger contemporaries of Emerson, Hawthorne, and Holmes. How both William and Henry grew up in a home expectant of greatness, with images of greatness around them from youth through college, we may gather from the vivid pages of *Notes of a Son and Brother*.

William James knew that the science of man was still unready to answer the question, "Is the great man the gift of nature, or as Herbert Spencer claimed, merely the focus of social forces?"—so unready indeed as not to be a science at all. From art, physiology, and medicine he had turned to psychology, placing now a reliance on sensory verification that no philosophical search could afterward dislodge. In 1891, at the end of his great work on psychology, James disclaimed the word *science* as applied to his book. No psychology, indeed, was as yet any more than the "hope of a science," in the sense of possessing laws as invariable as the laws of physics. To James the science of man was no more advanced in 1891 than physics had been before Galileo or chemistry before Lavoisier. To accelerate the development of a science of man, James insisted that we must first "understand how great is the darkness in which we grope." Such an attitude in itself denoted one necessity in the pursuit of the science of man: let the searcher wait; let him be humble; in the vast darkness a chink of light may open the way into a brighter passage.

The emergence and the production of great men were the central passion of James's intellectual life. What the vision of a world without povery was to George, the great Over-Soul to Emerson, the riddle of free will to Oliver Wendell Holmes, the fertilization and the growth of greatness were to William James. In "Great Men and their Environment," which was in part an answer to the extreme environmentalist position of Herbert Spencer and Grant Allen, James set forth his views at eloquent length. Some great men, he asserted, such as Shelley and Carlyle, had such strong genetic vitality that their genius would have flowered in any society, however barbarous or retarded; others were elevated to greatness only by the social emergencies with which they grappled, as with Cromwell and Washington, or the tasks they found congenial, as with Galton and Spencer. A genius was more likely to emerge from the mysterious womb of nature than from the impact of social forces. The greatest men sprang from impenetrable physiological mutations, like those of the animal world postulated by Charles Darwin. Once launched, the authentic geniuses impregnated their lesser fellows with the yeast of greatness, creating a ferment that to James was the most precious ingredient of an advancing civilization.

The core of William James's argument for the initiative of great men in changing the direction of society is the assumption of a physiological mutation which is usually more powerful than social forces. These mutations are not constant in number, but vary—contrary to Galton's view—from era to era. A period fruitful in geniuses, such as that of Pericles, owes its burden of great men in good part to a series of physiological accidents converging in time and place. It is the accidental gift of geniuses in a group that sets up a ferment which in turn creates a new series of exceptional people, some of them as great as those produced by physiological mutations. Were it not for the initiative of the first group of geniuses, those produced by nature in unpredictable batches, the secondary great men would not emerge. At such moments "the mass of the nation grows incandescent."

But how does a genius make his impress on the life of his time? How does he channel the forces of his environment, helping to create great men and movements? This mind of genius, asserts James, does not receive all of its ideas from its environment; such a mind has an exciting life of its own independent of its surroundings, full of spontaneous variations, flashes of insight, wit, humor, eloquence, inventions, daydreams, and meandering streams of thought that bear new ideas into the world. Such a mind, continues James, can be no mere echo of a voice or receiving mechanism for the messages of its environment. The brain of each genius has an independent uniqueness that operates in spontaneous variation through the molecular accidents of random images and a thousand sudden combinations of images that the genius transforms into ideas. In one of a thousand dissimilar instants, the idea "flashes out of one brain, and no other." Once born, the idea flowers or withers as the environment welcomes or discards it. Environment can only preserve an idea, not bring it to birth. If society accepts the idea, the genius has a profound effect on his contemporaries. His ideas change the environment and make society's incandescence glow more brightly. "The community may evolve in many ways. The accidental presence of this or that ferment decides in which way it *shall* evolve." Thus does James trace a parallel between Darwin's selection in the natural world and selection in the social world.[1]

James had found an oblique answer to this theory in the writings of Herbert Spencer and Grant Allen, who were his chief targets in his paper on the environment of great men. Spencer and Allen asserted that social and geographical forces, not physiological variations, brought forth great men in proportion to the intensity and pervasiveness of intellectual life. In his emphasis on geographical conditions, Allen was more extreme than his teacher Spencer. In his article "Hellas and Civilization" (*Gentleman's Magazine,* August, 1878), Allen had set forth the theory that the closeness of the islands and peninsulas of Hellas, in a climate varying, in six degrees of latitude, from subarctic to subtropical weather, had made inevitable a variety of products and an easy access of communication and trade which to Allen were the main early factors in intellectual and creative fertilization. An island civilization made political and intellectual independence an attainable goal; no king could easily impose his rule on cities and citadels surrounded by water and protected by mountains. In the earliest stages of navigation, Hellas had incomparable advantages for building up a prosperous society and an intellectual life enriched by communication with other countries. To Allen the main key to Hellas' cultural superiority was her trading prosperity, as with Holland in the seventeenth century and England in the sixteenth. "If any man really doubts," wrote Allen, "that literature, science, and art do in fact follow the course of commerce, let him consider wherein does the Greece of today differ from the Hellas of Pericles, and wherein does the Spain of Alfonso differ from the Spain of Lope and Calderon and Cervantes." These were the grounds of Grant Allen's extreme position which aroused James to his brilliant sally on the environment of great men.

In his reply to James, "The Genesis of Genius" (*Atlantic Monthly,* March, 1881), Allen agreed with his American opponent that great men have changed their environments, citing, among others, Wickliffe, Luther, and Calvin. But geniuses such as Pericles and Shakespeare could not have emerged except from societies which, thanks to their favorable geographical placement, had attained a high level of cultural and artistic ferment among the average citizens. It is the high level of interest in intellectual things among the citizens at large that makes the outcroppings of genius inevitable. "Except in a generally mechanical race," asserted Allen, "you will not find a Watt or an Edison: except in a generally literary one, you will not find a Shakespeare or a Goethe; except in a generally aesthetic one, you will not find a Leonardo or a Beethoven."

Between the genius and the mass of bright men in such a society is but a small gap. A genius needs then but a short leap to scale a new peak in the history of art or science. How, asks Allen, can an inborn Raphael discover in Memphis the laws of perspective in a flash of insight? Would you find a Cimabue among the Veddahs? "The something that made the many into art critics made the few into artists." The intellectual power necessary to the genius, asserts Allen, is potentially present at birth in many men, but can be developed only by a tremendously accelerated action in the brain cells induced by a climate charged with intellectual electricity, a sudden advance beyond the achievements of many distinguished colleagues working in the same field. When a mass of citizens rise to a high level of aspiration and achievement in any field, geniuses, in the view of Allen and Spencer, are certain to emerge. A high degree of development is, in their view, the product of an extraordinary multiplication of brain cell connections induced by the intellectual ferment made inevitable by geographic and economic conditions. To them a genius was one who "possessed a few more elements of mind than most other people his contemporaries."[2]

James did not answer Allen's article on the origin of genius with a new assertion of his belief in physiological variation. His reply, "The Importance of Individuals," which the *Atlantic Monthly* refused to accept, insisted on the study of genius as one of the most fruitful of all philosophic inquiries, rather than the study of statistical averages of achievement preferred by the sociologists. To two of Allen's most striking statements, "Both genius and milieu are products of the geographical conditions," and "If you can account for the average, you can account for the exceptions," James made no reply. Cannot more enlightenment be gained, asked James, from a study of great men as individuals than from a statistical survey of the society that surrounded them?

If it is assumed that genius is the product of both biological and social factors, then the cleavage between James and Allen was one of emphasis rather than polarity. Each believed in individual biological differences. Each believed in the crucial impact of great men. Whereas to Allen, however, a genius could arise only from a society of superior economic opportunities and intellectual movement, to James a genius was more often than not a physiological variation. True, the environment had to select and accept him. But in posing the belief that genius is in the main genetically derived, James violated the main principle of his scientific method as later set forth in his manifesto, *Essays in Radical Empiricism.*

All generalizations were to be distrusted, insisted James, that could not be supported by particulars observed and recorded by the senses. But to James particulars came first. They were vital for the future even if no concept followed. A part of radical empiricism was the reluctance of the philosopher to generalize on the basis of recorded particulars. Like Bacon, William James realized the dangers of the method which flew to conclusions before the evidence in the form of exact observations was overwhelming. Now in accounting for the origin of genius by genetic variations, James faced an insuperable obstacle. It is impossible to examine the genetic makeup of man under the microscope. The physiological accident imposed by nature and assumed by James and Galton remains even today beyond the reach of sensory verification. It is true that microscopes of the present day can discern the chromosome structure of the fruitfly. It is even possible to point to the minute link in the chain of genes that determines the color of the fruitfly's wings. But unfortunately for the theory of physiological variations, no science yet exists that can point to the link in man's chromosomes and say, "Here is the key to this baby's intellectual pre-eminence," or "Here is the gene that spells genius in music."

In attempting an analysis of genius, then, on the basis of genetic mutation, as assumed by Darwin for physical variations only, William James was for the moment repudiating his own scientific method in his search for the nature of man.

Certainly man inherits a uniqueness that makes him physically and psychologically different from each of his fellows. But the genetic transmission of this uniqueness, except for physical characters explainable by Mendel's law, remains a mystery to the followers of both William James and Grant Allen.

The debate between James and Allen on the origins of genius poses problems that only a science of man can ultimately resolve. Alfred Kroeber, after long studies of the clustering of genius in various civilizations, but especially the Periclean, has estimated that one in several hundred thousand is born a genius. Out of a hundred men and women thus gifted by nature, seventy-five to ninety, in Kroeber's judgment, are prevented by conditions from attaining the stature of genius promised by heredity. Kroeber finds it impossible to believe that heredity plants great men in clusters, turning the flow of genius off and on "like a playful faucet." Vital as these speculations are, we have as yet no means of testing them by the unassailable criteria of science. No means has as yet appeared for testing James's assumption of "physiological variations" as the primary source of great minds.

On the other hand, though a great many environmental factors in the lives of great men open themselves to inspection, a science of man is needed to assess their significance in the order of more crucial and less crucial effects. Of what importance, for example, is the habit of watching for an original idea, "that gleam of light," as Emerson wrote, "which flashes across the mind from within"? In a society of talented men, and appreciators of talented men, posed by Grant Allen, can such a habit be taught? "Every scientific conception," wrote William James, "is in the first instance a 'spontaneous variation' in some one's brain ... Their genesis is strictly akin to that of the flashes of poetry and sallies of wit to which the instable brain-paths equally give rise." The conditions under which such ideas are most likely to be born have never been tabulated, though hundreds of writers have testified to the stimulation of congenial company, the necessity of a relaxed frame of mind and of freedom from pressing worries for creative contemplation.

As boys Henry and William James lived under constant intellectual excitement at home, a home in which the father refused to advise an early devotion to any career, wanting only for his sons a rich variety of travel, experience, and leisure, as did also the father of such a contemporary mind as Robert Oppenheimer. Thus far, in speculations about the origins of genius, the various factors of such a home atmosphere have not been tabulated, much less assembled in the order of crucial impact. Among America's literary great, few have worked in solitude; almost all, under the spur of fame, have sought out their great contemporaries before their own fruition, as Whitman went to Emerson, Twain to Bret Harte, Melville to Hawthorne. This also is a phenomenon not yet tallied by the oncoming science of man. Nor has any attempt yet been made to test Grant Allen's assumption about the correlation of commerce and prosperity with the clustering of genius. The granting of leisure to talented people, as by various foundations, represents as yet the tapping of only a trickle of our resources. Only a science of man can answer the questions raised by William James's own years of early leisure at home and abroad, made possible by the fortune of his grandfather and the insight of his father. The study of biography recommended by James in itself offers a multitude of clues to the conditions of creative action. Only a science of man, shaped and informed by many disciplines, can place in a hierarchy the various conditions that bring greatness to birth in societies or men.

1915
A World War and Straws in the Wind

In 1915 America was at peace, her masses complacent in isolation, her factories running day and night to supply the armies of Britain and France. To the average American the trenches of France were a remote and improbable dream. Only dimly did men sense the nightmare of slaughter that two years later was to become a stark reality to many American soldiers.

In All Quiet on the Western Front, *Erich Maria Remarque pictures in a single scene the essence of murder and love, remote poles in the nature of man, coalescing in a pinpoint of time. After a night attack on the French trenches, the German hero falls into a shell hole. In the counterattack he is in danger: a French soldier may jump or fall into his refuge. Instantly he makes up his mind that if this happens he must stab his enemy through the throat. When, shortly after, a French soldier falls into the shell hole, the hero acts with almost mechanical frenzy. Then he hears the gurgles of his enemy, and waits for him to die. When the clear gray morning comes, the Frenchman, still conscious, looks at him in terror, but the hero only wants to give his enemy first aid. Suddenly he feels that this man is a comrade. When at last the Frenchman dies, the German finds in his pockets pictures of his wife and child. At last the hero speaks to his dead enemy, saying,*

Comrade, I did not want to kill you. If you jumped in here again, I would not do it, if you were sensible too. But you were only an idea to me before, an abstraction that lived in my mind and called forth its appropriate response. It was that abstraction I stabbed. But now, for the first time, I see you are a man like me. I thought of your hand-

257

grenades, of your bayonet, of your rifle; now I see your wife and your face and our fellowship. Forgive me, comrade. We always see it too late. Why do they never tell us that you are just poor devils like us, and that your mothers are just as anxious as ours, and that we have the same fear of death, and the same dying and the same agony—Forgive me, comrade; how could you be my enemy?

On May 1, 1915, Washington newspapers carried a notice warning American citizens to avoid the war zone and especially pointing out the dangers of crossing the Atlantic in English ships. On May 7, 1915, the Lusitania, carrying both passengers and war supplies, was torpedoed without warning off the coast of Ireland, with a loss of 1,200 men, women, and children, including 114 Americans. As much as any action, the sinking of the Lusitania crystallized American sentiment against Germany. The cries for vengeance were heightened by Germany's delay in accepting responsibility for the disaster. The event played into the hands of those who believed in preparedness as a way of national life; into the hands, too, of the investors who had helped to finance the war against Germany. It also prepared the public mind for what many people thought was a righteous war against German militarism, the militarism that was best exemplified in the invasion of neutral Belgium in 1914.

The sinking of the Lusitania drew men's minds again to the impenetrable phenomenon of courage in the presence of imminent death. Men remembered the brave men and women of the Titanic, who had three hours to prepare for the icy waters, whereas those on the Lusitania had only thirty minutes. On the Titanic Mr. and Mrs. Isidor Straus had sat calmly in deck chairs, he refusing to leave until the last man had preceded him, and she until her husband could come with her. On the Lusitania, as the waters rose higher, Charles Frohman gave his lifebelt to a hysterical woman, and repeated to Rita Jolivet a line from Peter Pan: "Why fear death? It is the most beautiful adventure in life." The courage of the men and women in the steerage, as on the Titanic, went for the most part unrecorded. As the Lusitania went down, the boiling waters were filled with *wreckage and bobbing bodies alive and dead, children, women, and men. One woman in the water was giving birth to a child. Of the 129 children on board, ninety-four perished.*[1]

In 1915 the Allies suffered a crushing blow to their hopes when the Russian armies in Poland were defeated by the German forces of Von Hindenburg and Mackensen. In April, 1915, Hindenburg had massed nearly one million men in Galicia, an army strengthened by picked assault troops under the command of Mackensen. On May 1, Hindenburg's artillery threw 700,000 shells into the Russian trenches, after which the assault troops under Mackensen attacked across the Dunajec. Przemysl, the Russian defense, collapsed at the point of the break-through. Przemysl was evacuated June 2. Lemberg fell June 22. By the Battle of Dunajec Germany recovered Galicia for Austria, even as Hindenburg had recovered East Prussia by the Battle of Tannenberg. By July, 1915, Russia had lost all her advantages of position and fortification. After the fall of Warsaw on April 5, great masses of the terrified Polish population filled the roads, preventing an orderly retreat and communicating new terror to the towns into which they flowed.

Writing in the New Republic for September 18, 1915, Gerald Morgan attributed the disintegration of Russian morale to one main factor: the poor quality of Russian officers, 80 per cent of whom, like the men they commanded, could not read or write. But the full impact of Russian illiteracy, hunger, and apathy was yet to come. Lenin watched and waited from his exile in Switzerland, assessing the collapse of Russian arms in the timetable of revolution, the world yet oblivious of his power. Had the democracies, despite their pockets of poverty, been too prosperous to understand the effect of hunger on the nature of man? The Communists understood the defeat of the Russian armies even more clearly than did the New Republic. In this knowledge lay their ammunition and the portent of future Russian power.

In 1915 the status of black Africa stirred the thoughts of American critics. What had Europe done to liberate the Africans? In the Atlantic for May, W. E. Burghardt Du Bois wrote,

Twenty centuries after Christ, black Africa, prostrate, raped, and shamed, lies at the feet of the conquering Philistines of Europe. What shall the end be? The world-old and fearful things, war and wealth, murder and luxury? Or shall it be a new thing—a new peace and new democracy of all races: a great humanity of equal men?

II

In 1915, as in former decades, optimistic social critics rejoiced in the wealth of foreign cultures thrown into the American melting pot. Writing in the Nation *for February 25, Horace Kallen spoke of the American future in a Whitmanesque manner. Indeed, Kallen looked to the future of America as "an orchestration of mankind," with each people an instrument of unique timbre blending its music with the stream of other voices. In such a mingling there would be both harmonies and dissonances, but to Kallen no other nation than America offered the potential of a cultural future embodying the rich strains of many nations in its symphony.*

In the Atlantic *for June, 1915, Owen Wister satirized the quack novels of his day, particularly such works as* Their Yesterdays *and* Eyes of the World, *by Harold Bell Wright. While denying that there existed an essential American hostility to literary art, as the English critic Edward Garnett claimed, Wister was forced to admit a pervasive immaturity in the average American attitude toward literary values. He quotes in despair one critic who, writing in the* Oregon Journal, *averred that Harold Bell Wright had "an almost clairvoyant power of reading the human soul." Wister is at a loss to understand the concurrent popularity of Harold Bell Wright and such works of art as Wharton's* The House of Mirth. *The popularity of trashy best sellers Wister traces to the essential vulgarity of the democratic taste. "Publishers cowardly; critics worthless; novelists false; why? Because it is successful to be so. But why should it be successful? The answer leads us straight back to the American people, to our garbled version of democracy."*

Nor would the same vulgar public allow a wholesome frankness such as Fielding was able to exercise in the eighteenth century.

Though Wister regards Hawthorne as America's greatest genius, was not even he limited in his penetration of truth by the essential immaturity of his American readers? In Wister's view, had Balzac or Turgenev written The Scarlet Letter, *he would have included many acute revelations of life which Hawthorne omitted. In such a capitulation to low taste by publishers and critics, could America sustain artists of transcendent quality? The American renaissance, Wister feared, must await the heightening of standards in the democratic mind.*

III

In 1915 the science of man made a decisive advance in the researches of the Yale geographer, Ellsworth Huntington. Physical vigor, according to Huntington, is at its highest on days when the temperature fluctuates between 50° to 55° at night and 60° to 70° by day. He found mental energy to be at its greatest when the average temperature is a little over 40°. Since human energy is a combination of physical and mental, Huntington concluded that the best climate would be one in which the average temperature in winter is about 40° and the average temperature in summer is approximately 60°.

In establishing his data on optimum temperature, Huntington investigated the daily work of about 2,500 factory workers in Connecticut, the Carolinas, Georgia, and Florida. He also traced the fluctuations in the marks of students at West Point and Annapolis. All of these investigations showed that "both mental and physical activities depend closely upon conditions of weather and climate." Huntington found also that in an ideal climate a stable temperature is undesirable for acceleration of mental activity. A fluctuation of temperature is a necessary condition of climate to sustain human energy. Still another factor is humidity, but it is less crucial than storminess and daily or seasonal fluctuation. Of the various climatic factors, mean temperature is easily the most crucial.

Convinced that his method was sound and fruitful, Huntington now drew a map of human energy as determined by climatic condi-

tions. He found that only a few countries and continents possessed the ideal climate for maximum human activity. England, New England, the northwest coast of the United States, Germany, France, Holland, northern Italy, Japan, parts of Scandinavia, Africa, South America, and New Zealand—these were some of the regions and nations which were blessed with the ideal climatic determinant of energy.

Huntington's next step was to make a map of the relative density of civilization as defined by fifty specialists chosen from various countries and from representative fields such as anthropology, history, and geography. With some variations and exceptions, the map of civilization in the main followed the outlines of the map of human energy. This correlation not only convinced Huntington that a strong correlation exists between human energy and exceptional achievement; it also convinced him that his method of quantitative analysis of energy and climate was a sound approach for further investigations.[2]

Huntington did not deny that other factors than climate were sometimes crucial in the production of superior and uncommon men. However, by applying his principle of ideal climate t the density of superior individuals, he was able to show a further correlation between personality development and the potential of human energy as affected by the ideal climate. Among the eminent persons listed in Who's Who in 1912, Huntington found that out of a population of 1,147,000 from 1840 to 1870, Massachusetts produced an average of 98 eminent persons per 100,000, whereas in the same period South Carolina produced 39.4 eminent persons per 100,000 and New Mexico in the same period produced only 1.5 eminent persons per 100,000.

Concentrating on the one criterion of climate, Huntington did not take into account a condition of civilization such as association in equality, such as George describes in Progress and Poverty. Nor did he take into account the necessity for the extension of political opportunities, such as George and Bellamy regard as crucial in the production of great men. But the high value of Huntington's analy-

sis lies in his quantitative measurement of human energy as affected by climate. Among the critics of human nature America had produced, none before Huntington's time had attempted such a quantitative analysis. Whatever the conditions a future science of man might describe as crucial for the development of uncommon men, Huntington's condition of climate as set forth in quantitative terms opened new vistas in the search for certainties about human nature.

XIII

On the Ways of Man: Darrow, Steffens, and Broun

> *Let society be the friend not the tyrant, the brother not the jailer, and the feeling will be retained a thousandfold. No man or society ever induced love with clubs or guns.... No amount of treatment can reclaim an evil heart if the treatment is administered without love.*
>
> —Darrow

IN THE AMERICAN search for certainties about human nature, no single discipline will avail; the scientists of the future must trace the thoughts of their predecessors in many fields: lawyers and doctors, historians and biologists, philosophers and chemists, poets and economists, preachers and engineers. Only by the co-operation of many disciplines and the merging of many insights can the science of man be developed. Do most criminals, as Clarence Darrow thought, suffer from a defective nervous organization? The specialized knowledge of neurologists and surgeons can provide a partial reply to such a question, but only a science of man can furnish a complete answer. As long as economic prizes such as public lands or monopolies or natural gas are available through legislative bribery, is the temptation for most men too great to be resisted, as Lincoln Steffens thought? Does economic gain invariably possess more constant and persuasive appeal than ethical teachings? A science of man, informed by the researches of the statistician and the sociologist, is needed to answer. The dreams and visions of sages and saints, asserted Heywood Broun, can be a reality in private and public life. Is this sort of assumption, fos-

264

tered by many educators and thinkers like Emerson and Mann, a perpetual delusion? Some will say that such a question cannot be resolved by a science of man. Nevertheless a great body of evidence already exists to show how certain people, among them the masses of India, have responded to the ideas and images of a Ghandi, an Emerson, or a Henry George. No biography of a man great by Broun's definition is without its instruction for the science of man to come.

In their probings of the nature of man, no three thinkers could have approached the problem with more dissimilar temperaments than Lincoln Steffens, Clarence Darrow, and Heywood Broun. Steffens was cool, dispassionate, disciplined. Darrow was full of a sad pessimism, skeptical of life's central meaning. Broun was impetuous and whimsical. Of the three Darrow was most persuasive, infusing whole courtrooms with the aura of his warmth, searching for the weak points of the hard human armor, leading his juries and judges into ugly corners whence criminals had emerged. Of the three men Steffens possessed most theoretical insight into human nature, Broun the most faith in its potential of altruistic energy. Whereas Steffens and Darrow gauged the impact of daily batterings on the human organism, Broun sought for himself and others those moments when an indelible vision triumphed over circumstance. Each of the three men had dipped deep into the stream of American hopes; each in his own life had embodied the distinction of obdurate love for a weaker fellow. If Darrow was skeptical of democracy's survival, he was naïvely confident that keeping one's brother healed the keeper as well. He conceived man's nature to be too deeply rooted in nature's animal forms to follow the visions of superior men. Steffens and Broun caught and held contradictory visions of man's central nature—Broun his elastic radiance, Steffens his impersonal plastic response.

II

From his childhood in San Francisco Lincoln Steffens was abnormally susceptible to the power of ideas—ideas of strengthening his mind, being thoroughly honest, and leaving his mark on the world. "Go to, boy," Evelyn Nixon would say to him. "The world is yours. Nothing is done, nothing is known. The greatest poem isn't written yet, the best railroad isn't built yet, the perfect state hasn't been thought of." A horse that required in Steffens perfect self-discipline; an imaginative railroad watchman; the Neely farm; a year of military school; the freedom and trust of a wise father; but best of all Nixon and the Oxford men—these were the ingredients of his boyhood world. Every Saturday evening he would go to Nixon's house to hear them talk:

It was conversation I was hearing, the free, passionate, witty exchanges of studied minds as polished as fine tools. They were always courteous; no two ever spoke together; there were no asides; they all talked to the question before the house . . . When the differences rose the urbanity persisted.[1]

Then followed unsatisfactory years at Berkeley, his curiosity whetted but unsatisfied; then Berlin and Europe through his father's bounty; and then he was back in New York at twenty-six, his honesty unmitigated. "I was just a nice, original American boob," he wrote later, "about to begin unlearning all my learning." But this is too modest. In those years of leisurely loafing Lincoln Steffens had polished a whole kit of intellectual tools with which to disentangle myth and reality in his study of human nature.

For nothing so fascinated Lincoln Steffens as the nature of man shaded in many colors and wrought into strange shapes. At bottom he sought an ethical constant; for two years in Germany he had listened and studied in vain for an ethics grounded in scientific surety. But if he had gained no new belief, he had learned to demolish his old ones without regrets, without insecurity; for he knew that he was slowly building the intellectual foundation on which the dartings of his mind could raise a structure symmetrical and firm. Meanwhile Steffens had acquired an urbanity, a charm, a confidence that most people, even in his early weeks on the *New York Post,* found irresistible. Faced with disillusionment in people, or with the vanities of the mighty, his choice spirits, he did not lose faith in himself. He expected clay in every marble, especially after that day in Munich when he had seen his hero Ibsen smirk and grin at a mirror hidden in his hat. When full of fear, he would be bold; when confident, he would speak softly. To men in high places, as to clubbed strikers, he spoke as an equal, never subservient, never superior. And from the beginning of his reporter's work, people talked easily to Lincoln Steffens. The police station was a better school than Heidelberg: "Many a morning . . . I stood and saw the police bring in and kick out their bandaged, bloody prisoners, not only strikers and foreigners, but thieves, too, and others of the miserable, friendless, troublesome poor."

Early in his reporter career Lincoln Steffens began to adopt what he thought was a scientific attitude toward human nature. *Good* and *bad,* he concluded, were meaningless terms: he looked behind men for the pressures that created them. He learned to like strong men, whether crooked or respectable, whether criminals, bosses, or reformers. What made "strong" men he did not fully elucidate; but he saw in them the drive and energy and resolution necessary to batter down resistance and lead their fellows toward corruption or honesty. To Steffens the supreme virtue was intellectual honesty, wherever found; and next in order of value moral and physical courage; both of these virtues he incorporated in the adjective *strong.* Captain Schmittberger of the New York City police embodied in some degree the strength of personality Steffens admired; and though he was a self-confessed collector of graft, Steffens urged Theodore Roosevelt as police commissioner to put him back on the staff. Steffens argued that because Schmittberger had been absolutely honest in reporting all the graft money he had collected from gambling dens and houses of prostitution, he would be just as reliable in carrying out the orders of superiors who wanted him to find the crooks and bring them in. Schmittberger, insisted Steffens, was strong; with the utmost tenacity he would carry out orders against all opposition. When Steffens' plan of "saving Schmittberger" was finally approved, the "strong" policeman proved his worth: he was absolutely incorruptible; he carried out the most difficult missions with persistent success. Time after time Steffens returns to that theme: that the strong men, especially if they possess imagination, can be channeled into constructive careers; but the rewards of the economic system lie all too frequently in the buying of privilege or the twisting and breaking of the law. "There are outlawed criminals," he wrote, "whom I would like to have in office under me if I were a responsible mayor or governor; as a voter I would prefer certain bold, intelligent bandits to a 'good man' like Mayor Strong or a 'good-natured' general like Commissioner Grant."

As a young reporter Lincoln Steffens observed human nature in abject degradation; and gradually, imbued with the belief that circumstance shapes the lives of men as the sea shapes the line of the shore, he ceased to condemn or praise. One evening an old woman of the slums called him into her one-room apartment to see a prostitute across the way who would not draw her blinds. The old woman's child had crowded to the window and had counted, one night, ninety-three customers. Horrified, the mother could do nothing; her oldest girl had decided upon the prostitute's business herself; when she grew up she too could have beautiful clothes and plenty of food. Then Steffens talked to the prostitute and found that the old woman had reported her and her girls to the police; this degradation of the children was the prostitute's retaliation. Only after threats from Steffens did she agree to cover her window again. But he did not condemn her. To Steffens she, like other criminals, in prison and out, was merely an extension of her environment, inevitably shaped and molded. In Minneapolis and other cities he found that leading citizens had protested the closing of houses of prostitution: it had eliminated the high rents on some of their properties. But Steffens did not condemn the respectable landlords, or any others who corrupted government. He did not condemn the McNamara brothers, who in their despairing hatred of injustice had dynamited the *Los Angeles Times* building. As he sat down to talk with a political boss, a rich corruptionist, or a criminal, he always talked as "one crook to another," conscious always of the conditions, not the merit, that separated one soul from another.

Now and then the skeptical Steffens found a man in whom the persuasion of ideas was infinitely more powerful than the rewards of business, politics, or crime. Tom Johnson, for example, the son of poor parents who had risen to great riches through monopoly, found his soul in torment after reading Henry George's *Social Problems*. To his attorney he said, "I want you to answer that book for me. I can't. And I must. For if that book is right I am all wrong, and I'll have to get out of business." Dissatisfied with the lawyer's answer, Tom Johnson called together a group of rich friends in New York; they, too, read the book and argued over it all of one night; but in the end Henry George had won them over, too. Returning to Cleveland, Tom Johnson sold his business and gradually became, as a disciple of Henry George, the symbol of reform. None of the old rewards could tempt him now; he wanted to make Cleveland a city without corruption, without monopoly. He found not only that "the ethics and morals of politics are higher than those of business," but running a great city like Cleveland, of which he became the mayor, was more of a challenge to intelligence than even the largest private business. It was more fun, too; for fat Tom Johnson was a jolly reformer, and for him the wine of life was always red. Though in the end he was defeated, and Cleveland returned to corruption, Tom Johnson had made his mark upon a turbulent democracy. "Honesty is not enough," wrote Steffens; "it takes intelligence, some knowledge or theory of economics, courage, strength, will power, humor, leadership—it takes intellectual integrity to solve our political problems. And these Tom Johnson had above all the politicians of my day."[2]

Other men Lincoln Steffens found, too, in whom the vision of a better world wrought more magic than the glistening rewards of the real one. There was Rudolph Spreckels, for example, who had also deserted his class to make his vision a reality. No baseness in the nature of man could surprise Spreckels; as a youth he had seen his father's machinery destroyed by the paid agents of his competitor, his own employees; he had known his father's bookkeeper to provide his competitor with valuable information. Yet Spreckels was not deceived into bitterness and cynicism; he knew the compulsions that make crooked both the rich and the poor; he was an idealist with no illusions. Then there was the elder LaFollette; Steffens went to him cynical but came away trustful and humble. By sheer tenacity and fanatic sincerity LaFollette had beaten one machine after another. Not only that: in Steffens' view he had built up a machine of idealists as staunch as himself. In the audiences he would watch for the faces that lighted up, for vigorous young men who also hated injustice; these he would call together after the meeting and organize them into a local unit to support his policies.

Still another idealist was Judge Ben Lindsey. One day in Denver, after he had pronounced sentence upon a boy, the boy's mother gave forth a cry that stabbed the judge's heart. After a retrial, with the mother as a witness, he let the boy go; then he went to see the jail to which he had been sending Denver's young delinquents, a graduate school of crime and vice; he visited the homes and the slum neighborhoods where the boys grew and breathed and thought. The trail of evil led back not to people, but to *conditions*, conditions that would have to be transformed if delinquency were to vanish. The bad boys had only copied the beliefs and attitudes of their elders. At first Ben Lindsey won many victories, even against conditions; but when at last the word was passed along by the political bosses to the economic bosses that they could no longer control votes if Lindsey won, respectable people turned against him, and even the ministers attacked his applied Christianity. But Ben Lindsey did not retreat; he carried his fight to the legislature; he fought the utility bosses and the coal bosses, patiently explaining his aims to the workers and their growing children. He was an idealist who would not quit; an idealist who traced back one effect after another to the impersonal causes, the evil soil from which bad boys and bad men grow.

Whereas other intelligent men, even Mark Twain in his deepest pessimism, sought to explain political corruption in terms of man's innate greed and selfishness, Lincoln Steffens probed deeper into

the heart of things. As he went from city to city, from St. Louis to
Minneapolis to Pittsburgh to Philadelphia to Cincinnati, he discovered patterns repeating themselves. In each city he found bribery,
corruption, protection of crime, as in New York; in each city he
found a political boss by whom the graft was distributed and
appointments made; in each city a traction company, a railroad, a
bank, real estate owners, in various combinations, who supplied
money to the political boss, their agent. The really big corruption,
the buying of a franchise, a public service commission, the buying
of judges and governors, he traced inevitably to respectable businessmen who needed a political boss and votes to gain their
ends. Economic power, in Steffens' view, normally overrides political
power; the few men with money, as Charles Beard was to show in
The Economic Basis of Politics and William Allen White in *A Certain Rich Man,* can buy enough votes or legislatures or judges to
win the prizes they covet, despite the intermittent protests and
victories of the reformers. Here and there, yes, one finds a Bob
LaFollette or a Tom Johnson with the intelligence, the appeal, and
the tenacity to win a victory over the economic interests, or even a
series of victories; but in a short time after any such victory has
been won, with the economic interests, the respectable businessmen,
applying the money pressure in season and out, the wheel turns
at the slightest public relaxation, and the oligarchy of wealth puts
its men in office again.

But Lincoln Steffens found that he liked the political bosses and
the businessmen who paid their bills for the buying of privilege.
He found them no better and no worse than himself or other people
in what were considered more respectable walks of life. He liked
the rich timberman, Weyerhauser, who had the courts declare logs
boats so that he could float them down the rivers; he liked the
bosses, Cox of Cincinnati, Croker of New York, Lomasny of Boston,
Durham of Philadelphia, Herrin of California; he liked Patrick
Calhoun, the immaculate southern gentleman, skilled in the manners and customs of corruption, who came to San Francisco to break
simultaneously the labor unions and the graft prosecution then in

progress. Given the situations in which these men found themselves, and the training to which they had been subjected, Steffens felt that he would have directed his energies in the same channels as they. C. P. Huntington and William F. Herrin of California found it necessary to control first the legislature and then the commission that in theory regulated their railroads. "So they are going to regulate the railroads, eh?" said Huntington. "Well, then, the railroads must regulate the regulators." Lincoln Steffens "admitted the compulsion" of this process; he looked for evil not in men, but in things, in the availability of prizes and rewards. "All discussion of public ownership is foolish," wrote Steffens: "either the State will own and operate the railroads and other public utilities or these public corporations will own and govern the State." To cut the root of evil, Steffens continued, was to put temptation beyond reach: "To put in prison a man who bought government to get a street railway franchise was wrong; we should put the franchise where men can't get it."

Steffens came to regard evil as the impersonal system which dominated the lives of men; it was not men who created the evil; it was the system which stamped men in its image, the system of purchased privilege. In explaining this process, Tom Johnson was Steffens' best teacher. "First you thought it was bad politicians," Johnson told him,

who turned out to be pretty good fellows. Then you blamed the bad business men who bribed the good fellows, till you discovered that not all business men bribed and that those who did were pretty good business men. The little business men didn't bribe; so you settled upon, you invented, the phrase "big business" . . . Hell! Can't you see that it's privileged business that does it? Whether it's a big steam railroad that wants a franchise or a little gambling-house that wants not to be raided, a temperance society that wants a law passed, a poor little prostitute, or a big merchant occupying an alley for storage—it's those who seek privileges who corrupt. . . . It is privilege that causes evil in this world, not wickedness; and not men.[3]

And privilege was impersonal, like a waterway, or a street with thousands of people, an alley for storage, or a franchise for fifty years, or a monopoly of copper or wheat, or a mortgage foreclosure.

Nowhere did Lincoln Steffens state his theory of the impersonality of evil more dramatically than in his talk with the business leaders of Los Angeles. To this select group he spoke what was to him a central reality: "You cannot build or operate a railroad, or a street railway, gas, water, or power company, develop and operate a mine, or get forests and cut timber on a large scale, or run any privileged business, without corrupting or joining in the corruption of the government." The question of the group was, "Who started the evil?" Steffens replied that the enemy was not *who* but *what*, not a person but a thing: "If it was some Thing that hurt us we could be Christians and forgive sinners; we could cease from punishing men and develop an environment in which men would be tempted to be good." But this kind of reasoning was lost on the businessmen; they wanted Steffens to place the blame on the politicians for allowing themselves to be corrupted, and they feared the inefficiency of public ownership. But William Milholland, manager of Los Angeles' public waterworks, was in the room; formerly manager of the privately-owned waterworks, he had frequently testified that public ownership had taken him and the waterworks *out* of politics. Still, everyone except Steffens wanted to pin the blame for existing evil on people. "Who started it all?" they would ask. Then Steffens told his story of the apple. In the Garden of Eden story, Adam said Eve was to blame, but Eve blamed the serpent. Thereafter the theologians blamed Satan. But Steffens had a different version; the real villain of the Garden of Eden was the apple itself.

From his long observation of human nature Lincoln Steffens emerged with impulses of hope and promise as well as of tolerance and sympathy. To him the deficiencies of democracy lay not in men, but in circumstance. And the circumstance was the lack of democracy, not the excess of it, the national failure to extend into the economic realm the fine theories of political declarations; in short, placing the rewards of economic power beyond the reach of men. As the roots of evil men lay in circumstance, to transform them meant only to change the circumstances.

III

Bending early, like Lincoln and Holmes, toward a rational and skeptical explanation of human behavior, Clarence Darrow for over half a century probed ceaselessly into the nature of man. From boyhood, under the example of his learned, inquisitive father, he had espoused submerged causes in community life; when he turned to the law, and studied the lives of criminals under the manifold buffets of circumstance, he had no heart for the prosecution; rather he taught his jurymen, and eventually millions of Americans, to trace the roots of human aberrations to the terrible impersonal soil from which they sprang. In such a mind as Darrow's the search for truth was never final; after infinite toil and patience his knowledge of the human organism was still murky and clouded. But like Lincoln, Holmes, and Steffens, he emerged from his inspection of man with a renunciation of human responsibility and an enlargement of his charity. If no one could trace the infinite variations of heredity in fashioning the human structure, and no thoughtful man could blame the criminal for his early environment, who was to judge with certainty the guilt of the human vessel? For the undeniable weaknesses of man's nature, whether manufactured or inborn, Clarence Darrow felt only infinite patience; but unlike Bellamy and Broun, he expressed no great hope for the ultimate extension of man's rational faculties to the soul of institutions.

In *The Story of My Life*, praising Warren Harding for pardoning Eugene Debs, Darrow wrote, "The truth is, no man is white and no man is black. We are all freckled." No words Darrow spoke epitomize more exactly his justification of man's ways before the tribunal of opinion or a jury of his peers. To Darrow, as to Whitman, men are roughly equal in moral stature; no man was to him a criminal, and no man a saint. A criminal was merely the transmitter of evil, not its origin; he was in fact in no way responsible for the crime, just as the upright man could claim no merit for his blameless life. The upright man was a transmitter, too, a transmitter of a cultural outlook he did not create through a brain he was not responsible for. "We are all freckled." In answer to the question, "Is man fundamentally dishonest?" Darrow again put forth his belief that man is an agent without moral color, like a steam boiler. The boiler "is neither honest nor dishonest,—it stands for a certain pressure, and no more. Man cannot be classified as honest or dishonest—he goes along with the game of life and can stand a certain pressure for his ideals, but at a certain point he can stand no more."

To Clarence Darrow man had arisen from the animal world stamped so irrevocably with the physical processes of the animal organism that "reason has little to do with human action." The activity of the reason is spasmodic, that of man's animal functions constant and powerful. Like Holmes, Darrow pointed to the many processes of the body altogether untouched by human decision— the automatic actions of the heart, the stomach, the intestines. The first instinct of man is to preserve his life; the second, to perpetuate his kind. Not only does nature incorporate in man's structure physical processes and needs that easily overwhelm his acquired rationality; she determines in advance the quality of his adaptatory equipment. "Life begins with the cell," wrote Darrow in *Crime, Its Cause and Treatment,*

and evolves according to pattern. If the cell is that of a human being, it will be black or white, male or female, tall or short, intelligent or stupid, sensitive or stolid; it will develop a large or small brain, a fine one or a poor one, a sensitive nervous system or a defective one. . . . The whole structure, potentially, is in the original cell.[4]

In creating a defective nervous system, a faulty brain structure, or abnormal glands, nature takes the first step in creating a potential criminal; that is, nature makes adaptation to *any* environment enormously difficult. Such a man, limited by nature, responds more readily to criminal influences than does a perfect human structure.

Though Darrow denied the existence of a criminal type, he was always conscious of the insistent push of heredity including the activity of intelligence; he assumed what twentieth-century psychologists were to postulate with less and less assurance: that intelligence cannot be heightened or diminished by environmental fac-

tors. "Heredity," wrote Darrow, "has everything to do with making
the machine strong and capable, or weak and useless; but when
the machine is made and thrown on the world in its imperfect
shape, environment has everything to do in determining what its
fate shall be." What struck Darrow as an almost universal phenomenon was that criminals appeared to have faulty mental and
physical equipment; he noted also that they spent their formative
years in impoverished homes; but he did not record any belief that
their poverty had diminished their intelligence. "In a broad sense,"
he wrote, "some criminals are born and some are made. Nearly all of
them are both born and made. This does not mean that criminality
can be inherited, or even that there is a criminal type. It means that
with certain physical and mental imperfections and with certain
environment the criminal will be the result." Darrow's assumptions
about the genetic imperfections of man's nature correspond roughly
with those of Holmes and Lincoln; he is strikingly less sanguine
about the pervasive conquests of environment than Mann, Bellamy,
and John Dewey. "Crime," Darrow concluded, "results from defective heredity when applied to the environment. It comes from the
inability of the machine to make the necessary adjustments of life."
Though he admitted the prevalence of organic deficiencies among
criminals, he noted also the tendency of inheritance to maintain
normal intelligence. In a *Preface to the Universe* he made one of
his most optimistic statements about human nature: "Nature, the
great communist, provides that the treasures of genius, like her
own bountiful gifts of sunlight, rain, and air, shall remain the common property of all her children."

Darrow ventured no estimate on the relative weight of heredity
and environment in the scales of human destiny. Far from an
unswerving environmentalist, he had repeatedly blamed structural
deficiencies for the adaptatory ineptitude implicit, he thought, in
most criminal patterns. But in a brilliant analysis of the Jukes and
Edwards families published in the *American Mercury* for October,
1925, he subjected the conclusions of the geneticists to devastating
scrutiny, denouncing the simplification of genetic theory to explain

either brilliance or depravity. How can anyone trace the influence of original germ plasm through forty thousand Edwards descendants and cull its effects from those of other family strains? The irrefragable proof of genetic strains Darrow found shaky with superstition. The depravity of the Jukeses could not be shown to be hereditary; even feeble-mindedness, the geneticists now admitted, was not necessarily inherited. To Darrow the poverty, ignorance, and isolation of the Jukeses was sufficient to explain their long history of delinquency and squalor. Of both the Jukeses and the Edwardses he concluded, "Why go out of the way to even infer that the germ-plasm had anything to do with either case?" But this conclusion, however compelling in a particular argument, we cannot accept as final in Darrow's thought; he was too deeply aware of the inherent structural blemishes of the men he had defended; he constantly assumed, moreover, the doubtful principle that the organic deficiencies of men make them more susceptible to the temptations of crime than they are to the appeal of constructive remunerative endeavor.

However doubtful and shifting the proportionate powers of heredity and environment, Darrow believed man responds mechanically to the pressures of circumstance, transmuting food, instincts, ideas, images, into inevitable action and speech. Debating with Will Durant in 1927, Darrow affirmed that man, like a tree, like an animal, is a machine; that is, "an apparatus so designed that it can change one kind of energy into another." In the body food and drink are transferred automatically into energy to move arms and legs, energy to think, to feel. Alfred Asgis interpreted Darrow's position with rough accuracy when he accused Mark Twain of believing that "the exuberant vitality of Tom Sawyer was simply the effervescence of a carbon compound!" Evading the issue of man's unmechanistic powers of growing and reproducing, Darrow called man "a mechanistic organism." He had shown, it is true, that life cannot exist without fuel and that many of the processes of the body, as Holmes had said, function automatically; but he had not proved that life and reproduction can be reduced to physical and chemical explanations. Nevertheless, like Thomas Huxley, Darrow would be content with no other elucidation of the roots of life; he awaited an extension of Huxley's description of protoplasm as the logical probing of the mystery of renewal. To Darrow the words *will* and *consciousness* were meaningless terms. Man was a machine, or an organism, if you will, with his innermost mechanical parts still untallied. When Durant asked, "Is human behavior of the same order as the erosion of the hills, or the flight of the winds, or the obstinate tides of the sea?" Darrow did not reply aloud; but his definition of man compelled an emphatic assent.[5]

Darrow did not expand to logical lengths his conception of man as an energy-transforming machine; nor, like Henry George, did he apply the conception of quantitative intellectual power to the ebb and flow of civilization. As an organism man requires food for survival and perpetuation. But food is only one form of energy. Streams of nervous energy converge on the growing youth—the energy of parents, community, teachers, all seeking his intellectual or emotional allegiance. Upon the youth no impact of personality, no glance, no image, word, admonition, is wholly lost; to them all he responds with the energy of thought, action, belief, gestures, emotions, yielding, resisting, combining, absorbing.

When energy is applied to materials, when bricklayers, carpenters, plumbers, apply their energies to the building of a house, no blow is lost, no fling of the trowel, blow of the hammer, turn of the wrench. Similarly, when energy gained from food processes is applied to personality, every impact leaves its mark: a glance at the dinner table, an erect posture of a teacher, the reading of a poem. Even the reading of a book may bring tears to the eyes, a fast beat to the heart, a resolution to the mind; and tomorrow's action presses hard upon the thought of today. If, then, man's organism responds with mechanical certainty to the application of energy, his plasticity, his education—in the sense of constructive conditioning in the direction of Aristotle's ideal man—or any other ideal may be accelerated and intensified by the further application of energy to his personality. Only the energies of chemistry can push him to the peak of his physical powers; only the energies of superior teachers can project him into new intellectual and creative attainments. The energies of the state's material resources may be transformed not only into rare teachers, but also into travel, into music, into the glorious portraits of the Louvre, or into the incomparable splendor of the Grand Canyon, with no image wholly lost, no color wholly faded.

To Darrow, then, all human actions spring from a chain of cause, some links plainly discernible, others hidden in a past infinitely remote. No thought exists without an origin, a whole chain of ancestors; no response without a stimulus; no stimulus without the impact of energy. "Each human soul," he wrote in *Resist Not Evil*, "is the irresponsible, unconscious product of all that has gone before." Caught in the stream of sequence and consequence, of responses he cannot govern and stimuli he did not create, man is like "a grain of sand tossed by an angry sea." Man is a compound of mechanical responses to the capricious streams of the world's energy. "A man is like a tree," wrote Darrow, "bent back and forth by the storm. If a storm is hard enough, sooner or later it will break. Which way a tree falls has nothing to do with the consciousness of the tree, but has to do with the prevailing and contrary force." Man is a focus of forces, forces antagonistic or friendly to each other, but in the words of Thomas Hardy loveless and hateless; man's choice is only the expression of the superior force.

If man is such an organism, responsive only to energy and circumstance, the way to the creation of a more humane citizen is by a reorganization and redirection of the forces that control his personality. This was the hope of Jefferson and Mann, George and Bellamy. But Darrow proposed no educational or social blueprint for the redistribution of society's energies. The shaky points of the social structure he pointed out unerringly; but he was pessimistic about either amelioration or reconstruction. He had observed that the number of criminals increases with the price of food; he had voiced his belief that if work were plentiful, jails would close; he had pointed out that the ownership of men and the ownership of land and necessities are inseparable; he had asserted that every mechanical invention rivets more surely the power of the owners over the lives of the propertyless. But Darrow had neither any expectation of peaceful change nor sympathy with revolution; his only concrete proposal was the elimination of expenditures for the armed services, which he claimed would alone be sufficient to banish dire poverty and crime.

IV

When Heywood Broun died, on December 18, 1939, his spirit was still youthful, his faith in man still eager. Since 1927, and his words on the Sacco-Vanzetti verdict, "It is death condemning life!" Broun had sounded day by day an indomitable naïve assurance of the march of the humble from obscurity to fulfilment. Unlike that of the skeptical Darrow and the surpriseless Steffens, Broun's faith in the magic of images never wavered; the slow inexorable grind of economic motives would ultimately yield its course before the ringing onslaught of ideas.

To such an idealist as Broun the brotherhood of man was a reality sired by dreams and pregnant with the limitless progeny of an Athenian America. To the scientific validity of the potential of uncommon men in the American experiment, Broun gave not a fragment of his energy. Rather he was an asserter, an affirmer of hopes, pointing his daily column with the resolutions of his heroes—Jesus, Jefferson, Lincoln, John Brown, Bellamy, Wilson, Debs, Sacco and Vanzetti. But ageless enigmas spoke with the voices of humbler heroes, too—the voice of the redcap, the Harvard scrubwoman, the first robin, the unknown soldier, Ruth Hale, and Wesley Hill, the Gabriel of *The Green Pastures*.

Unlike Zola, Dreiser, and Farrell, Heywood Broun found no lasting fascination in plumbing the animal depths of man's nature or tracing in his behavior the pulls and strains of an ugly world. Not that he was unaware, or that he was always voiceless in explaining the roots of man's cruelty. "On the night Dillinger was shot," he wrote, "any man from Mars could have pointed out to you upon this earth a thousand incubators in which his successors were being reared." For the evil in man's nature Broun looked, like Darrow and Steffens, to the impersonal inexorables. "Public Enemy No. 1 is not a man," he wrote. "It is a tenement house . . . a farm precariously held, or indeed any spot or spots where misery is salted into the wounds of the desperate and the despairing." In capital punishment Broun, like Darrow, saw the focusing of community savagery, the release of primitive sadism flowing back again from the cell of the criminal to the heart of the public: "We are all a little dirtier and meaner and more cruel because of the shock." When had the condemned murderer ever been free to choose a better life? The straps of the electric chair were only the last of the tight, warping bonds that had confined his spirit from the day of his birth. We should weep, not for the criminal, but for the world that fashioned him.

Nor was Broun willing to put responsibility on the leaders in high places, warped and twisted as he conceived them to be. For them, too, the excuse of circumstance obtained. On occasion, it is true, Broun attacked with the ardor and scorn of a prophet. When President Lowell, after serving on Governor Fuller's commission, expressed no dissent from the condemnation of Sacco and Vanzetti, Broun wrote: "What more can these immigrants from Italy expect? It is not every prisoner who has a President of Harvard University throw the switch for him." Henceforth Harvard should be known as "Hangman's House." Of Governor Fuller Broun said, "The justice of the business was not his concern. He hoped to make it respectable." Five years later, however, when Broun reviewed his old columns on the Sacco-Vanzetti case, he found that he could not hate even A. Lawrence Lowell; he found it impossible to fix responsibility on a few people, or even a few thousands. "My whole idea of human motivation and of the nature of the whole broad road to salvation," he wrote, "has changed utterly. No longer do I believe that the fault lies with individual tyrants and gross villains." The death of the innocent men he now traced to the hate, the passion, the hysteria of the hour; from these springs of poison might have emerged a thousand Lowells. "The poor fish peddler and the good shoemaker were victims of hate. I know that more hate will not bring them back."[6]

Broun was a less realistic calculator of the virulence of hatred than Mark Twain or Clarence Darrow or Lincoln Steffens; nor could he visualize, as had John Dewey in *Human Nature and Conduct*, the sturdy repetitiousness of institutionalized behavior. Against these patterns, molded not by fixed elements in human nature but by the continuance of institutions, the fists of the idealist pound in vain. But Broun drew so constantly upon his heroes of love and tolerance, set their ideal so persistently before his readers, that he could visualize neither the ultimate extensions of human cruelty nor the limitations of good will. In his recurring dreams for a rational world to come, the symbols of brotherhood writ themselves too large.

At times, it is true, Broun was overwhelmed by the long gap between the vision and the reality. In his memorable essay, "There Is a Ship," he flounders in despair, almost too bitter to unburden his heart. Nine hundred passengers on the *St. Louis,* men, women, and children, homeless and nationless, are seeking one oasis of good will in the Western Hemisphere. But no country will enfold or even tolerate them; they must return to the maelstrom of horror. "There is a ship," he wrote. "And almost two thousand years have elapsed since the message of universal brotherhood was brought to earth. What have we done with the message? . . . Nine hundred are to suffer a crucifixion while the world passes by on the other side." A sudden sinking would be more merciful than our averted eyes. For are we not imposing upon them a death infinitely more horrible than the oblivion of the sea?[7]

But in the mind of Heywood Broun the whisper of faith would not be stilled. Like a candle out of a dark room, mankind would some day emerge, after the example of some of its members, from the caverns of savagery to the embodiment of brotherhood. Like Bellamy in *Looking Backward* and Howells in *Altruria,* Broun spoke always for potentialities rather than the actualities of the human organism. Reason may be only one small part of man's ends. In his essay, "In the Image of God," Broun affirmed again the triumph of the human spirit over agony and catastrophe. However many people may "cast man down rather than raise him up," human beings are infinitely resilient: "Who says that man is puny? He falls asleep and dies awhile and then he is up again." He survives floods, earthquakes, desolation, sorrow, the eternal hostility of nature. After each flood of water or flood of despair man gathers his hopes, plants his feet, looks up to the sun again. Survival of the flesh embodies the survival of man's dreams, and "all men live with the hope that one day they may touch greatness."

The projection of Broun's hopes for man's realization of himself came to rest insistently on the personality of Jesus. Here was a man who embodied all the cures for a sick world. In his imaginative sketch of Pilate, "The Procurator Writes," Broun characterizes Jesus as the destroyer of both classes and nations, the destroyer of hate itself. As Pilate chooses between the world of the Roman sword and Jesus' dream of brotherhood, the old wound in his shoulder begins to ache and he remembers the glory of Roman arms, the proud march of Roman feet. Nationalist and oppressor that he is, Pilate understands the power of agitation: "An idea can cut through shields which javelins would never pierce." And before him stands a man speaking for a "world in which the meanest slave could pluck a Roman by the sleeve and call him brother." As Pilate hesitates, Jesus smiles. "It was a friendly smile," wrote Broun, "almost as if he were saying. 'Make either choice, I will understand.' "[8]

The compassion of these words, undiminished by the renunciation of Pilate or the taunts of Jesus' enemies, Broun hugged to his heart as the supreme virtue, the goal of ethics and institutions, the solvent of all conflict and the salve of all wounds. He called Jesus "the first and greatest teacher of democracy." To Broun the compassion of Jesus was infinitely more revolutionary than the fiery fervor of communism. Yet in what country had love triumphed? Its yield seemed worlds remote from the deeds of churches or the

actions of the State Department. Still, year by year, almost month
by month, Broun returned to his vision of triumphant love. In his
essay, "Even to Judas," he asserted anew the triumph of compassion over the betrayal of Judas at the Last Supper. "Good-will toward
men," concluded the dominie, "means good-will to every last son
of God. Peace on earth means peace to Pilate, peace to the thieves
on the cross, and peace to poor Iscariot."

To many critics Heywood Broun's exaltation of compassion as
the supreme virtue possessed no more validity in a world of conflict
than the visions of Shelley or the romantic quest of St. Francis.
Notwithstanding the noble sentiments of manifestoes, victories in a
democracy are won only by the marshalling of forces, the extensions
of economic pressures into political advantages. Good will is only
weakness; good will and compassion mean annihilation. But Broun
denied that the tactics of democratic forces are incompatible with
the gospel of love. Defeat your enemy; but love him still. "I admit,"
he wrote, "that maybe it is a mean and most annoying attitude not
to give back hate for hate, but I could name upon my toes and
fingers a score of individuals to whom I could earnestly say, "Why,
damn your dirty hide, I love you." Like Darrow, Broun asserted
that the human organism for its blossoming, for its health, requires
the food of love. Like Darrow also, he insisted that a law impelled
by hatred and cruelty is twisted, as Emerson said, into a rope of
sand, or reaps in turn only bitterness and despair. Is love an unsci-
entific medicine for the criminal or the slum dweller? "I see no
reason," wrote Broun, "why we should go on constantly engaged in
the wholesale manufacture of a criminal class. We plant the seed
and reap the crop and in our city slums there is never a field which
lies fallow for a season." On erring man should fall the love and
good will we mouth on Christmas Day. The courts should love, too,
and the police, and the judges in high places; and laws should be
bright with the love of erring man.

In their analysis of the nature of man, Darrow, Broun, and
Steffens struck common ground at two points: each believed that

conditions shape the destiny of men; and each believed in the efficacy of compassion. In their rejection of man's free choice Steffens and Darrow are categorical; Broun makes clear his position only in his analysis of crime.

Of the three men Darrow was most aware of the limitations of the human organism, Broun of its potentialities. To Darrow man was three-fourths selfish, one-fourth unselfish; to Broun man's aspirations soared without effort, his rational faculties expanded with easy leaps. "Man is nature's last and most perfect work," wrote Darrow,

but, however high his development . . . , he is yet a child of the earth and the rude forces that have formed all the life that exists thereon. He cannot separate himself from the environment that gave him birth, and a thousand ties of nature bind him back to the long forgotten past and prove his kinship to all the lower forms of life that have sprung from the great universal mother, Earth.[9]

A deeper student of biology than either Steffens or Broun, Darrow also knew "the stages of all life" more intimately than they. Whereas he drew his portrait of man from the courtroom and the prison, Broun was ever seeking embodiment of the high reaches of the human spirit. On his fifty-first birthday, only nine days before his death, Broun wrote: "At fifty-one I have more faith than I ever had before. People are better than I thought they were going to be, myself included." More assertive and buoyant than either Darrow or Steffens, Broun was less scientific and thorough than they in his study of human nature.

Steffens' long study of man led him always to the conditions beyond; for the unlocking of man's secret chambers, for illumination of his strange contradictions, Steffens studied the intricacies of the imagery that fashioned child and man, rejecting as undecipherable or relatively impotent the impact of genetic characters. Of the three men Steffens possessed the most disciplined mind, the superior poise and judgment in social analysis; of the three men he was the surest architect of his intellectual structure, secure in his few premises, neither wavering nor retreating, his resolute probing of motives neither colored by extreme hopes nor diminished by despair. As clearly as any writer of industrial America, Steffens fused the scientific probing of man's nature with the great backlog of democratic expectations—expectations that Darrow distrusted and Broun maintained.

1924

The Loeb-Leopold Case

On May 21, 1924, on the South Side of Chicago, Nathan Leopold and Richard Loeb got in a rented car, with Leopold driving and Loeb sitting in the back seat, and drove along Ellis Street and around the Harvard School. They had planned a kidnapping together, had already written a ransom note, and were looking for a small boy as their victim. When Bobby Franks (thirteen years old) came along on his way home from school, Leopold stopped the car beside him. Loeb, whom Bobby knew, persuaded him to drive with them around the block. Bobby Franks got into the front seat beside Leopold. Within ten minutes after the car moved off, Loeb struck Bobby over the head with a taped chisel. When Bobby struggled and fought, Loeb grabbed him, pulled him into the back seat, and stuck a gag into his mouth. In a few minutes the boy was dead. After wrapping their bleeding victim in a blanket and waiting for half-darkness, Loeb and Leopold drove to a secluded place in the marshes, undressed their victim, poured acid over his face and genitals, and stuffed his body into a culvert in a swampland near 118th Street and the Pennsylvania Railroad tracks.[1]

A pair of eyeglasses dropped by Leopold near the culvert led eventually to the identification of the murderers. Under questioning Loeb was the first to confess. When Leopold heard that Loeb was confessing, he also broke down and gave a much more explicit and detailed version of the story than that of Loeb.

The confessions were made on May 31, 1924. The trial of Loeb and Leopold began on July 23, with a plea of guilty on the part of the defense led by Clarence Darrow. Since a plea of guilty legally

287

assumed an admission of sanity and the avoidance of a jury trial, Darrow confined his defense to a plea for mitigation of sentence, a normal procedure in such cases. Although the boys, he maintained, were not legally insane, they were emotionally abnormal. In his plea for mitigation of sentence, Darrow analyzed the reports of the various alienists and psychiatrists who had examined both boys. Leopold, who was nineteen at the time of the crime, had been a precocious baby, having taken his first step at two months and uttered his first words at four months. In intelligence tests his score was between 200 and 210.

Possessed of enormous mental and physical energy, Leopold grew up undersized, moody, and introspective, resenting the derision of his older brothers, and concentrating even in his early years on attaining intellectual superiority, stifling normal expression of his feelings in favor of a rigid intellectual self-discipline. Darrow called him a "half-boy"; he was never a boy's boy. Neither he nor Loeb learned as children the consequences of lying, sadism, deceit, or hatred. Leopold graduated at nineteen and was doing graduate work in law at the time of the murder. Generally unpopular socially, he had become an expert in bird lore and had made hundreds of trips for the study of birds in the marshes where the body of Bobby Franks was stuffed into the culvert.[2]

Unlike his friend Leopold, Richard Loeb was relatively tall, broad, and athletic. As a child he also had been precocious. Like Leopold, he entered the University of Chicago at fourteen, graduated at eighteen, and was doing graduate work at the university at the time of the murder.

From an early age Loeb had been fascinated by detective stories. He often pictured himself as a detective outwitting the criminal. As he grew older and mastered one subject after another, he nevertheless always preferred detective stories to literature, history, or psychology. The fantasies of his childhood about committing the perfect crime never lost their hold upon his imagination.

Loeb and Leopold were both sons of lawyers and knew each other through social contacts. Loeb was extremely popular with both boys and girls. Thrust into the sophisticated atmosphere of college students when he was fourteen, Loeb had had his first sexual experience at fifteen. When he was sixteen, Loeb became the idol of Leopold, who, though more brilliant than his friend, felt that Loeb possessed everything worth-while that had been denied to him. Loeb was popular, handsome, dashing, daring, imaginative. Leopold was not handsome; he was reserved, combative in conversation, unpopular with girls, often arrogant in his discussions with minds he considered inferior. Leopold became increasingly devoted to Loeb, finally agreeing to carry out any order that Loeb might impose upon him.

By this time, through imitation of Loeb, Leopold had experimented sexually with various girl pickups near the campus. Neither Loeb nor Leopold was a true homosexual. They did, however, experiment with sexual relations, which gradually became from all accounts much more important to Leopold than to Loeb. Leopold so idolized Loeb that, although he had no stomach for criminal action, he agreed to commit any crime as directed by Loeb on condition that this crime would be followed by a sexual experience with him.

In their early criminal escapades together Loeb and Leopold stole automobiles, smashed windshields, threw a brick through a store window, set fire to an abandoned shack, and stole valuables from fraternity brothers at the fraternity house. When the two easily escaped detection in these crimes, Loeb then proposed to Leopold a perfect kidnapping and murder. Leopold was so completely attached to Loeb that he agreed unhesitatingly to this action. Later, after many years in prison, Leopold affirmed that the sexual association he had with Loeb was of supreme importance in his willingness to commit the crime.[3]

In the trial of Loeb and Leopold, the confessed murderers reacted to everything with levity or contempt. One photograph of the trial shows Loeb grinning broadly and Leopold smiling while behind him sits Leopold's gray-haired father looking at the floor, his head in his hands. In the joint medical report issued under the

*leadership of Dr. William A. White, the psychiatrists declared that
Leopold "conceives himself as a superior being, quite set apart and
not called on to be amenable to the social regulations or legal
restrictions which govern the ordinary human being."⁴ As a child
he did not have the normal sympathy for animals, children, or
human beings. The joint report declared that Leopold early rejected
"God, conscience, sympathy, social responsibility and loyalty as
being thoroughly unnecessary to him."⁵*

*As Leopold grew older and absorbed Nietzsche as one would
a prophet, he thought more and more of himself as a superman
whose pleasure and ego were of such dignity and meaning as to
obliterate all ordinary considerations of responsibility. At the age
of nineteen, according to the medical report, his emotional development was comparable to a nine-year-old's. He was proud of being
cold and distant. Moreover, "he had considerable interest in the
thought of observing himself as a murderer."⁶ In his conversations
with psychiatrists Leopold said that he wove Loeb into his life of
fantasy as an ideal man. He made a chart of the ideal man in
which Loeb scored 90, Leopold only 62. Leopold told the physicians
that he had an "almost complete identification of myself with Dick.
It was a blind hero worship."⁷*

*In Clarence Darrow's summation to the court, which occupied
several days, he attempted to show that the planning and execution
of the crime were the products of diseased minds. As he spoke,
Darrow was in a sense synthesizing not only his knowledge of this
particular crime but also his knowledge of the nature of man in
criminal action. What makes a boy a criminal? What made these
boys criminals? They were highly intelligent; in fact, thought Darrow, they had been "crowded like hothouse plants, to learn more
and more and more."⁸ To Darrow the important thing in creating
a responsible person was not the developing of the intelligence but
the training of the emotions. "It takes something besides brains,"
he said to the court,*

to make a human being who can adjust himself to life. . . . Brains are not the chief essential in human conduct.... The emotions are the urge that makes us live; the urge that makes us work or play, or move along the pathways of life.... The question of intellect means the smallest part of life. Back of this are man's nerves, muscles, heart, blood, lungs—in fact, the whole organism; the brain is the least part in the human development. Without the emotion-life man is nothing.[9]

Darrow pointed out that neither Loeb nor Leopold had normal emotional responses. In terms of emotional growth they were stunted and deformed—so much so, in fact, that they could not understand why people were so horrified at their action.

In analyzing the deficiencies of Loeb and Leopold, Darrow returned to the theme of the relative nature of man's responsibility, a theme which he had argued again and again in courtrooms across the land. Who or what was responsible for Loeb's unscrupulousness, his ingratitude, his disloyalties? Who or what was responsible for Leopold's obsessions with his own genius, his own fleeting satisfactions at the expense of a little boy's life? Of all the many factors and combinations of factors that made Richard Loeb, which one was to blame? Was Loeb to blame if he had been born with a deficient nervous system? As for himself, continued Darrow, he did not feel that he was wise enough to fix the blame or even to identify the crucial weakness:

It may be defective nerves. It may be a defective heart or liver. It may be defective endocrine glands. I know it is something. I know that nothing happens in this world without a cause.... Intelligent people now know that every human being is the product of the endless heredity back of him and the infinite environment around him.... Under the same stress and storm, you would act one way and I act another, and poor Dickey Loeb another.[10]

At no time in his long career did Darrow point more dramatically to the lack of a true science of man than in his summation at the Loeb and Leopold trial. "We have not been able," he said, "with any satisfaction to peer into the brain and see its workings; to analyze the human system and see where it has gone awry."[11] *The word* mind, *Darrow pointed out, has as yet no specific meaning.*

"Whether it exists or not no one can tell. It cannot be found as you find the brain. Its relation to the brain and the nervous system is uncertain."[12]

Nor do we yet know, insisted Darrow, exactly in what way the emotions and the mind interact with each other. The riddle of human conduct, in Darrow's view, could not be unraveled until science had traced a more accurate picture of the nature and mechanisms of the brain. How do emotions come to birth, grow in volume and intensity, and burst forth in a blaze of violent action? Science as yet could not answer.

Knowing that part of the abnormal interest in the Loeb-Leopold trial was concentrated on the riches of the two boys' families, Darrow spoke on this problem as follows: "The great misfortune in this terrible case is the money. That has destroyed their lives. That has fostered these illusions. That has promoted this mad act. And, if your Honor shall doom them to die, it will be because they are the sons of the rich."[13]

The personalities of Loeb and Leopold brought into focus the necessity for a new search for the origin of violence in adolescent youth. The science of man as yet had very little knowledge of the effect of endocrine glands on the personality of adolescent boys. In a medical sense both boys were abnormal. Leopold had a premature involution of the thymus gland. His thyroid gland was overactive. His adrenal glands did not function. Medical tests showed a "premature calcification of the pineal gland." In the opinion of the physicians, one effect of these abnormalities was to accelerate sex development and precocity about sexual matters. Yet in the several decades that have passed, no study of criminal action has been made which would lead to greater light on the crucial relationship between endocrine glands and personalities capable of violence.

Loeb also showed marked physiological deviations from the normal. He had a subnormal blood pressure. The carbon dioxide content of his blood was low. He had a basal metabolism of -17. Subject to fainting spells, as many as six in one day, Loeb suffered

*tremors, twitchings of the lips, frothings at the mouth in moments
of fainting. Such symptoms indicated in Loeb physical abnormalities that may have been responsible for the unique perversity that
seemed to mark his actions from the time he was a small child.
Medical experts could not agree on the relation of these abnormalities to his criminal tendencies. As his brain developed unusual
powers, his emotions resisted any penetration of normal values, any
initiation of generous action.*

*When Theodore Dreiser said early in his career, "We are only
spring-mouths through which subterranean fluids arise and bubble,"[14] he was thinking of the relentless flow of sexual energy. What
was the relation of sexual energy to high metabolism, such as
Leopold possessed, or to low blood pressure, such as Loeb had?
In what way, if at all, did Leopold's immense sexual drive obliterate
the calculation of possible consequences in the workings of his
superb mind? Science cannot yet answer. It is in the main denied
that either Loeb or Leopold was a true homosexual; yet the immense
sexual energy of Leopold as a boy of sixteen and seventeen was
concentrated on Loeb in both a physical and psychological sense.
This attachment, as Leopold said, more than anything else was
the determining factor in his being willing to join Loeb in the
kidnapping and murder of Bobby Franks. Neither the hereditary
forces of sexual and endocrinal energy, nor the influence of two
malign personalities in the early years of Leopold and Loeb, can
yet be charted, measured, or compared. Certain it is that both boys
were abnormal in nervous organization, a condition Darrow found
in greater or less degree in most of the criminals he had known. It
is also certain that each suffered a block to normal mother-son
relationship in early years through a possessive relationship with a
governess. Leopold's governess came to him when he was three or
four, staying until he was fourteen, an ignorant amoral woman
apparently without scruple, though warm and affectionate, who
aroused Leopold sexually while he was still a child.[15] Loeb's governess came to him when he was eleven, a highly intellectual
person, stern and implacable, who pushed him forward daily into*

new intellectual achievement, not seeing the void in his emotional
life, not knowing the origins of his wilful personality. But the
exact influence of each governess is yet to be described or weighed
in total effect in comparison with other forces, either environmental
or genetic. The methods of Freud, however valuable as half-dogma,
half-science, could as yet suggest only the direction, not the volume,
of subterranean emotional life, especially the hidden life of adolescent youth.[16]

XIV
Veblen and the Mystery of Behavior

> *The instinct of workmanship brought the
> life of mankind from the brute to the human
> plane, and in all the later growth of culture
> it has never ceased to pervade the work
> of man.*
>
> —Veblen

No ECONOMIST in American thought has sought
more painstakingly than Thorstein Veblen to ground his conclusions about society in the science of man, particularly in the
anthropologist's distinction between behavior fixed in the womb
and behavior that is acquired. "A meticulous discrimination between
the two concepts—of habit and heredity—" wrote Veblen in
Imperial Germany and the Industrial Revolution, "is the beginning
of inquiry into human behavior." Hence in all his books Veblen
scans, according to his lights, the original nature of man in primitive society, seeking for that hereditary constant untouched as yet
by cultural strata, even by the concept of ownership.

In this process of reaching back to primitive society for hints
on man's original inheritance, Veblen relied very little upon the yet
scanty investigations of primitive societies by cultural anthropologists. Rather, like Rousseau in his *Essay on the Origin of
Inequality,* he trusted unhesitatingly to his own speculations, speaking with a tone of easy authority on the hereditary constant of man,
citing no scholarly predecessors for his main assumptions, but
nevertheless grounding one economic argument after another on
his portrait of primitive life. Veblen knew that his ultimate position
as an economic thinker would depend on this highly speculative
analysis of man's original equipment. Whether his assumptions

about man will be incorporated into the biological science of the future is still undetermined. But until the prenatal origin of the behavior of man has been traced precisely by the biologists, the speculative thinking of Veblen, even to a greater degree than that of Dreiser, Holmes, and Tocqueville, deserves close scrutiny. For with Veblen the discovery of the original nature of man, in a scientific sense, was a goal of constant search and unremitting reflection; whereas to many of his great predecessors, it was a bypath of conscious endeavor.

The son of immigrants whose families had suffered dispossession of farms in their native Norway, Thorstein Veblen was born on the Wisconsin frontier July 30, 1857, the fourth of twelve children. Like his family and neighbors, Thorstein as a youth was proud of his Norwegian background and made little attempt to speak English until he entered Carleton College Academy at the age of seventeen. He was a lank, ungainly, peculiar lad, unpredictable and queer even to his family, who early recognized his superior intelligence and feared his caustic tongue. At Carleton College, where he began his undergraduate work three years later, he made no friends except Ellen Rolfe, niece of the president, and John Bates Clark, his professor of political economy, both of whom perceived the remarkable intellectual qualities behind his eccentricities. Reared in a rural atmosphere of distrust for Yankee lawyers and bankers, Veblen was already sympathetic with the advanced agrarian aims of the Populist movement and eagerly absorbed Henry George's *Progress and Poverty*.

Aware of his superior gifts, Veblen now began a career of teaching and studying in which his genius ultimately flowered, but his strange, proud spirit never came to rest. Speaking irony and double meaning with a slow nasal twang, he was attractive intellectually only to a few, and seldom made warm friends. After teaching a year at Monona Academy, Veblen joined his elder brother Andrew at Johns Hopkins for graduate study. Within a year he transferred to Yale, where he found a more congenial intellectual atmosphere and was graduated as Doctor of Philosophy in 1884. Unable to secure a college position despite enthusiastic letters of eminent professors, Veblen returned to his father's farm, where he continued zealously an immense range of reading. In 1891 Veblen went to Cornell University to study under Professor J. Lawrence Laughlin. The following year, when Laughlin was appointed to head the economics department at the University of Chicago, Veblen went with him on a fellowship paying $520 a year. In 1895 he was made an instructor, but not until 1899, when he published *The Theory of the Leisure Class*, was he made an assistant professor.[1]

Veblen, now forty-two, was a master of irony and understatement, a thinker determined at all costs to express his concept of economics, already basing many of his conclusions on the findings of anthropologists and his own evaluations of the life of primitive man. From this point on Veblen did not expect recognition from the academic world. Rather he concentrated on articles and books which he felt would in time bring him vindication. *The Theory of Business Enterprise*, which was published in 1904, was followed in 1914 by *The Instinct of Workmanship and the State of the Industrial Arts* and in 1915 by *Imperial Germany and the Industrial Revolution*. Meanwhile Veblen had left Chicago for Stanford University. There, however, he refused as usual to accustom himself to the mores of academic life. By his long silences he embarrassed friends and acquaintances who endeavored to help him; and in December, 1909, he was forced to resign. In 1911 he was divorced from Ellen Rolfe Veblen, whom he had married in 1888; in 1914 he married Mrs. Anne F. Bradley, who had been his student in Chicago and California. The second Mrs. Veblen looked after her husband devotedly until her mental breakdown in 1918.

In 1919 Veblen began the most productive period of his intellectual life, joining the faculty of The New School for Social Research with John Dewey, Charles A. Beard, James Harvey Robinson, and Wesley C. Mitchell. Even in the informal atmosphere of The New School Veblen made no effort to win the friendship of either students or colleagues; but freed from academic restraint and suspicion, he now had more time for writing than ever before, and published five books in the next six years. Among these were *The Vested Interests and the State of the Industrial Arts* (1919), *The Place of Science in Modern Civilization* (1919), and *The Engineers and the Price System* (1921). His last book was *Absentee Ownership and Business Enterprise in Recent Times* (1923). In the final years of his life Veblen was able to lecture only irregularly at The New School, where his salary was paid in substantial part by one person, a former Chicago student and colleague. He died of heart disease in Stanford, California, on August 3, 1929.[2]

II

As early as 1898, in his "Instinct of Workmanship and the Irksomeness of Labor," Veblen had formulated his theory of a hereditary instinct in man that strives to reduce chaos to order, war to peace, waste to conservation, barrenness to pregnancy, conflict to co-operation. This trait Veblen did not attempt to describe in biological terms; he later denied, in fact, that it had any specific neurological or genetic origin. The instinct of workmanship he described as a trait developed in primitive man by the need to survive; it is the capacity to analyze the material circumstances of a man's environment and his own thinking resources, and to make them serve desired ends.

Veblen asserts that primitive man—to whom he always returns as justification for his analysis—was peaceful, not warlike; he was an animal with a mind and body eager to act, but not destructively; he had yet acquired no sense of emulation, ownership, conquest, glory of battle, conspicuous waste, invidious comparison, or sportsmanship. He had not yet settled in fortified communities or made claim to particular land or women; he did not enjoy killing or the sight of blood. Being relatively weak and defenseless, man "was of a peaceable and retiring disposition by force of circumstances." Originally he was without tools or armor or weapons of defense. Only after he developed tools did he become a predatory animal. But by virtue of his instinct of workmanship, the functional content of which was "serviceability for the ends of life," man deplored war and waste and destruction, and continued to do so even in later ages, when it was assumed by most economists that he was by nature predatory and warlike.

Primitive man was a member of a small wandering group; in order for the group to survive, asserts Veblen, it was necessary that each person think not only of his own interests but of the life of the group as well; Veblen unhesitatingly denies, therefore, that exclusive self-interest is an original trait of human nature. To him it was difficult to draw a line between the instinct of workmanship and that of parenthood, which had as its aim not only the rearing of one's own children and concern for them, but a protective solicitude for all other children as well. The yielding to the instinct of parenthood is a purposeful action by which life is created or maintained; in Veblen's view it is both an end implanted genetically and a workmanlike use of the materials at hand for the furtherance of life.[3]

This view of a peaceful and constructive bias in the nature of primitive man Veblen incorporated into *The Theory of the Leisure Class* (1899), in a chapter entitled "The Conservation of Archaic Traits." Later he expanded the same main assumptions into a book entitled *The Instinct of Workmanship* (1914), an analysis infinitely superior to his earlier statements in his use of supporting evidence, including the testimony of a few anthropologists. In *The Theory of the Leisure Class* Veblen contrasts in general terms the peaceful uses of the instinct of workmanship in primitive societies with the predatory necessities of human habits in later eras. This master instinct, in which Veblen included the tendency to "good-nature, equity, and indiscriminate sympathy," is not useful to modern man in competitive situations. To Veblen such an instinct must have stemmed from very ancient roots of human nature to have survived at all.[4]

When it comes to accounting for the instinct of workmanship as the product of heredity or environment (and he considers it always imperative to make the distinction), Veblen finds himself in an intellectual dilemma. To him the origin of man was the end result of a long process of natural selection whereby the creatures with most adaptability and intelligence (mysterious offshoots of the animal world) survived by virtue of their superior resourcefulness and propagated their kind. The era in which man first made his appearance was relatively peaceful; and in the centuries after neolithic man appeared (ten or twelve thousand years ago) the psychological processes necessary to securing food and clothing and propagating the young in a peaceable manner were imbedded in man's biological structure. Thus runs Veblen's analysis in some parts of his writings; yet he denies that the instinct of workmanship has any neurological origin; it uses the resources of many instincts, gaining its result by indirection, not by a simple automatic response to stimulus: a psychological process rooted in some degree in man's biological structure, yet impossible to isolate as a Mendelian factor.

Elsewhere Veblen accepts the conclusion of James Harvey Robinson that we are all barbaric at birth, with all the resources of civilization to learn anew; in this sense the instinct of workmanship is merely the impress of a cultural inheritance, taught by the love and care of the mother for the child, and learned from the solicitude of the family and the application of intellectual resources to the furthering of life that the child sees from infancy. To Veblen the instinct of workmanship is both habit and heredity. He is certain that it exists as persistently as a biological constant, but he is uncertain whether its pervasive aspects of order, peacefulness, efficiency, and solicitude for others are cultural traits learned anew by each generation. But the root of man's instinct of workmanship remains the inherent plasticity of his organism, without which the habits of culture would bounce off his personality like acorns off a rock.

Curiously enough, Veblen finds an exemplification of the instinct of workmanship and the nature of neolithic man in the morality of early Christianity. In his ironic essay, "Christian Morals and the Competitive System" (1910), Veblen is more emphatic than ever in his delineation of the peaceful, constructive, even compassionate qualities of original man, in the centuries before he was

In the decade of the 1880's well over 5,000,000 new-comers entered the United States. America, with its many sparsely settled areas of great fertility, could still afford to serve as a land of refuge. (Puck, *April 28, 1880*)

New York City health officers vaccinate Russian and Polish immigrants on board a steamship in quarantine. (*Library of Congress*)

Strikes and riots resulted in a number of deaths in Chicago in 1886. On May 4 an anarchist threw a bomb into a crowd of unemployed workers in Haymarket Square, killing seven policemen. (*Library of Congress*)

In his quest for a science of history, Henry Adams was always aware of the unprecedented social forces in America at work on the nature of man. (*Harvard University Archives*)

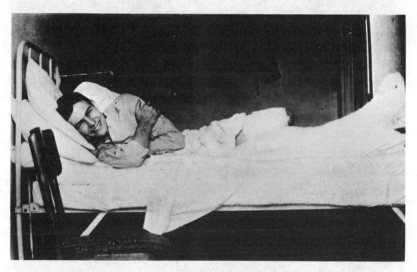

Ernest Hemingway was wounded while serving as an ambulance driver on the Italian front during World War I. Hemingway's war experiences provided the basis for *A Farewell to Arms*. (*Henry S. Villard*)

An idealized picture of a country school by Winslow Homer. (*City Art Museum of Saint Louis*)

A young Negro mother teaches her two children at home in Louisiana. (*Photograph by Russell Lee—Library of Congress*)

Christmas dinner, December, 1936. (*Photograph by Russell Lee—Library of Congress*)

President John F. Kennedy and Attorney General Robert F. Kennedy confer during the 1962 Cuban missile crisis. (*United Press International*)

Dr. and Mrs. Martin Luther King officially start the last leg of the Selma-to-Montgomery civil rights march on March 25, 1965. Dr. Ralph Bunche and Rev. Ralph Abernathy are on King's right. (*United Press International*)

A demonstrator is wrestled down the Harvard University Administration Building steps by Massachusetts state troopers. State and local police were called in to clear some five hundred student demonstrators from the building on April 10, 1969. (*United Press International*)

corrupted by a predatory existence—a corruption later heightened by capitalistic mechanization. Two unmistakable teachings of Christianity especially prominent in the early believers, insists Veblen, were nonresistance and brotherly love, neither much honored in the competitive era, but both still dominant in Christian theory. Among the early Christians, who were oppressed and propertyless, the teaching of mutual service found eager response. Nevertheless, asserts Veblen, it had long before impressed itself whenever circumstances permitted, especially in peaceful savage settlements: "Brotherly love or mutual service appears in its elements at least, to be a very deep-rooted and ancient cultural trait, due to an extremely protracted experience of the race in the early stages of human culture." Christianity merely gave a new name to an ancient impulse so universal as "would argue that it is an elemental trait of the species, rather than a cultural product of Christendom." Here Veblen, like Rousseau in *Essay on the Origin of Inequality*, makes the spirit of compassion a hereditary constant in man—a spirit reinforced, it is true, in the concepts of both men, by the care and protection of the young. To Veblen compassion is really a part of the instinct of workmanship: to use the materials of environment, whether animate or not, for the furtherance of life and the avoidance of waste and suffering.

Similarly, Veblen thought, though to a lesser degree, the doctrine of nonresistance, though not so elemental as that of mutual service, had served in the eras of savagery to maintain the ends of life. To the savage, as Rousseau points out, to flee from a marauder was not to give up property but to move on to equally accessible food or lodging. Under the Roman oppression, asserts Veblen, the vast hordes of subject peoples had lost all sense of social distinction and all hope of victory by the traditional weapons or succor from the Roman religion. Beaten and robbed and brutalized by their oppressors, the vast masses of the poor had sunk into a state of relative savagery. Thus psychologically prepared, the downtrodden poor eagerly accepted the Christian doctrine of nonresistance, and its exaltation of patience and humility as a way of life. In the words of Veblen: "The pride of caste and all the principles of differential dignity and honor fell away, and left mankind naked and unashamed to follow the promptings of hereditary savage human nature which make for fellowship and Christian charity." The more prevalent the spirit of defeatism among the lower orders, asserts Veblen, the more likely is the spirit of nonresistance to be embraced as a moral code. The more nearly a people approaches a primitive or savage way of life (and there are such groups in all modern countries), the more widespread is the acceptance of the lowly Christian virtues of patience and nonresistance, as well as of mutual solicitude.[5]

Thus Veblen upheld with tenacious analysis in book after book his concept of neolithic man not only as using the materials around him imaginatively and constructively toward the ends of life, but also as possessing the dominant traits of impulsive brotherhood and a strong preference for a peaceful way of life. Whether or not Veblen was indebted to Rousseau's great essay, he accepted many of Rousseau's conclusions about the virtues of the primitive savage; he believed with Rousseau that original human nature has been corrupted by faulty institutions, and that once the institutions are changed, man quickly reverts to his primitive sense of brotherhood and peaceful way of life. Even in the midst of predatory habits, insists Veblen, the original hereditary propensities of savage man assert themselves in aversion to war and bloodshed, spontaneous solicitude for the young, and impulsive comradeship whenever artificial barriers and distinctions are temporarily annihilated.

III

Veblen's concepts of original man stand in striking contrast to those of his great colleague at The New School, James Harvey Robinson. In 1921 Robinson published his seminal work, *The Mind in the Making,* a classic of even wider illumination than *The Theory of the Leisure Class.* In setting forth his concept of primitive man, Robinson did not attempt as had Veblen to trace the impact of the neolithic age as distinct from the barbarian. It was enough for Robinson that of the 500,000 years in which man had existed as man, he had passed all but the past ten thousand as a wandering savage hunter, naked and speechless—a biological variation capable, unlike the animals, of imaginative imitation of his fellows, but fumbling, timid, suspicious, routinized, conservative, seeking no new way of life, rooted and wedded to the habits of his youth.

As to man's original resourcefulness Robinson does not speculate; it is enough for him that man lived almost five thousand centuries before he even learned to write. Nor does he deal with man's original impulse to compassion or peacefulness. To Robinson we are animals as well as human beings; as animals we "know of blind animal rage, of striking, biting, scratching, howling, and snarling, of irrational fears and ignominious flight." Like animals man is curious and easily bored, and demands sexual release. But man is at once an animal, a child, and a savage. Like a child, he is playful and changeable; like an animal, he exhibits highly emotional traits (Robinson does not mention parental solicitude exhibited by all the higher animals); like the savage, he is timid, fearful, superstitious, imprisoned by habit and routine. As a savage, man possesses the power of comprehending and imitating an action that gives a better result than previous means to the same end. If, says Robinson, a savage in a restless moment sharpened a stick with the edge of a shell or stone, and impulsively thrust it into a fish or a snake, he would have invented a crude spear, whether or not he recognized the advantage of his chance device. Another savage, perhaps more alert and intelligent, may have imitated the action forthwith, recognizing its superiority to his own methods. This capacity for imitation is to Robinson the margin of savage superiority; no other animal is capable of such imitation and simultaneous analysis.[6]

This concept is close indeed to Veblen's instinct of workmanship, in some of its narrower aspects. But it is plain that Robinson believes such actions possible only in the most unusual savages, whereas Veblen considered the instinct of workmanship pervasive and persistent in neolithic man. To Robinson, then, original man possessed almost no originality in the mass; nor did he exhibit any more peaceful attitudes in the mass than do primitive tribes of the present day, which differ widely in their social attitudes. Robinson implies that the savage hunters, through half a million years, might have varied widely in habits and customs within family and tribe. But man today is born totally uncivilized, his mind and organism at birth differing no whit from those of his savage ancestor.

Like Veblen and preceding thinkers on the science of man, Robinson sought to identify a hereditary constant. Whereas Veblen conceived this constant to be a pervasive, instinctual attempt at improvement of ways and means together with a bias toward mutual aid and good will, Robinson conceived man's hereditary instincts as essentially aimless in his uncritical acceptance of his environment. By nature savage man, in Robinson's view, was neither good nor evil, but merely impulsively slavish in his acceptance of the status quo: "Mankind is conservative by nature and readily generates restraints on himself and obstacles to change which have served to keep him in a state of savagery during almost his whole existence on the earth, and which still perpetuate all sorts of primitive barbarism in modern society." It was natural for the savage man to imitate and accept; it was unnatural for him to imagine a departure from custom or act upon it.

Whatever the ultimate decree of biological science, Robinson is more plausible than Veblen in his analysis of the hereditary constant in man. Had savage man possessed the instinct of workmanship as pervasively as Veblen visualized it, he would not have propagated his culture relatively unchanged for half a million years. The instinct of workmanship, as Veblen conceived it, presupposed a willingness, even a daring, to attempt new methods and means of serviceability. The facts appear to be, however, that only after many centuries did even exceptional savages depart from custom. Veblen's assumption of a hereditary proclivity toward mutual succor and parental solicitude, however, Robinson neither affirms nor repudiates. Among some savage tribes good will and a

peaceable way of life undoubtedly prevailed; among others cannibalism, torture, and warfare were both customary and righteous.
To Robinson originality in the sense of examining and doubting
the mores one has been trained to accept is the rarest and most
productive intellectual trait in man's history. But this habit of
questioning is likely to be pervasive only in a society such as that
of the early Greeks which possessed fewer fixed customs at the time
of its flowering than any preceding civilization. To extend Robinson's assumption, it is true that each man has the capacity to
doubt the teachings of his youth, whether educational, social, or
religious, but in Robinson's view the average man, whether savage
or modern, clings as do the animal, the child, and the savage to
repetition rather than to experiment. This is his original nature,
and only to the extent that man escapes the rigorous impress of
custom and habit does he realize his creative potentialities.

Thus far we have analyzed the search that Veblen and Robinson made for the constant elements of man's biological inheritance.
On one point they were agreed: whatever his instinctual equipment, man by nature makes a decisive response to environmental
stimulus. Indeed, in Robinson's view, it is the automatic certainty
of this response that requires man to imitate rather than depart
from the life he has known. And to Veblen the plastic mechanism
in man was sufficiently evident in the terrible ease with which the
habits and requirements of a predatory society molded man's
motivations in a form often contrary to his original savage impulses. To Veblen habit impressed by social custom was the
irresistible agency of human action, a thousand times more decisive than the genetic structure in man's range of thought and
feeling.

So crucial was this point with Veblen that he was always dis-
contented with his statement of the impact of habit on behavior.
In book after book he returned to the theme: Man's environment,
human and material, shapes his thinking habits with drastic
thoroughness, leading him to conspicuous, dramatic waste of
human energy in sports, war, dress, and useless possessions, and

leading him, most wastefully of all, to an uncritical acceptance of the mores of a predatory economic system. In *The Theory of the Leisure Class* Veblen demonstrates how the customs of the feudal era have implanted themselves in the thoughts and habits of the machine age, requiring its members to prove by waste and useless display their superiority in the social scale. Even the sense of ownership, which in Veblen's view originated in the ownership of women, he saw as a cultural fact that had to be learned. Woman's tendencies to seek respectability in the affectation of idleness, and to dress with the conspicuous uselessness of high heels, for example, were traits irresistibly enforced by custom and habit.

In perspective, however arresting Veblen's speculations on the nature of man, it cannot be said that he contributed, even in one minute particular, an illumination of the central problem he posed for himself: the certain distinction between the inherited and the acquired. He posed assumptions rather than evidence of the nature of primitive man, projecting conditions and attitudes in his imagination rather than assembling facts by sensory verification. What Veblen projected as facts, cultural anthropology was already attempting to prove or disprove by expeditions among primitive peoples. If observation of primitive peoples still existing left many problems unsolved, it offered at least the opportunity for sensory evidence. Veblen's speculations, on the contrary, possessed only scattered reports of life among primitive peoples, such as Herbert Spencer had used in his *Sociology*.

Yet for future searchers for a science of man, Veblen's ideas of original nature, of a benevolent co-operation enforced by need and circumstance, command a respectful and provocative attention. If Veblen found no verifiable answer to his own crucial question, he pointed, like many fellow-searchers in the stream of American thought, to the need for a vast mass of evidence that only the disciplined training of the biologist and the anthropologist could eventually bring forth.

XV

John Dewey and the Plasticity of Impulse

Breach in the crust of the cake of custom releases impulses; but it is the work of intelligence to find the ways of using them. There is an alternative between anchoring a boat in the harbor till it becomes a rotting hulk and letting it loose to be the sport of every contrary gust.

—Dewey

To the American search for a science of man, John Dewey brought no great gift of specialized learning, such as the knowledge of biology possessed by Oliver Wendell Holmes or William James; no experimental background such as that of Franz Boas or Ruth Benedict; no deep knowledge of history or economics such as that of Henry Adams or Charles Beard or Henry George. Though he recognized that a science of man had ultimately to deal with measurable human energy as the physical sciences deal with measurable electrical and chemical energy, he made no quantitative analysis of man, as Alfred C. Kinsey was to do in his studies of American sexual behavior. Yet despite these deficiencies of specialized knowledge, Dewey sketched a portrait of man more far-reaching in its effects than that of any of his predecessors.

A catalyzer rather than an innovator, Dewey embodied in his analysis of human nature a synthesis and judgment of special learnings such as none of his contemporaries could muster, inviting his readers to test his theories in the classroom, most rigorous of all laboratories in the continuing search for a science of man. Like his teacher William James, Dewey sought for final answers in the crucible of experiment rather than in theory, however logical. Of one thing Dewey was certain: the classroom is a reservoir of energy, awaiting diversion from old channels to new, or continuance in the old. A teacher in control of such energy is the key experimenter with the potential of change in the lives before him. In the classroom the flow of child energy might be diverted from routine imitation to creative action, from hidden thoughts to freedom of speech, from resentment to friendship, from self-abasement to confidence in the growth of one's mind. The complex of Dewey's theories about man arose from his remarkable synthesis of philosophy, psychology, political science, biology, logic, and anthropology. The quality of his insight in this synthesis was such as to persuade thousands of teachers and specialists to try his theories of the redirection of human energy in the classroom. Without acceptance of such a pragmatic test, John Dewey's portrait of man would have had relatively little effect on American life.

The impress of Dewey's youth and upbringing in Burlington, Vermont, where he was born in 1859, was a mingling of outdoor hardihood, the hopeful seriousness of a bookworm, and small-town simplicity still infused with the democratic manners of pioneer life. From early years John rowed with his brother Davis on Lake Champlain, was bashful in the presence of girls, lost himself easily in his studies. Graduating from high school at fifteen, he entered the University of Vermont, where he first grappled with required courses in Greek, Latin, ancient history, analytic geometry, and calculus. Dewey studied Huxley's physiology, read Frederic Harrison's articles in the *Fortnightly Review* and Harriet Martineau's condensation of Comte's *Positive Philosophy*. So far Dewey had shown no great promise as a brilliant student or an iconoclastic mind. He was "painfully . . . average," a rather shy man ("I was abnormally bashful"), with no fixed purpose and no estimate of himself as a potentially great thinker.

Upon graduation, Dewey taught for two years in a Pennsylvania high school, then entered Johns Hopkins University, where he engaged for the first time in an accelerated, fruitful intellectual life. Though he wrote his thesis on Kant, he soon found himself drawn to the pragmatism of C. S. Peirce and William James. The latter's *Principles of Psychology* was to prove the most decisive influence in his intellectual growth.

Dewey now began a career of teaching and writing unequaled for its persuasive impact on American education. After teaching at Minnesota and Michigan, he was called to Chicago, where, beginning in 1894, he served for ten years as head of the department of pedagogy, philosophy, and psychology. In 1904 he began a new career at Columbia that lasted until his retirement in 1929. After 1929, however, Dewey's creative life was more active than ever, continuing almost until his death in 1952. In 1930, when the University of Paris conferred a degree on Dewey, it called him "the most profound and complete expression of American genius." By 1942 he had published 36 books and 815 articles and pamphlets, without, as he himself said, "a quotable sentence."[1]

In 1926 Waldo Frank visited Dewey at his summer home on Long Island, where, Frank wrote, he "squats on the backporch at twilight, and cleans the chimney of the parlor lamp. There is a smudge of lampblack on his nose." To Frank, Dewey was "tall, awkward, atrociously groomed, exquisitely bashful. The gray head, for all its intellectual force, has a lamblike look which at times becomes sheepish." One essential quality of John Dewey was to Waldo Frank his acceptance of reality, however painful: "The world is noisy, stupid, ugly—yet it *is*. Now find a reason for it."[2]

II

Dewey sketched his portrait of man most compellingly in his classic of social psychology, *Human Nature and Conduct*. In this book he deals at length with the most baffling of all questions: "What elements of man's nature are genetically transmitted? What elements are acquired?" Many a present-day searcher has said that these questions are meaningless because they assume a separation that does not exist. The attempted distinction, nevertheless, was pointed to by Franz Boas as the heart of research in anthropology.

Environment, it is agreed, does not begin to act until conception; but at the moment of conception, the influence of genetic transmission is complete and unalterable. Therefore there is a separation of genetic and environmental influence; what scholars refer to as meaningless is the separation of the two influences after birth. Even here, however, the distinction is full of meaning for the pragmatist; and it is to this problem that Dewey addresses himself in *Human Nature and Conduct.*

In 1922, when Dewey's classic appeared, each psychologist gave a different answer to the question, "What instincts are inherited?" Though the psychology of instincts has long since passed out of favor, this has not stopped the flow of assumptions about what is inherited, whether the term is *instinct, impulse,* or *tendency.* A hundred years before Dewey, Horace Mann used the term *propensity.* No two psychologists agree on what is inherited; this is one of many reasons why psychology as a science lags even farther behind mathematics than does biology or sociology. Yet each psychologist continues the search for the nature and divisions of that energy which each child brings into the world. All are agreed on one thing: the child does bring energy of muscle, nerve, feeling; but beyond this point no psychologist can be dogmatic. What organized forms of energy man brings into the world are still in the main conjectural. When the study of man can answer this riddle, and prove its answer in quantitative terms, it will for the first time have deserved the name of *science.* Like his predecessors and successors, Dewey was limited in his search by the most crucial of all factors: he could not examine the fixed genetic structure of man under the microscope in such a way as to link particular genes with behavior after birth. The gene in the fruit-fly chromosome that determines eye color can be identified; not so, however, the gene that fixes eye color in man, much less a gene that determines his fear, pugnacity, sexual desire, or anger.

In his treatment of instinctual behavior Dewey's main assertion is that although such a thing as innate fear may exist, it cannot be isolated or defined except in terms of environmental particulars.

Thus, to such an extent as fear exists as an innate tendency, in actual experience it becomes particularized as fear of falling, fear of darkness, fear of fire, and as a child gets older, fear of another boy's fists, fear of superiors. In the adult man whatever remnant is left of innate impulse may be expressed in fear of policemen or, in China, fear of the spirit of one's ancestors. No two people, in Dewey's view, whatever their original equipment of fear, have exactly the same particularized fears because each moment of fear takes on the coloring of the unique circumstances in which it appears.

Similarly Dewey does not deny that such an instinct as pugnacity may be present in the unborn child. But pugnacity, though it might be expressed through kicks of the feet and blows of the fist, might also be expressed in creative competition to build a statue, coach a football team, or engage in a great social struggle to extend the suffrage, abolish the slums, or provide new educational opportunities for brilliant boys and girls. To Dewey, then, pugnacity as an instinct is so general as to be meaningless. The nature of such an instinct as belligerency can never be isolated in the embryo. It can be isolated only by tracing the flow of energy into particular environmental channels. One man may realize the energy of belligerency in killing an enemy in war. Another man may realize the energy of belligerency in saving an enemy's life by carrying him from the battlefield to the nearest hospital. In Dewey's view, then, there are no such things as separate instincts. For the word *instinct* Dewey consistently uses the word *impulse*. "Impulses," he says, "are too chaotic, tumultuous and confused to be able to know."[3]

Assuming that anger also is an inherited impulse, continues Dewey, can it really be defined except in social terms? In a simpler organism, such as the eagle or the tiger, anger is easier to isolate as a flow of energy almost always dispersed in attack or defense. But in a human being fear is "as meaningless as a gust of wind on a mudpuddle" apart from the environmental particulars that called it forth. Fear has more meaning for us as we understand more fully the circumstances of people and conditions, when it "becomes a smouldering sullenness, an annoying interruption, a peevish irritation, a murderous revenge, a blazing indignation." Whatever the broad impulse or energy of anger provided by genetic transmission, in actuality it is a habit shaped and colored by circumstance.

The central fact about human nature is to Dewey its limitless modifiability. The original plasticity of man is his most vital inheritance. "The existence of almost every kind of social institution at the same time and place in the history of the world is evidence of the plasticity of human nature." To Dewey this is not to deny individual differences, but to place them in proper perspective. There is no doubt a limit to plasticity, but it has not yet been traced. A man may be born with a capacity for musical expression. What would have happened to Beethoven had he been born in a savage tribe? In such a situation Beethoven "would doubtless have been outstanding as a musician, but he would not have been the Beethoven who composed symphonies."[4]

To Dewey only one thing is certain about inherited impulse. It is energy which may take many forms in actual behavior, depending upon the environmental stimuli. Even sexual energy, to Dewey, may be the origin of many nonsexual creative actions and feelings, depending upon the impingement of circumstances. The loose energy of impulse may take the form of habitual capitulation to custom. On the other hand, it may take the form of continuous flow of fresh and original ideas. To Dewey the flow of energy into originality and inventiveness may become just as habitual as the flow of energy into unquestioning obedience in civil or military life. It is the function of education to use the impulses of the child to make him a creative human being with a habit of spontaneous expression. Impulses are indeed, then, a completely fluid raw material which may flow in many directions new or old. The loose inherited instincts of man are the most modifiable part of his organism. Indeed, writes Dewey, "original modifiability has not been given a fair chance to act as a trustee for a better human life."[5]

Not the instincts themselves but their plasticity is the root of both destructive and creative behavior in adult life. Impulses are the raw material of habits, but it is not necessary that habit be a slave of custom. Habit may be, in Dewey's view, a constant questioning of custom and an intellectual drive toward a more creative life, personal and social. "The most precious part of plasticity," writes Dewey, "consists in ability to form habits of independent judgment and of inventive initiation." The energy of many young people is now in the main directed toward absorbing and reproducing the thoughts of other people. Such energy, in Dewey's view, might as easily be directed toward "exploration, discovery and creation." Dewey never loses sight of this fundamental approach to instinctual energy. To him democracy "should be a means of stimulating original thought, and of evoking action deliberately adjusted in advance to cope with new forces." In contrast to this ideal purpose of democracy, writes Dewey, our society at present is "still so immature that its main effect is to multiply occasions for imitation."[6]

III

The child's immense plasticity, Dewey believes, is the key to the production of a community of uncommon men and women. In his early years the child may be trained to conform, to imitate, to follow, to accept; similarly, he may be trained to inquire, to examine, to question, to create. A child may be taught to think of himself in expansive or restrictive terms, as possessing greater or less inventiveness or capacity for learning, than his earlier years had taught him to believe. Dewey does not underestimate the tenacity of custom; what many would term the innate deficiencies of children he would call the decisive impress of home conditioning before the child reaches the schoolroom. Nevertheless, the plasticity of human nature is such that a habit of intelligent speculation may gradually overcome the habit of routine and imitative thought. In a society of equals, such as a classroom may become, widespread creativity may become a habit, and the child may be trained to think of himself as an individuality. Though it is true that few boys and girls can become inventors or creators in a superlative sense, the schoolroom's hospitality to original ideas, however limited, is the nation's most fertile seed ground for the cultivation of uncommon men and women.

To Dewey, the heart of the democratic principle is the recognition of each child as a unique individual, to be cherished by his teachers and peers and invited to contribute freely to the flow of ideas and impressions around him. Whatever a child's limitations, the expression of his uniqueness must be sought in "a free and enriching communion." In such an intellectual climate, each individual may experience a new heightening of his own powers in the very pooling and stirring of ideas. Each child has needs to which only a community of equals can minister; each community, on the other hand, finds itself enriched by cherishing the personality and gifts of its humblest member. Social communion for mutual growth is an art each child can learn. To Dewey these principles of democratic action appear to have a realistic justification in the plasticity of the human organism.

As the child can contribute to the pool of ideas by speaking and writing, his individuality may also find expression in other arts. Dewey writes that

the function of art has always been to break through the crust of conventionalized and routine consciousness. Common things, a flower, a gleam of moonlight, the song of a bird, not things rare and remote, are means with which the deep levels of life are touched so that they spring up as desire and thought.[7]

In the forms and colors of a child's drawing the unique elements of his personality come into focus, symbols of individuality to be cherished if not completely understood by his teachers and peers.

In his analysis of the nature of man, John Dewey did not succeed in isolating specific impulses. He made no exploration of the intricacies of man's genetic constitution, an inquiry upon which all speculation must ultimately depend. His analysis of impulses as forms of unchanneled energy too chaotic to have meaning rests only upon assumptions, not upon the proof of the laboratory. The definition of *impulse* and *instinct*, after the notable work of John Dewey, still awaits the resourceful experimenter: the conclusive work of the geneticist, the biochemist, or the biophysicist.

Nevertheless, Dewey's concept of plasticity, a theory derived from his diverse and profound learning, has been the most persuasive force in twentieth-century American education. Like Jefferson's unproved assumption that the average man has the political intelligence to preserve himself at the polls, Dewey's assumptions have become a broad reality in American education. They have become a reality partly because the American people are committed by faith, not by science, to the democratic experiment of expanding each child's powers. In the American mind each child's powers are elastic enough to be stretched a long way: if not by college, then by high school; if not by high school, then by elementary training; if not by academic subjects, then by vocational; if not to an A or B average, then to a C average. If his mind cannot be stretched far, one superb teacher may channel the energies of his feelings into creative human relationships.

As Aristotle spoke for the potential of Athens' privileged citizens, so John Dewey speaks for the potential of the democratic experiment—an experiment extending more fully each decade into the laboratory of the schoolroom. How many uncommon men and women can spring from the ideal democratic classroom is still a mystery; no systematic plan for the conscious production of creative minds has yet been adopted, though every college, graduate school, and scholarship testifies to the unending search for talent and superiority.

When Dewey affirms that environment has never really been tested, he means in the main a classroom laboratory and a community life which would bring to bear on the child all the energy of beneficence and imagination society can muster or money can purchase. To him the science of human nature is fundamentally the art of directing human energies toward ends that are creative and inventive in the fullest sense. In the classroom, with the encouragement of the community, a child can be stimulated to become, in small part or large, an artist, an inventor, a unique individual who cherishes the similar development of every other child.

Dewey himself represents an average man become extraordinary by his power of tenacious concentration. To what extent can hard work make an ordinary mind extraordinary? No one yet knows. A science of man is needed to provide the answer to this riddle alone. Dewey lacked the brilliance of Jefferson and was far inferior to Emerson as a critic of literature, of the nature of genius, and of the meaning of civilization. But unlike Emerson, Dewey saw that the schoolroom might breed self-reliance, not imitation; creativity, not servility. Whereas Emerson distrusted all education except the solitary, Dewey realized like Horace Mann that the manhood and womanhood of America would inevitably be shaped by classrooms and teachers provided by the state. The burden of Dewey's message was pragmatic: What happens when you ask a child to paint a picture, write a poem, give his opinion? Direct his energies to creative ends in art, in human relations, in exchange of ideas: help him to cherish uniqueness. When inquiry into man becomes a science, wrote Dewey, our "problem will be the problem of how human nature is most effectively modified." We find Dewey's realism in the pragmatic refrain of Bacon, "Let the experiment be made."

XVI
Theodore Dreiser and the Human Enigma

Oh, life! oh, death! oh, mysterious, inex-
plicable forces by whose tolerance we are,
and in whose giant keep we move!

—Dreiser

AMONG THE NOVELISTS of twentieth-century America no one has attempted a more prolonged or rigorous examination
of the nature of man than Theodore Dreiser. Through *Dawn, A Book*
about Myself, Hey, Rub-a-Dub-Dub, Tragic America, America Is
Worth Saving, as well as in his novels and short stories, Dreiser
renews and continues his search for the permanent and transient
forces that shape the actions of men. From his early youth, as he
shows in *Dawn*, he found himself fascinated by the study of plants
and animals, always hungry for the sharp, clear test of sensory evidence, suspicious of philosophical and theological assumptions. Like
Mark Twain and Thomas Hardy, he rejected the concept of a world
benignly planned. Like Clarence Darrow and Oliver Wendell
Holmes, he was eager for new evidence that would uncover the
deep springs of human motives. Dreiser continued his search for
certainty about man's nature in vain until the end of his life. He
was not systematic; he was forced to discard in part his early premises; he accepted the dictates of science without training himself
to probe her secrets. But no one among his contemporaries, except
perhaps Farrell in *Studs Lonigan*, has left a more exactly documented record of the behavior of man in selected milieus of American life.

In *Dawn*, recalling the restlessness of his sister Amy, Dreiser
wrote, "But against youth of such chemic unreasonableness and
force, of what avail are threats, pleas, tears? Forever and ever life

317

goes its chemic way, unmindful of anything save attractions and repulsions. Blood will tell and have its way, the iron, sodium, carbon, hydrogen, of endless suns."[1] This concept, that man is driven by inborn chemical mechanisms (by which Dreiser means essentially the compulsions of sexual energy), is easily the most dominant of his explanations of human nature. To him, the sexual drive, which he called a "race-producing force, fumbling like a blind man in a cave,"[2] asserts its supremacy over all other life forces, breaking through the fabric of social restraints, driving its vessels in mad pursuit of power, beauty, and the most insistent harbor of all, love's supreme welcome.

In his early youth Dreiser watched the chemic impulse of love drive his sisters away from the moral walls of home and church; he had seen his brother Paul driven to overflowing warmth, breaking forth in song, as joyfully pagan in his pursuit of love as any Athenian youth untouched by the Hebraic code. How the chemic impulse beat and twisted Dreiser himself he has traced with informing detail in *Dawn* and *A Book about Myself*. Of no other American novelist do we have, as yet, so revealing a record of the mingled hopes and dreams, the awakening lust for flesh, the moments of desperation, the moods of torment, as in Dreiser's history of himself. "Like the rest of the flora and fauna of the world," he wrote, "I was growing toward fruition or bloom without knowledge of the processes involved."[3] Again he wrote, "We are only spring-mouths through which subterranean fluids arise and bubble."[4]

To Dreiser the biological and chemical forces implanted in man by nature easily nullify by one neurotic path or another the thin conventions of legality. Man wishes to fulfil his own utopian planning for self-restraint. But, says Dreiser, "His sheer, rank human nature, which sinks deep below into mechanistic, chemical and physical laws and substances, will not let him."[5] Side by side with noble laws, man has developed devices for the release or diversion of sexual energy—houses of prostitution, the secrecy of the automobile, the universal visualization of nudity, the feverish night clubs. Those who impose serious restrictions upon themselves in obedience to the social code find themselves driven into neurotic despair or into absurd and ridiculous sublimations.

For the extremes of sex repressions Dreiser would substitute the utmost sexual freedom, a freedom which he conceives to be the inherent command of nature for the preservation of her race. Violently as he condemns the pretensions of chastity and monogamy, however, Dreiser at no point delineates in detail the social concomitants of his sexual utopia. He is content to condemn the suffering and terror and fear caused by sexual frustration, and labors his main contention: sex as a normal and vital compulsion has its roots in the machinery of nature. Sex he calls an "all but dominant force in life."[6] In "Neurotic America and the Sex Impulse" he writes, "Protean as this impulse may be, and it takes many forms, it stands revealed as the underlying reality of a thousand astounding impulses or disguises—pathetic, lying, simulating, denying, but the same old impulse everywhere."[7]

How the hereditary compulsion of sex dictates events with remorseless power Dreiser dramatizes in the memorable portraits of his heroines. In *Jennie Gerhardt* Jennie's need for love drives her into her clandestine union with Senator Brander, as it later compels her indestructible loyalty to Lester Kane, culminating in her friendless vigil at the church service and her farewell to his body on the station platform. In *Sister Carrie*, when Carrie leaves her Indiana home for Chicago and meets on the way the salesman, Drouet, she falls an easy victim to his pleas; her body is ripe for love and no memory of church or home deters the processes of nature. Like Roberta in *An American Tragedy* and like Etta in *The Bulwark*, Aileen in *The Financier* is impelled by physical need into the arms of her lover. In all these portraits Dreiser paints the inevitable pressures of nature bursting the fragile bonds of family and community conventions. To him no obloquy attaches to Jennie or Carrie or Aileen; the obloquy is instead on society for its retention of unworkable and unnatural bonds. "Love should act in its own heat," wrote Dreiser, in *A Book about Myself*, "not when its bank account is heavy. The chemic formula which works to reproduce the species, and the most vital examples at that, is not concerned with the petty local and social restraints which govern all this. . . . Nature's way is correct, her impulses sound."[8]

Not only is the sexual drive a part of man's inheritance from nature; any great talent or spark of genius is also the gift of heredity. In his essay on "Personality," written in 1919, Dreiser is very explicit on the dominance of nature in the shaping of exceptional minds. He ridicules the American assumption that we are all "lazy Napoleons, idle Hannibals," that each man "contains within himself the seed or the mechanism for producing endless energy and ability, providing he can only be made to realize that he has it."[9] Such a dream is sheer nonsense; nature "sends bubbling up from her inexhaustible springs an infinitude of creatures who are of small import,"[10] many with no more brains than a cat or a wolf, destined from the womb to submergence in the mediocre. A painter, a general, a statesman, a prophet, an architect are born, not made; and Dreiser quotes with approval the question of Jesus, "Who by taking thought can add a cubit to his stature?"[11] "For every one of the first order," he asserted, "a million of a weaker, fumbling character. For every tender, Christ-like soul, how many of another kind—avid, selfish, cruel."[12] To Dreiser this proportion of genius to blindness, gentleness to cruelty, is unalterable by man's devices.

In his attitude toward genius, then, Dreiser in effect nullifies the influences of environmental factors; he runs counter to the tradition of Thomas Gray's "Elegy," the beliefs of Jefferson and Henry George. George's optimistic assertion, "As the common worker is on need transformed into queen bee, so, when circumstances favour his development, what might otherwise pass for a common man rises into a hero or leader, discoverer or teacher, sage or saint,"[13] was to Dreiser, at least until middle age, an absurd falsification of life's realities.

Not only does nature endow the average man with a fierce sexual drive and a dull brain, but also, in Dreiser's view, with hatred and savagery as well. In "Secrecy—Its Value," he characterizes the race as "poor, spindling, cowardly, scurrying man, dodging perpetually here and there between the giant legs of chance."[14] There are many exceptions to this characterization, it is true; man is infinitely various; but it must always be remembered that "Nature makes and regulates man, and She makes him any way She pleases—vile, lovely, strong, weak, simple, complex."[15] Eight years after the publication of *Hey, Rub-a-Dub-Dub*, when Dreiser visited Russia, he looked upon the Russian experiment as an attempt to change the nature of man, "to educate out of the child, and so the race," the "immemorial traits of avarice, cruelty, vanity, and what not else."[16] To the confidence of the Soviet leaders in the pressures of education, Dreiser opposes the conclusions of Darwin, Spencer, Haeckel, and Voltaire about the nature of man.

In his assumptions about the dominance of heredity—formulated, for the most part, before 1920—Dreiser was not consistent either in the treatment of the subject in his novels or in his later utterances just before his death. As he often reiterated, he knew at bottom only intellectual uncertainty; though he leaned to the theory of a human nature fixed and essentially unalterable, he was eager for new evidence. In *Dreiser Looks at Russia*, when he speaks of the great hope that savagery can be educated out of the race, he concludes doubtfully, "I wonder." Curiously enough, in view of *An American Tragedy* and its pressures of circumstance, Dreiser makes no distinction between the power of heredity over sex and intelligence, and its power over selfishness and hatred. Certainly Darwin and Spencer made no such claims for man's inherent greed. To those most sympathetic with the theory of hereditary dominance, the genetic determination of intelligence is a truism; but the most ardent believers of this doctrine do not make such claims as Dreiser did for the extent of nature's domination of man's conduct, benign or evil.

Nor did Dreiser see any contradiction between his belief in hereditary dominance and his conception of man as a physicochemical mechanism. If man responds mechanically to physical and chemical forces, we may ask, are these forces not the products of his environment as well as of the glands with which he was born?

Dreiser was in thorough sympathy with Jacques Loeb's hope that "ultimately life, i.e., the sum of all life phenomena, can be unequivocally explained in physico-chemical terms."[17] But it is evident that though he mentions Loeb and George Washington Crile, he had not applied Loeb's conclusions in *The Mechanistic Conception of Life* (1912) or Crile's in *Man—An Adaptive Mechanism* (1916) to his own reflections on the nature of man. Both authors were research physicians of long experience, Loeb for the Rockefeller Foundation and Crile for Western Reserve University Medical School. Crile traces with great care the response of contact, distance, and chemical ceptors in the various organs and tissues of the body, comparing them with similar reactions in plants and animals. Each emotion— fear, anger, worry, jealousy, joy, hatred—has an inevitable physical or chemical effect. The responses to all such stimuli Crile and Loeb believed to be mechanical and automatic. "The human organism," asserts Crile, "like plants and other organisms, is fundamentally a transformer of energy, this energy being derived originally from the external environment and returned ultimately to the environment, in the form of heat, motion, electrical energy, mechanical work performed, etc."[18] To Crile environment is "the master artificer," impressing its chemicals, its language, morality, fears, values, even changes in physiognomy upon the child's responsive mechanism, the chief marvel of which is "the plasticity of the brain." In *The Mechanistic Interpretation of War and Peace* (1915), Crile reasserted his concept of the dominance of environment:

The brain of man may be likened to a moving-picture film running from birth to death. Among the numberless pictures some obtain possession of the final common path, or become adequate stimuli. Those that become adequate stimuli produce action patterns, the responses of which to repetitions of the stimuli by which they are produced make up the conduct of the individual. In other words, man's action patterns reflect as in a mirror his environment.[19]

Though both Dreiser and Crile defined man as a physico-chemical mechanism, Dreiser conceived the chemical direction of man's nature to be determined at birth, whereas Crile believed in the dominance of environmental forces. If Dreiser leaned to a belief in man's inherent depravity, Crile leaned to a conviction of his inherent neutrality in the scales of good and evil. In Crile's belief the actions of man are powered and directed by environmental energy, which he transmutes into thought, feeling, chemical change, gestures, posture, speech, expression, movement. If a child, by conscious or unconscious effort, is taught peace, good will, co-operation, he will pour out his energies in these directions; if he is taught war, hatred, fear, suspicion, competition, his energies will inevitably be patterned in these molds. "If a colt grows up in the wilds," wrote Crile, "it becomes a wild horse; if bred by man, its action patterns are domestic. The young of all animals is plastic."[20] A corollary of Crile's conclusions is that the child of man cannot be inherently good or evil; in the beginning he is as neutral as his thyroid gland, his liver, his kidneys, his bones and muscles. Through this plastic neutrality the child's environment shapes inexorably the fate of men and nations.

Profoundly as he believed, then, in biological and chemical forces and a scientific analysis of man's nature, Dreiser was in these fields a sporadic and undisciplined thinker. Though he mentions the early influence of Huxley, Darwin, Spencer, Crile, and Loeb, it is evident from his fragmentary and often contradictory analysis of man's nature that he had not extended his ideas to their logical extremes. He possessed the spirit of rational inquiry without either the time or the inclination for a prolonged examination of the evidence at hand. Had he read Crile's books with care, he would have been forced to revise whole sections of *Hey, Rub-A-Dub-Dub*. Preoccupied with sexual freedom, Dreiser traces the necessity for sexual expression to man's inherent chemistry. As man unfolds, his sex secretions require release; nothing can stop this process of nature. Nevertheless, as Dreiser's novels show, the restraints, the taboos, the excuses, the feelings of guilt, frustration, and dismay, the sublimations, the wooings, all these pressures, in some minds permanent and decisive, are the creation of society, not the creation of nature.

II

Whatever his categorical statements on the dominance of heredity, Dreiser has woven into his novels, consciously or unconsciously, intricate and devastating evidence of environment's heavy stamp upon the thoughts and actions of men. No other American novelist has attempted such a minute record of conflicting and interweaving human motives born of the social scene. In the meditations of Rufus Haymaker, the growth of Frank Cowperwood's financial dreams, the disintegration of George Hurstwood, in the revealing pressures of his own boyhood and youth, but most compelling of all, in the actions and thoughts of Clyde Griffiths in *An American Tragedy,* Dreiser has documented with superb fulness the social compulsions of American life. "I understand that a man is born into the world with his own pair of eyes," wrote Stephen Crane, "and he is not at all responsible for his vision—he is merely responsible for his quality of personal honesty."[21] No reporter of American life has had more impartial vision than Theodore Dreiser; without passing judgment on Lester Kane, George Hurstwood, or Clyde Griffiths, he sought a complete image of the inner man. In this search for detached completeness of portrayal, so richly fulfilled in his portrait of Clyde Griffiths, lies the genius of Theodore Dreiser.

In *Jennie Gerhardt* Dreiser explains Lester Kane as the product of environmental forces. "We live in an age," he wrote, "in which the impact of materialized forces is well-nigh irresistible; the spiritual nature is overwhelmed by the shock."[22] The idealism that Kane might have felt toward Jennie is stultified in part by the hard compulsions of the commercial world, the snobbishness of his family, the thousand glittering images of glamour and success. Battered daily by these forces, confused by their kaleidoscopic brightness, confused, too, by the conflict between marriage conventions and his own desire for continued freedom, Kane in Dreiser's view could not be expected to evolve a constructive outlook when faced by his desperate need for Jennie. "I tell you I'm crazy about you," he says to her. "I've got to have you," and again, "You belong to me."[23] Like Tocqueville and Horace Mann, Dreiser was aware of the extreme solutions often induced by the spirit of personal freedom in American life. To Dreiser the very mass of impressions was inimical to integration. "The whole body of things material, social, and spiritual," he wrote of Lester Kane, "had come under the knife of his mental surgery and been left but half dissected."[24]

How the pressure of convention combines with the impulse of compassion to continue marriage long after it has failed is a favorite theme with Dreiser, nowhere more poignantly depicted than in the story, "Free." To the world about, even to the children and their mother, the marriage of Rufus and Ernestine Haymaker has been happy and successful. Only Rufus himself, standing vigil now in his wife's last illness, knows the inner truth: he has never really loved his wife, he has longed from the first months to be free again, to seek the crystal moments of a new love, the wine of strange sunsets, the solitude of expectancy. Even before their marriage he had wished to break off; but he had been bound by his sense of honor. Had he not promised? Besides, he found himself incapable of inflicting pain. "After the marriage it was too late. He feared to wound her, to undo her, to undo her life."[25] So Rufus Haymaker in his compassion and his confusion had left honesty behind, allowing himself to be domesticated and directed according to his wife's conventions, dreaming lonely dreams, letting pass the springtime of his life without the search, the expectancy, the fulfilment for which he hungered. Now, at sixty, he still wishes to be free . . . perhaps a few years . . . But at the moment of Ernestine's death he looks in the mirror in dismay, and the bitterness of his agony overwhelms him: "Free! I know now how that is. I am free now, at last! . . . Yes—free . . . to die!"[26]

Dreiser also portrays the forces of religious convention as having drastic and far-reaching effects on the minds of youth, leading now to blind obedience, now to neurotic rebellion. Against the Catholicism of his youth Dreiser is particularly bitter and outspoken in *Dawn* and *A Book about Myself*, where he pictures his father as dogmatic and narrow solely because of the power of the

church. Dreiser hated the parochial schools of his Indiana years
with an almost ferocious intensity. As he grew older, and began to
consider the release of sex as normal and ethical, he began to hate
all religious teachings for their repressive and secretive attitude
toward sexual life. But Dreiser's intellectual grievance against
religion was even more profound. He looked upon religion as the
enemy of the scientific outlook on life,[27] as the opponent of sensory
proof, as an illusion that distracts the mind from the reality of its
misery or from an objective analysis of life. So at the end of his life
Clyde Griffiths seeks escape in the Protestant faith of his youth,
unprepared as he is to trace the forces of his life that led inexorably
to his plan for drowning Roberta, ready to grasp at any straw that
will resolve his dread of dissolution. Jennie Gerhardt derives her
measureless tenderness not from religion, but from nature. It is
not his Quaker faith, relatively noble though it is, that teaches
Solon Barnes the great lesson of his life; his conversion to love is a
revelation of nature's benign law.

Yet Dreiser, realist and artist that he was, could not be blind
to the beauty of religious imagery, or to the inner core of compassion that no Christian church repudiates as the heart of its message
to the world. How beautiful and soothing is the funeral mass of
Lester Kane! To such a funeral, says Dreiser, "The Church made no
objection, of course. The family was distinguished. What more
could be desired?" But later he writes, "Jennie watched all this
with wondering eyes. Never in her life had she been inside a
Catholic church. The gloom, the beauty of the windows, the white-
ness of the altar, the golden flames.... To Jennie the candles, the
incense, the holy song were beautiful."[28] To compassion, as to
beauty, in any alien way of life, Dreiser's eyes were always open.
No story in American literature portrays more vividly the spirit of
compassion than his "Sanctuary." As Madeleine Kinsella returns,
time after time, from her disastrous sallies into the world's cruelty,
she finds always the same little bed, with the lamp beside it, and
the gentle voice of the welcoming nun. This is her sanctuary, her
utopia, where no one accuses and no one questions. In Solon Barnes

and his grave way of life, too, we hear an overtone of Dreiser's admiration for the tenacity of human love as the supreme value, whatever the roots of its compulsion.

The impact of poverty on human action is to Dreiser far more profound than that of social or religious convention. The bitter poverty of his own youth, the stealing of coal, the thin clothes in the Sullivan winters, the meal of fried mush or fried potatoes, the drab floors and walls, his mother washing and ironing to keep the family together—all these distilled in his mind an acute, ever returning pain. "Even so late as my thirty-fifth or fortieth year," he wrote in *Dawn*, "the approach of winter invariably filled me with an indefinable and highly oppressive dread. . . . At such times I felt not only an actual physical heart pain but a heavy, sinking sensation at the pit of my stomach, which all but unfitted me for any serious work I might have in hand."[29] The insistent sting of poverty caused conflict and unhappiness in the Dreiser household— broken now and then, it is true, by a visit of the prosperous Paul. In the homes Dreiser afterward pictured, the Gerhardt home, the Hurstwood home, the Griffiths home, poverty left its mark of misery and heartbreak. When Jennie yields at last to Lester Kane, the image of a home for her mother is foremost in her mind. Step by step with his persistent failures, with his descent in unaccustomed poverty, Hurstwood's personality cracks and breaks. In *An American Tragedy* Clyde suffers acute pain from the poverty-stricken position of his family, from the denial of clothes, drugstore glitter, and money for sweethearts and good times.

III

The pressures of circumstance, of poverty and religious teachings and the beckoning of purchasable pleasure, pound with remorseless power on Clyde Griffiths in his early days in Kansas City. In no other personality of Dreiser's novels does inborn chemistry count so little and environment so much. From his early years Clyde is struck by the contradiction between the goodness of God, never to be questioned, and the wretchedness of his home. Why are some people rich, like his Uncle Samuel, and some people so poor? He is ashamed of his poverty, his home, his parents; he cannot bring his friends to meet them. As he stands on the street corner singing hymns with his parents, he hates the jests of the onlookers; he hates to be part of a show, an amusement; he feels ashamed for the whole family and their queer drab place in community life. As Clyde switches from soda fountain clerk to bellboy at the Green-Davidson Hotel, he breathes for the first time the air of luxury; he becomes acquainted with soft rugs, deep chairs, shining bathrooms, the clink of glasses. "Who were these people with money," Clyde asks, "and what had they done that they should enjoy so much luxury, where others as good seemingly as themselves had nothing?"[30] Who among us, indeed, Dreiser implies, is free of such meditations? Clyde begins to yearn for and to envy the luxury he sees, the dazzling life with girls only money can buy. And thus his soul is shaped—a soul little different, indeed, from millions of others, stunted by the same poverty, excited by the same conflicts, yearning for the same fulfilment, a soul neither evil nor benign, its destiny a feather in the compulsive winds of chance.

In his years from seventeen to twenty-one, after his flight from Kansas City, the forces around Clyde remind him always of the superiority of wealth and social position. The gap between the bellhop and the great man sets his soul in a turmoil of envy and emulation. Those who live in great houses and lavish hotels carry on their faces the mark of authority and prestige; those who serve them and arrange their comfort bear on their faces and in their eyes the guilty admission of their inferiority. "Each man," wrote Emerson, "carries in his eye the exact indication of his rank in the immense scale of men, and we are always learning to read it."[31] But from whom does he learn his rank? How does a man acquire a sense of his own worth and transmit it through his voice, his eye, the slant of his shoulders? Dreiser makes clear that the values Clyde sees exhibited in the faces around him are grounded, in the main, on the prestige of wealth or the lowliness of poverty. But the poor will not accept their lot; in the American scene, as Tocqueville had shown, the poor might rise and the rich might fall. Deficient in education, in the kindling of creative or professional ambitions such as one or two teachers inspired in Dreiser himself, Clyde yearns, like every youth he knows, for the superior values embodied in the power of wealth.

At Lycurgus, working in his uncle's family, living in the shadow of riches, Clyde is subjected to the same forces with greater intensity. The dominance of wealth and position hc, like everyone else, accepts as rightful and unassailable; the values of Samuel and Gilbert Griffiths he grafts easily to his own. His rich relatives can open the door of economic advancement. When they make him the head of the collar-stamping department, at twenty-five dollars a week, he regards them almost with reverence. "By blood," his cousin tells him, "you're a member of this family. And to our help here, and especially in a position of this kind, you represent us. . . . Not the least thing must occur in connection with you that any one can comment on unfavorably."[32] One of the family! As Clyde acquiesces humbly before this youth, he begins to dream of social advancement too, of entrance into the dazzling world of Gilbert Griffiths, revolving now on the fringes of his life, the magical name of Sondra Finchley resounding in his ears. Why may he not marry a girl like Sondra? For his entry into a world like this, his relationship to the Griffiths is indispensable. True, Clyde is handsome; this is an asset; but as the malicious Gertrude Trumbull reminds him, "People like money even more than they do looks."[33]

In his love affair with Roberta, from his first greeting in the collar-stamping shop until her last moments on Big Bittern Lake, Clyde yields to the dominance of the Griffiths family and their world. Following the suggestions of Gilbert about the danger to family prestige, he looks upon Roberta as a social inferior, avoiding public appearances with her at his side, sloughing her off without a qualm when Sondra beckons. His mind is filled with envious images of "Gilbert Griffiths racing in his big car, Bella, Bertine and Sondra dancing, canoeing in the moonlight." From these thoughts

Clyde turned almost in hatred to Roberta: "For after all, who was she? A factory girl! The daughter of parents who lived and worked on a farm and one who was compelled to work for her own living. Whereas he—he—if fortune would but favor him a little—!"[34]

Step by step, as Roberta becomes more dependent upon him, her dependency enhanced not only by her love but now also by her pregnancy, Clyde finds himself pulled more and more irresistibly toward Sondra's enchanting world. As Sondra draws close to him, gay and warm and glittering, the image of Roberta is a hateful millstone dragging him back from that great eminence on which his dreams are fastened. Clyde's first desperate thoughts of murdering her did not spring, as Dreiser shows, from his evil nature; they were a spike driven deep into his soul by the heavy hammer of circumstance, the Griffiths world, the Green-Davidson world, the spiritual and material poverty of his early years. "He could not murder anybody—not Roberta, anyhow. Oh, no! Surely not after all that had been between them. And yet—this other world!— Sondra—which he was certain to lose now unless he acted in some way—."[35] And thus is Clyde impelled, little by little, image by image, toward the tragic boat ride on Big Bittern Lake. In his choice of action, or series of choices, it is not the chemistry of sex, but rather the clash and grinding of relentless social machinery that dominates the last months of Clyde's free existence.

Nowhere in American literature are the infinite complexity, the intricacy, and the manifold roots of human motives more closely traced than in *An American Tragedy*. The confusion, the criss-crossing of impulse, the hammering of countless images, all these Dreiser delineates with a genius for life's infinite shadings. The multitude of influences bearing upon Clyde, gripping his mind in an agony of conflict, make integration impossible. Even at the fatal moment, though he desires and has planned the death of Roberta, the conflicting compulsions of his life freeze him in fear and torment: he cannot act. Dismayed by the confusion on his face, Roberta takes a step toward him in the boat. "And Clyde," writes Dreiser, as instantly sensing the profoundness of his own failure, his own cowardice or inadequateness for such an occasion, as instantly yielding to a tide of submerged hate, not only for himself, but Roberta—her power —or that of life to restrain him in this way. And yet fearing to act in any way—being unwilling to—being willing only to say that never, never would he leave here with her to marry her—that he was in love with Sondra and would cling only to her—and yet not being able to say that even. But angry and confused and glowering.[36]

In this depiction of Clyde's mind appear only a few of the mingled pressures beating upon his brain: his love for Sondra, which is really not so much a passion for her as for the world in which she moves, his pity for Roberta, his hatred of her as the obstacle to his dreams, his hatred of himself, his fear of the consequences, his awareness of imminent failure, his resentment of circumstance. In his conversations with Reverend McMillan in the death cell, when Clyde attempts again to unravel the skein of his many-colored motives, to determine in his heart whether or not he is really guilty, he becomes lost again in the complexity of his feelings. "But can you say now truly and positively . . . that you wanted to save her then?" asks McMillan. Clyde answers:

It all happened so quick, you see, that I'm not just sure. No, I don't know that I was so very sorry. No. I really don't know, you see, now. Sometimes I think maybe I was, a little, sometimes not, maybe. But after she was gone and I was on shore, I felt sorry—a little. But I was sort of glad, too, you know, to be free, and yet frightened, too—[37]

But Clyde is sure that before the blow murder was in his heart, whereupon the Reverend McMillan sadly begins to pray.

Clyde's life, then, contrary to Dreiser's conception of inborn chemical processes, is guided to its tragic end by the pitiless forces of his American milieu. It is true that in his affair with Roberta Clyde was driven by his sexual needs; but his attitude toward her place in his life and his frantic pursuit of Sondra were created by environmental values. Like millions of other American poor boys, Clyde was denied in his youth the fascination of great minds, the example of exceptional friends. No years at college for Clyde, no

days with Socrates before the judges or in his cell, no hours in the
utopias of More, Campanella, Bacon, or Bellamy, no dreaming with
Jefferson at Monticello, Lincoln in his cabin, Thoreau on the banks
of Walden. His mind was shaped, his soul stirred, by images of
American plenty, position, power, authority. What American boy,
indeed, has not yearned for wealth, power, the love of a glamorous
Sondra? The dreams of books may fade into smoke; but images of
life press relentlessly on the mind. The average youth's yearnings
do not end in murder, and seldom result in illicit pregnancy; but
in his heart he is an image of his world; he is often no better and
no worse a man than Clyde Griffiths. And though he may live out
his three score years and ten, and may attain a competence, at the
end he is no richer in mind or nobler in motive than the forces
that ringed him around and stamped him in his youth.

IV

Impressively as he has pictured the destructive forces in American life, stamping deep the minds of Clyde Griffiths, Lester Kane,
and Frank Cowperwood, Dreiser has expressed little confidence in
the ultimate impress of constructive pressures on a national scale.
No such utopian seer of these forces as his teacher Crile, Dreiser
was for most of his life pessimistic about the response of man's
mechanism to an improved environment. He saw no correlations
between the automatic response of Clyde Griffiths to the material-
ism of his world and the automatic response of Jefferson or Emerson
or Theodore Dreiser to beneficent pressures. How powerful such
pressures were on Dreiser's plastic youth he tells us in *Dawn*, particularly in his characterization of Christian Aaberg. Dreiser was
sixteen, Aaberg forty-five; together in a hardware store, they made
piles of bolts, rivets, buckets, pots and pans. A man of amazing
depths and breadth of reading, Aaberg introduced Dreiser to the
concepts of Aristotle, Ibsen, Goethe, and Schopenhauer. Dreiser
began to read with feverish eagerness; Aaberg had convinced him
that "mind, and mind alone, makes the essential difference between

the masses and the classes.... Either I had it· or I did not have it. If I had it, I might do much; if not, nothing."[38] As Dreiser read, his estimate of himself mounted. However low his salary, he had a mind! He pictured to himself the heights of greatness. "One could rise! One could rise!" Dreiser did not translate the import of such an accidental beneficence into social terms; he did not visualize the calculated pressure of such experiences which society might impose on a thousand Theodore Dreisers or a million Clyde Griffithses.

Despite his pessimism about the nature of man, Dreiser in his later years showed glimmerings of hope for social reorganization. As he points out in *Dawn*, he could never see misery and poverty without wishing "to point out a way by which life might be better organized, [without] wishing that it would not permit the untrained or the inadequate to stew so persistently and helplessly in their own misery." Further: "While I see no change in the rate of those who must die unfed in the west as well as the east, in Russia at least; is there not a light feebly beginning to glow? I wait to see it flame brightly, illuminating a stubborn, selfish, greedy world."[39] Though these statements reflect Dreiser's hope for the amelioration of misery, they do not express any confidence that a new social organization will create new motives or changed aspects in the nature of man.

Not until 1941, when he published *America Is Worth Saving*, did Dreiser express a thoroughgoing conviction that man will respond inevitably to the constructive pressures of a more equitable and democratic environment. His insistence on the hereditary limitations of man, on the working of inborn chemical processes, so pronounced in *Hey, Rub-a-Dub-Dub*, had now faded into relative insignificance. The theory of the survival of the fittest, in an era "when all of life, because of our acquired store of knowledge, is organized socially," was now an anachronism. For the first time he points to those constructive forces that the American democracy can yet bring to bear with undreamed-of power on the nature of man. Though as yet "the majority of poor people as well as the rich are mean and cruel," Dreiser lays the blame not on the nature of man but on the "brutality of our standards" and the chains of ignorance. But these chains, this brutality, are not inevitable. To Dreiser, now, as to Lincoln and George, there must be a new concept of equality adjusted to the industrial age; he calls for a guarantee of work, the reward for which must be "a basic minimum share of the nation's products sufficient to end undernourishment, preventable diseases and bad housing." To justify this beginning, insists Dreiser, we have only to look again at the Declaration of Independence and the Constitution: "The thoughts and wishes of America's founders, for all the promise of the Declaration of Independence and the rules and laws of the Constitution, have never been implemented. The conception of equal chances for ALL has never come to life."[40] Does not the Declaration embody a revolt, asks Dreiser, against the idea that man makes himself, that man deserves the place in society into which he is born?

Thus did Theodore Dreiser turn in his later years to the belief, so profoundly documented in *An American Tragedy,* that the dominant motives of man's actions are rooted in his environment. If his genius is nature-made, still his poverty, his hopes, fears, and values, his hatreds, his chance to rise, all these society impresses upon him with relentless stamp. Nowhere did Dreiser (however unwittingly) portray more exactly the plastic nature of man, his automatic response to love and hatred, than at the end of *The Bulwark,* when Solon Barnes meets the puff adder in his garden. To fright and fear the adder replies with a vicious, towering head and swollen neck. "However," said Solon afterward to Etta, "I decided to speak to it and did so, telling it that I knew it was harmless and that it could go its way without harm or interruption from me." The adder lowers his head and retreats, whereupon Solon steps forward again, and again the adder lifts its head in anger like a cobra. But once more Solon soothes the adder with his voice; and once more the adder makes friends with him, coming close, finally crawling across his foot. "And then," concluded Solon, "my intent being not only good but loving, it understood me and had no fear,

but came back to me, crossing the toe of my shoe." Solon's experience with the adder aroused him to "the need of love toward all
created things."[41] It could not have symbolized less, in his old age,
to the soul of Theodore Dreiser.

V

For the well of compassion in Dreiser's heart was deep and
sweet until the end of his life. In it lies the secret of his objectivity,
his understanding of what Browning called "the stages of all life";
to his compassion we may trace his superiority in analyzing human
motives to Lewis, Hemingway, and Faulkner. When Dreiser
was a little boy, as he tells us in *Dawn*, he was one day playfully
examining his mother's worn shoes, when she said, "See poor
mother's shoes? Aren't you sorry she has to wear such torn shoes?
See the hole here?" Upon which the child examined them with
new care, and suddenly burst into tears and could not stop. Of this
incident Dreiser writes, "That was the birth of sympathy and
tenderness in me."[42] But in an intellectual sense Dreiser's compassion, like that of Lincoln, Holmes, Darrow, Hardy, and Steffens,
had its source in the conviction that no man in his own substance
is good or evil, no man makes himself, no man can choose, no man
can break through the pressures, inherent or social, that guide his
destiny. Not to condemn man, or to praise, but to understand, was
the central aim of Dreiser's life and art. What he wrote of Eugene
Witla in *The Genius* was true also of himself:

With Eugene convention meant nothing at all, and his sense of good
and evil was something which an ordinary person would not have comprehended. He was prone to like all sorts and conditions of human
beings—the intellectual, the ignorant, the clean, the dirty, the gay, the
sorrowful, white, yellow, black.[43]

No estimate of Dreiser better symbolizes his compassion than
the words of Sherwood Anderson:

Theodore Dreiser is old—he is very, very old. I do not know how many years he has lived, perhaps forty, perhaps fifty, but he is very old. Something grey and bleak and hurtful, that has been in the world perhaps forever, is personified in him. . . . Long ago, when he was editor of the *Delineator,* Dreiser went one day, with a woman friend, to visit an orphan asylum. The woman once told me the story of that afternoon in the big, ugly grey building, with Dreiser, looking heavy and lumpy and old, sitting on a platform, folding and refolding his pocket handkerchief and watching the children—all in their little uniforms, trooping in. "The tears ran down his cheek and he shook his head," the woman said, and that is the real picture of Theodore Dreiser. He is old in spirit and he does not know what to do with life, so he tells about it as he sees it, simply and honestly. The tears run down his cheeks and he folds and refolds his pocket handkerchief and shakes his head.[44]

VI

Among the American thinkers on the nature of man, Dreiser takes his place with the rationalist critics who believe in a scientific examination of man's motives. Though he lacked, it is true, the training in biology and anthropology that Holmes and Crile possessed, he rejected early all supersensory explanations of man, applying himself steadily to traceable roots of human behavior. More artist than thinker, Dreiser did not construct, as did Holmes and George, a hierarchy of conclusions about man, built solidly upon a few basic premises. For most of his life Dreiser overestimated the power of hereditary chemical forces, particularly the sexual drive, to scatter and nullify ecological patterns.

Dreiser's contribution to the literature of man is to be found not in the consistency of his interpretation, but in his massive and powerful record of American men and women struggling with forces they do not understand. Gifted as he was with astonishing powers of observing and reporting, Dreiser concentrated his energies, especially in *An American Tragedy,* on the forces and patterns in American life that warp and destroy. In thus laying bare destructive forces, Dreiser has probed more objectively and more minutely than Mark Twain in *The Gilded Age,* Upton Sinclair in *The Jungle,* or Sinclair Lewis in *Main Street.* His examination of sexual and marriage patterns, however wide of the mark in quantitative significance, was pitilessly honest, something relatively unknown in American novels before his day, though anticipated in a pale sense by *The Scarlet Letter*. Lacking Mark Twain's humor and deftness, Hawthorne's subtlety, Lewis' electrical style, Cather's gift of pathos and tragedy (except in *Jennie Gerhardt* and "Sanctuary"), Dreiser worked unwearyingly at the massing of honest detail, the constant pressures that drive and bind and break the heart. His plots, like Zola's and Balzac's, have no sudden, whimsical reversals; in each is one long, inevitable curve—the slow bereavement of Jennie, the descent of Hurstwood, the gradual crystallization of Clyde's temptation. In these portraits, and in those of himself, so gradually and inexorably evolved through his genius for cumulative detail, Theodore Dreiser has illumined deep recesses of the nature of man.

1935
Hunger, Tyranny, and Hope

In 1935 the depression in America was five years old and deepening. America had over 19,000,000 people on relief, one in every six or seven of the population. As FERA administrator, Harry Hopkins had spent $323,890,560 on relief in the first ten months of 1934, almost a third more than in 1933.[1] In 1935 Congress appropriated $4,880,000,000 for the Work Relief Bill.[2] Time estimated uncomfortably that of the 19,000,000 on relief, 20 per cent were unemployables, or "chronic dependents."[3] Over the country the debate ran, "Most people out of work couldn't hold jobs if they had them." For the first time since 1911, marriages had fallen in 1932 below the one-million mark, though the population had risen from 93,000,000 in 1911 to 125,000,000 in 1932. In 1935, according to the President's inaugural statement of 1937, one-third of American families were "ill-fed, ill-clothed, and ill-housed."[4] The mean income of 13,000,000 families was $471 annually, including income from gardens and part-time labor. For these families the average expenditure for food was $206 annually. The middle third of American families received a mean income of $1,076; the upper third received an average of $2,100.[5]

In 1935, 50 per cent of the heads of families on relief in New York State had been unemployed three years or more. In New York City the relief rolls in 1935 included 13,000 executives and professional people. Among their numbers were 927 actors and actresses, 72 advertising men, 18 architects, 512 artists, 47 auditors, 28 bank executives, 27 stockbrokers, 103 chemists, 1,875 comptrollers, 99 lawyers, 82 ministers, 1,568 musicians, and 5,453 sales-

men.[6] The relief allowance in New York City for one meal per person was 6.97 cents.

On September 8, 1935, the fiery career of Huey Long came to an end with shots from the pistol of Dr. Carl A. Weiss in the state capitol at Baton Rouge. The Atlantic *wrote, "The share-cropper, the poor white, the Negro who found a ray of hope in the Kingfish, are now voiceless."[7] To the recurring accusation that Louisiana's schools and roads were built on the dunghill of graft and corruption, Huey Long said, "We got the roads in Louisiana, haven't we? In some states they only have the graft."[8] To the* Nation *Long's deepest urge was his desire for personal power. Long's control of a whole state was the more ominous because he was "dangerous . . . an expert rider of our social chaos."[9]*

In 1935 Westbrook Pegler attacked the Townsend Plan with ancient and persuasive rhetoric about the inborn corruption of human nature. "There is a sentimental . . . tradition," he wrote, with characteristic fervor,

that people of 60 years and up are uniformly wise and sweet and kind, and also pathetic. There is a conspiracy to write off all the laziness, incompetence, wastefulness and all-around uselessness of which they may have been guilty while putting in their time. The Townsend Plan makes no discrimination. It would pension, at the rate of $200 a month, a vast number of itchy old loafers who never were willing to pack their own weight and earn their room on earth.[10]

In 1935 a Plymouth cost $510, a Pontiac $615, a Hudson $585, a Packard $980.[11] In Pittsburgh a loaf of bread cost 10 cents, a pound of butter 25 cents, a pound of round steak 25 cents, a quart of milk 12 cents, a pound of apples 5 cents. In New York City long queues formed, often a block long, to buy day-old bread at 4 cents a loaf.

In 1935 Richard Harrison, seventy years old, was still playing the part of De Lawd in The Green Pastures. *The play had opened on Broadway February 26, 1930. In five years two million people in thirty-nine states had seen* The Green Pastures.

In 1935 Gary Cooper played in The Lives of a Bengal Lancer,

Freddie Bartholomew in David Copperfield, *Ronald Colman in* Clive of India.

On January 5, 1935, at Flemington, New Jersey, Bruno Richard Hauptmann went on trial for the kidnapping and murder of the Lindbergh baby boy. When Hauptmann was found guilty, partly through the positive identification of his voice by Charles Lindbergh, the New Republic wrote, "In the Hauptmann trial both the defendant and society were found guilty.... What we had at Flemington was less a process of justice than a mass orgy of hatred and revenge."[12] The passions aroused in the Hauptmann trial recalled the outbreak of mass passion at the murder and kidnapping of Bobby Franks. Eleven years had passed. Leopold was now thirty years old, Loeb twenty-nine. What scientist could explain the impulse to murder that existed in Loeb and Leopold, or the savage mass hatred for a murderer rather than for the roots and soil that created him?

In 1935 the dictatorship of Adolf Hitler was two years old. On June 30, 1934, he had purged by assassination several of his colleagues, among them Ernst Roehm, his closest friend. Though he had been born and brought up a Roman Catholic, as pointed out by John Gunther in Harper's, he had a deep hatred of all religion: priests he called "black moles." Though he avoided and evaded women, many women found him sexually attractive. Austere in his habits, cold and distant to his subordinates, Hitler identified himself with the German people more than with any single man or woman. In this identification, communicated with a psychic power still unexplained, lay Hitler's greatest political weapon. When he came to power, Germany was in economic chaos. He gave men work, hope, and tyranny. Not once had he thus far deviated from the program described in Mein Kampf, which had sold 1,930,000 copies since its publication in 1925.[13] Of the sixteen million Jews in Europe, thousands were already dead, six million were to die in obedience to his command. With gradual German thoroughness the tyranny hunted down the Jews, sent them to the concentration camps and thence to the death chambers.

In 1935 Leon Trotsky, an exile in Mexico, wrote an article in the Atlantic full of curious and perceptive comment on the nature of man. What American critic would have written a more compact summary of Céline's Journey to the End of the Night?

A Parisian student, who comes from a family of little men, a rationalist, an anti-patriot, and a semi-anarchist . . . enlists, to his own astonishment, at the very first trumpet call, as a volunteer in the army; he is sent to the front, and in the mechanized slaughter finds himself envying the horses who perish as men do, but without mouthing false phrases; after being wounded and be-medaled, he wanders through the hospitals where successful doctors exhort him to speed his return to the "flaming cemetery of battles"; as an invalid, he is discharged from the army; he departs for an African colony and there pines away from human baseness, from the heat and the malaria of the tropics; he makes his way illegally into the United States, and finds employment in Ford's plant; he finds a true mate in a prostitute (these are the genuinely tender pages in the book); he returns to France, becomes a physician to the poor, and, soul-sick, wanders through the night of life among the sick and the hearty, all equally pathetic, depraved, and miserable.[14]

Trotsky was fascinated by the revolutionary power of Céline to strip himself and his art of the influences of French society. It is evident to Trotsky that no writer can pierce to the heart of life without a ruthless and implacable search in the abyss of man's darkest nature: "It seems almost as if the moralist who is so ruthless to himself had been repelled by his own image in the mirror, and smashed the glass, cutting his hands. . . . Either the artist will make his peace with the darkness or he will perceive the dawn."[15]

In 1935 Robert Briffault, writing in Scribner's, posed anew the question, "Is man improving?" Briffault denied that primitive man and modern man differed appreciably in original mental equipment. The most remarkable discovery of modern times, according to Briffault, was the realization that the "human mind is a social product."[16] It is not man's brain structure that makes him peculiarly human, insisted Briffault; it is rather the accumulation of social habits and attitudes which his mind gradually absorbs. "What is mind?" Clarence Darrow had asked. No scientist could yet answer.

Briffault asserted that Darwin could not account for the evolution of man's mind. To define mind in terms of physiological structure was a basic fallacy. In recent decades men had realized that the word mind could be analyzed only as a product of social forces. To Briffault the corollary of this conclusion that the human mind was a social phenomenon was that the salvation of the individual soul was a much less crucial aim than the salvation of the social organism. In Briffault's view it was impossible for the individual man to "effectively improve himself while the social structure remained unimproved."[17] Man was improving, but only as the society around him improved in the influences and habits it incorporated into his personality. "The isolated and self-sufficient human individual is a chimera which has never existed.[18]

In 1935 some easy assumptions about human nature held by literate Americans deteriorated before their eyes. "Any man who really wants to work can find a job" and "Those out of work are lazy and incompetent" gradually lost their meaning. Social decencies broke down under the stress of hunger, foreclosures, months or years of unemployment, the acceptance of charity or work relief. Prolonged hunger and privation could turn an educated man into a savage. Threat to his family's survival could turn a man everybody trusted into a thief or an embezzler. People became less certain about the fixed habits and thoughts of their neighbors, friends, and children. Like combat veterans, Americans bitten hard by the depression were better prepared to accept the contradictions in human behavior within themselves and their neighbors, the origins of which they could trace in part to the cataclysmic blows of an economy suffering progressive disorganization. In London, the most popular play of 1935 was Love on the Dole, at the end of which the heroine sells herself to a local official so that her brother may have a job to support the family. Such a play was not yet possible on the American scene, though The Grapes of Wrath was in the offing; Love on the Dole faced bitter realities too plainly, and perhaps the depression in America was not so harsh and prolonged as the depression in England. Many Americans went to bed hungry every night, but not two-thirds of them, as in India, China, and many other countries.

In 1935 the Jeffersonian image of the nature of man as a plastic reasoning mechanism found itself justified in a thousand protests that could not be quelled except by Congressional action that gave men jobs. Unions began to flourish. Civil liberties expanded in waves of meetings, protests, assemblies. Whatever the ultimate dangers in the expansion of popular power, the laborer became his own spokesman more fully than ever before in American life; the lower his income, as Fortune was to show, the more certain he was to vote for Franklin Roosevelt. For the first time in American history, the federal government subsidized artists and writers, dramatists and historians. In the common war against poverty, joblessness, and insecurity, social inequalities lost their meaning; and Tocqueville's image of the rise and fall of personal fortunes repeated itself in endless patterns.

Never before had the American heart felt such uneasiness before the prospect of disaster. But the citizen felt a new pride, too, in the deep heritage of democratic values, of the equal worth of himself and his neighbors in the eyes of his mayor, his governor, his congressman. In the crisis of depression and misery, when the German sought a Führer at any cost, the American looked to the democratic process for salvation. In America in 1935, the Ku Klux Klan was silent; in years of misery, except for minor prophets, few Americans blamed their plight on the Jews, the foreigners, the Negroes, or the merciless rich. Emerson's picture of the nation in a crisis finding its way with unerring collective insight found a new justification in the maturity of democratic action. Instead of retrogressing to savagery and mass insanity, the American public advanced into an outlook of a more creative rationality than pessimists had hitherto thought possible. What forces, genetic or environmental, could account for the differences between German and American solutions in time of national crisis? The science of neither country could yet resolve the riddle.

XVII
Faulkner and Hemingway: Image of Man's Desolation

> *I believe that man will not merely endure: he will prevail. He is immortal, not because he alone among creatures has an inexhaustible voice, but because he has a soul, a spirit capable of compassion and sacrifice and endurance.*
>
> —Faulkner

No two American novelists of the twentieth century have probed more deeply into man's despair and cowardice than Ernest Hemingway and William Faulkner. Perhaps to a greater degree than Faulkner, Hemingway accepts the perverse and cruel in man's nature as a normal and inevitable effect of a world scarred by war and tension; but to Faulkner the irrationality of man's impulses is genetically inevitable. In his portraits of man's cruelty and inner chaos we may trace a hundred times more shades and colors than in those of Hemingway. Faulkner's world is an ominous medieval castle of many levels, filled with a thousand faces stricken with unique horrors, writhing and twisting in their cells; whereas Hemingway's world is a bull ring, where all is meaningless except the ritual of combat and the courage of the fighter. To Hemingway the sexual man is not beautiful; but like any clean-limbed animal, a man takes his mate as he takes his drink, hard and fast, as the primitive woman prefers it; whereas the men and women of Faulkner's novels are beset by the poison of incest, impotence, or bitterness: the ecstasy of simple mating is denied to them all.

Nevertheless, Faulkner is a greater artist than Hemingway, in the sense that his images of his people, predominantly sick in mind or spirit, are more fully differentiated than those of Hemingway. To Faulkner the blood of man is ever hot and wild and pregnant with monstrosity and hatred; witness Addie's reverie in *As I Lay Dying*. That the blood might carry the impulse of gentleness toward a son or a husband, as in Anderson, Lawrence, or Whitman, or even in the Hemingway of the later chapters of *A Farewell to Arms*, is an assumption largely foreign to Faulkner's image of human nature. Nor can Faulkner's concept of man's blood as an unwavering symbol of irrationality be traced, as some critics would suppose, to the South's pervasive guilt for mistreatment of the Negro. In Faulkner's favorite novel, *As I Lay Dying*, neither Addie's family nor her forebears have close relations with Negroes. Man's blood is poisonous in its original essence and effects: this appears to be Faulkner's central conclusion about the nature of man, and no American artist has left to posterity a more compelling gallery of portraits to support his synthesis.

No American writer has explored so fully as Faulkner the deviations of sexual behavior in a particular milieu. Even his first novels, which do not have their setting in Yoknapatawpha County, show the fascination Faulkner felt for sexual aberrations. In *Soldiers' Pay*, his first novel, the hero seduces the childhood sweetheart of a dead soldier as he is being buried. The hero concludes his seduction with the thought, "Sex and death: the front door and the back door of the world. How indissolubly are they associated in us!"[1] In his second novel, *Mosquitoes*, Faulkner pictures a group of young people in New Orleans all suffering from sexual frustration. On the first page of the novel Mr. Talliaferro says, "Frankness compels me to admit that the sex instinct is perhaps my most dominating compulsion."

Though neither the hero of *Soldiers' Pay* nor Mr. Talliaferro of *Mosquitoes* finds any joyous release in sexual intimacy, in the perspective of Faulkner's works they appear healthy and normal as compared, for example, to the incestuous-minded Quentin of *The Sound and the Fury*, a boy driven to suicide on his seventeenth

birthday by the picture of his beautiful sister Caddy in the arms of
another man. In *As I Lay Dying*, where Faulkner for the first time
makes death a theme of great dignity, we see the pregnant Dewey
Dell appealing to a drugstore clerk for medicine with which to
induce an abortion. The drugstore clerk exacts as his payment a
sexual intimacy with Dewey Dell in the cellar of the drugstore
after hours. Even in the last sentence of *As I Lay Dying* we have
what appears to be an ironic aberration in sexual impulse—the marriage of the father simultaneously with the purchase of long-needed
teeth on the day of his first wife's funeral. In *Sanctuary* Faulkner
pictures a remarkable array of aberrations in the impotent Popeye,
the nymphomaniac Temple Drake, and the incestuous father,
Horace Benbow. In *The Wild Palms* a sex attraction between a man
and woman who meet at a cocktail party destroys the career of
the man and the marriage of the woman, who finally dies of an
attempted abortion induced by her doctor lover.

One has the feeling in reading Faulkner that the sexual drive
in man can never be reconciled either with the impulse of love
and kindness or with reasonable and responsible action. It is always
to Faulkner a symbol of primitive delirium gushing forth from a
great well of evil. As Elizabeth Hardwick has written, Faulkner is
possessed and maddened by his absorption with his characters:
"He is authentically, romantically possessed by his genius; he can
lose himself not only in the act of writing in the world his imagination has created and populated. He believes all of it, concretely,
amazingly."[2] In no department of his art does Faulkner show more
versatility or greater certainty of the original contamination of man's
soul than in the breadth and variety of his unique images of sexual
experience. One of Faulkner's great gifts is his ability to possess
the reader's mind with a conviction that whatever the furious,
demented compulsion experienced by the character, he is a personality completely believable and individualized, living in a place
differentiated from all others in shape, smell, and mood.

Though everywhere in Faulkner we find a pervasive assumption
that the blood of the father will visit its poison upon the blood of

the children, this belief is nowhere so plainly stated as in the characterization of Addie in *As I Lay Dying*. The very concept of a mother dying with her children round her, one of them making her coffin, has an elevation somehow incompatible with the belief of Addie in her poisonous heritage. On each page we expect a higher reach of human nature that never comes, a strain of poetry as in Melville's *Pierre*, a stab at the sky as in Ahab's magnificent rhetoric, the wild cries of the older Gant, the humility of an Oedipus or a Lear. The poison blood of one's ancestors not only takes its toll in sexual aberrations; it carries with it, too, an impulse of hatred boiling in Addie's breast against herself, her father, and her children. "My father used to say," said Addie, "that the reason for living was to get ready to stay dead a long time."[3] Such a blind rejection of life Faulkner assumes is in Addie's blood also. As she hated her father, so she hates herself and her children:

When I would have to look at them day after day, each with his and her secret and selfish thought, and blood strange to each other blood and strange to mine, and think that this seemed to be the only way I could get ready to stay dead, I would hate my father for having ever planted me. I would look forward to the times when they faulted, so I could whip them. When the switch fell I could feel it upon my flesh; when it welted and ridged it was my blood that ran, and I would think with each blow of the switch: Now you are aware of me! Now I am something in your secret and selfish life, who have marked your blood with my own for ever and ever.[4]

This passage, spoken by Addie, is perhaps the chief text in the strange Faulknerian bible of man. At no time does he exhibit faith in life or the creation of life comparable to his faith in the power of blood to transmit hatred and despair. It is impossible to imagine the Faulknerian concept of blood as a serious intellectual belief. If one were to have asked him, "Do you believe this hatred of her children came down in the blood stream from her father?" one cannot imagine his answering, "Yes, of course." Yet in *As I Lay Dying* we have in several places such an emphasis on the genetic transmission of hatred that the reader is forced to accept this implication of Faulkner's characterization. "My children were of me alone, of the wild blood boiling along the earth, of me and of all that lived."[5] To Faulkner it seems evident that the blood of the human race has always been wild, that it has never permitted a rational organization of life infused with the love of children or parents or human beings at large. Only at isolated moments does Addie feel the surcease of the wild hatred in her breast. "The wild blood boiled away and the sound of it ceased. Then there was only the milk, warm and calm, and I lying calm in the slow silence, getting ready to clean my house."[6]

So real is Addie despite the theory of wild blood that we accept her with a willing suspension of disbelief. Because of Faulkner's genius for tracing the unique symbol in human speech, the differentiated image of the eye or the slope of chin or shoulder, we believe that Addie lived and died.

Though Faulkner's novels all vacillate in tone between elevation of phrase and the bottomless indignity of man's behavior, this contrast is particularly dramatic in *As I Lay Dying*. When the men of the family put Addie's coffin on a wagon and begin their long trek to Jefferson, the novel possesses a mood of tragic dignity. As Addie's body begins to smell, the buzzards circle overhead. The very tenacity of the father makes the situation credible and compelling. But somehow in the latter part of the novel, when the wild blood of the drugstore clerk requires payment of Dewey Dell and the father marries while the earth is loose and fresh above Addie's grave, the novel assumes an emotional shapelessness utterly unlike the firm progression of the opening chapters. Thus in *As I Lay Dying* we have two strains of wild blood, both of which are pervasive in Faulkner's novels. We have the wild blood of hatred creating a family of pitiful and divided members, each of them subject also to that other wildness which is dramatized in Dewey Dell, but which is reduced to final contempt for man in the action of the drugstore clerk and in the marriage of Pa Bundren in the last scene of the novel.

Only in *Light in August*, possibly his greatest work, does William Faulkner diverge from his habit of attributing evil to ancestral blood taint or sexual abnormalities. In this, his tenth novel, Faulkner for the first time traces evil to its relentless impersonal roots. Early in the story, Joe Christmas savagely murders his middle-aged mistress, almost severing her head with an ax. In other Faulkner novels the inexorable determinants that link by link formed the chain of causation in Joe's mind would have remained forever sealed from the inspection of the reader. Not so with *Light in August*. As a boy of five in an institution, Joe Christmas has heard within a few steps of his hiding place the love-making of a man named Charley and the dietitian. Falsely believing that the boy understands what he has heard, the dietitian skilfully maneuvers the removal of Joe Christmas from the orphanage by a farm couple, named McEachern, who are willing to adopt him. Under the McEachern roof life poisons Joe in two ways. The father beats him into insensibility while preaching religious duty. The mother secretly and guiltily feeds and comforts Joe, arousing in him not love but only contempt for her cowardice. By the time Joe is ten his soul has crystallized into a fusion of numb hate and mechanical, passive obedience.

Gradually the Faulkner magic penetrates the deepest impulses of hatred aroused in the soul of Joe Christmas by the relentless stabs and lashes of his environment. When the first woman he loves, a prostitute, believes falsely that Joe is part Negro, she curses and rejects him, renewing Joe's conviction that the world around him spews only hatred upon its members. This betrayal of Joe's adolescent impulse to love is the ultimate warping which makes his murder of Mrs. Burden almost an automatic action when he hears from her the admonition to pray: "She ought not to have started praying over me." This admonition to prayer from his mistress reminds Joe of the admonition from McEachern to learn the catechism, Joe kneeling before him, feeling the blows of his father's strap upon his back, later fainting and falling senseless to the floor. As a crowning irony McEachern had forced Joe to kneel with him while he asked God to quell the boy's stubborn heart. The scenes

of Joe's life with McEachern rush like great shafts of light and
health from the mind of William Faulkner: for the first time the
evil he pictures has a source within the reader's ken. In *Light in
August* alone does evil emerge from mysterious, unexplorable depths
to the inspection of rationality.

In Faulkner's depiction of human nature the infrequent presence
of rationality in his characters coincides with the escape of man
from the fierce tides of sexual energy. The boy-hero of "Barn Burning" is only ten years old. At the beginning of the story he is already
in revolt against the crimes in which his father has forced him to
participate. At the trial the boy thinks, *"He aims for me to lie . . .
And I will have to do hit."*[7] Already the boy says to himself, "They
wanted only truth, justice."[8] Where the boy's concept of justice
comes from Faulkner does not say, though certainly he is no Words-
worthian worshiper at the shrine of childhood glories. Was the
hero's sense of justice innate, or was it derived from his mother,
who also resists unavailingly the father's crime? At least the boy
does not yet show the deep, explosive anger which Faulkner infers
is inherent in his father's blood and presumably in time will burst
out again in the son.

Meanwhile, in resisting the father, the boy acts from a sense of
justice, the origin of which Faulkner does not attempt to trace.
When the boy realizes that his father is going to burn Major de
Spain's barn, he is outraged that his father does not at least give
Major de Spain warning, as he has on other occasions. " 'Ain't you
going to even send a nigger?' he cried. 'At least you sent a nigger
before!' "[9] When the boy warns Major de Spain and then runs
away from home, his sense of justice triumphs over his deep love
for his own blood. He justly admires his father's courage. "He was
brave! . . . He was in the war! He was in Colonel Sartoris' cav'ry!"[10]
In no one of the immense gallery of Faulkner's characters do we
feel the presence of rationality, of the "hope and pride and compassion" of which he spoke in his Nobel Prize speech, so fully as in
the boy-hero of "Barn Burning." But a few years later, when the
hero of "Barn Burning" has thrust upon him the immense energy

of awakening manhood, will he have lost his sense of justice in the seething cauldron of sexual fires?

To Faulkner irrationality of action is pervasive and inevitable, a kind of projection of cosmic hysteria to which mankind is doomed. It is true that in such a portrait as that of Dilsey in *The Sound and the Fury* we have a mature, healthy Negro woman whose sexual vitality has become wholly subordinated to maternal ideals. Her magnificent mental health alone battles against the psychotic derangements of the family she serves. In most other instances, however, the virtues described in Faulkner's acceptance speech exist only in men and women on whom the insanity of sex has lost its hold. One of the few memorable characters endowed with dignity and compassion in Faulkner is Miss Worsham in "Go Down, Moses." Even in Faulkner's first sentences about her, we feel the presence of a gentility electric with courage: "She was quite old too—thin, erect, with a neat, old-time piling of white hair beneath a faded hat of thirty years ago, in rusty black, with a frayed umbrella faded now until it was green instead of black."[11] Miss Worsham is indomitable in helping to bring about a respectable funeral for the grandson of a local Negro woman, a young criminal who has been executed in Illinois.

As Faulkner knows, the concept of a fairness and justice unswervingly executed in the presence of a hostile community is one of the great traditions of the South. But it appears only rarely in his novels, as in the remarkable characterization of Uncle Ike in "Delta Autumn." To old Uncle Ike conscience is still a working mechanism which he believes pervasive despite all cheating and killing and broken promises. "I still believe. I see proof everywhere .... I didn't say all men ... I said most men. And not just because there is a man with a badge to watch us."[12] The old man's sense of calm fidelity Faulkner pictures against a background of a violent, hopeless love and a younger generation accustomed to broken laws and broken promises. The old man's conscience will not even permit him to own the land on which he has hunted. "It belonged to all; they had only to use it well, humbly and with pride."[13] But Uncle Ike is a rare phenomenon among Faulkner's portraits. One has the feeling that the ideals in man that William Faulkner cherishes most are those that he believes doomed by the sexual man to still-birth, impotence, or swift annihilation.

Faulkner's explicit statements about the nature of man show a belief in actual and potential rationality largely foreign to the assumptions about human nature pervasive in his works. It is true that in Faulkner's later novels, such as A Fable, Requiem for a Nun, and Intruder in the Dust, he has portrayed figures which suggest, if they do not fulfil, his own ideal of heroic and tragic stature. Faulkner's most revealing statement about the nature of man was spoken in a conversation with Henry Nash Smith: "There is the first stage when you believe everyone and everything is good. In the second you believe no one is good. Then at last you come to realize that everyone is capable of almost anything—heroism or cowardice, tenderness or cruelty."[14] At what point in Faulkner's career, if at all, has he portrayed human nature on the basis of his third assumption? Certainly by common consent Faulkner's best novels are those written in his early career, among them The Sound and the Fury, As I Lay Dying, and Light in August. In none of these novels do we see embodied Faulkner's principles of extreme rationality and irrationality combined in one character. Such a depiction of the cruel and the tender in one person as we find in Dmitri in The Brothers Karamazov is absent from Faulkner's gallery of portraits. When Dmitri drags an old man by his beard through the mud and during a prolonged period of self-inspection finds himself overwhelmed with a sense of guilt, his mind now troubled by images of cruel poverty witnessed in a dream, he finds in himself those extremes of which Faulkner says every man is capable. Yet nowhere in Faulkner's art, profound and moving as are many of his characterizations, do we find a sense of bottomless evil combined in the same person with a "spirit capable of compassion and sacrifice and endurance."

Despite his statements about potential opposites in human nature, therefore, one cannot evade the conviction that to Faulkner

evil is so deeply inherent in human nature, especially the irrationality of the sexual man, that he cannot compellingly portray
a character of tragic dignity and weakness half so easily as he can
picture a man with a death instinct or a woman who would
sacrifice everything to her obsessive sexual need, such as a Char-
lotte of *The Wild Palms*. In his Nobel Prize speech Faulkner said
that the only thing worth writing about was "the problems of the
human heart in conflict with itself." Yet with such conflict—between,
for example, the extremes of tenderness and cruelty, love and hatred
—Faulkner has dealt only seldom and then without success. The
milieu in which he is most completely at home is that of a madness
engendered by sexual agony and frustration. One cannot escape the
conviction that Faulkner has portrayed life according to his central
vision of cosmic cruelty and irrationality rather than according to
his stated principle of the author's duty to present a balanced view
of the inner man, his capacity for order and chaos, cruelty and
tenderness, love and hatred—perhaps, if one may extend Faulkner's
thought, within the same day or the same hour.

Indeed one of Faulkner's deep convictions, the concept of inherent evil in man without an accompanying assumption of inherent
benevolence, may actually have prevented him from writing his
greatest novel. No one in American literature has been more richly
or fully equipped with the magic electric phrase that makes not
only a moment but a face, a honeysuckle bush, an eddy in a flood,
a hand, even a strand of hair, unique in the reader's experience.
Yet one cannot escape the conviction that Faulkner's superb art
was profoundly influenced by a diseased and irrational exaggeration
of the inherent evil in man's nature. No searcher for a science of
man wishes to evade or underestimate the manifold origins and
effects of evil; to depict its dark, persistent tentacles requires limitless patience and imagination. But Faulkner has only rarely traced
the origins of evil to verifiable parallels in the reader's experience.
His descriptions of sexual behavior do not help us to understand
either ourselves or the citizens of Mississippi. It is easy for the
average American, when he reads about Clyde Griffiths, to put

himself in Clyde's place as he sees Clyde within reach of Sondra's social eminence. But how many readers ever discover their own baseness, their own irrationality, in the strange world of Faulkner's people? The sexual world of Studs Lonigan is a more readily verifiable world than that of Quentin or Candace Compson, Horace Benbow or Temple Drake or Harry Wilbourne. Even the conflict in the mind of Dimmesdale in *The Scarlet Letter* has more illumination for the present-day American than the strange frenzies of Faulkner's heroes in *The Sound and the Fury* or *The Wild Palms.*

II

Though no true artist can fail to have worked out for himself an expectancy profile of the average man's behavior, it is in a sense unfruitful to trace this concept in such writers as Hemingway and Faulkner. Neither Hemingway nor Faulkner is an intellectual in the tradition of Henry James, Zola, Camus, or Thomas Mann. Indeed, Faulkner has proudly said of himself, "I ain't no intellectual." Perhaps no artist can at once unfold the world of his imagination and observe a consistent discipline of abstract intelligence. Hemingway's pride in physical courage is infinitely greater than his understanding of the polarities in man or of the artist's synthesis of the forces that shape him. It has been said that Hemingway writes from his hips, as Faulkner writes from the energy of his obsession with the world of his imagination. Though Faulkner is a greater artist than Hemingway, he has been less involved than Hemingway with the social upheavals of war and revolution. The romantic conception of Hemingway as one of the lost generation who recovered some of his ideals in the Spanish Civil War has presented to a whole generation of American intellectuals an image of man's nature more assiduously admired and imitated than any other: the valiant man immune to both hope and suffering, disillusioned, cynical, devoted with equal intensity to women, liquor, and the clean courage of combat. The very romanticization of Hemingway has done him a disservice by exaggerating the quality of his art and the validity of his portrait of the ideal man.

If Hemingway has an attachment to courage as a primary virtue, he also has a conviction that the intellectual man must live in perpetual disillusionment, scarred by wars without purpose or meaning. In *The Sun Also Rises* the hero, Jake Barnes, is represented as spiritually as well as physically castrated by his war experiences, living among a group of disillusioned comrades for whom nothing in life has any very deep meaning except alcoholic annihilation of reason and the release of the sexual man. Hemingway, unlike Faulkner, is unable to individualize his hero. We do not see why he placidly accepts anti-Semitism in himself and his friends, a token of the rootless irrationality that pervades the novel. Of Richard Cohn, Jake Barnes says, "He had a hard, Jewish, stubborn streak."[15] When Brett says, "that damned Jew," she echoes the feelings of Jake and his friends. Did Jake's castration by bomb work any magic of internal change? We have no evidence of this except that his Catholic faith helps him to bear his infirmity. Jake ridicules Cohn for aspiring to a titled mistress; yet what is it in the depths of Barnes that makes him love Brett? Is he also thinking of Brett's title? We never get deep enough to know. Perhaps at bottom Jake is only a sentimental, shallow barbarian, as his meditation during the mass suggests, with no sense of European society and the history of which he is a part. The introspection at mass is a masterful stroke of characterization; Jake faces himself honestly, but fails to ponder why he loves Brett, or why his love for bullfighting and fishing is of great moment to him, or what is the deepest meaning of his impotence. We can only conclude that Jake Barnes, humble and appealing as he is in his friendly acceptance of lost, drunken souls, thinks only with his hips about the war and its aftermath.

If the characters of *The Sun Also Rises* are of a lost generation, the book contains no hint of the hopes or dreams they have lost. One cannot say from the story that they ever possessed—except perhaps for Cohn and Jake—anything of value to their fellow-men. They have no hope for the future because they have no roots in the past of home or country or the soil of great books and ideas. Nowhere in the book does it appear that either Barnes or Heming-

way has any real insight into the legacy of war wounds, the impact
of Italian fascism, the bitterness of the German poor, or the background of the general strike in Great Britain. Unable to cope with
personal dilemmas, oblivious to social and intellectual ones, the
characters of *The Sun Also Rises* take refuge in drinking, quarreling, fishing, and watching bullfights. If this is an implied defense
of the manly virtues, as many critics and young writers have been
led to believe, then books like *The Magic Mountain, Bread and
Wine,* and *All Quiet on the Western Front* are frauds and delusions
in their definitions of courage and manhood. The more deeply an
artist penetrates his characters, the more explicitly he must portray
the environment that shaped them, and the more permanent will
be the propaganda for his values. But by this test *The Sun Also
Rises* is not a study of a lost generation or any generation; no
character in the book comes alive either in his internal life or in
the milieu from which he grew.

The pre-eminence of courage as the ultimate virtue in a chaotic
world Hemingway represents nowhere more dramatically than in
"The Short Happy Life of Francis Macomber." When Mrs. Macomber hears that her husband has flinched in the presence of a
charging lion, she exclaims, "I wish it hadn't happened! Oh, I wish
it hadn't happened!"[16] and begins to cry. Not only does Mrs.
Macomber at this moment cease to love her husband; she turns her
affection to Wilson, the iron-nerved hunter who had saved her
husband's life. Still not content, Mrs. Macomber resolves to kill
her husband. She cannot bear to live with a coward.

In *The Green Hills of Africa* Hemingway tells of finding in a
tree a "Kudu skull with one beautiful, long, curling horn."[17] In the
grass below the tree M'Cola and Hemingway find the missing horn,
and Hemingway screws it back into the skull of the Kudu. As he
handles the horn, Hemingway notices that it has an abominable
stench, though the skull itself is clean and fresh from sun and rain.
This small incident in *The Green Hills of Africa* is a fitting symbol
of Hemingway's concept of manhood. An animal, like a man, is
beautiful in death, especially if the death has been imposed by

violence in an encounter in which the man, like the animal, stands up bravely at the end.

The image of man traced by Hemingway is full of a naïveté remote from the great tradition of Hawthorne, Melville, and Dostoevski. One cannot imagine Melville reading Hemingway except with recurrent gasps of pain. Though he did not pass through the shocking war experiences of Hemingway, Melville was a man hardened by life before the mast, accustomed to the sight of incredible cruelties and contrasts, such as the flogging of old Ushant in *White Jacket*. The naïveté of Hemingway lies in his inability to portray a human being of the stature and complexity of Ahab, White Jacket, or Lord Jim. The counterpoising of the abasement and elevation of human nature, as in *Victory,* requires a grasp of the novelist's art foreign to Hemingway's creative outlook.

To the average critic Hemingway is merely portraying the hard facts about the men and women he knows, facts representative of a world shattered by war and broken dreams. If this is true, if Hemingway never encountered a human being of the stature of Dmitri in *The Brothers Karamazov*, then his naïveté, though understandable, is still remote from the vision of a great artist. For thousands of young Americans, for hundreds of writers, Hemingway's portrait of the nature of man calls forth an electric recognition of the hazards by which one must live in a nihilistic universe. The more chaotic and meaningless the world we live in, to Hemingway and his followers, the greater the necessity for the virtue of naked courage, as in the last moment of Robert Jordan's resistance in *For Whom the Bell Tolls*. But Hemingway in his naïveté fails to place the superb courage of Robert Jordan in the proper scale of human values. Is this not the same Robert Jordan who carefully calculates the moment when he must dispose of one of his comrades? Is there any difference between this Robert Jordan and the hero of *A Farewell to Arms,* who casually and cold-bloodedly kills his sergeant merely to be rid of his presence? It is true that the hero of *A Farewell to Arms* rises to a certain tenderness at the end of the novel when he realizes belatedly the majestic quality of the woman he has loved so casually. This is the only moment in Hemingway's novels when his hero assumes a stature even remotely comparable in complexity and polarity of motives to a Michael Henchard, a Clyde Griffiths, or an Arthur Dimmesdale.

To Hemingway the essence of manhood is to seek out danger and face it unwaveringly; to his art it is irrelevant that the emergency probe another deep recess of the human heart. The death of a man in a bullfight is no less worthy a payment for courage than the death of a man in saving a friend. In *The Old Man and the Sea* Hemingway's image of courage shadows forth a mood of grandeur in the fisherman's long struggle with the great fish. The old man struggles with himself, too, with his hunger and weariness and the pain of his hands cut by the racing cord. But to compare the invincible courage of the old man with the complex heart of Captain Ahab is to see in one image Hemingway's limitations as a searcher for the nature of man. Ahab also has a fierce courage, but Melville places it in perspective, picturing the frenzied captain in revealing action among his men, showing us the great depths of Ahab's mind, depths in which courage is an element of manhood subordinate to his search for life's central meaning. When we compare Hemingway's preoccupation with courage in *The Old Man and the Sea* with Conrad's absorption with the same virtue in *Lord Jim,* we comprehend instantly Hemingway's deficiencies as an artist. Certainly the old fisherman, like the simplest man, is infinitely complex, and Hemingway's portrayal of his relations with the little boy is a new dimension in his range of creative vision. But the courage shown by the old man does not contain the complexities of *Lord Jim's* great interior struggle. In *Lord Jim* we have a much more piercing analysis of courage than exists in any Hemingway novel precisely because Conrad shows the many shadings of Jim's cowardice at war with his great ideal to stand up well when the chips are down.

In the perspective of American thought Hemingway's preoccupation with courage as the supreme virtue is a simplification of

human nature that in reality poses an escape from more fundamental dilemmas. The courage of the bull ring, the elephant hunt,
the fishing boat, and the barricade symbolizes to Hemingway an
essence of man cut off from social meaning and the intellectual
consequences of other crucial passions. The polarities of human
nature in daily conduct, the wavering between cruelty and tenderness, hate and love, and the many shadings of these emotions
escape the inspection of his art. Hemingway pictures man as a desolate creature who is devoid of hope, as a ruthless pagan who is
lacking in any sense of intellectual perspective—either of social
forces of his own milieu, or of his own responsibility in shaping
or resisting them.

Like Hemingway, Faulkner has also failed, though to a lesser
degree, in tracing the polarities of human conduct in the great
tradition of Mark Twain, Hawthorne, and Melville. Yet in the field
of sexual behavior Faulkner has added a dimension of permanent
worth to the literature of the nature of man. In no other American
have the aberrations of the sexual man found such a relentless por-
trayer as in William Faulkner. In this field he has no equal in either
the range of his insight or the varied resources of his art. In
Winesburg, Ohio, Sherwood Anderson traced some variations of
sexual motivation with deeper perception than Faulkner has done
in any of his novels. Anderson's sexual man is on the whole robust
and healthy, a surge of sap from the tree of earth; but Faulkner's
sexual man is often like a rat with three eyes or a dog with two
tails. In the whole range of bizarre and unnatural sexuality Faulkner is unsurpassed. His weakness as a searcher of human nature,
like that of Hemingway, lies in his reluctance to probe the rational
complexities of man's strivings as relentlessly as he does the depths
and shadings of irrational behavior.

In *You Can't Go Home Again* Thomas Wolfe sets down in a
few pages a perspective on the nature of man denied to Hemingway and Faulkner, but common to Abraham Lincoln, Henry
George, and Mark Twain. When Wolfe asks himself, "What is
man?" he replies with a chronicle of contrasts and polarities such

as that posed by the surpriseless minds of Steffens, Darrow, or Dreiser. "This is man," wrote Wolfe,

who will steal his friend's woman, feel the leg of his host's wife below the table cloth, dump fortunes on his whores, bow down in worship before charlatans, and let his poets die. . . . This is man, the great warrior with the flaccid gut, the great romantic with the barren loins . . . a stench in the nostrils of the Bull, the Fox, the Dog, the Tiger, and the Goat.[18]

When Wolfe writes that no one can exaggerate the worst of man, he states an extreme as realistic as those of Hemingway and Faulkner, but without being blinded to its opposite. For this view of the ugly depths of man Wolfe qualifies with a glance at his spasmodic reach toward rationality and art: Man "needed speech to ask for bread—and he had Christ! He needed songs to sing in battle —and he had Homer! He needed words to curse his enemies—and he had Dante, he had Voltaire, he had Swift!"[19] It is easier also for Wolfe as an artist to portray the many actualities of man's senseless cruelties than the few burning examples of his potential creativeness in many fields. But in our search for the crucial and manifold contradictions in man's nature we may find in Wolfe a more balanced analysis, if, as some would say, a lesser art, than in William Faulkner. What essence of insight escaped both Faulkner and Hemingway, Wolfe grasped at least in part when he wrote that man's belief in life is perennially triumphant and unquenchable. Faulkner and Hemingway also loved life, Faulkner at least sufficiently not to dispatch himself into the unknown. But Wolfe went further. He saw that man loves man because he believes in life. "At his best," wrote Wolfe, "he *is* love. Without him there can be no love, no hunger, no desire."[20] But this pole of man Hemingway and Faulkner left largely unexplored and unrecorded: a weakness of their art and a gap in the artist's faithful record of human fiber. If no single being like Prince Myshkin or Jennie Gerhardt existed, the necessities of his art would force the novelist to invent one.

1945
Victory and Hiroshima

On March 24, 1945, more than a million Americans launched with their allies a final push against Nazi Germany. For three days and nights 7,000 Allied planes had bombed fifty-three targets in the Ruhr Westphalia section of Germany. Finally, on March 24, after 2,000 bomber planes had advanced before them, some 3,000 transport planes had landed men and gliders on German soil. Before nightfall the airborne infantrymen had captured 4,000 troops behind the German lines. By 6:00 P.M. the airborne troops had taken all their objectives, including bridges over the Yssel River, the next line of Nazi resistance after the Rhine. American casualties mounted. Before the big push the total casualties had numbered 859,587, twice the total casualties of World War I.[1] Parachute troops caught in the trees were shot to pieces by German machine guns. To a father, mother, buddies, whether American, French, English, or German, a soldier dying was a unique pregnant world in himself, a world of hopes and dreams of a mind unstretched, a world of fatherhood and husbandhood still unfulfilled. But in the stony moat of war the soldier in death was like a marble dropped into the sea or a flaming match flicked into the street.

II

In April, 1945, as the American armies advanced toward the Erla concentration camp, the Nazi guard herded 295 men into a barracks room, hurled in cans of acetate, set the acetate ablaze, and killed all but a few of the screaming prisoners who ran from the inferno. A handful who escaped over the electric fence were shot to death *by Hitler Youth manning a tank. Only four prisoners survived. At Belsen, in a six-mile-square enclosure, the Nazis had imprisoned 60,000 men, women, and children. During March, 17,000 had died of starvation. After their release by the Americans in late April, they still died at the rate of 300 to 350 every four hours. A correspondent for* Time *wrote of the liberated prisoners:*

The living tore ragged clothing off the corpses to build fires over which they boiled pine needles and roots for soup. Little children rested their heads against the stinking corpses of their mothers, too nearly dead themselves to cry. . . . The living lay side by side with the dead, their shrivelled limbs and shrunken features making them almost indistinguishable. Women tore away their clothing and scratched the hordes of lice which fed on their emaciated bodies; rotten with dysentery, they relieved themselves where they lay. . . . Over all this the SS *guards—both girls and men—had watched coldly and unmoved.[2]*

Nine days after Buchenwald was liberated, correspondent Percival Knauth wrote as follows of the death ovens: "In some of them there are still charred remains, a grinning, blackened skull, a chest from which the flesh was still not fully burned away, skeletons half melted down."[3] The ovens consumed 150-200 people daily. Two hundred died daily after liberation. Knauth described the piles of bodies stacked like cordwood: "Yellowish or brownish skin stretched tightly over bones and cavities and all their members hung down loosely." Twelve hundred citizens of Goethe's Weimar were ordered by General Patton to march through the Buchenwald camp. Captured Nazi soldiers buried the pitiful corpses of the starved ones. The mayor of Weimar and his wife committed suicide by slashing their wrists. At Leipzig, when the Americans entered the Rathaus, they found Mayor Alfred Freiburg motionless in his official chair, his wife and daughter in chairs near by.[4] All three had taken poison, their suicide a token, most correspondents felt, not of responsibility for German crimes but of despair in the face of defeat.

In 1945 Meyer Levin wrote for the Nation *an article entitled "What's Left of the Jews." Of the 16,000,000 Jews in Europe, as-*

serted Levin, not many more than half still remained. Of the
350,000 Jews in France, 175,000 survived. Of the 140,000 in Holland, 25,000 still lived. In Belgium, of 90,000 Jews, one out of three
or four remained. Only in Rumania, where they numbered 600,000,
did the Jews escape a mass slaughter. Of the prisoners at Belsen,
reported Levin, 12,000 died after the Americans liberated the
camp.[5] Six weeks later the liberated ones were still dying at the
rate of fifty a day. In their associations with the German people,
American correspondents found no sense of personal guilt or responsibility. The Germans were afraid, angry, servile, helpless,
ashamed; but they did not feel any personal guilt for the deaths of
millions who had died defenseless, without benefit of weapons,
law, courts, food, medicine, kind words, a cup of water, or a
cigarette.

III

On April 12, 1945, at 3:35 in the afternoon, Franklin Roosevelt
died at Warm Springs, Georgia, of a massive cerebral hemorrhage.
In the morning he had signed several documents brought to him
by William Hassett, among them a bill to extend the life of the
Commodity Credit Corporation. Grinning at Hassett, Roosevelt
said, "Here is where I make a law." Mrs. Elizabeth Shoumatoff, who
was painting a portrait of him, was in the room, as was also his
cousin, Margaret Suckley. "He was so gay," said Mrs. Shoumatoff.
Suddenly Roosevelt slumped sidewise in his chair and muttered,
"I have a terrific headache." He fainted away. Within a few hours
he was dead.[6]

On April 18, 1945, Ernie Pyle, aged forty-four, was killed by a
Japanese machine-gun bullet. "It's not that I have a premonition
that death is going to catch up with me," he had said. "You begin
to feel that you can't go forever without being hit. I feel as if I have
used up all my chances."[7]

On April 29, 1945, Benito Mussolini was shot to death in Milan
by Italian guerrilla soldiers.

On or about May 1, 1945, Adolf Hitler took his own life in the rubble of a Berlin bunker.[8]

IV

In 1945 Americans debated in thousands of angry discussions the question of Germany's collective responsibility for the crimes of Adolf Hitler. One after another German intellectuals denied the possibility of collective guilt. At the University of Marburg the rector said: "The rule of an authoritarian regime, which assumed all responsibility, relieved the German people of all blame for whatever took place."[9] *This authoritarian regime, he maintained, was responsible for the atrocities. Some American commentators looked upon such a statement as symptomatic of a diseased mentality. An article in* Harper's *entitled "Germany's Deformed Conscience" asserted that the individual German who subordinated his will to that of Adolf Hitler believed that he therefore had the right "to commit any act at all, criminal ones included, and not be held morally or otherwise responsible for them."*[10]

In their hour of victory Americans did not pause to contemplate to what extent an American soldier also "abdicated his private judgment and placed his conscience on deposit"[11] *with his superior officer. An American soldier who killed helpless prisoners normally felt that he was not morally responsible for this action if it was done at the order of his superior officer. As the Germans denied responsibility for the murder of Jewish citizens, so the American airmen who bombed Hiroshima felt that they were not morally responsible for the annihilation of many thousands of people including women and children. Hiroshima was bombed by airmen under orders from superior officers who could court-martial them for refusal to drop the bomb. Did the airmen who carried the bomb, or the President who ordered its use, feel the compunction of conscience or guilt?*

In 1945, before the dropping of the atomic bomb, Tokyo had been scourged day after day by the American Air Force. Of its

7,000,000 inhabitants, 3,000,000 had been killed or evacuated. Three other key cities of Japan—Osaka, Kobe, and Nagoya—had been similarly demolished and reduced in population.

On the morning of August 6, 1945, American airmen dropped the atomic bomb on Hiroshima. Of its 245,000 people, nearly 100,000 were killed or died within a few hours or days. Another 100,000 were wounded.[12] Of the total number of inhabitants, no more than one in six remained unscarred. In a factory library of Hiroshima a young woman of twenty was buried under books toppling from the shelves. People lay on the ground amid the rubble, dazed and burned. If a rescuer took hold of a hand, the skin pulled off like a glove. By evening 10,000 men, women, and children sought help at the Red Cross hospital. One physician worked for nineteen hours without stopping.

A strange new menace accompanied the blinding flash. Rays from the bomb destroyed body cells. About ten or fifteen days after the catastrophe, hair began to fall out. Then came diarrhea and fever. Four weeks after the explosion gums began to bleed and the proportion of white blood cells fell sharply. This drop in the white-cell count reduced the victims' resistance to infection. Wounds healed but slowly. Sore throats and sore mouths multiplied. If a patient's white-blood-cell count fell below 1,000, or if his fever stayed abnormally high, there was little hope for his survival. If a patient survived the high fever and the low blood count, he was next stricken with anemia. If the anemia could not be remedied, other infections developed, such as infections of the chest cavity. The atomic bomb had therefore released upon the world strange and fearful effects never before felt by man—not only mass deaths never before known, but also strange ills and bodily symptoms induced by radiation.[13]

American leaders on the whole justified the dropping of the atomic bomb on Hiroshima without seeing in it a parallel to the systematic annihilation of Jews by the Nazi government. The atomic bomb was justified as a measure of competition with German military research, but mainly as a means to a quicker ending of the war and a saving of American lives. "I realize the tragic significance of the atomic bomb," said President Truman.

Its production and use were not lightly undertaken by this government. But we knew that our enemies were on the search for it. We know how close they were to finding it. And we know the disaster which would come to this nation, and to all peaceful nations, to all civilizations, if they found it first. . . . We must constitute ourselves trustees of this new force—to prevent its misuse, and turn it into the channels of service to mankind.[14]

On the question of American collective guilt for the use of the bomb, Bruce Bliven wrote in the New Republic, *"The general sadness, I believe, came less from the application of the atomic bomb in the Japanese war than with thoughts of its future use elsewhere and specifically against ourselves or our children."[15] Only in a few cases did Americans accept the implications of guilt at America's being the first nation to use the bomb. Speaking for the Federal Council of Churches, John Foster Dulles and Bishop G. Bromley Oxnam said, "If we, a professedly Christian nation, feel morally free to use atomic energy in that way, men elsewhere will accept that verdict . . . the stage will be set for the sudden and final destruction of mankind."[16] But few Americans associated the use of the atomic bomb on Hiroshima with the mass cruelties at Dachau and Belsen. The death chambers in the concentration camps satisfied only the lust of hatred; the bombing of Hiroshima, it was claimed, relieved both Japanese and American suffering by shortening the war. To the Japanese suffering from radiation, however, this distinction in motive and method was too subtle to be comprehended. To the Japanese at Hiroshima it was difficult to distinguish between the American airmen who dropped the bomb and the German officials who, acting under orders, herded their victims into the gas chambers. The ultimate meaning of the bomb, as expressed in the words of Freda Kirchwey in the* Nation, *was "one world or none." In such a dilemma the question of relative responsibility for atrocities in war assumed a complexity undecipherable by even the most advanced architects of a science of man.*

XVIII

Terman and the Definition of Genius

> *Who has found the boundaries of human*
> *intelligence? Who has made a chart of its*
> *channel, or approached the fountain of this*
> *wonderful Nile?*
>
> —Emerson

HOW COULD America identify its crops of uncommon men? In terms of intelligence, however defined, what were the early indicators of genius? These questions, more than any others, agitated the minds of Lewis M. Terman and his associates at Stanford University. If, with the aid of the developing science of psychological testing, scholars could seek out the most promising youth, could they then also devise elements of an environment in which such youth would flourish? Terman believed that genius was mainly the gift of nature, not of parental training or magnificent teachers. No one, in his judgment, could become a genius without having given certain signs of precocity in early youth. Whatever environment genius needed in order to flourish, its roots lay in a high intelligence which to Terman was inescapably genetic in its origin.

In 1926 appeared Catharine Cox's *The Early Mental Traits of Three Hundred Geniuses,* a memorable landmark in America's search for a science of man. By examining the behavior patterns of childhood and youth, Cox and her associates established what they believed was inescapable evidence of mental ability that could be translated into quantitative terms. The intelligence quotients of the three hundred geniuses averaged above 160. A few of the I.Q.'s were below 140; a few were above 180. To Bunyan, Cervantes, and Cobbett the raters ascribed an I.Q. of 105; to Cromwell, Raphael,

367

and Rembrandt, 110; to Goldsmith, Luther, and Swedenborg, 115; to Cranmer and Defoe, 120; to Addison, Lincoln, and Swift, 125; to Balzac, Rousseau, and Savonarola, 130; to Beethoven, Darwin, Erasmus, Franklin, Hamilton, Napoleon, and Leonardo da Vinci, 135; to Agassiz, Hobbes, and Montaigne, 140; to Bacon, Dickens, Emerson, Galileo, Jefferson, and Milton, 145; to Byron, Hugo, Mendelssohn, and Mozart, 150; to Condorcet, Hume, and Tennyson, 155; to Chatterton and Voltaire, 170; to Coleridge and Schelling, 175; to Macaulay, Pascal, Goethe, and John Stuart Mill, 180 or over.[1] This quantitative approach by I.Q. procedures was no doubt a relatively crude instrument in the measurement of the intelligence of genius. It made no effort to gauge environmental impact on the growth of intelligence. But it was the first attempt to establish a quantitative analysis of behavior through a close study of biographical evidence, a study which Terman had anticipated in his analysis of the early mental traits of Francis Galton.[2]

The behavior patterns used as evidence by the co-operating scholars were of many kinds. The searchers found, for example, that Coleridge at age three could read a chapter from the Bible; that Mozart composed a minuet when he was five; that when Goethe was eight, he wrote literature judged superior by adult standards; Schelling at eleven had as classmates boys of eighteen and nineteen who recognized him as their equal; Milton at twenty-one wrote "The Nativity Ode," one of the finest in the language; when he was thirteen, Velasquez made rapid strides in the study of art. Emerson entered Harvard when he was fourteen. At age ten he had written a long poem, "The History of Fortus," containing some lines of remarkable power. When Henry Fielding was twenty, he wrote a comedy which was judged worthy to be presented by a famous cast at the Theatre Royal in London. At eighteen Franklin wrote *A Dissertation on Liberty and Necessity, Pleasure and Pain.* Several of Heine's poems were published when he was just nineteen. Aubrey records that by the time Thomas Hobbes was fourteen he had translated Euripides' *Medea* into Latin verse. When he was sixteen, Hegel translated Longinus' *On the Sublime.*[3]

One persistent early sign of high intelligence was a voracious appetite for reading in diverse fields. By the time she was seven or eight, George Eliot had read many of the works of Scott, Daniel Defoe, and Samuel Johnson. She was so fascinated by Scott's *Waverley* that at age eight she wrote out the story from memory. Milton was so enamored of books, "so eager to learn and know," that by the time he was twelve he seldom went to bed before midnight. As a boy Jefferson was an omnivorous reader of his father's books, among them the works of Swift, Pope, Addison, and Shakespeare.

In their study of biographical evidence, the searchers discovered a close correlation between high intelligence and constructive character traits—traits named and described under some sixty-seven headings. The genius in early life was more companionable, cheerful, and consistent in mood than less promising minds, more generous by habit and impulse, more responsive to beauty in varied forms, less liable to anger, depression, and egotism, more accurate in rating his superior talents. The genius as a child had a keener sense of justice, was more athletic, lively, and good-humored than youth of less intelligence. As a citizen, son, husband, brother, the genius was more consistent in meeting his responsibilities than minds of lesser promise. At the same time the youthful genius was more independent of mind than average boys and girls, less conventional in his thinking.

In their interpretations of their findings, Cox and her associates state as their most important conclusion that *"the extraordinary genius who achieves the highest eminence is the gifted individual whom intelligence tests may discover in childhood."*[4] Assuming that nature bestows the gift of high intelligence, the authors are careful to point out that heredity is not sufficient in itself to bestow greatness. Most of the geniuses studied had *"superior advantages in early environment."* Cox does not make any attempt to evaluate the weight of nature and nurture in the formation of genius. It is evident to the authors that a high I.Q. is almost invariably the accompaniment of genius, but they make no claim that the high

I.Q. alone assures the accompaniment of greatness characterized in their study of the chosen three hundred. It is true that more often than not geniuses have appeared in superior families. They have displayed in childhood not only superior intelligence but also superior traits of character. Whether or not the qualities of persistence and force of personality are inherited, the authors do not attempt to decide. Nor do they conjecture that the sixty-seven character traits in which the geniuses were found superior may have been the fruit of unconscious imitation of remarkable people in and around the family of the genius. As a final concession to the powers of heredity, however, Cox and her associates subscribe to the sentiment of Horace:

'Tis only from the sturdy and the good that sturdy young are born; in steers, in steeds, appear the merits of their sires; nor do fierce eagles beget timid doves. Yet training increases inborn worth, and righteous ways make strong the heart; whenever righteousness has failed, faults mar even what nature had made noble![5]

Yet what magic of growth enabled Cervantes to write *Don Quixote* with an I.Q. of 105, or Bunyan his *Pilgrim's Progress* with the same average intelligence, no one yet knows. To Emerson a genius was one who, like del Sarto, did with a few swift strokes what others struggled for months to bring forth. "Shakespeare made his Hamlet as a bird weaves its nest." Can a boy of limited intelligence become a genius by force of will and energy and ambition alone? Another careful study like that of Cox, applied to geniuses of limited intelligence, was needed to answer.

II

Simultaneously with the research and preparation for the Cox report on three hundred geniuses, Terman and his associates had selected in 1921 one thousand gifted children with I.Q.'s of the genius level. It was necessary to examine 250,000 pupils in California schools in order to find about fifteen hundred with I.Q.'s over 140, of whom about one thousand formed the main experimental groups.[6] It was an arresting fact in itself, though one that Terman has not dwelt upon, that one school child in 250 in the communities chosen could qualify in measurable intelligence as a potential genius. The average age was ten years. The purpose of the search was first to gather many types of information about children of genius intelligence, then to follow the careers of the one thousand into maturity to see what aspects of genius would appear as they grew older. The ratio between boys and girls was 134 to 100. Terman points out incidentally that the ratio of male geniuses to female geniuses in the past has been approximately 20 to 1. Does nature grant greater genius potential to the man than to the woman? This is a significant query yet to be answered by historians of genius.

As with the investigation of the three hundred geniuses, it was found that the one thousand gifted boys and girls were superior not only in intelligence but in personality traits as well. Early in life they showed more pronounced curiosity, better memories, larger vocabularies, and a fascination for knowledge in itself as found in atlases and encyclopedias. These abilities and interests were a natural outgrowth of the gifted children's wide-ranging mental acquisitiveness, not of efforts by parents to interest their children in extracurricular development. Seventy per cent of the parents reported that the gifted child had proceeded at his own pace. Two parents in ten said they had encouraged intellectual acceleration, but one parent in ten said he had tried to delay the child's immersion in free reading of his own choice. In school achievement the gifted children were two full years ahead of their grade placement, but in actual mastery of subject matter they were 44 per cent beyond their years.

The gifted children were shown to sleep more hours per day than unselected children. The diet for the gifted children was above average. Gifted boys reached puberty earlier than average boys. The mean of first menstruation of girls was at 13.02, a somewhat lower age than the mean age for American girls in general. There were fewer physical defects among the gifted children than in the general child population. Among the gifted the searchers found all the maladjustments present among average children; the difference was that the maladjustments occurred less frequently.[7]

The 1921-22 analysis of the gifted boys and girls was confirmed in a series of tests given them in 1927-28, when the subjects were in most cases sixteen years old. Similar follow-up tests were given again in 1936, 1940, and 1945. In 1947 appeared *The Gifted Child Grows Up*, a report by Terman and his associates on the accomplishments of over one thousand gifted people, most of whom in 1945 were thirty-five years old.

The most striking fact of the 1945 review of accomplishments was that no authentic genius had yet emerged from the one thousand—though it was still too early to say that among these gifted people, whose accomplishments were very substantial, no genius would ever appear. The time of greatest qualitative productivity in the life of genius, according to Harvey C. Lehman's investigation, has been between the ages of thirty-five and forty.[8] The gifted children in Terman's study were thirty-five years old in 1945, forty-five years old in 1955.

In tracing the careers of their subjects, Terman and his associates have rendered an inestimable service to the emerging science of man. If the history of each gifted child is followed even until he is age fifty, the scholars will have at hand a repository of invaluable information, including the impressions of the subjects themselves as to the reasons for their fulfilment or relative lack of accomplishment.

In analyzing the achievements of their subjects in 1945, the searchers came across a startling fact: though all the men had an intelligence of the genius level, in terms of achievement they were widely separated. In vocational success, writes Terman, some were internationally eminent; others were semiskilled laborers. In order to show the differences in achievement among the gifted men of his study, Terman selected the 150 most successful, designating them as the A group, and the 150 least successful, designating them as the C group. Comparison of A men and C men brought into focus some striking contrasts. Though the A and C men had similar records in elementary school and even in high school, they began to diverge when they reached the college level. Ninety per cent of the A men graduated from college, and 76 per cent of them had one or more years of graduate work. But only 37 per cent of the C men graduated from college, and only a seventh of them had one or more years of graduate work. Whereas all of the A men attended college, a sixth of the C men did not attend college at all. In college, though their intelligence was roughly on the same level, the A men made much better records than the C men and received many more honors. Only 10 per cent of the C men were awarded scholarships, compared to 30 per cent of the A men. In terms of vocational distinction, Terman found that among the A group were twenty-seven college teachers, twenty-four lawyers, sixteen physicians, eleven engineers, ten writers and journalists, seven chemists. But the C group had produced only fourteen professional people, as compared to 103 in the A group. Among the C professional people were three writers, two teachers, three engineers, three chemists, one clergyman, one lawyer, and one artist.[9]

Terman found that over half the A men had married women who had also graduated from college, whereas only one-fourth of the C wives were college graduates. In testing personality traits of A and C men as described by themselves, their parents, and their wives, Terman did not find substantial differences except in three traits, which he describes as perseverance, integration toward goals, and self-confidence. In these three categories the A men were statistically superior. To themselves the C men appeared to believe more in conforming to authority than the A men, whereas ratings by their wives and parents reveal no differences on this point. In another test of personality traits, however, the A men were markedly superior to the C men in appearance, attractiveness, poise, alertness, curiosity, and originality. In only one respect, that of freedom from vanity, was the C group superior to the A. In personal traits such as frankness and talkativeness there was very little difference between the two groups.

In summarizing the differences between gifted men of the A group and gifted men of the C group, Terman points out that in intelligence scores alone the two groups remained roughly equal from age ten to age thirty-five. The differences in accomplishment and earning power could not be attributed to differences in physical health. Between the two groups there were no significant differences in physical health in 1922, 1928, or 1940. From 1922 to 1940, between the ages of eleven and twenty-nine, the mental health of the A group increased appreciably. The mental health of the C group in the same period deteriorated, and social adjustments became increasingly difficult for them. In terms of social acceptability the C group was at a disadvantage. Though fewer of the C men were married in this period, the number of divorces among the C's was more than double that of the A's.[10]

In seeking explanations for the relative lack of accomplishment on the part of the C group, Terman and his associates made many other comparisons. They found, for example, that whereas half of the fathers and 18 per cent of the mothers of the A men had graduated from college, in the C group the situation was very different. Only 15 per cent of the fathers had graduated from college, and 11 per cent of the mothers. Another factor the searchers considered was the accomplishment of the siblings. In the A group 62 per cent of the brothers of the gifted children graduated from college; in the C group, only 31 per cent. Twice as many sisters of A men attended college as sisters of C men. Moreover, at least a third of the A brothers did two or more years of graduate work, while only 8 per cent of the C brothers had done graduate work to this level.[11]

III

In 1959 appeared *The Gifted Group at Mid-Life,* based on information gathered in 1955. The average age of the group was now forty-five. In general they had fulfilled their early promise—as measured, for example, by listings in *American Men of Science,* in which seventy-seven of the names were now on record, as compared with nineteen in 1945. Although there were in 1959 a number of writers that the editors of the study could call successful, there were no more than four "with a high order of literary activity." Except for one composer, no rare creative artist had emerged. Unfortunately the study of 1959 does not compare the achievements and characteristics of the A and C groups, as was traced in the 1947 report.

Every quantitative analysis of human action marks an advance in the American search for a science of man. The great accomplishment of Terman and his associates is the measurement not only of the intelligence but also to some degree of the personality traits found to correlate with exceptional native ability. From Terman's researches it is evident that at least one child of genius potential may be found among 250 pupils in many communities of average American citizens. By tests of proved efficiency Terman and his associates have been able to follow the careers of over one thousand gifted children over a period of thirty-five years. This in itself not only represents a substantial mass of statistical information, but also provides a token for similar investigations to come. Although no authentic genius has yet emerged from the group, many distinguished men have in large part fulfilled the promise of childhood brilliance. By and large the one thousand gifted children now grown up have become superior citizens as workers, husbands, and fathers, even though their intelligence of the genius level has not been translated into inventions, poems, scientific discoveries, paintings, or novels which would stamp gifted people as geniuses comparable to the three hundred who were analyzed by Catharine Cox.

The great puzzle emerging from Terman's work, however, and still to be solved, is this: What were the factors, personal or environmental, which prevented gifted men of the C group from realizing a potential at age thirty-five comparable to their promise at age ten? At age ten, though the C group was inferior to the A group in appearance and appeal of personality, there was no marked difference in personality traits between the A group and the C group. The environmental factors which prevented the C group from becoming distinguished have yet to be identified. From

Cox's study of the three hundred geniuses a fact emerged time after time which Terman and his associates did not attempt to measure. The three hundred geniuses were associated as children with remarkable people. What were the aspirations created in the minds of the three hundred? What were the aspirations created in the minds of the 150 relative failures among Terman's gifted children? Terman himself writes, "Often the difference between a C and an A is little more than a difference in level of aspiration."[12] What conditioning of genius as described by William James was lacking in the lives of the gifted children, especially the boys of the C group? Terman does not attempt to describe these deficiencies in environmental stimulus. They can only be described in terms of the environment of great men such as those analyzed in part by Catharine Cox.

Cox's investigation, however, fell far short of tracing crucial motivations felt by great men in their childhood. She and her associates traced the accomplishments rather than the motivations which released streams of energy in the childhood of genius. Similarly, in Terman's study of the one thousand, we do not as yet know what moments in childhood released the energies of gifted children toward those goals compatible with the intelligence of genius. From the A group of gifted children have emerged a substantial number of men already distinguished at the age of forty-five. But in this group gifted with the intelligence of genius were there incitements to creative actions consonant with their superior mental equipment? As yet, perhaps, we know too little about the creative process to set it moving in the gifted child. If he has the mind of a genius, should he travel to the homes of great men and talk with them about his future? Should he visit such men as Isaiah Berlin, William Alfred, E. M. Forster, Pablo Picasso, Alvin Johnson, Wallace Stegner, Linus Pauling, Leonard Bernstein?

Terman has traced the growth and development of the gifted child in American society as it exists. One next step in a search for the science of man is to show how gifted children may aim not merely at high vocational goals but at levels of creative thinking already achieved by authentic geniuses among their contemporaries.

XIX
Biology and the Quest for Certainty

> *A truly biological analysis of human so-*
> *ciety must build on the recognition that man*
> *is the most teachable of animals. This is a*
> *profound truth which the eugenist has neg-*
> *lected.*
>
> —Hogben

AMONG American social thinkers from Jefferson to Franklin Roosevelt, a belief in the plasticity of man's organism has emerged from experience and awareness of democratic hopes rather than from the irrefutable proof of science. In the Declaration of Independence Jefferson based his claims for "life, liberty, and the pursuit of happiness" not on scientific data about man's nature, but on his natural rights as endowed by the Creator. When Lincoln called for the testing of illiterate Negroes in the hard school of army life, he expressed a belief in experimentation with human tissue, but no assurance of the scientific fact. As free high schools sprang up in the 1840's, expanding decade by decade into a net-work nation-wide, Americans everywhere assumed the elastic response of the average mind to books, teachers, and ideas; but this assumption was buttressed by no scientific certainty about the nature of man. When Henry George, in 1870, wrote, "The influence of heredity, which it is now the fashion to rate so highly, is as nothing compared with the influences which mould the man after he comes into the world," he spoke without the evidence of biology and anthropology; Darwin's *The Origin of Species* was only eleven years old, and cultural anthropology was yet unborn. The right to vote, to speak freely, to assemble, to travel without restraint, to choose one's own occupation, to attend a free high school and a free college—all these assume a confidence in humble minds un-paralleled in the history of the world; but it is a confidence which is justified, even now, by no categorical evidence of the scientific method.

The question, then, as to whether or not the concepts of democratic thinkers are founded on an illusory image of man's nature is yet to be answered with mathematical finality. That it will be answered in time admits of no doubt to those who believe, as do Julian Huxley, Lancelot Hogben, and John Dewey, that the criteria of the scientific method can be applied as surely to the study of human beings as to the study of inorganic matter. But the science of man, requiring as it does the services not only of biology and psychology but also of sociology and anthropology, is still in its infancy. In relation to mathematics, biology is still in the Newtonian era; in relation to chemistry and physics, in Huxley's opinion it is no farther advanced than in 1850; sociology he maintains will not reach a status comparable to the chemistry of today until a century hence. To what extent is intelligence (as defined by intelligence quotients) genetically determined? To what extent is the incidence of genius determined by environment? Is such a trait as ambition to succeed or desire to excel a specific of genetic inheritance? Is musical talent or sculpturing talent inborn? Can the impact of ideological influences, however communicated, be tallied and measured? What happens to identical twins in radically different surroundings? How pregnant with meaning these questions are to America's democratic decisions no one can doubt. As yet, however, science can reply to them only with tentative conclusions or contradictory evidence.[1]

Following the trail opened by Mendel, biologists since 1900 have sought to trace in man's inheritance the genetic formulae of Mendel's laws. This has been the field of concentration despite the fact that experimentation cannot be carried on with human beings; the life of man is seventy years, that of the fruit fly ten days. Productive as have been T. H. Morgan's researches on the fruit fly, the correlation between fruit fly and man in terms of genetic characters rests thus far on assumptions rather than upon evidence. Morgan himself has made no such assumptions. Granting that the fruit fly and the man are alike in Mendelian inheritance of physical characters, what nervous structure in the fruit fly can be compared to the structure of the cortex? Man's breathing, like that of the fruit fly, is fixed and automatic in the nervous system. But the cortex is the area, the measure, of man's plasticity, of billions of brain connections yet to be formed. Nothing exists in the fruit fly comparable to the cortex in man.

Yet, as Pavlov points out, no physiological study of the hemispheres was begun before 1870. Few biologists until the time of Pavlov gave any attention to the biology of the cortex—to that area of man's mechanism, in short, that separates him most completely from the animals. In the words of Hogben: "Man inherits an immensely developed forebrain; and this circumstance frees him from many of the restrictions which heredity imposes upon the brute creation."[2] Surgical exploration of the cortex is in its infancy.[3] Instead of concentrating on the forebrain, wherein resides man's unique inheritance, biology has devoted its researches to the relatively fixed and socially unalterable mechanism of genetic transmission. "Heredity," wrote Arthur Thomson, "implies inertia, but variability implies creativeness."[4] In solving the basic problems of society, "a study of the central nervous system," asserts Hogben, "will have far more to contribute than the study of reproduction."[5] Yet in twentieth-century biological science the energy and resources devoted to research on the nervous system have by no means equaled the effort expended on the study of the genetics of transmissible characters.

To the question of the inheritance of instinct or temperament biology and psychology today can make no answers with categorical assurance. As long ago as 1924 J. Arthur Thomson attacked as fallacious McDougall's assumptions about inherited instinct. Sexual behavior in birds and animals is inborn: "But where man has ritual in this connection it is prescribed, not by inborn instinctive pre-arrangements of the brain and the mind, but by tradition."[6]

The old concept of inherited instincts has been effectually modified
by the researches of Pavlov and the gradual acceptance of his
theory of conditioned reflexes. In place of long lists of generalized
instincts, such as pugnacity, fear, anger, etc., science today finds
such unconditioned reflexes as seizing and biting. Extreme behavior-
ists maintain that the unconditioned child is afraid of only two
things: falling and a loud noise. In his illuminating researches on
the fruit fly T. H. Morgan has discovered the position of genetic
units within the chromosomes that determine the growth of various
fruit-fly organs.[7] Presumably the genes of the human being may
in time be similarly identified; but meanwhile the genetic determinism of fear of falling or a loud noise is yet to be established.
Environment begins at conception; in the womb the child lives
in a soundproof world; he becomes accustomed physiologically to
quiet and stability of position. Even so, would a child born and
kept for the first month of his life among loud noises be afraid of
them? Or would a child accustomed to falling in the first month be
afraid of falling? No experiments have yet been carried out to
provide the answers to such questions. Meanwhile such cautious
biologists as H. S. Jennings make claims for the inheritance of
"temperament," without defining that elusive term; Jennings goes
so far as to state that "imperfect genes . . . taken alone would yield
an irritable, lazy or stupid person."[8] For such a statement, however, Jennings submits no experimental evidence; no one has yet
isolated the genetic determinant of laziness or irritability.[9] Though
the effect of the endocrine glands on personality is indisputable,
this effect is now quickly alterable by the use of chemicals. Little
is yet known in a genetic sense about endocrine functions; certainly
their genetic determinants are yet to be isolated.[10]

In the past several decades the assumptions of psychologists
and biologists, founded on the researches of Alfred Binet and Lewis
M. Terman, that inherited intelligence can be precisely measured,
have been found so faulty as to be no longer tenable. No longer
is the claim made that intelligence (however defined) is a pure
product of genetic determinism and hence unchangeable from birth

to death. Feeble-mindedness is no longer traced to organic weakness alone. "Until some more satisfactory definition can be given as to where feeble-mindedness begins and ends," wrote T. H. Morgan in *Evolution and Genetics*, "... it is extravagant to pretend to claim that there is a single Mendelian factor for this condition."[11] The distinguished record of the Edwards family and the sad history of the Jukes are no longer set forth as proof of hereditary determinism. One review of the available evidence estimates a maximum change of 24 I.Q. points traceable to environmental factors.[12] Evidence has been brought forth to show that the more isolated the community, the more remote from city stimuli, the lower will be the I.Q. of its citizens.[13] The long isolation of feral man, as shown in Petroff's study, is an extreme example, as yet more suggestive than authoritative.[14]

The researches of Otto Klineberg, thus far unchallenged, afford striking new evidence of the effect of environment on intelligence.[15] In the Army Alpha Tests of World War I, when 14,994 southern and 8,165 northern Negroes were examined, it had been found that the intelligence of southern Negroes lagged far behind. White soldiers of the same state, whether South or North, ranked higher in intelligence than Negroes; but the Negroes of Pennsylvania, New York, Illinois, and Ohio ranked higher in median scores than the *whites* of Mississippi, Kentucky, Arkansas, and Georgia. Was this increase due to the better environment of the North or to the superiority of Negro emigrants? In Tennessee the average I.Q. of Negro children was found to be 58; in Los Angeles, 105. From intelligence tests given to southern children who had migrated to New York City, Klineberg found that the longer they remained in a city environment, the higher their I.Q.'s rose. Those who had been in the city only one or two years had an average score of 94. A similar trend was observed in southern Negro children who moved from rural areas to towns and cities. In Klineberg's view, then, the correlation between environment and I.Q. is indisputable.[16] Such studies throw further doubts on the extent to which heredity determines intelligence.[17] They stress anew the importance of quantitative studies of human interactions in the development of intelligence.

One hope of scientific certainty in calculating the relative roles of heredity and environment in shaping intelligence and personality has been the study of identical twins. The difficulties in this field have been so numerous, however, that until 1940 fewer than a hundred identical twins had been observed and tested in the United States. The tabulated results thus far have been indecisive; thousands more identical twins must be discovered, tested, and observed before the present data can be implicitly relied upon. The most comprehensive study thus far, that of Newman, Freeman, and Holzinger, *Twins: A Study of Heredity and Environment* (1937), though indecisive on an absolute basis, yielded a few positive results. Nineteen sets of identical twins living apart showed differences in intelligence, the highest being .791 on the Binet I.Q. test. One invariable trend was the correlation between intelligence and the amount of education each twin had received. "In the case of the intelligence tests," write the authors, "consistent and significant positive correlations with educational ratings are found."[18] As might be expected, the study showed physical traits of the separated twins to be less variable than intelligence: "It appears that the physical characteristics are least affected by the environment, that intelligence is affected more; and personality or temperament, if our tests can be relied upon, the most. This finding is significant, regardless of the absolute amount of environmental influence."

If biologists no longer insist upon a genetic equivalent to intelligence, and have in part relinquished the conception of inherited instincts, still less do they now claim that heredity in any quantitative sense determines social conduct. Galton's sweeping assertion of 1901 is no longer tenable: "Whether it be in character, disposition, energy, intellect, or physical power, we each receive at our birth a definite endowment, allegorised by the parable related in St. Matthew, some receiving many talents, others few."[19] Jennings, it is true, leans to the belief that even selfishness and unselfishness may have genetic origins.[20] But no biologist now maintains, as formerly, that a criminal tendency appears in human beings in accordance with Mendel's laws. Lombroso's conception of the criminal type has long since been discredited.[21] Father Flanagan's assertion, "There is no such thing as a bad *boy*," which is a contemporary equivalent of "Man's character is made for him and not by him," is a conclusion accepted now by biologists and sociologists.

Forty years ago, in his study of the Jukes family, Dr. Estabrook maintained that "there is an hereditary factor in *licentiousness*."[22] As Hogben indicates, Estabrook does not define *licentiousness;* neither, of course, does he identify the place of genetic licentiousness in the linear arrangement of human genes; no biologist at the present writing, as Weinstein points out,[23] has even seen genes under the microscope. The idea that the Negro by virtue of his color possesses an inborn savagery inimical to civilized practices, or that the white race possesses more inborn chivalry toward women than the yellow, is not seriously credited by biologists today. All men, as James Harvey Robinson points out in *The Mind in the Making*, are born completely uncivilized.[24] Our social attitudes are not inborn. "We humans," says Robinson, "accept our breakfasts, our trains and telephones and orchestras and movies, our national Constitution, or moral code and standards of manners, with the simplicity and innocence of a pet rabbit."[25]

With the gradual reduction of the claims of heredity, the eugenic concept of the improvement of the race has also suffered deterioration. In his brilliant essay, "Eugenics and Society," Julian Huxley delineates the environmental factors which the eugenist has hitherto neglected in his plans for genetic selection. "Our schemes for improving the genetic qualities of the nation or the species are meaningless," he asserts, "except in relation to some particular environment, present or future."[26] A eugenics plan in a slave order will be very different from a plan in a socialist order. In England, Huxley notes, the class system works to encourage achievements in art, science, and mathematics in the upper classes, and to discourage independence and initiative among unskilled laborers. The class system conceals rather than uncovers true genetic differences.

Insufficient food and vitamin supply has reduced the mental energy of large numbers of impoverished children; under such conditions intelligence tests are not dependable. Even under the present environmental discrepancies, one-half of the most brilliant school children of England come from wage-earning families. "The fact that an undue proportion of artists, writers and scientists come from the upper strata of society would not then mean that these strata were proportionately endowed by heredity—merely that in the rest of society the Darwins and the Einsteins, like the Miltons, were mute and inglorious."[27] Thus eugenists must work to equalize environment; for only then will the gifts of hereditary talent open themselves to the world.

In withdrawing, at least in part, its conclusions about the genetic determination of instinct, intelligence, and temperament, biological science presents a much less fixed image of the nature of man than it did half a century ago. The area of man's genetic unalterable determinants is still unknown; but in the concepts of science it has narrowed with each passing decade, while the area of man's plasticity looms larger and larger.

The evidence of Loeb, Crile, Sherrington, and Pavlov demonstrates as never before the quantitative magnitude of the brain's responses. "The incomparably greater development of the cerebral cortex in man," writes Pavlov, "is pre-eminently that factor which has raised man to his dominant position in the animal world."[28] Yet the study of the cerebral cortex, the organ of man's plasticity, is only in its infancy. The cortex is a thin brain cover of gray matter, about one-fifth of an inch thick; if taken off and rolled in a ball, it would be about as large as a plum or a walnut, weighing perhaps half an ounce. The cortex is made up of tiny nerve cells, estimated at 9,200,000,000, arranged in regular patterns. Between the cells are stretched countless nerve fibers carrying the almost instantaneous impulses of thought, making an innumerable number of combinations, establishing habits of thinking that eventually become mechanical.[29] "It is obvious," writes Pavlov, "that the different kinds of habits based on training, education and discipline of any sort are nothing but a long chain of conditioned reflexes."[30]

Such an extreme statement must be studied, of course, in the light of the conclusions of more conservative scientists like E. L. Thorndike, Lewis M. Terman, and Arnold Gesell. Yet no biologist or psychologist has yet set limits to the work of the cortex as the instrument of man's plasticity. In *The Human Brain* John Pfeiffer asserts that man's only inborn trait may be his teachability.[31] The most amazing function of the cortex is its infinite capacity for receiving and sorting and storing away messages from the world outside man's skin. In some unknown way its mechanism allows man to imitate the speech of others and finally comprehend ideas expressed in words. The cortex is the measure of man's learning powers: how many images he can remember, how many ideas he can absorb, how many mental habits he can establish, to what extent the stimuli of his environment can direct his emotions and govern his conduct, the chemical and physical constituents of thought— these have been only imperfectly recorded, much less measured.

The idiot and the genius are rough extremes of man's potential; but we have given little quantitative attention to the brain responses of the average man when placed in a superior environment. If man is a mirror of his environment, as Crile asserted, then the learning that takes place in the cortex is the pre-eminent factor in his destiny. The assumption by Arnold Gesell, that genius is only a further step in the unfolding of genetic patterns,[32] inspires the question: "Then does every man who is born a genius inevitably reach the goal?" Perhaps one in a million, or one in several hundred thousand, as Galton asserted, is born a genius.[33] If so, the loss of genius through lack of a favorable environment is three-fourths of their number. Whatever part genetics may play in the formation of a genius, few biologists now claim that there is a Mendelian factor for character traits as well. Man will be hateful or compassionate, prejudiced or tolerant, peaceful or warlike, as his environment decides. Only through the yet unmeasured plasticity of the nervous system can Jefferson's concept of the common man find scientific justification or demolition.

Postscript

I N an age when biology has been gradually reducing its claims based on genetic determinism (at least as applied to character and personality traits), a new claim for inherited instincts appeared in Robert Ardrey's *African Genesis* (1961), followed in 1966 by the same author's *Territorial Imperative* and Konrad Lorenz's *On Aggression*. From observations of animal life (as well as the life of fish and birds), both men argued that man is also by instinct aggressive. Ardrey, though not a trained biologist, was a close observer of animal life in Africa; Lorenz was already renowned as an ecologist. Man not only inherits a strong aggressive instinct from his animal ancestors, in Ardrey's judgment; he also inherits an instinct to defend a certain bit of land as his territory. "If man is a part of the natural world," wrote Ardrey, "then he possesses as do other species a genetic inheritance as long as life itself. The territorial urge, as a part of that inheritance, may in the human species be wrong or right, bad or good, destructive or constructive, wasting or conservative."[34] Genetically transmitted, such an urge cannot be erased by the teaching of civilized customs and attitudes over the centuries. It is intellectual folly, in Ardrey's judgment, to assume that "environment must be held responsible for human aggression."[35] Ardrey's view of man, according to Gerald Gorer, was of "a killer with an innate propensity for using weapons against his fellowman."[36] Ardrey maintained indeed that man has an "aggressive imperative" and that he needs warfare and its weapons in order to survive.

Such a bold claim for genetic determinism of instinctual behavior involved conclusions which leading anthropologists and biologists had thought amply refuted decades ago. In reviewing Ardrey's *Territorial Imperative* in *The New York Times,* Loren Eiseley called Ardrey "a Calvin resurrected in modern guise."[37] It was obvious to both Eiseley and Ashley Montagu that Ardrey's interpretation owed much to Freud's analysis of man's primary nature. "Men are not gentle creatures who want to be loved," Freud had written. Rather they are "creatures among whose instinctual endowments is to be reckoned a powerful share of aggressiveness."[38] Does man not exploit his neighbor, seize his possessions, humiliate, torture, and kill him? To Freud no commandment was so absurd as the one to love one's neighbor as oneself. Is there indeed any commandment, asked Freud, that runs counter to man's nature more than this one? *Homo homini lupus* (Man, a wolf regarding man).

"Who, in the face of all his experience of life and history, will have the courage to dispute this assertion?" Freud had asked.[39] Looking backward through the ages of man's evolution, Loren Eiseley responded: "Who would have thought that incipient man on the Pliocene uplands frequented by Ardrey's murderous apes would eventually evolve a capacity for compassion? Yesterday on the streets of New York I saw a young man stop a line of traffic and gently toot a horn to coax a reluctant pigeon out of his path."[40]

Man and Aggression, a collection of fourteen articles and reviews of the three books by Ardrey and Lorenz, appeared in 1968. In this compilation edited by Ashley Montagu, several authors call attention to the failure of Ardrey and Lorenz to define such crucial terms as *instinct, aggression,* and *territorial.* Is aggression a spontaneous release of energy, as Lorenz has claimed, or is it release triggered by a challenge, a movement, a chemical change, the pain of a blow? "Thus," writes J. P. Scott, "we have a mechanism which prolongs and magnifies the effects of external stimulation but no mechanism for building up the first stimulation from within. There is no internal change corresponding to the change in blood sugar which results in hunger. In short, the physiological evidence is against Lorenz's notion of the spontaneity of aggression, and indeed, it is difficult to see how such a mechanism for spontaneity could have evolved."[41] In the article "War Is Not in Our Genes," Sally Carrighar points out that the apes, nearest to man in evolution, are the least aggressive of all animals; they do not fight, either collectively or singly. In his essay "The Nature of Territorial Aggression," John Hurrell Crook asserts that "there is no theoretical requirement for aggressive behavior to well up spontaneously without prior stimulation."[42] Such behavior is not an ineradicable or innate force requiring periodic release in explosions of fighting or anger.

The arguments of both Ardrey and Lorenz suffer from too close identification of animal nature with human nature. "There is little doubt," writes Kenneth Boulding, "that the oriole's genes build into the bird itself both the knowledge and the desire to build an oriole nest and that this knowledge comes from the information in the gene rather than information coming into the bird through its senses."[43] But man, asserts Boulding, unlike the oriole, has an enormously expanded nervous system of perhaps ten billion components, representing a capacity for learning denied in large part to the animal world. It is true that man often suffers from genetic defects which reduce his ability to learn; but in general his range of learning sets him completely apart from the animal world. The one thing that makes man completely different from the animals is the teachability with which he is genetically endowed. Yet Ardrey and Lorenz assert that human beings are cruel and savage by instinct—that in this they are like their animal ancestors. Montagu and his fellow anthropologists believe that this is a slander not only of human life but also of animal life. Most wild animals are not ferocious, even in the defense of territory; Montagu names the chimpanzee, the orangutan, the gorilla, and many small animals which have no sense of territorial ownership, such as the northern plains red fox, the California ground squirrel, and the Iowa prairie spotted skunk. Montagu has dealt at length with the cooperation that exists in all animal life outside captivity. Upon this cooperation of activity depends the adequate care of the young and, indeed, the very survival of the species.

XX
Heredity and Sexual Behavior: Alfred Kinsey

> *In the main a man's sexual constitution*
> *is all-pervading, deep-rooted, permanent, in*
> *large measure congenital. At the same time*
> *. . . we have to recognize, on the one hand,*
> *that the acquired may go much farther*
> *back than was once believed, and, on the*
> *other hand, that the constitutional is often*
> *so subtle and so obscure that it remains*
> *undetected.*
>
> —Havelock Ellis

No TOPIC has been so elusive in American thought about the nature of man, or so long postponed, as the inquiry into sexual behavior. The revelations of Pepys have no parallel in early American letters. Such a notation as that of Aaron Burr in his *Journal*, "Four francs for a prostitute and brandy; two for benevolence," is a record strange and rare in American diaries. As in other fields, however, so in sexual behavior: the inquiries of the poet and the novelist have preceded the quest of the scientist. When Emerson stated that the sexual man was a remnant of the chimpanzee, he gave voice to a distaste that suggested a progressive rejection of the sexual man by exceptional human beings. Mark Twain's heroes betray as few thoughts about sexual life as those of Dickens. Whitman, on the other hand, set down in page after page his exultation in the release of sexual energy—the first poet in American life to disassociate sexual release from the morality of the Christian code. Though to Whitman sexual release was a joyous experience, fit companion to his poetic flights, he was realistic enough to assert that the average young American had recourse to houses of prostitution. Apparently Whitman saw no contradiction between the expectancy of release in "To a Common Prostitute" and the transcendental vision of "Passage to India." With the advent of Theodore Dreiser came what we may call the first amoral conception of sexual behavior, remote alike from the exultation of Whitman and the distaste of Emerson: to Dreiser the sexual man embodied an almost impersonal outpouring of energy that easily demolished all social barriers in its path. Like many of the ancient Greeks, and unlike Americans as a whole, Dreiser believed that no code of morality could be based on the variegated needs and desires of the sexual man.

Since Dreiser's early novels and the advent of Sherwood Anderson the documentation of sexual life in American literature has widened and deepened to a degree unthinkable half a century ago. To read *Sister Carrie* six decades after Doubleday withdrew it from distribution, and to compare it with such a novel as *The Naked and the Dead,* is to trace an enlargement of literary freedom unequaled on the American scene, an enlargement not without its penalties of inferior fiction as well as its rewards of a few superb novels. Without such an enlargement of creative documentation of sexual life, the American public would have been ill prepared for a scientific scrutiny of its most private behavior.

The distance traced by Dreiser and Anderson between the actuality of this private behavior and the moral codes of American life was recorded with scientific precision in 1948-53 by Alfred C. Kinsey and his associates at Indiana University. From the beginning of his researches Kinsey divorced himself as far as possible from all considerations of ethical or religious sanction. His aim was merely to record the actuality of events in the most mysterious domain of the nature of man. The attempt to reduce sexual behavior to quantitative evaluation, as though it were divorced from human choice and the influence of family, community, or church, was without parallel in the growing search for a science of man. To many social critics the researches of Freud, revolutionary as they had seemed in his time, held little promise of factual certainty as compared with Kinsey's objective quantitative procedure.

One of Kinsey's most significant conclusions is that man is born with a potential of sexual energy that throughout his life may be roughly measured by the number of times it requires release to the point of ejaculation. The ways and means by which the American male releases his sexual energy depend in substantial part on his environment. But the lifelong quantity of sexual energy and the frequency of its release over this long period are by Kinsey's finding hereditary in origin. The words *sexual outlet* or *total sexual outlet* occur on hundreds of pages of Kinsey's study. Thus, between the ages of sixteen and twenty the "mean frequency of total outlet" for single men is 3.3 orgasms weekly. Boys who have a first orgasm by age eleven have on the average three orgasms weekly between ages eleven and fifteen. Boys who have a first ejaculation at fifteen or later have a weekly average of 1.74 orgasms in the first year of adolescence. How these orgasms are effected depends upon circumstances. But the timing of the first orgasms and the frequency thereafter are determined, in Kinsey's view, by hereditary mechanisms.[1]

Kinsey defines adolescence, with appropriate qualifications and exceptions, as the time of first ejaculation; the average age at which American males arrive at this point is thirteen years and seven months. By Kinsey's definition over a third of all boys are adolescent by the end of the seventh grade, and over 96 per cent by the end of the eighth grade. Why some boys become adolescent at ten, others at thirteen, and still others at seventeen or even eighteen is still unexplained. But to Kinsey it is obvious from the statistics of adolescence that environment has little or nothing to do with such criteria as the growth of pubic hair and the first ejaculation. The onset of adolescence is a factor primarily of the male's age and the functioning of biologic mechanisms relatively independent of social conditioning or even of the kinds and quantity of food to which he is accustomed. When the development of the boy's body reaches the point requiring the release of sperm, masturbation is the means used to this end in more than two-thirds of American boyhoods. Though the boy at this point has some choice of sexual outlet, he has little or no control of the energy itself. If his training is such as to prevent masturbation, his body seeks an outlet in nocturnal emissions, which are themselves a symbol of the male's helplessness to control the energy generated by hereditary mechanisms that were set in motion long before his birth.[2]

Kinsey's studies show further that boys who reach adolescence at age eleven have a higher frequency of sexual release throughout life than boys who reach adolescence at fifteen or later. In the history of married males, boys who reached adolescence at eleven had an average of six orgasms weekly from ages sixteen to twenty; whereas in the same period boys who reached adolescence at fifteen had an average weekly release of 2.5. Between the ages of twenty-one and thirty-five, the difference between the two groups has sharply lessened: 2.38 to 2.20 orgasms weekly. Though the difference in total sexual outlet of the two groups steadily decreases from the third decade of life onward, the significant fact is that it persists throughout life, despite the immense range of environmental influences. In the history of single males, the difference between the two groups follows an almost identical pattern. Thus it appears that the frequency of sexual expressions is governed by a hereditary mechanism that requires release generally independent of moral, religious, or parental teachings, and that is equally active among married and single men.[3]

One of the most arresting of Kinsey's findings is that boys who reach adolescence at eleven but never go beyond the eighth grade in school have a higher frequency of sexual release than boys who go to high school and beyond. Boys who will not go beyond the eighth grade have an average of 5.1 ejaculations a week between the ages of eleven and fifteen; those who will never go beyond high school have an average of 4.2; and boys who will go on to college have an average of 3.3. These differences in frequency persist in manhood, though in diminishing ratio. Thus between twenty-one and twenty-five, the male who reached adolescence at eleven and left school in the eighth grade has a frequency of 5.46, whereas the high-school graduate in these years has an average of 3.87 and the college male a frequency of 2.79.[4]

Kinsey has found no evidence that "sublimation" is a reality in sexual experience; he is at a loss, therefore, to account for the phenomenon of a higher frequency of orgasm in boys who will finish eight years of school than in boys who will complete twelve or sixteen. When a boy of eleven has five ejaculations weekly, Kinsey's findings would assume that he will attend neither high school nor college. If this assumption is correct, what hereditary factor is responsible? What environmental factors impinging on the sex drive may be isolated? Sociologists say that more than half the students who drop out of high school or never go on to college act for economic reasons. But is the need for satisfying sex hunger related to the need for a job? Such questions the embryonic science of man is not yet ready to answer.

The researches of Kinsey and his associates make it overwhelmingly clear, however, for the first time in the search for the science of man, that environmental forces are powerless to stop the periodic flow of sexual energy. This is not to say that the teachings of parents, teachers, and clergymen are helpless in all instances to restrict the release of sexual energy to the ends they describe as acceptable or righteous. Among the overwhelming mass of citizens, however, the teachings of family, church, and community are as powerless to prevent the release of sperm outside of marriage as to prevent the menstrual flow. This conclusion of the Kinsey researchers is supported by such incontrovertible evidence as to give it epochal validity in the American search for the science of man. Environment can stretch the mind, shape the thoughts of youth, change the common into the uncommon man, direct the channels of energy into hate or love, establish modes of dress and morality a thousand times more easily than it can stop the periodic release of sexual energy. The gap thus created between the facts of sexual behavior and the moral assumptions of church, school, and family life is so wide that it cannot be bridged for generations to come.

What Whitman and Dreiser and Lawrence have recorded in literary terms Kinsey has documented with the factual accounts of thousands of human beings. One effect of these researches is to support the main thesis of Freud—that the rebellious sexual nature of man expresses itself in one way or another even when the patient believes he has, in the words of Plato, "set in order his own inner life and is at peace with himself." The reason for this turmoil is gradually emerging: the sexual element in man is the least educable. Nature wants children to repeople the earth. She cares nothing about society's responsibility to the child, but only about his entrance into the world. It is the conflict between the desires of nature and the teachings of society that Freud describes in variegated manifestations, and Kinsey sets down in cold statistical fact.

The conclusions reached by the Kinsey researchers have a validity denied, however, to the methods of Freud. Epoch-making as Freud's investigations are, they cannot compare in significance to the quantitative procedure of Kinsey and his associates. Like every science, the science of man must wait for the final and indisputable evidence of mathematical record. What was formerly the most obscure and private part of American life has suddenly, through the Kinsey report, become the most fully described and tabulated. It is plain from this tabulation, moreover, that in no other department of the nature of man is heredity so powerful as in that of his sexual behavior.

1955
Poverty, Science, and Hope

In 1955 the national income of the United States was $330,000,-000,000, ten times the money value of goods and services produced in 1935, when one-third of the nation, 13,000,000 families, had been "ill-fed, ill-clothed and ill-housed," with an average family income of $744 a year. By 1955 the population had risen to 164,000,000. Of the 43,000,000 families, 18,000,000 had annual incomes of $5,000 or more. One-fifth of all American families, despite the enormous advance in prosperity, had incomes not exceeding $2,000 a year, an income that would provide no more than three dollars a day for food.[1] More than 8,000,000 families, comprising some 30,000,000 individuals, were still "ill-fed, ill-housed, ill-clothed." In America's most prosperous decade there were more than a few scattered pockets of poverty: every fifth American knew it to be a stark reality. How many uncommon minds lost their original luster under the daily cloud of poverty, no one could tell.

In 1955, in an article titled "America's Next Twenty Years," Peter Drucker prophesied that by 1975 America would have a population of 220,000,000. Between 9,000,000 and 12,000,000 young people would be college students. By 1975 America's productivity may have doubled. "Today," wrote Drucker, "every American at work supports himself and one-and-a-half other people besides. Twenty years from now every American at work should produce enough to support, at today's standard of living, himself and three-and-a-half other people. And he will have to do this in fewer working hours."[2] In 1955 one farm family could grow enough food for itself and seven other families, as compared to one other family *in 1870.³ By 1975, if Drucker's prophesies are accurate, one farm family will grow enough food for itself and fourteen other families.*

In 1955 the Supreme Court decision on segregation was one year old. The North found to its dismay that despite decades of self-approval, its own schools by no means embodied the reality of the great decision. In New York City, as in most other northern cities, schools had been skilfully located to concentrate Negro children in Negro sections of town, and white children in white sections. Though the New York State law provided for a mingling of blacks and whites in every school, many school boards had devised ways and means to subvert the intent of the law. Desegregation was a national problem, not a southern one only. Each state and each community, North or South, responded to the Supreme Court decision in a way peculiar to the roots of its past. Some border states proceeded immediately toward elimination of segregation, whereas Georgia, South Carolina, and Mississippi contemplated the abolition of public schools as the alternative to the abolition of segregation.⁴ The Supreme Court decision was often only a rope of sand; but it did uphold an ideal of justice for the Negro child, appealing to the great chivalrous tradition of fair play which has a strong hold on thousands of southern whites.

Fewer Americans in 1955 than in 1855 would claim that the Negro's blackness was the badge of his genetic inferiority. In a hundred years the color stamp of servitude in American minds, as described by Tocqueville, had loosened its hold. Year by year, partly as a result of war employment policies, professional doors were opening to Negro talent. In 1948, 2.4 per cent of the total Negro population held professional jobs. By 1955 the proportion had risen to 3.5 per cent.⁵

In 1955 an ever increasing number of young people, white and black, sought admission to American high schools and colleges. Eight and a half million boys and girls were enrolled in high schools, 22,000,000 in elementary schools. In the nation's colleges and other institutions of higher learning, which numbered 1,858, there were 2,700,000 men and women enrolled.⁶

In 1955 the Ford Foundation granted funds to Portland, Oregon, and Reed College in partial support of a five-year study to devise a superior educational program for Portland's gifted children.[7]

In 1955 the British Eugenics Society recommended the identification of England's most promising school children, aged eight to thirteen, "exceptional in scholarship, good fellowship, and sports." Parents of gifted children, in the opinion of the society, should be encouraged by government grants to have more children.[8]

In 1955 juvenile delinquency took a high toll among American youth. In United States District Courts alone 1,235 defendants were tried and 734 of them sentenced to federal imprisonment.[9]

In 1955 research in the functioning of the human brain advanced apace, yet the knowledge it brought was still remote from the completeness of a trustworthy science of man. The workings of man's brain differentiate him more conclusively than any other function from the dog or the ape. Yet the mechanisms of the brain are still mysterious and in most ways inexplicable. In surgical terms, "The exploration of the frontal cortex of man has just begun."[10] The question of Holmes a century ago, "What is the chemical equivalent of thought?" is still unanswerable. Relatively little is known about brain chemistry. Apparently the circulation of the blood in the brain has more to do with high intelligence than its size, weight, or structure. Every minute a pint of blood circulates through the blood vessels of the brain.[11] Prolonged nose stoppages from adenoids or colds reduce the supply of blood and oxygen to the brain and are known to retard children in school achievement.[12] The brain requires one-fourth of all the oxygen the body absorbs. Thyroid extract and iodine are known to improve the mentality of cretins and idiots. The energy for the work of the brain comes from glucose, which is broken down in fourteen chemical steps in the blood-brain barrier.[13]

In 1955 the study of the effect of drugs and injuries on brain function gave new hope that some main sources of mental illness may be found in the chemistry of the brain. It is claimed that blows on the head may produce "practically every symptom known to psychiatrists."[14] Similarly chemicals such as mescaline can break through the blood-brain barrier and produce symptoms of great violence. Barbiturates, nitrous oxide, carbon dioxide, and alcohol all disturb the oxygen supply of the brain and its absorption of energy-producing glucose. Why is diabetes thirty times more prevalent among average healthy people than among schizophrenics?[15] Physicians have concluded from this fact alone that a chemical lack or excess may be at the root of schizophrenia. Injections of sodium cyanide have produced remarkable temporary relief from schizophrenic symptoms.[16] In 1955 Serpasil and Thorazine alone had been found so efficacious in treating mental illness that some physicians had come to regard all such illness as being chemically reversible.

On April 18, 1955, at 1:15 in the morning, Albert Einstein died in his sleep. He was seventy-six years old. To Einstein the chief ingredient of genius was concentration. Genius he called "a demoniac possession . . . like that of a lover."[17] At twelve he had read Euclid with feverish delight. No country and no family could he call his own with such devotion as that with which he clasped to himself the life of the mind, the gradual miracle of his genius. Because he feared that the Nazis would develop the atom bomb before the Americans, he had urged President Roosevelt to initiate the bomb. Yet when the bomb was dropped at Hiroshima, Einstein was horrified at what he had helped to accomplish. "Ach," he said, "the world is not yet ready for it."[18] With many of his fellow-scientists he opposed persistently the making of the hydrogen bomb. To Einstein the scientist was responsible not to one nation, but to all mankind.

In 1955 the Salk vaccine brought within sight the conquest of the dread paralytic polio. Up to April 12, when Dr. Thomas Francis made the announcement at Ann Arbor, 1,836,000 children, including Salk's two sons, had provided proof that the vaccine worked.

In 1955 William Faulkner, writing in the July Harper's, indicted the American denial of the right of privacy to the country's uncommon men: "America has not found any place for him who deals only in things of the human spirit."[19] Was a democracy, then, incompatible with the growth of a creative elite?

XXI
Anthropology and Man's Changing Image

> Biologically we know that hereditary races are constant to the degree that if a thousand morons and one man of genius are born per million in this generation, the proportion is unlikely to be seriously different in the next generation or for a number of generations following. If Athens for a thousand years had no great men, began to have a few in the sixth century, produced an astonishing number of geniuses of absolutely first rank in the fifth and fourth centuries, tapered off in the third, then became sterile again and has remained so until now, there is no known mechanism of heredity which can explain this fluctuation of incidence of high ability.
>
> —Alfred Kroeber

As COMPARED to chemistry and physics, the science of man is perhaps conceived but not yet struggling to be born; much less is it a lusty child. The American search for such a science, like all such quests, has been spasmodic and unpredictable in its advance, preceded by the guesses and hopes of scientists and poets about the nature of man.[1] Each tradition is indispensable; neither is sufficient. The poet seeks for the thread of unity and purpose, the scientist for a short step ahead on the solid rock.

The great Declaration posed certain articles of faith about man, none of which has yet been tested in the crucible of science. One article of faith was an assumption of the plasticity of the common man's mind, a capacity for growth never admitted or tested in aristocratic countries. What would be the effect of economic opportunity on the energies of the propertyless? Henry Adams visualized the release of the energies of humble and obscure persons as the most remarkable phenomenon on the American scene. But no scientist has yet measured the energies thus released, or the energies of boys and girls with eyes suddenly opened to the humble and obscure origins, not unlike their own, of uncommon men. "One could rise! One could rise!" cried Dreiser at sixteen, his mind aflame with a new vision of its reach.

The biologists have not visualized a structure for a science of man or their own opportunities for its development. Nor has biology concentrated on the springs of energy or the limits of man's elasticity of behavior. Rather it has sought a more exact delineation of man's internal structure, concentrating on the genetic mechanism which is fixed and unalterable at conception. Biology seeks those hereditary constants without which, it is true, no science of man is possible. But the multitude of unconsciously imitated acts impressed upon the child from early years—the concepts of right and wrong, of religion, warfare, making love, marrying, making a living, caring for one's family: none of these things, profound and often decisive in the shaping of human destiny, has biological science sought to measure.

The dynamics of equality in frontier America, of expanded definitions of equality in the minds of Lincoln, George, Bellamy, and millions of humbler lives, all these intellectual forces possess a nongenetic reality biology does not deny and does not attempt to measure. A correlation of sciences is needed to measure the impact of these forces on American life. Until this measurement is made, we cannot know the tenacity and effects of hereditary constants; nor can we know the full reach of man's most crucial hereditary variable, his plasticity, his teachability, in a society embodying the calculated forces of enlightenment.

This need for a quantitative measurement of social forces has been anticipated by the developing science of anthropology. Though little more than half a century old, cultural anthropology has already provided a mass of valuable data about the nature of man.

In this search American anthropologists have been foremost; the names of Lewis Morgan, Franz Boas, Ruth Benedict, Margaret Mead, Robert Lowie, and Ralph Linton are already world-renowned. Rejecting no correlative science, the anthropologist employs the findings of biology, chemistry, geology, psychology, and economics in delineating man's changing image. The anthropologist is not concerned with the individual, but rather with the mass man, the collective product of organic and social patterns. In order to achieve his aim, the anthropologist believes it imperative to immerse himself from time to time in societies alien to his own, divorcing himself from judgments of ethics and custom, observing man afresh in a milieu of extreme simplicity. The anthropologist, as Ruth Benedict says in *Patterns of Culture,* wishes to tally human behavior shaped by a variety of cultural traditions, not by one only.[2] Unlike some commentators on the uselessness of inquiry into the division of function between heredity and environment, the anthropologist regards this search as central and primary. "One of the fundamental aims of scientific anthropology," writes Boas in *Anthropology and Modern Life,* "[is] to learn which traits of behavior, if any, are organically determined and are, therefore, the common property of mankind and which are due to the culture in which we live."[3]

One of the decisive contributions of anthropology has been its painstaking analysis of so-called racial characteristics. Beyond the distinction of skin color, all attempts even to define the word *race* break down in the study of physical characteristics alone. In *The Nature of Human Nature* Ellsworth Faris asserts that race "is not a fact; it is a concept." As Boas points out, vastly more numerous physical differences exist within a race than between races. Negroes as a group have slightly smaller brains than whites, but the brain sizes of both Negroes and whites have remarkable variation; there is, moreover, no proof that brain size has any relation to intelligence. If races are thought of as white, yellow, and black, it is not true that all black men have kinky hair and flat noses, or that the nose bridge of the white man is always high.

Since Boas' study of 1911, a series of investigations have brought general agreement that cranial length and breadth, among other physical characteristics, can be modified substantially by environment.[4] Boas found that the longer European families (Bohemians, Sicilians, Hebrews, Hungarians) remained in the United States, the greater the differences in the children's head measurements, height and weight, and hair color from those of the immigrant parents. "All the evidence," concluded Boas, "is now in favor of a great plasticity of human types, and the permanence of types in new surroundings appears rather as the exception than as the rule."[5] In the words of W. M. Krogman: "A race is at best not a clearly defined biogenetic entity; it is now seen to have a transitory definition as well. It is plastic, malleable, varying with time, with place, and with circumstances."[6] The white race includes the Egyptian, the Moor, the Mexican worker, the English aristocrat, the Junker general, the French artist, the American mechanic, the Russian farm worker, and a thousand other types separated by vast differences in hair color, skin color, height, weight, leg thickness, nose breadth. In view of these physical differences within the race, the very classification of races according to skin color fades into scientific insignificance. In Robert Redfield's judgment color is no more an index of a human being's merit than the color of an automobile is an index to its mechanical excellence. Race, he asserts, is the product of social imagination rather than scientific investigation: "Race is, so to speak, a human invention."[7]

Whatever slight physical differences exist among races, anthropology presents indisputable proof that color is no criterion of intellectual power. "If we were to select the most intelligent, imaginative, energetic and emotionally stable third of mankind," writes Boas, "all races would be represented."[8] In no country does a black skin suggest mental inferiority more powerfully than in the United States. Yet the innate mental inferiority of the Negro is, according to the anthropologist, a pure myth; the researches of Otto Klineberg alone have established beyond reasonable doubt the environmental origins of most race differences in intelligence tests.[9] The researches of Melville J. Herskovits show no correlation whatever between the relative blackness of a Negro and his intellectual attainments.[10] When we turn to the yellow race, the Chinese and the Japanese, the investigations are less extensive; but the evidence is in the same direction. The record made in the schools of California by first-generation Americans born of pure Japanese parents, together with the brilliant record of the Nisei in World War II, testify to their range of intellectual adaptation. "The claim is not tenable," concludes Boas, "that mental qualities of races are biologically determined. Much less have we a right to speak of biologically determined superiority of one race over another."[11] There is no such thing as Negro blood, Italian blood, Jewish blood, Chinese blood; it is human blood, with all blood types represented in most races.

If race superiority is a myth, if a Negro is by reason of his color neither physically nor mentally inferior to the white, then it follows that primitive man is essentially the same at birth as the most privileged white child of the Main Line. His attitude toward religion, toward his parents, toward sex and marriage, toward warfare, toward foreigners, toward making a living, even his motor habits, are all induced not genetically but culturally. In order to test this conclusion, one anthropologist after another—Malinowski, Benedict, Mead, Lowie, Kluckhohn—has immersed himself in primitive societies, societies untouched by the complexities of the machine era and uncomplicated by the absorption of diverse customs. Anthropology is still young, and its methods of research are complicated.[12] But thus far at least the overwhelming evidence from the documentation of primitive societies is that the behavior of primitive man has its roots, like that of civilized man, in social determinants.

The primitive child, like the civilized child, learns customs and emotions and habits first from unconscious imitation; in plasticity of mind they are exactly alike. "An important change from primitive culture to civilization," writes Boas, "seems to consist in the gradual elimination of what might be called the emotional, socially determined associations of sense-impressions and of activities, for which intellectual associations are gradually substituted."[13] The primitive man, not having access to books, ideas, schools, or educated people, cannot possibly substitute intellectual associations for emotional ones; the extent to which civilized man succeeds in the same process is no mark of his innate superiority; but as to how rarely it is accomplished in race-saving attitudes the genius and persistence of fascism are an impressive testament. What is true of the primitive mind is true of our own; it has no existence in inheritance as such. "Much has been said and written on the hereditary character of the Italian, German, Frenchman, Irishman, Jew, and Gypsy," asserts Boas, "but it seems to me that not the slightest successful attempt has been made to establish causes for the behavior of a people other than historical and social conditions."[14] Thus it is with civilized man, and thus it is with the primitive. Primitive societies differ in striking fashion; but they differ by compulsion of social determinants.

Among the most suggestive and informative studies of primitive culture are those of Margaret Mead. In *Coming of Age in Samoa* and *Growing Up in New Guinea*, she recorded the life of adolescent girls in roughly divergent primitive cultures; in these studies she established the value of her results and the soundness of her methodology, resolving her findings in quantitative as well as qualitative record. In 1935 appeared a still more significant study, *Sex and Temperament in Three Primitive Societies*, describing the temperament and sexual behavior of three New Guinea tribes structurally similar but socially divergent: the gentle Arapesh, the violent Mundugumors, and the aesthetic Tchambuli.

The docile, affectionate Arapesh temperament Dr. Mead traces to the early milieu of tribe and family. From earliest months the Arapesh child meets only gentleness, warmth, love; she is fed often, carried about, surrounded with soothing tones, comforted instantly when she cries. As the child grows older, she is never scolded or beaten; she is taught to find everyone a friend and comforter, even dogs and pigs. By the age of eight, the child's personality is already molded by the happy, trustful behavior of friends and family.[15]

To the Arapesh girl, as she becomes ready for love, each step is gradual and confident; she meets her husband's family, lives with them, participates in their daily routine, long before the marriage consummation. Not passion, but tenderness, is the key to Arapesh love life; not play, but children, is its goal. No more aggressive in love-making than his wife, the Arapesh man is restrained, solicitous; the marriage act is preceded by long and tender preparation. With the first signs of pregnancy, all love-making ends; the child must rest and grow undisturbed. When the child is born, it may or may not be allowed to live; but if it lives the husband shares with the wife the care and affection surrounding the new-born. In the Arapesh community life there is no fighting, no quarreling, no competition for food or wives; docility, patience, good will prevail.

No people could be more unlike the peaceful Arapesh than their tempestuous neighbors, the Mundugumors, who numbered in 1935 no more than a thousand people. Sturdy and fierce, they possess the best land of the area and earn their living with comparative ease, each family its own provider. The very organization of Mundugumor society, Dr. Mead reports, sets up frictions and antagonisms within the family. A man's property passes first to his daughters, then to his daughters' sons, next to the daughters of his daughters' sons, etc. Such a family linkage is called a *rope*. The mother's property and loyalty, on the other hand, go to her sons, her sons' daughters, the sons of these daughters. A father hopes for a daughter, whom he may trade for an extra wife; but a brother also hopes for a sister, as he possesses in theory the same right as his father to give her away. Hostility between fathers and sons, between fathers and mothers, is the inevitable outcome. To the taboo-minded father, pregnancy is hateful; to the mother it is hateful, too, bringing the reproaches of her husband and the danger of desertion; and whether the child is a boy or a girl, its birth is the occasion for further hostility between father and mother.

In the early months of life the child is not cuddled, as in the Arapesh community, but hung up in a rough uncomfortable basket. When he cries too loudly, his mother scratches on the basket to divert his attention, suckling him only as a last resort, and then as briefly as possible. The attitude of the mother toward the child is one of anger and exasperation; the child soon learns to respond in kind. When he is old enough to walk, and wanders toward the dangerous river, the mother screams and scolds. He is weaned with harsh suddenness. As the child grows older, he learns he must refrain from weeping, be bold, aggressive, and suspicious like his elders. In contrast to the Arapesh habits, the love-making of the Mundugumor boys is quick and violent; in manhood their language is sadistic and coarse, particularly toward young lovers. Nor are the women more soft and yielding than the men; they also are harsh and violent, seeking, like the men, power, dominance, quick satisfaction of desire.

Utterly dissimilar in temperament from both the Arapesh and the Mundugumor, the neighboring Tchambuli find in ceremony and art their central motivation. This is true, however, of the men only; the Tchambuli women, unlike the Arapesh and the Mundugumor, have developed temperaments of strikingly different flavor from their husbands'. They are steady, efficient, cheerful breadwinners and organizers; the men are ceremonial, dramatic, quarrelsome, art-loving. This contradiction in temperament Dr. Mead traces to the structure of Tchambuli society, in which men and women are separated in economic function and competition for approval.

In his early months and years the Tchambuli child is conditioned to laughing attention, frequent feedings, and good humor; he is weaned with careless ease, never with harshness, never with extreme solicitude. The girl continues to live in this safe milieu. But as early as eight the Tchambuli boy begins to separate himself from the world of women and explore the provinces of the men's ceremonial life; no longer does he have a secure place at his mother's knee. This is the beginning of three or four years of frustration and defeat that affect his whole life; excluded from his old world and not yet admitted to the new, he develops habits of resentment, insecurity, quarrelsomeness. Though meanwhile he is learning to adorn himself, to dance, to speak gracefully, to play flutes of varied and wonderful tones, he is too young to engage in a man's sexual life, with which girls of his age are already familiar. In the Tchambuli courtship the girl selects an older lover before she yields to her future husband; the sting of rejection and secrecy finds no compensation in loving explanations, as in the Arapesh tradition. Boys and men quiver in resentment at slight hurts and often burst into hysterical anger. Notwithstanding the purchase of wives, and assumed masculine government, the women dominate by virtue of the superior fiber of their personalities, a fiber strengthened by consistent affection and purposeful activity of the woman's world. For them the men act and dance and play the flute; for their approval they adorn themselves and expend their energy in lavish ceremony, losing a sense of reality, even of emotional reality, in the never-ending drama of make-believe.

In these three New Guinea tribes, then, tribes possessing a common geographical environment and racial ancestry, Dr. Mead has documented personality types utterly dissimilar. Her conclusion is that these temperaments are, in effect, the creation of tribal patterns of culture. So plastic, indeed, does human nature appear from this documentation, that even the terms *male* and *female* as applied to temperament have no decisive meaning. The approved traits and attitudes in both the Arapesh and the Mundugumor tribes appear in approximately equal intensity in men and women, boys and girls. The docile, compassionate temperament of the Arapesh appears in both sexes; the Arapesh man is no braver, gentler, more competitive, or less maternal than his wife and daughter. Sex as a powerful determinant of either masculine or feminine action is reduced among the Arapesh men and women to a role of inconsequence. "I was innocent of any suspicion," writes Dr. Mead, "that the temperaments which we regard as native to one sex might instead be mere variations of human temperament, to which the members of either or both sexes may, with more or less success in the case of different individuals, be educated to approximate."[16] Such a plasticity of temperament, however, she found to be the fact: "Neither the Arapesh or the Mundugumor have made any attitude specific for one sex."[17] This is not to say that genetic differences are absent; they are as plentiful in each of the tribes as in a civilized community; but the mass of each group, whether men or women, are *molded in the temperament* that the tribe prescribed. In the Arapesh tribe the aggressive, tempestuous man is out of place; among the Mundugumors he is normal and respectable.

The conclusion of Dr. Mead, that the nature of man is malleable and plastic to a degree never fully visualized or measured, is the central significance of social anthropology. "The vast proportion of all individuals who are born into any society," writes Ruth Benedict in *Patterns of Culture*, "always and whatever the idiosyncrasies of its institutions, assume . . . the behaviour dictated by that society."[18] The *chameleonship* of man, in Mark Twain's word, is inherent in this conclusion. The normal unborn child can be made as easily into the Mundugumor as the Arapesh, the American lawyer as the Japanese soldier, the Russian doctor as the Tchambuli dancer, the London banker as the African cannibal, the Jew as the Catholic, the Good Samaritan as the Levite, the disciple of Jefferson as the disciple of Hitler. The uniqueness of man is the inheritance of plasticity. Whatever habits, feelings, drives, impulses man may inherit genetically are as a pinpoint to his immense receptiveness to the social impress. In Ruth Benedict's judgment, based upon her examination of primitive societies, Dewey is on solid ground in his comparison of the child's cultural contribution to the few words of baby talk that the family adopts as part of its own language; this is the child's contribution as compared with the total vocabulary of his mother's language built up by custom, tradition, and association. The findings of Benedict and Mead, of Kluckhohn and Boas, sustain the analysis of Hocking, set forth in his *Human Nature and Its Remaking:*

As to structure, human nature is undoubtedly the most plastic part of the living world, the most adaptable, the most educable. Of all animals, it is man in whom heredity counts for least, and conscious building forces for most. Consider that his infancy is longest, his instincts least fixed, his brain most unfinished at birth, his powers of habit-making and habit-changing most marked, his susceptibility to social impressions keenest,—and it becomes clear that in every way nature, as a prescriptive power, has provided in him for her own displacement. . . . To any one who asserts as a dogma that "Human nature never changes," it is fair to reply, "It is human nature to change itself."[19]

The fundamental sameness of the races of man, and the common gift of his plasticity, however distant the scientific fact from cultural acceptance, have far-reaching implications. The gulfs that separate African savage and English aristocrat, Polynesian native and American scientist, Chinese coolie and German architect, the anthropologist attributes to the accidents of geography and culture, and not to any unalterable arrangement of genes. A New Guinea cannibal, if brought at birth into the home of a Sorbonne professor, would grow up speaking French, attending the Catholic church, making love in the manner of his friends, and going to the university of his choice. Had George Bernard Shaw been transported at birth to the heart of Africa, he would have become the intellectual leader of his tribe, presumably speaking the native tongue, carrying a harpoon like his fellow-tribesmen, but illiterate and savage, a foreigner to the world of books, remote indeed from the creative synthesis of *Saint Joan* and *Heartbreak House*. If races are equal, then all men, as Robinson asserts, are born completely uncivilized; a New Guinea baby at birth is fundamentally similar to a German, a French, an American baby. Recently a blond and blue-eyed American boy appeared in New York speaking perfect Chinese but unable to articulate an English word; he had been brought up from birth by a Chinese family. In the light of anthropological fact, the sameness of races, Mark Twain's story of Pudd'nhead Wilson and the comments of Tocqueville and Henry George about Negro nature assume a new vitality in American life; and the assumptions of democratic thinkers may yet emerge tough realities from the crucible of science. Realities they even now appear to American anthropologists, with only the late E. A. Hooton voicing a vigorous dissent.

It would be a presumptuous error, however, to assume that the central conclusion of anthropology has won wide acceptance even in the scientific world, much less in the mind of the average citizen still deluded by the prejudices of color and nationality learned at his mother's knee. The incredible persistence of anti-Semitism, of national paranoia, the assumptions of racial or national superiority, can be accounted for only by a tenacity of custom not yet measured. To be effective on a national or international scale, the central teaching of man's plasticity as the origin of his differences must be woven anew each generation into the fabric of custom until it nullifies or reverses, in land after land, the teachings of untold centuries. The researches of the anthropologists, to be effective even among the physicists, chemists, doctors, engineers, biologists, psychologists, require expansion a thousand fold if they are to be as fully accepted as the efficacy of aureomycin or the Salk vaccine. To the informed few the plasticity of man, assumed for fifteen decades by many American intellectuals, now possesses an unquestioned scientific validity. But to make the implications of anthropological science as dramatic a reality as asphalt or steam turbines to Americans at large, whether scientists or schoolboys, requires resources and imagination comparable to those bestowed on the atom bomb. The dropping of the bomb is its own persuasion, instantaneous and irrefutable, like the magic of the needle of morphine; but the teachings of the anthropologists are thus far as unreal to the average American as the forests of Tibet or the customs of the Tchambuli.

In the tallying of human behavior under the pressure of cultural traditions, anthropology has made no attempt to account for individual differences. Each person inherits a genetic uniqueness and is subjected to a unique combination of environmental colorings. Within each warlike tribe is a nonwarlike member whose lack of masculinity may be genetic in origin. A man's body build has a relation to his personality; some evidence exists that a man's body build has its origin in the endocrine glands, which are the product of genetic determinants.[20] There is also evidence that schizophrenia is inherited. Some differences in the energies of men, especially the differences in sexual energy, appear to be genetic in origin. The question of whether musical talent is inherited as eye color is inherited anthropology does not seek to answer.[21] The individual differences among men may be traced only by a combination of sciences, of which genetics is the chief resource, and anthropology only the handmaiden.

However remarkable the advances anthropology has made in tracing the diverse extensions of man's plasticity, it has not yet sought to measure the origins and roots of the uncommon man. Only one American anthropologist, Alfred Kroeber, has seriously studied what he calls "the clustering of genius." What in man's plasticity can account for the crops of genius reaped in the Athens of Pericles, the London of Elizabeth, the New England of Emerson, Alcott, and Thoreau? In 1848 Walt Whitman was twenty-nine years old, a respected man of average talent as a newspaper editor. By 1855 he had changed into a poet of rare genius. From no American life of such beginnings was genius less expected.

A science of man is needed to tally the roots of talent from which the flower of genius has emerged in the lives of Hawthorne and Melville, Cather and Faulkner, Edison and Oppenheimer, Dreiser and Wharton, Frank Lloyd Wright and Marian Anderson. In no country so frequently as in America have uncommon men and women emerged from the great mass of the obscure and undistinguished. A true science of man will not be content to trace the behavior of societies remote and strange from our own. It will seek also to discover what patterns of behavior impinged on the plasticity of a Mark Twain, an Abraham Lincoln, a Sherwood Anderson, to precipitate them beyond the fences of mediocrity into the fields of creative splendor. For this end biography, though indispensable, awaits the tools, the experimentation, of a true science of man.

American anthropology has succeeded in establishing a body of factual data undreamed of six decades ago. Yet thus far it has not initiated any controlled experiment to determine man's plastic response to the vision of uncommon achievement, such as the dream of Milton, of leaving "something so written to aftertimes, as they should not willingly let it die." In a sense every college, every classroom, may hold for the youth many fragments of such a dream. But no one has yet sought to mine in an average American town or county the utmost gold of uncommon talent that may lie hidden among its people. To dig for such talent in a controlled experiment is as yet foreign to the aims of cultural anthropology. But only with the knowledge amassed by anthropology could such an experiment go forward, or a true science of man emerge from the myths, the dreams, and the delusions of American ideas about human nature.

1969
March of Events

In early January, 1969, America was still elated by the flight of Apollo 8 around the moon and back to earth. Archibald MacLeish praised the feats of the astronauts in a burst of poetic rejoicing in the ties that bind mankind together. "To see the earth as it truly is," he wrote, "small and blue and beautiful in that eternal silence where it floats, is to see ourselves as riders on the earth together, brothers on that bright loveliness in the eternal cold."[1] Arnold Toynbee, however, writing in the London Observer, at once raised the historian's questions of the priorities that most benefit mankind. Could not man find better uses for his wealth? Even in America 10 to 20 per cent of the population lived in slum poverty and ugliness. America's scientific efforts, like those of other nations, had been dazzlingly successful; her grappling with social ills had been weak and ineffectual. Toynbee then quoted President Johnson: "What really counts is whether we can keep people from dying on the Vietnam battlefield." Not Americans only were the President's concern, wrote Toynbee; the emphasis was on "people." Ironically, continued Toynbee, Apollo 8 had returned to earth on the same day that China had monitored her eighth nuclear test in Sinkiang and America had sold fifty jet fighter planes to Israel. Our first priority as world citizens, in Toynbee's view, was to avoid nuclear annihilation; our second, to feed the planet's burgeoning population.

On January 5, 1969, the undeclared war in Vietnam was eight years old—the longest war in American history. In the week of January 5-11, no fewer than 151 Americans lost their lives in Vietnam; in the week of January 12-18, 196 were killed. The American death

414

toll in Vietnam from January 1, 1961, to January 15, 1969, was 31,181.

In 1969 Michael Harrington's The Other America *was over six years old. Harrington had lived for two years in a Catholic Worker house on Chrystie Street, one block from the Bowery. He and his fellow workers had no money and received no pay; they accepted the philosophy of voluntary poverty, sharing the living conditions which they provided for the desperately poor and the drunken ones: the soup line, the rough clothes, the simple bed. Often the Workers took in a besotted drunk, shaved and bathed him, gave him warm food and a clean bed.[2] From these experiences and his intense study of other types of American poverty, Harrington was admirably fitted to write* The Other America—*a passionate tract, but fully documented. More than any other book, it helped to spark the first official "war" on poverty in America's history. Only three days before his assassination on November 22, 1963, President Kennedy had given orders to his chief economic adviser, Walter Heller, to set forth proposals for submission to Congress. As Kennedy's successor, President Johnson pushed forward measures for relief of the poor more far-reaching than any in the history of the nation. In 1933 President Roosevelt had said that one in three Americans was "ill-fed, ill-housed, and ill-clothed." In 1963, according to Harrington, despite America's vast wealth one in four citizens—40,000,000 to 50,000,000 of her people—lived in poverty; Robert Lampman estimated 32,000,-000.[3] But what is poverty? Harrington provided an illuminating appendix of definitions of poverty, a handbook in itself to America's most baffling dilemma.[4] For the first time in American life, thanks to the incredible productivity of farm and factory, a land without poverty was within the reach of democratic aspirations.*

On January 16, 1969, *President Johnson's Council of Economic Advisers presented its annual report to Congress. The nation as a whole, asserted the President in his accompanying message, was now in its ninety-fifth month of continuous economic improvement: "The prosperity of the last five years extends to every corner of our national life."[5] More than 8,500,000 additional workers had found* *jobs. In 1968, 4,000,000 Americans had "escaped from poverty, the largest exodus ever recorded in a single year." Unemployment dropped from 5.7 per cent of all workers to 3.3 per cent. The average family income had risen from $6,210 in 1959 to $7,974 in 1967 ("in constant 1967 prices"), a gain of 28 per cent.[6] One in seven white families still lived in poverty, compared with one in three nonwhite families. In proportion to their incomes, poor families paid a higher share of taxes than more prosperous neighbors. A total of only $9.7 billion additional yearly income (5 per cent of the nation's budget), asserted the council, would lift the nation's twenty-two million low-income persons out of poverty in six to eight years. The nation, insisted the President, "cannot afford to have any citizen in poverty."[7] The report of the council was unique in American annals; never before had the conquest of poverty seemed so imminent. Nor had any previous president and his colleagues grappled so realistically with the basic dilemmas of the nation's economic life.*

On January 20, 1969, Richard Nixon was inaugurated in Washington as the thirty-seventh president of the United States, having won the election by a margin almost as narrow as that with which John Kennedy had won the presidential election of 1960. The margin of Nixon's victory was less than 300,000 votes out of more than 70,000,000 votes cast. In the count of electoral votes, however, Nixon received 302 from thirty-two states—or 32 more than needed for election. Of the popular votes counted, the losing candidate, Hubert Humphrey, won 43.2 per cent; Nixon received 43.6 per cent.

On March 28, 1969, Dwight Eisenhower died in Bethesda Hospital, his wife Mamie, his son John, and John's wife Barbara at his side. Eisenhower had made a gallant fight for life, having suffered seven heart attacks. On August 5, 1968, Eisenhower had made a televised speech to the Republican National Convention—a speech remarkable for its clarity, force, and precision of diction. On March 29 Eisenhower's body was moved from the funeral home to the Washington National Cathedral, where, after a ten-minute service attended by family and close friends, it was put on public view. On March 30 the coffin was moved in a military procession along Con-

stitution Avenue to the Capitol; during the next twenty-four hours some 55,000 persons filed past the bier. At the ceremony in the Capitol's rotunda, President Nixon eulogized Eisenhower as "one of the giants of our time." On March 31 religious services were held at the National Cathedral, attended by the family, foreign dignitaries such as President Charles de Gaulle of France, and members of the Cabinet, Congress, and the diplomatic corps. After the services Eisenhower's body was taken to Washington's Union Station and placed aboard a train for Abilene, Kansas, where he was buried on April 2. Thus the farm boy came home, having embodied in his life something of the essence of democratic hopes and dreams—a soldier turned statesman, shaping in part and then writing the history of his time.

April 4, 1969, was the first anniversary of the death of Martin Luther King, Jr. Over the country—even in Washington, D. C.— dozens of streets were lined with windowless ruined buildings: homes, churches, businesses which had been destroyed by fires following King's assassination. Thousands of devoted followers gathered in Atlanta for services commemorating his contribution to the cause of peaceful resolution of racial strife in the United States. A great leader, a great pacifist, an opponent of all violence, was more alive than ever in the affections of both black and white Americans.

In 1969 student agitation in American colleges continued, with San Francisco State College in an intermittent state of siege, and the administration building at Harvard occupied by militants who forced the administrators to leave their offices. On April 19 Negro militants at Cornell University occupied Straight Hall and forced twenty parents (who had been visiting the campus for Parents' Weekend) to rise, dress, and leave the building. After discussion with Dean Robert D. Miller, the militants agreed to surrender the building on the condition that the university would provide legal assistance against any "charges arising out of the occupation of the [building]."[8] To this the dean agreed, subject to the approval of the faculty; he agreed also that he would recommend that the university press no charges, whether civil or criminal. At this point the mili-

tants left Straight Hall, several of them carrying loaded guns. When a full faculty meeting refused to accept the terms agreed to by Dean Miller, he resigned. In a later full faculty meeting, however, the members reversed their original decision and accepted the terms imposed by the militants. Professor Walter Berns called the reversal by the faculty "abject surrender"; another distinguished professor, Arch Dotson, called it "surrender to intimidation." Professor Allan P. Sindler resigned in protest.[9] President Perkins, who later resigned under pressure, defended the reversal by the faculty as a peaceful solution to an explosive situation that might have ended in violent confrontations between police officials and Cornell students.

However reluctant to call in local authorities in time of disturbance, Harvard had done so on April 9, for the first time in three hundred years. On May 1, 1969, Judge M. Edward Viola of Cambridge, Massachusetts, found 169 persons guilty of criminal trespass in entering and occupying a Harvard University administration building on April 9. One of the defense attorneys, John G. S. Fry, said in his final appeal against the charge: "It doesn't simply involve a fine. It involves a criminal record."[10] Of those convicted, 141 men and women decided to appeal the verdict. On the same day, May 1, in a nine-hour meeting, the trustees of Cornell University declared that disruption and "tactics of terror" on the campus would be met with "firm and appropriate response." Further, said the trustees, "the university is not a sanctuary from the law."[11] Thus one university after another, however reluctantly, was now appealing to the local authorities to maintain peace on the campus. On May 1 about one hundred Columbia University students left two buildings they had occupied, within a few minutes after they learned that warrants for their arrest had been signed by the State Supreme Court.[12] Meanwhile, however, in a scuffle between the white militants and Professor James S. Young of the Department of Government, Dr. Young was struck in the face with a stick while another youth held one of his arms behind his back.[13]

On April 27, 1969, Negro leader Bayard Rustin, who had organized the March on Washington in 1963, declared that college offi-

cials should "stop capitulating to the stupid demands of Negro students" for courses in "soul" music and poetry. Rustin deplored courses for blacks only and self-segregation in dormitories of their own. How could Negro students overcome the inferior education with which they entered college? Rustin's answer was that the Negro students must recognize their needs and take remedial courses, especially in English and mathematics. "What in hell are soul courses worth in the real world?" asked Rustin. "The easy way out is to let them [the Negro students] have black courses and their own dormitories and give them degrees." Colleges, he maintained, must not give students degrees until "they have been brought up to par." Only in this way could they prepare for the real world. Viewing campus disturbances as highly destructive, Rustin asserted that "a multiple society cannot exist where an element of that society, out of its own sense of guilt and masochism, permits another segment of that society to hold guns at their heads in the name of justice."[14]

In 1969 classicists revolved anew Plato's analysis of the anarchy preceding the transition from democracy to tyranny. Family life in a democracy, said Plato, becomes more and more anarchical. Indeed, "the father grows accustomed to descend to the level of his sons and to fear them, and the son is on a level with his father, he having no respect nor reverence for either of his parents; and this is his freedom." As for education, continued Plato, "in such a state of society the master fears and flatters his scholars, and the scholars despise their masters and tutors; young and old are all alike; and the young man is on a level with the old, and is ready to compete with him in word or deed; and old men condescend to the young and are full of pleasantry and gaiety; they are loth to be thought morose and authoritative, and therefore they adopt the manners of the young."[15] In 1969 such a book as Wallace Stegner's All the Little Live Things *threw into sharp focus Plato's timely analysis—in which, however wide of the mark in many particulars, literate Americans of the twentieth century might find a mirror of some of their own dilemmas.*

On April 29, 1969, Democratic Senator George S. McGovern proposed a frontal attack on hunger through the medium of $1.8 billion in free food stamps to be distributed annually to some 5,200,000 persons at the bottom of the economic scale—many of them members of families with incomes of $80 a month.[16] *The bill, as introduced, also called for increasing the face value of the stamps to a level that would provide for a minimum wholesome diet. The two Republican cosponsors of the bill were Senators Theodore F. Stevens of Alaska and Mark O. Hatfield of Oregon. In the ranks of the Democrats, some twenty-nine other senators agreed to support the bill. Senator McGovern pointed out that President Nixon had asked for an addition of only $15,000,000 for food programs initiated by the government in the coming fiscal year. The additional $15,000,000 was to be used, however, not to buy more food but to teach the recipients how to buy and what foods to select. President Nixon's budget revisions on behalf of food for poor families, asserted Senator McGovern, despite the promise that the administration would never turn its back on the growing needs of the American people, "were only the barest nod to the hungry."*[17] *America's priorities, acknowledged the Senator, were peace and the ending of inflation; still, could not the military budget be reduced by $10 billion for the sake of America's poverty-stricken families?*

On May 12, 1969, Howard A. Hill, the first Negro mayor of Chapel Hill, North Carolina, was sworn into office. "I've got to be good," he said. Mr. Hill, the thirty-four-year-old son of a sharecropper, was director of employee relations at Duke University, fifteen miles from Chapel Hill. He had a master's degree in social work from the University of North Carolina. Four years earlier Mr. Hill had bought a house on Tinkerbell Road in the Colony Woods section of Chapel Hill. At first there had been a few anonymous telephone calls; but the Hills, who had two children, stayed on. The mayor's salary was $100 a month. Negroes made up only 10 per cent of the population of Chapel Hill. As for the campaign, Mr. Hill asserted: "It was the cleanest ... I ever had a part in. It was a campaign settled on the issues, and a lot of credit is due my opponent."[18]

June 5, 1969, was the first anniversary of Robert Kennedy's death. His book Thirteen Days, *published in 1969, which traced the almost hourly events of the Cuban missile crisis of 1962, revealed afresh the piercing depth of his understanding—and that of President John Kennedy—of American responsibility at the brink of nuclear war.*

On April 20, 1969, Sirhan Bishara Sirhan was convicted of the murder of Robert Kennedy in the first degree. Efforts of the defense lawyers failed to win him a life sentence by virtue of insanity or extreme emotional turbulence.

In 1969, whatever the turmoil on the campuses, the cause of free higher education advanced apace. Indeed, the growth of free public colleges countrywide corresponded in its remarkable momentum and community acceptance to the development of free public high schools a century earlier. In 1969 New York City supported nine senior colleges, six community colleges, and a graduate center, each a part of the City University of New York. Except for graduate work and fees in the various two-year community colleges, tuition was free. Each student in the senior colleges was in effect a scholarship student, having earned his place by his high school grades. At Brooklyn College, as in the other senior colleges, a student whose grades were too low to admit him to day school might pay tuition and go to school at night; then, when he could show several semesters of "B" work, he might matriculate in day school, where tuition was free. Of the various states California had made the greatest advances in establishing free colleges. California now supported eighty-nine free community colleges (to enroll in which only a high school diploma was necessary); some nineteen four-year state colleges; and nine divisions of the University of California, including Davis, Santa Cruz, Los Angeles, Santa Barbara, San Diego, and Berkeley. In 1969 Texas supported six public universities, sixteen four-year colleges, and forty two-year colleges.[19] No phenomenon in the sixth decade of the twentieth century more fully justified American democratic expectations than the advance of free education on the college level—unparalleled in the history of the West.

On Sunday, July 20, 1969, at 4:17 P.M. (EST), the strangely crab-like lunar module "Eagle" landed on the moon near the southwest shore of the Sea of Tranquillity. Directing the descent of "Eagle" from the spacecraft Apollo 11 to the moon's surface were copilots Neil A. Armstrong and Colonel Edwin E. Aldrin, Jr. After a rest of more than six hours Mr. Armstrong, at 10:56 P.M., stepped slowly down the ladder, his movements recorded by television and viewed by millions of people around the world. As he stepped onto the moon's surface, Armstrong declared: "That's one small step for a man, one giant leap for mankind." On July 21, at 1:55 P.M.—after twenty-one hours and thirty-seven minutes on the moon—"Eagle" blasted off the surface and rose into lunar orbit to rejoin Colonel Michael Collins and the command module of Apollo 11, "Columbia". The linkup was achieved at 5:35 P.M., some sixty-nine miles above the moon's surface. On July 22, after jettisoning "Eagle" at 12:56 P.M., "Columbia" blasted out of lunar orbit and started for home, where a jubilant world awaited.[20]

XXII
Intelligence and the Conquest of Hunger

THE assumption that man's intelligence is genetically determined long before birth and remains constant during the productive decades of his life has a long and honorable history. Plato's parable of the metals, teaching that golden or iron parents will normally have children of similar talents, has been verified in thousands of deep-searching minds. "But as all are of the same original stock," asserts Plato, "a golden parent will sometimes have a silver son, or a silver parent a golden son."[1] Even the exceptions to Plato's main assumption, then, that "the species will generally be preserved in the children," are themselves the fruit of genetic determinism. Down through the centuries, despite probings by great scholars, the fragmentary science of man has not yet brought forth a confident analysis of the origins of intelligence.

Whatever a child's inherited gifts, recent evidence shows that the growth of his intelligence depends also on proper nutrition, even before birth. According to Dr. Charles Upton Lowe, Chairman, Committee on Nutrition, American Academy of Pediatrics, poverty and consequent malnutrition affect a child's life from conception onward. "Malnutrition during the last trimester of pregnancy," wrote Dr. Lowe, "and, certainly during the first months of life, may seriously compromise ultimate intellectual achievement." Moreover, "when a fetus receives inadequate nutrition in utero, the infant is born small, the placenta of his mother contains fewer cells than normal to nourish him and his growth will be compromised."[2] What happens when an infant lacks proper nutrition in the first few months of life? The child's brain "fails to synthesize protein and cells at normal rates and consequently suffers a decrease as great as 20% in the cell number."[3] It is to the advantage of the child that he spend the full nine months in the mother's womb because "during the last trimester of pregnancy, protein synthesis by the brain is proceeding at a very rapid rate."[4] After birth, although protein synthesis by the brain continues, it does so at a much less rapid rate than during the last three months of pregnancy. Thus the prematurely born infant may often start life with a handicap to the growth of his intelligence, having missed weeks or months of the most rapid growth of protein synthesis by the brain. "As many as 50% of prematurely born infants," wrote Dr. Lowe, "grow to maturity with an intellectual competence significantly below that which would be expected when compared with siblings and even with age peers."[5]

Among America's poor citizens the rate of prematurely born infants is four times as high as that found among middle-class families, which in suburban communities is only 5 per cent. But in some urban slums the rate of the prematurely born is 25 per cent. Moreover, as Dr. Lowe pointed out, 75 per cent of all infant deaths in the first months of life result from immature growth. High mortality in infancy is, in Dr. Lowe's judgment, the "hall mark of poverty."[6] Another penalty of poverty among deprived Americans is mental deficiency, which is three to five times as frequent in poverty-stricken families as in prosperous ones. Of all mentally defective children, 75 to 85 per cent are born in poverty.[7] The penalties of poverty and hunger are linked in an ever-tightening circle, preventing poor children from long concentration on basic skills and often from attending high school or college (or both)—by which attendance well-fed children may prepare to enter useful occupations. In America one third of all families containing four or more children are victims of poverty. As between black and white citizens, poverty afflicts 40 per cent of the blacks and 12 per cent of the whites— totals of 21,000,000 and 10,000,000 people, respectively.[8] If American children and pregnant mothers were on the whole well fed, the country could surely break the chain of causation by which malnutrition widens catastrophe over the generations in a continuing destruction of human fiber.

For an auspicious beginning of the child's brain development, he needs rich nourishment in the mother's womb for the full nine months of pregnancy. After birth the child needs the kind of careful feeding care that millions of mothers stricken by poverty are unable to give. The younger the child, the more vulnerable he is to conditions of care and nutriment that are irreversible in their effects, whether beneficent or destructive. The younger the child, the less the state can intervene to help him receive nutrients he needs for the development of his intelligence. As much development of intelligence takes place in the first four years of life as in the thirteen years following.[9] But in the first four years of a child's life the state or community, however beneficent, is powerless to intervene. The more poverty-stricken the family, the less likely (despite Medicare) the children during these first years can have the attention of a skillful and dedicated pediatrician. The deprivations of the mother create in turn the deprivations of the child—and the cycle continues generation after generation, with the intelligence of the children no further developed than that of their parents in *their* earliest years.

Nutritive food for children, according to Dr. Lowe, is not simply that for adults scaled down: "The nutritional needs of the infant are unique and bear only tangential relations to those of the adult."[10] For example, the average adult has no need "for Vitamin D as a dietary supplement. Were the infant to be reared without such supplement, he would develop rickets in a matter of months. The requirement for Vitamin C by the adult may be as low as 10 mgs. per day. If the young infant were given amounts of Vitamin C this low, he would undoubtedly develop an aberration in protein metabolism known as tyrosyluria and, in addition, might go on to develop scurvy. Because of his very rapid growth, the infant's requirement for iron is approximately equal to that of a full grown woman and approximately twice that of a full grown man."[11] Such examples show the need for the use of experienced nutritionists in the direction of food programs. Striking differences in nutritional needs have been observed among ethnic, racial, and geographic groups. In Texas, for example, a dietetic survey showed a Vitamin A deficiency: "Among the Mexican-American groups, Vitamin A deficiency was severe. Among the black population surveyed, Vitamin A deficiency was mild or non-existent. Among the white population, Vitamin A deficiency was at an intermediate level," depending on food chosen for home consumption. "In Louisiana, salt is iodized; in Texas, it is not."[12]

On February 16, 1969, appeared the first of five *New York Times* articles in a series titled "Hunger in America." The relation between hunger and the retardation of intelligence has seldom been more graphically depicted (though not explicitly stated) than in these articles. Dr. Donald E. Gatch was pictured in a Negro home in Pritchardsville, South Carolina, holding a little child who was suffering from rickets (caused by Vitamin D deficiency) and scurvy (lack of Vitamin C). According to the *Times* reporter, Homer Bigart, Dr. Gatch took a seven-month-old girl from the mother's arms and pointed out symptoms of kwashiorkor and scurvy. The baby's hair had thinned, the hairline had receded, and the hair color had turned to gray; her skin was extremely dry. The baby's diet was deficient in iron, causing the hemoglobin count to fall to one half of normal. "Will the child live?" the doctor was asked. The reply was in the affirmative; but Dr. Gatch feared that the child had "suffered irreversible damage through growth retardation and [loss] of brain cells."[13] This child was only one of several nearby who were blighted with rickets—an affliction that could have been avoided if the family had been provided with Vitamin D–enriched dry milk, which, the *Times* pointed out, had been shipped abroad since 1965 through American aid programs. Other victims of hunger were two afflicted old ladies, one bedridden with rheumatoid arthritis, the other by the Wernicke syndrome. Pellagra, caused by dietary deficiency in the essential nutrients niacin, thiamine, riboflavin, and folic acid, also was prevalent in the community.

In 1968 there had appeared a valuable survey of the nation's food deficiencies titled *Hunger, U.S.A.*, with a foreword by Robert Kennedy. Published under the auspices of the Citizens' Board of Inquiry, the study identified 280 "hunger counties" in twenty-four states. Florida had nine such counties, Arizona one, Texas thirty-five, Tennessee eleven, New Mexico seven, Oklahoma five, Georgia fifty.[14] Every state, however prosperous, had its pockets of desperate hunger that did irreversible damage to the brains of infants. A typical hunger county—such as Autauga County, Alabama—was found generally to have no federal food programs. In Autauga only 19.6 per cent of the poor had the benefit of welfare assistance. The county mortality rate of babies one day to one year old was 15.5 per cent per thousand, more than twice the national average. In 1968 almost half (48.2 per cent) of the incomes of the county's families fell below the poverty line.[15] "Our government's efforts to reach the hungry," wrote Robert Kennedy, "through the Commodity Distribution and Food Stamp Programs, reach only 18 per cent of our poor. The School Lunch Program—the same kind of program which increased school attendance 35 percent in Latin America—reaches only two of the six million children of poor families—and most of those reached were not among the poorest of our children."[16] The School Lunch Program, when properly administered, was able to reach the hungry child, on a daily basis, at age six or over. It could provide food free or at a reduced price to those unable to pay, and serve as a means of distributing fortified foods and of teaching the principles of nutrition. But unfortunately the state had to put up $3 for every $1 of federal money; and the state's share was too often raised through price charges passed along to the children. Moreover, when first implemented the program provided very few hot breakfasts for those children who needed them most. Finally, though advantageous in several crucial ways in combating the hunger of the young, the School Lunch Program as set up intervened too late in the child's life to prevent brain damage caused by malnutrition. The battle against hunger, in order to ensure the rich flowering of intelligence, must begin at the time of conception; this battle requires a national plan of benefits reaching into the humblest homes in the most remote towns and villages of every state.

On February 19, 1969, President Nixon presented a message on poverty that emphasized anew the factors of environment in the growth of intelligence. "In recent years," said the President, stressing the Economic Opportunity Act, "enormous advances have been made in the understanding of human development. We have learned that intelligence is not fixed at birth, but is largely formed by the environmental influences of the early formative years. It develops rapidly at first, and then more slowly; as much of the development takes place in the first four years as in the next thirteen. We have learned further that environment has its greatest impact on the development of intelligence when that development is proceeding most rapidly—that is, in those earliest years."[17]

The prospect of the conquest of hunger on the American scene is an opportunity without parallel in the history of the nation—one that would call forth an upward push in the level of intelligence and creative achievement among citizen groups hitherto deprived generation after generation. The food supply is overwhelmingly plentiful. The 6 per cent of Americans engaged in farming produce enough food not only for 200,000,000 citizens but also for 160,000,000 people in other parts of the world.[18] America's food supply is so bountiful that every child can have ample and appropriate nutrients. In England, the moment a woman becomes pregnant she is entitled to food and vitamin supplements at the local government food station. There she is received as a welcome guest, with a courteous official eager to answer her questions. Thus the unborn child begins at once to build a resistance against the ravages of hunger and its toll of lowered intelligence. Members of the royal family set a good example by calling at the food station for the supplements due them on such occasions. Those who remember the London of 1940 will recall the pinched faces, the scrawny frames, of children on the way home from school. Now for the most part the poor boys and girls of London have rosy cheeks and vibrant health, thanks to the school nutrition programs uniform throughout the nation. America, on the other hand, has no national plan for the abolition of hunger beginning with the unborn child. Beyond the conquest of this earliest hunger through vitamins and timely food supplements lies a new surge of intelligence; a new will to learn, to try for college; a new flow of mental and physical energy. Could not America provide every child with a warm, nutritious breakfast at school as well as a hot lunch? But the earliest years are the most crucial ones; even age six may be too late. The conquest of that hunger which lowers the level of a child's intelligence must begin first in the poorest home, with nutritious food for the mother and hence for her unborn child.

On November 12, 1968, C. P. Snow spoke at Westminster College in Fulton, Missouri, analyzing the problem of hunger as the most crucial of the world's dilemmas.[19] In some countries the population was expanding faster than the supply of food to keep it alive. The indication was, asserted Snow, that we might be moving into large-scale famine—perhaps within ten years. In Snow's view there was no possibility of curtailing population growth within ten years. If the world had twenty or thirty years in which to prepare against the catastrophe, Snow believed, an apocalyptic crisis might be avoided. But there seemed to be no way at present by which the expansion of the world's population could be slowed down or reversed. Looking ahead, Snow envisioned that the first step toward the catastrophe of world hunger would be local famines. These local famines, in his judgment, would appear between 1975 and 1980. By that time the countries with plentiful food supplies would still be able to feed their people, but the food-hungry countries would have reached the impasse of starvation. Lord Snow believed that it was not possible for poor countries themselves, such as India and Pakistan, to revolutionize their food production soon enough to head off a wave of hunger engulfing the whole population. If the rich countries were to take a realistic view of the catastrophe ahead, they would need to devote 20 per cent of their gross national product to feeding their poor neighbors over a period of ten to fifteen years.

XXIII
Conclusion: The Plastic Mind Under Glass

> *The great object of Education should be*
> *to inspire the youthful man with an interest*
> *in himself; with a curiosity touching his own*
> *nature; to acquaint him with the resources*
> *of his mind, and to teach him that there is*
> *all his strength.*
>
> —Emerson

O<small>N THE AMERICAN</small> scene the science of man may still be justly defined, in Holmes's phrase, as the topography of ignorance. Americans have not yet produced or even projected a co-ordination of disciplines directed toward the accumulation of certainties about human nature. Nevertheless, despite the sporadic nature of the advances toward a co-ordination of scientific purpose, the American search for the science of man has accumulated a body of assumptions and guesses some of which have been tested, not with the precision of laboratory analysis, but by pragmatic application in the crucible of social experiment.

"Ah! what a plastic . . . creature he is!" wrote Emerson of man. When the first elementary schools were established in Massachusetts in 1634, the colonists acted on the assumption that each child, however limited, was plastic enough in his response to ideas to justify the attention accorded him in the classroom. Twenty to twenty-five decades later, when Americans had spanned the continent, they applied the same assumptions in setting up free high schools to which attendance was often made compulsory. By the middle of the twentieth century the same principle of the plasticity of response in the average person's mind was being applied to the development of junior colleges and universities open, in many states, to students of merely average high-school records. Indeed, in some states—notably Ohio, Indiana, and Illinois—any student who is graduated from high school is upon application admitted to the state university. Those unready for college, often as many as one-third, fail and fall by the wayside in the first quarter. Nevertheless, the assumption obtains that a student's plasticity of mind cannot be fully tested except in a university atmosphere, in which for the first time he may feel an exciting and prolonged stimulation of his faculties.

In recent decades, educators have become more and more reluctant to pigeonhole any intellectual destiny by I.Q. tests or high-school averages. Man, as "a fagot of thunderbolts" (Emerson's phrase), is as yet unmeasured. How is a thunderbolt born? The acceleration of mental energy, of purposeful action, of imagination, is a mysterious process not yet traced. The extent to which a fanatical desire to learn or act can overcome an inherent deficiency of intelligence is also still unknown. A man of rare intelligence may feel no incentive to creative action; a man of limited intelligence may be fired with unquenchable creative zeal.

Moreover, the education of the emotions may be more crucial even on the college level than the expansion of intellectual skills. "No single thing is so important to every man," wrote Bellamy, "as to have for neighbors intelligent, companionable persons." Was not each child entitled to refined and cultivated parents? Bellamy believed, like Emerson, that the nation was involved in the education of the whole citizen—his emotions and his sense of responsibility to others, as well as his mind. Man's plastic response to the training of his emotions seemed to both Emerson and Bellamy to offer unlimited vistas in the extension of man's faculties. The whole trend of American education, despite deficiencies, has been moving toward advanced training of some kind for those between the ages of eighteen and twenty-two. Bellamy's dream of a whole society of educated men and women has come nearer to complete fulfilment than anyone could have prophesied even a half-century ago. Each new expansion of high-school or college opportunities represents an investment in perhaps the most fundamental of all unproved assumptions on the American scene: that children and adults are more plastic and malleable in their response to books, teachers, and ideas than any scientist has yet suspected.

The philosophy of a free public school education extending from the first grade through the university, however fragmentary in its realization, has been a challenge unique in the history of the world to the aristocratic concept that blood will tell. No science of man has yet evolved to state decisively what elements in the nature of man are fixed mainly by heredity and what elements mainly by environment. Though twentieth-century Americans lack, as did those of the seventeenth century, an answer to this question, they have extended the public school system on the assumption that genetic patterns play a much smaller part in the molding of human nature than their ancestors in aristocratic countries had assumed. The emergence of uncommon men from relatively democratic societies, such as the Athens of Pericles, the Florence of Michelangelo, and the London of Shakespeare, made no significant impact on the educational practices of aristocratic societies. Though the idea of a fixed human nature was challenged in the English revolution of 1642-49, when, in Cromwell's army, English soldiers of humble origins were able for the first time to become officers, the American Revolution was explosively decisive to a much greater degree than those of England or France in its challenge to the dominance of genetic traits. Whereas France remained bound by its economic limitations, a whole continent of free-ranging opportunities opened to millions of American minds new visions of achievement unknown to their humble forebears. Achievements multiplied by imitation. It was impossible not to believe in oneself when one saw his humble neighbor or his neighbor's son transform his lot from poverty to affluence, from ignorance to awareness, from rural isolation to travel and association with other minds. "In England," wrote Emerson, "every man you meet is some man's son; in America he may be some man's father." Such a process which, as Henry Adams wrote, released men's energies like "the blast of a furnace," broke down in millions of lives the prevailing notion that human nature is fixed by the genetic limitations of one's ancestors. "One could rise! One could rise!" Dreiser's cry reverberated throughout the land.

Such realities early required the Americans to open their schools alike to rich and poor, washed and unwashed, weak minds and strong. "In America," wrote Emerson, "the poor boy puts his hand into the pocket of the rich and says to him, 'You shall educate me, not as you will, but as I will.'" It is true that the persistence of slavery over many decades confirmed in millions of minds the concept of genetic racial inferiority. It was easy alike for the aristocratic southerner, the Negro, and the poor white, in a society stratified securely from generation to generation, to believe that man was more fixed than plastic by nature. But with every march toward the West, where new frontiers opened daily to plastic adaptation, with the amazing extension of economic opportunities to humble people in the northern states, the irresistible forces of American society ranged themselves on the side of the unproved assumption of man's malleability.

Hence, while private schools remained the refuge of the great aristocratic traditions of the South, the public schools of the North and West progressed apace. With each westward advance, the support of free public schools became more inevitably entwined in American minds with the implicit rejection of the belief that men were limited in their achievements by the blood streams of their ancestors. The Americans did not pause to examine the foundations of these unproved assumptions. They erected a million crucibles of social experiment without first having proved the soundness of their investment in the teachability of human nature. "What untold waste!" some Americans exclaimed. "How can you make a silk purse out of a sow's ear? How can you expect any son or daughter of *that* family to respond to any teacher, however magnificently trained?" But such protests, however widespread among the intellectuals, presented little sustained obstruction to community support of free public schools.

Every classroom brought into action America's unproved assumption of man's extreme plasticity. Whatever was cruel or barbaric or tawdry in the child's home, or in the custom of his community, many a classroom stood ready to challenge. The guesses and assumptions of America's great thinkers spoke in the superb schoolteacher. If the child had a low opinion of himself, the primary duty of the teacher was a daily recognition of the child's unfolding uniqueness. Respect for the child's individuality was the core of enlightened teaching. The plastic child could be trained, as Emerson had maintained, to have a deep respect for his own thoughts, and this was a necessary prelude to the child's habit of creative thinking. Whatever elements of the uncommon man spoke in the words of the teacher, the books of her heroes, or the unfolding minds of her class, could take root in the gifted pupil. The classroom could invite the belief of the child, whatever his origin, in the potential growth of his mind and the worth of his unique personality to his friends of the class. The rotten fruit of American civilization, the filth of its slums, its unhappy homes, its ugly alleys, its bitter quarrels, also reposed in the hearts of its children. Each day the child was forced to mesh and reconcile the experience of the classroom, gray or bright, with the experience of his home, his street, his friends. To many thinkers it appeared that America was naïve to expect that the pressure of books and ideas in classroom life, however effective, could counterbalance the drag of barbaric custom imposed upon the child since the first months of his life.

Nevertheless the classrooms expanded, malign or benignant, each grounded on the unproved assumption that the substance of human nature is plastic. Whatever was inherent in human nature was but a fragment, a grain of sand, as compared to the child's native teachability. When John Pfeiffer wrote in *The Human Brain* that man is not anything innate "except perhaps teachable," he reflected in modern scientific terms the belief underlying America's greatest social experiment, the gamble in the classrooms on the plasticity of man.

II

Despite the fact that universal education has, over the years, brought many gifted children to the attention of discerning teachers, America's crop of uncommon men has remained scanty. In the national assumption of teachability, every scholarship in every university graduate school represents an investment in plasticity which may produce uncommon men. No one, however, who has studied the prevalence of uncommon men in Athens, Florence, or Elizabethan London can look with assurance on America's yield of remarkable people. With a population of only three millions, it is true, colonial America produced John Adams and his Boston, Thomas Jefferson and his Virginia; and in the many decades of America's national life uncommon men have appeared from time to time in peculiarly favorable soil and climate. Thus far, however, few scholars would claim that America has brought forth a quota of great men proportionate to its wealth, its incitements to intellectual growth, its masses of eager human beings, or the varied riches of its cultural backgrounds. In comparison to Periclean Athens alone, which had a population, including slaves, of only half a million, America has not produced a sculptor comparable to Phidias, a philosopher of the stature of Aristotle, a dramatic poet the equal of Sophocles or Aeschylus. To that inexplicable genius, Abraham Lincoln, Americans have erected a marble tribute derived not from a glorious new art, but from the classic models of ancient Greece. In the field of mathematics, despite the superiority of applied science, America has produced no genius comparable to Euclid. In the nineteenth century our poets, with the single exception of Whitman, were not equal to England's best: Wordsworth, Shelley, Keats, Byron, Tennyson, and Browning. In the past century our wealth and human materials doubled and trebled the resources of England; but our crop of great men (except in politics and statesmanship) was inferior both in stature and in numbers to hers. Though America has excelled in the novel, we have yet to produce a novelist with the inexhaustible humor of Dickens or the depths of insight possessed by Thomas Hardy. If *The Scarlet Letter* is the greatest American novel, it cannot be said that Hawthorne's range of achievement is equal to that of George Eliot or Gustave Flaubert. Aristocratic Russia in the nineteenth century, with its millions of submerged and illiterate toilers, produced two novelists, Tolstoy and Dostoevski, whom America with its vast range of opportunities has not yet surpassed. What American composers can compare with those of Czarist Russia or Bismarckian Germany? Nor have we produced architects comparable to those of aristocratic France, medieval Germany, or Renaissance Italy. The ugliness, by and large, of America's dwellings testifies to the understatement of Matthew Arnold's assertion that Americans "have no trained sense of beauty." With the richest human materials yet massed together in a single continent, America has not yet brought to light the quota of great men which have emerged in other lands that denied to their citizens not only free schools and economic betterment but also freedom of speech, movement, and vocational choice.

To gauge the process by which great men have emerged is beyond the present reach of experimental search for the nature of man. The stages by which nature and Elizabethan London combined to produce a Shakespeare are still a mystery. Though we may trace step by step the growth of Milton's genius, even the gradual crystallization of his ambition to be as great a poet for England as Homer was for Greece, David for Israel, or Virgil for Rome, we do not find the same clear evidence of the conditioning of genius in other lives. Nevertheless a great body of evidence about the true nature of genius lies unexamined in the biographies of great men and the histories of the societies that produced them.

Whether or not the conditioning of genius can be artificially duplicated by social planning is a question yet unanswered—some will say unanswerable. Despite the multitude of universities in which talent may flower in the presence of perceptive teachers, America has not yet projected, much less brought to culmination, any experiment in the production of genius. To those who reject the possibility of such an experiment the searcher for a science of man may point out the schools where great art flourished—the school of Rubens, the school of Rembrandt, the schools of Giotto, Titian, and Leonardo, the Academy at Athens from which Aristotle and Euclid emerged. It is no contribution to scientific knowledge to reject experimentation for assumptions, however obvious their truth may seem to the mass of uncritical minds. In no other field are the minds of intellectuals so uncritical as in the evaluation of evidence about human nature. For this reason alone, because the evidence is thus far so uneven and contradictory, America needs a large number of experiments in the conditioning of genius. In *The Advancement of Learning* Bacon outlined for his contemporaries a number of treatises yet unwritten that the world needed to provide a new foundation for scientific thinking in many fields. In a similar way a new *Advancement of Learning* is needed today to describe fifty or a hundred experiments to amass evidence about human nature possessing the authority of proof that exists in the natural sciences. Only by such experiments carried out on a scale hitherto undreamed of can America gauge the potential of great men among its mass of ordinary citizens.

III

Nothing is lacking to carry out such experiments except the imagination to use a fraction of our national resources, public and private, to this end. To what extent, for example, are the experiences of the child's first two years crucial in the development of his intelligence? Can his potential of learning power be accelerated or permanently retarded by environmental influences in this time? Of his early years, are these the most plastic and crucial?

Some years ago, to calculate the effect of isolation on newborn animals, the Rockefeller Foundation financed a five-year experiment in the psychological laboratory of McGill University. One group of seven Scottish terrier puppies was reared normally without control. Another group of terriers, eleven in all, was isolated, one dog to each cage. The restricted puppies had no communication with each other. Food and drink were given them through sliding panels, so that they did not see human beings. The experimental puppies were kept in isolation thus described until they were seven to ten months old. After this time they were exposed to the same daily exercises and stimulation as the normal puppies. The psychologists then observed and compared the two groups of puppies and gave them various psychological tests. The methods and results of this experiment were fully described by two of the experimenters, William R. Thompson and Ronald Melzack, in the *Scientific American* for January, 1956. In one experiment the dog was pursued by a toy car which upon touch caused electric shock to the dog. The normal dogs learned very quickly how to avoid this electric shock. After six shocks the normal dog grew so wary that the experimenter could not touch him with the toy. "In contrast," wrote the experimenters, "the restricted dogs behaved wildly and aimlessly. They jumped about, galloped in circles and actually ran into the car when it was held still in their path. It took these dogs an average of 25 shocks each to learn to avoid the car, and even then they became excited whenever they saw it." When the same test was administered to the same dogs two years after release from isolation, they still showed the same violent fear in response to the electric shock and "learned to avoid the car only after 23 shocks." The experimenters conclude that the very early period of stimulation is essential for normal development of nervous response. "The experiments bring out clearly that any animal needs varied sensory stimulation in order to develop normally, just as it needs food and drink."[1] The McGill experiment brings into focus our relative ignorance about the development of intelligence and emotional response in the human animal's first two years of life.

The experiments of Dr. Hilda Knobloch and her associates with one thousand infants show, according to her own statement, that "in the human organism with an undamaged central nervous system ... it is life experiences rather than hereditary influences which seem more important in molding intellectual functioning."[2] The study by Dr. Knobloch was carried on in Baltimore in 1952. Of the

992 infants in the group examined, 500 were premature. The general conclusion of Dr. Knobloch was that the children at age eight months are much more alike in intellectual potential than has hitherto been supposed. Dr. Knobloch's research and conclusions point the way to a need for more complete information than we now possess on this crucial period of infant development. Such experiments need to be extended a hundred fold in this one area alone if America is to conserve and nourish its most gifted children and develop the potential greatness in human beings.

IV

Experiments to test American assumptions about the nature of man could be planned by a panel of distinguished thinkers in many fields—social scientists, historians, poets, biologists, artists, educators, statisticians, meteorologists. One such experiment might be projected to answer the following question: Does a vastly expanded investment in average human resources, expended with the best available knowledge, produce a proportionate increase in remarkable men? Once a foundation or group of foundations has determined that such an experiment is justified, the leaders of the experiment may bring together specialists in many fields to trace in outline the ways and means to put the experiment into action. The first task is to select a small county of both rural and industrial occupations, peopled by families both old and new to American ways, a county subject to no extremes of climate, equipped with schools of moderate efficiency, embodying in a microcosm the American diversity of nationality backgrounds, occupations, and natural resources. The panel of experts would first take perhaps a year to tabulate the human resources of the community and the sums of money invested in them annually, either through voluntary action or taxation, toward the enrichment of life beyond the status of animal comforts and necessities. A citizen who uses part of his income to build a beautiful garden, plant a tree, pay for a stained-glass window in his church, a citizen who adds to his taxes for a beautiful new school building, who contributes books and working time to the town's free library, who purchases a recording of *Rigoletto* for his family, who takes his family to a drama which is a work of art—any citizen who makes such contributions is enlarging the volume of civilized practices in his neighborhood. Each of these small contributions to civilization exacts from him not only energy but also wealth. Would the multiplication of such expenditures also in time multiply the number of remarkable people in the community? This is the key question the experiment would seek to answer.

In taking an inventory of human and cultural resources, the panel of experts could draw up a list of subsidies to be granted to people and for services they considered most necessary to the production of remarkable personalities. In their discussions of the existing and customary subsidies, the experts would gradually shape a collective definition of the conditioning of talent and genius. Such an evaluation of human and social resources would in itself crystallize not only the ultimate goal of the experiment and the controls to be used, but also the ways and means by which boys and girls of talent could be identified in very early years and provided with numerous incitements to creative growth.

The table below, which is merely suggestive and exploratory, shows how the foundation experts might begin an inventory of the subsidies the hypothetical county already provides for its human and cultural resources. Each senior in college, for example, the experts may decide is subsidized by his parents or the county to the extent of one thousand dollars. Each senior in high school is subsidized by the county to the extent of three hundred dollars. This is in addition, of course, to the subsidy of board and room granted by his parents. An artist may already be living and working in the community, but he now receives no subsidy from the hypothetical county to grant him leisure time. The human resource might represent a service, such as a clinic, a library, or a food and vitamin station, rather than a person. All such services, however, would require a subsidy of human resources. Each inclusion in the inventory, such as that of clergymen, poets, or swimming instructors, might be the focus of fruitful discussion of values and resources which would prove to be helpful in the production of talented people.

PRESENT SUBSIDIES OF HUMAN RESOURCES

Seniors in college	25	$ 2,000 each
Seniors in high school	400	600
Artists	2	none
Architects	2	none
Works of art to beautify community	1	1,000
Public health nurses	1	8,000
Novelists	1	none
Libraries	2	6,000
Librarians	4	8,000
Teachers, elementary and secondary	500	8,000
Engineers	20	none
Physicians	25	none
Sculptors	1	none
Swimming instructors	1	9,000
Art galleries	1	10,000
College teachers	20	9,000
Music teachers	5	none
School psychologists	1	10,000
Physicians for prenatal care	1	12,000
Nurses for prenatal care	1	8,000
Food and vitamin stations for young children and expectant mothers	1	10,000
Poets	1	none
Great men in residence	1	none
Scientists	1	none
Clergymen	6	10,000

The panel of experts tabulating such resources could be a continuing body meeting every month or two to determine the policies of the experiment within the limits of the funds provided. The experts could decide to multiply some subsidies by five, others by ten, others perhaps by two or three, keeping in mind an arbitrary fivefold or tenfold increase in the total money investment of preceding years. If, as is conceivable, such an experiment could continue for two or three decades, the experts would want to give close attention to prenatal care of children and expectant mothers, as England is doing today through its health services, in order to insure each child before and after birth against the hazards of deficient diet and lack of medical attention. No one yet knows to what extent pronounced inequalities in the intelligence of very young children are due to a deficient or unbalanced diet from birth onward. The experts might feel that a series of nursery and kindergarten schools, manned by extraordinary teachers paid on the same scale as engineers in industry, would provide an opportunity for watching over the youngest members of the population and providing them with needed medical care, supplementary diet, and many creative classroom opportunities.

The complete co-operation of the experimental county's people and officials would, of course, be required. Only if the people were fully sympathetic toward the experiment could it go forward with assurance. Even so, several years of discussion and evaluation of the proposals might be necessary before such a county would co-operate imaginatively with the plans of the experts. Without an understanding of the purposes of the experiment, the selected county might feel hostile to both the planners of the project and the talented specialists employed to watch over its young people for potential and blossoming talent in many fields.

Would one aim be for every child to achieve a minimum proficiency in athletics, music, and art as a foundation for growth in talent? What ideal mass personality such as Whitman delineated would be the prelude to highly individual achievement? What sources and signs of talent would the workers watch for? With ample funds it would be possible for teachers to bring children and young people into association with remarkable children of other counties, states, and countries. The possibilities for exposing each child to an atmosphere of creative excitement would be limited only by the number of skilled teachers available. Certainly, from early years, visits to and residence in the experimental county by creative men and women of America and other countries would be a necessary condition of the experiment.

To visualize the acceleration of creative and intellectual life tested by such an experiment, we may project additions to the program decided upon by the foundation after a second or third year of the experiment.

NEW SUBSIDIES OF HUMAN RESOURCES

Twenty artists in residence	$10,000 each
Twenty poets in residence	10,000 each
Ten awards to citizens for beautification of buildings or landscape	6,000 each
Twenty architects in residence	10,000 each
Twenty noted musicians in residence	15,000 each
One hundred awards to high-school students for original paintings	200 each
One hundred awards to high-school students for original poems: trips to Concord and Boston	200 each
Fifty awards for designs of clothing, schoolrooms, gardens: high-school students	200 each
Fifty awards to college students for original essays on the arts	200 each
Ten sculptors in residence	10,000 each
Ten Shakespearean actors in residence	10,000 each
Ten scientists in residence	10,000 each
Seminars of college students: one week at Monticello	1,000 each

The possibilities for increasing the incentive to creative action, once such an experiment is under way, would be limited, of course, by the response of the community to the activities of cultural acceleration already in effect. One can imagine, however, that the association of artists, poets, musicians, and scientists in residence together, available for consultation with the young people of the community, would in itself set in motion a chain of incitements, large or small, to creative action. Until such an experiment is made, none can assume that the plasticity of human nature does or does not permit the artificial development of great men.

The possibilities for systematic subsidizing of human resources and services have not yet been visualized on the American scene as part of such an experiment. A few talented men have been, so to speak, subsidized in childhood by parents who were able to provide every cultural advantage. The problem of the experiment would be to provide similarly from foundation funds all opportunities that money could purchase for responsive boys and girls. The peculiar advantage of America in the production of great men is her possession of unlimited wealth, a condition never before exemplified in a country of such diverse human resources.

No experiment has yet shown whether or not brilliant boys and girls with difficult personalities, enmeshed in the explosive chemistry of adolescence, can be directed to creative pursuits. Is it possible to find a remarkable teacher whom a scarred but talented student would heed? With generous funds it is possible to experiment with such a student. To take him to many places and introduce him to talented boys his own age may have a decisive effect upon his aspirations. Can the ambition to become a creative person —a reformer, a poet, a great biologist—be communicated? Is such an ambition infectious or inherent? Such a question can be answered only by experimental action with a large and representative group of people. The impact upon young people of visits to historic places and homes of the great, of conversations with distinguished men, may be much more profound than has hitherto been realized. As Emerson wrote, "The earth is his who can go over it." Wealth, as Matthew Arnold asserted, is the indispensable machinery of culture. Every cultural or creative advance has its economic coefficient.

V

An indispensable resource in such an experimental county as we have described would be a college. Eventually, as need grew, perhaps a cluster of colleges might be created, each separately endowed, patterned architecturally after the colleges of Oxford and Cambridge. Each one would represent a link with the youth and dreams of great men. The college would be open, free of tuition, to the young people of the county—provided they had read certain great books, upon which the entrance examinations would be based. Each student would have a room for study and sleep at the college, even though he might live nearby. As at Oxford, he would have dinner with his teachers in the great dining hall of the college four or five evenings a week. The college dining room would also be open to teachers in the local schools; every effort would be made to glean some of the benefits of their rich backgrounds for the students and faculty of the college. The faculty would be selected with the greatest care and would be paid salaries among the highest in the land. At the end of the first year at college each student would be given a grant with which to spend two months at Oxford or Cambridge, meanwhile visiting the homes of great men—perhaps that of Milton at Chalfont St. Giles, or Disraeli's home at Hughenden Manor, or Carlyle's house in Chelsea. A program of visits to great living Americans, either singly or in small groups, would be an integral part of the college course. A study of the biographies of great men would continue in each year of the college offerings. At the end of the study the senior student would write a thesis upon the renowned man or woman of his choice.

A course of creative writing in depth, exploring the student's personality and tracing the crucial moments of his life, should be required in the freshman year and again in the junior year. When skillfully taught, no course is more vital to the growth of critical insight and self-confidence than creative writing. The more electric the student's creative diction (based on exact sensory observation of his own incandescent moments), the deeper his appreciation of the writer's craft and the emotional roots of creative energy— whether in *Look Homeward, Angel; Sons and Lovers;* or *Moby Dick.* A book such as *The Ordeal of Richard Feverel,* though quaintly elevated in style, speaks of the youth's own cruel dilemmas of love and loyalty and desire. Unless the teacher can call forth in his pupil the streams of energy that in turn summon up the most original images and unique sentence rhythms, he cannot prove the

student's ability to write. "No one ever forgets," wrote Emerson, "the
visitation of that power to his heart that creates all things new, that
was the dawn in him of music, poetry, and art." Of all his teachers,
the creative writing instructor probes most deeply into the psyche
of the student, helps him to come to terms with himself, and pushes
him forward into stages of accomplishment he never thought possible. A student may be weak in chemistry, analytics, even psychology and history, and yet be a first-rate achiever in creative writing.
Writing about himself summons up streams of energy and self-
knowledge uniquely beneficent in his college life and the adult
years to come.

VI

Such an experiment carried out over two or three decades
would bring into focus, as through a giant magnifying glass, the
conditions which foremost thinkers about the nature of man have
believed conducive to the awakening of genius. The conditions
outlined for this experiment have all existed spasmodically and
accidentally in American life, as in the boyhood associations of
Henry and William James, and in Henry Adams' lifelong access to
the great minds of his time. "Go to Cambridge," wrote Emerson to
Peter Hunt, ". . . and *think* your way up to your true place
among men." The aim of the experiment would be to concentrate,
magnify, and prolong over several decades for many people the
creative excitement present hitherto at scattered moments in a
few fortunate lives. The psychologist who believes that genius is
in the main a genetic gift would have an opportunity to search
out the child gifted by nature and watch over his intellectual
growth. The anthropologist would have an opportunity to observe
and record the plastic response of children to the words and the
behavior of magnificent teachers imbued with a fascination for
the historic emergence of greatness on the American scene. Perhaps in the experimental county one great man, "great" that is by
the collective definition of the group, had emerged in the last

hundred years. In two or three decades it would be possible for the experimentalists to say, "Has the county given birth to more than one great man? If not, is the county now sending forth poets, scientists, artists, teachers, musicians, architects of distinction, whereas when the experiment started it produced only a trickle of leaders?" Through the co-operation of psychologists, biologists, anthropologists, social scientists, and literary critics, the values sought in the terms *great man, great woman* could be delineated and sought after as a product of the incentives to achievement. In such an experiment the life of every great man might be examined for clues to the golden moments which nourished his ambition or banished his despair. Take, for example, the frenzy for art that gripped the Florentines of the fourteenth and fifteenth centuries—for an art equal to that of Athens and Rome. What was the origin of this madness? What was its spring and source? It is easy to say that it will not come again, but it is a task worthy of great men to want to recapture that madness for Americans of the future. Let tired nihilists go their way among the shattered lives and gray faces. The creation of genius can walk side by side only with a proud belief in life.

A hundred years after Emerson America is still not at the meridian, but only at the dawn of civilization. Even if the experiment outlined above were a total failure—if, after multiplying by five or ten those subsidies conducive to talent or greatness, the yield in distinction and talent were no greater than in previous decades—the world would still be richer than it is now in certainties about human nature. The controls in such an experiment would be difficult to design and maintain. From the point of view of the social scientist and the statistician, the task might appear difficult and cumbersome—some would say impossible. Only if the experiment failed to produce genius might the realist assert that greatness is a mysterious, untraceable emergence of talent that no human ingenuity can anticipate or cause to flower.

I do not claim in suggesting this experiment that it is scientific in its design. I claim only that some such experiment carried out by foremost thinkers in many fields can confirm or disprove the persistent assumptions about the nature of man upon which American education is based. Man is plastic. He is capable of a cruelty he never suspects in himself until an emergency makes him savage. He is also capable of a generosity, perhaps a heroism, he never expected in himself until a crisis calls it forth. To what extent can man's plasticity lead to greatness? When many boys and girls are given the subsidies now granted only to the fortunate few, what will be the fruit in uncommon men? To those who believe such questions are illusory and sentimental, I say, "You believe in the hard facts. Where are they? Where is your experiment that proves your ground? Where is your statistical analysis?" A true science of man yet eludes us, a science more desperately needed than any other in the history of the world. Only through a science of man can we prove or disprove our assumption of plasticity and test our hope for new crops of uncommon men from the average soil of American life.

Notes

Introduction

1. *New York Times Magazine,* July 6, 1947, p. 32.
2. *Samson Agonistes,* ll. 674-76.
3. *Ethics* X, 1179*a* (New York: Dutton, Everyman ed., 1911), p. 255.
4. *The Prince and The Discourses* (New York: Modern Library, 1940), p. 117.
5. *The Leviathan* (New York: Dutton, Everyman ed., 1914), p. 30.
6. For illuminating analyses of Darwin's influence, see M. F. Ashley Montagu, *Darwin, Competition and Cooperation* (New York: Henry Schuman, 1952); also Montagu's *The Biosocial Nature of Man* (New York: Grove Press, 1956).
7. *Progress and Poverty* (New York: Dutton, Everyman ed., 1911), p. 327.
8. *A New View of Society* (New York: Dutton, Everyman ed., 1927), pp. 16, 45.
9. *Ibid.,* p. 72.
10. Newman, Freeman, and Holzinger, *Twins: A Study of Heredity and Environment* (Chicago: University of Chicago Press, 1937).
11. *Anthropology and Modern Life* (London, 1930), p. 202.
12. *Abraham Lincoln: Letters and Speeches* (New York: Dutton, Everyman ed., 1907), pp. 26-27.
13. *The Republic,* III, 415 (New York: Modern Library, 1941), p. 125.
14. *Clarke Papers,* ed. Charles Firth (4 vols.; Camden Society Publication, 1891-1901), I, 304.
15. *Selections from the Writings of Thomas Paine,* ed. Carl Van Doren (New York: Modern Library, n.d.), pp. 149, 150.
16. *Ibid.,* pp. 149, 150.

I. Jefferson

1. *Writings of Thomas Jefferson,* ed. Paul Leicester Ford (10 vols.; New York, 1892-99), IX, 358. Hereafter referred to as *Ford.*
2. Ford, I, 4. For the background of Jefferson's childhood the most valuable source is Marie Kimball, *Jefferson: The Road to Glory* (New York: Coward-McCann, 1943). I have also consulted Francis W. Hirst, *Life and Letters of Thomas Jefferson* (New York, 1926); Henry S. Randall, *The Life of Thomas Jefferson* (3 vols.; New York, 1858), and Saul K. Padover, *Jefferson* (London: Jonathan Cape, 1942).
3. Ford, I, 4.
4. Ford, IX, 480.
5. *The Works of Alexander Hamilton,* ed. Henry Cabot Lodge (12 vols.; New York, 1904), X, 433; *The Life and Works of John Adams,* ed. Charles Francis Adams (8 vols.; Boston, 1851), VI, 234, 243.
6. *The Federalist,* Nos. 6, 63.
7. *The Federalist,* Nos. 11, 39. The

449

passage on acquired endowments in the next paragraph is from *The Federalist*, No. 35.

8. *The Writings of Thomas Jefferson*, Memorial Edition (20 vols.; Washington, 1923), XVI, 90-92.

9. Cabanis wrote (*Oeuvres Complètes* [5 vols.; Paris, 1824], III, 64, 65): "Nous sentons; et des impressions qu'éprouvent nos différents organes, dépendent à la fois et nos besoins, et l'action des instruments qui nous sont donnés pour les satisfaire. Ces besoins sont éveillés, ces instruments sont mis en jeu des le premier instant de la vie. Les faibles mouvements du foetus dans le ventre de sa mère doivent sans doute être regardés comme un simple prélude aux actes de la véritable vie animale, dont il ne jouit, à proprement parler, que lorsque l'ouvrage de sa nutrition s'accomplit en entier dans lui-même; mais ces mouvements tiennent aux mêmes principes, ils s'exécutent suivant les mêmes lois." See Marquis de Condorcet, *Outlines of an Historical View of the Progress of the Human Mind* (Baltimore, 1802), p. 7: "Man is born with the faculty of receiving sensations. In those which he receives, he is capable of perceiving and distinguishing the simple sensations of which they are composed. He can retain, recognize, combine them." For an analysis of Cabanis and Tracy and their influence on Jefferson, see Adrienne Koch, *The Philosophy of Jefferson* (New York: Columbia University Press, 1943).

10. Destutt de Tracy, *A Treatise on Political Economy* (Georgetown, 1817), p. 70.

11. *Notes on the State of Virginia* (Philadelphia, 1788), pp. 69, 70.

12. Ford, V, 377-79.

13. *Notes on the State of Virginia*, p. 173.

14. Ford, X, 25, 227.

II. Tocqueville and Mann

1. *The Life and Works of Horace Mann*, ed. Mary Tyler Mann (5 vols.; Boston, 1891), IV, 228. For the details of Mann's early life I have followed Mary Tyler Mann, *Life of Horace Mann* (Boston, 1904), pp. 10, 13-17, 26, 28.

2. *Ibid.*, IV, 160, 166.

3. *Ibid.*, III, 261.

4. *Ibid.*, IV, 131.

5. *Democracy in America*, tr. Henry Reeve and revised by Francis Bowen (2 vols.; Cambridge, 1863), II, 107, 406.

6. For details of Tocqueville's life I am indebted to *Memoir, Letters, and Remains of Alexis de Tocqueville*, ed. Gustave de Beaumont (2 vols.; Boston, 1862), I, 24-38; J. P. Mayer, *Prophet of the Mass Age* (London: J. M. Dent & Sons, 1939), pp. 1-14; George W. Pierson, *Tocqueville and Beaumont in America* (New York: Oxford University Press, 1938), pp. 13-19. Pierson traces in minute detail Tocqueville's research and travels in America.

7. *Democracy in America*, I, 416.

8. *Ibid.*, II, 266-67, 272.

9. *Ibid.*, I, 426.

III. Emerson

1. "Over-Soul," in *Complete Writings of Ralph Waldo Emerson* (New York: William H. Wise & Co., 1929), p. 206. For biographical details on Emerson, the studies of Van Wyck Brooks are indispensable: *The Life of Emerson* (New York: Literary Guild, 1932); *The Flowering of New England, 1815-1865* (New York: E. P. Dutton & Co., 1936).

2. "Over-Soul," *Complete Writings*, p. 206; "Nominalist and Realist," *Complete Writings*, p. 310; "Nature," *Complete Writings*, p. 22; "Civilization," *Complete Writings*, p. 629.
3. *Journals* (10 vols.; Boston and New York, 1909-14), III, 388.
4. *Letters of Ralph Waldo Emerson*, ed. Ralph L. Rusk (6 vols.; New York: Columbia University Press, 1939), IV, 87, 103, 369, 372.
5. *Complete Writings*, p. 574.
6. *Journals*, X, 125.

Vignette: 1855

1. *The Writings of Henry David Thoreau* (14 vols.; Boston and New York, 1906), XIV, 19.
2. George Fitzhugh, *Sociology for the South* (Richmond, 1854), pp. 89, 93, 179, 250, 251, 271.
3. Emerson, *Letters*, ed. Rusk, IV, 514, 530.
4. Margaret Fuller Ossoli, *Woman in the Nineteenth Century* (Boston, 1845), p. 37; *Harper's Magazine*, December, 1855.
5. *U.S. Magazine of Science, Art, Manufactures, Agriculture, Commerce, and Trade*, January, 1855.

IV. Lincoln and Emerson

1. *The Hidden Lincoln*, ed. Emanuel Hertz (New York: Viking Press, 1938), pp. 120, 308.
2. *Ibid.*, p 143.
3. *Autobiography of Abraham Lincoln*, ed. N. W. Stephenson (Indianapolis, 1926), pp. 4, 10, 11.
4. *The Hidden Lincoln*, pp. 233, 234, 247.
5. Emerson, *Journals*, IX, 375.
6. *Ibid.*, IX, 537, 556; X, 97; *Miscellanies*, in *Complete Works*, ed. Edward W. Emerson (14 vols.; Boston and New York, 1903-4), XII, 317, 335.

V. Lincoln

1. *Abraham Lincoln: Complete Works*, ed. John G. Nicolay and John Hay (2 vols.; New York, 1922), I, 178-79, 179.
2. William H. Herndon, *Life of Lincoln* (Cleveland: World Publishing Co., 1942), p. 339.
3. *Complete Works*, I, 179, 370.
4. *Ibid.*, I, 511.
5. Herndon, *op. cit.*, p. 354; *The Hidden Lincoln*, p. 142.

VI. Holmes

1. *The Writings of Oliver Wendell Holmes* (14 vols.; Cambridge, 1891-92), VIII, 325.
2. *Ibid.*, VIII, 293.
3. *Ibid.*, VIII, 263.
4. In *The Autocrat of the Breakfast-Table* (*Writings*, I, 185) Holmes writes: "Our brains are seventy-year clocks. The Angel of Life winds them up once for all, then closes the case, and gives the key into the hand of the Angel of the Resurrection. Tic-tac! tic-tac! go the wheels of thought; our will cannot stop them; sleep cannot still them; madness only makes them go faster; death alone can break into the case."
5. *Writings*, VIII, 285.
6. In *The Autocrat* (*Writings*, I, 196) Holmes wrote: "All uttered thought, my friend, the Professor, says, is of the nature of an excretion. Its materials have been taken in, and have acted upon the system, and been reacted on by it; it has circulated and done its office in one mind before it is given out for the benefit of others."
Again (I, 195): "There are half a dozen men, or so, who carry in their brains the *ovarian eggs* of the next generation's or century's civilization. These eggs are not

ready to be laid in the form of books as yet; some of them are hardly ready to be put into the form of talk."
7. Writings, VIII, 327.
8. Ibid., V, 227.
9. Ibid., VIII, 337.
10. Ibid., V, 226.
11. Ibid., V, 228.
12. Ibid., I, 86.
13. Ibid., V, 226, 228.
14. Life and Letters of Oliver Wendell Holmes, ed. John T. Morse (2 vols.; Boston, 1896), I, 263.
15. Writings, V, 323.
16. Ibid.
17. Ibid.
18. Maurice Kirkwood's antipathy toward girls, an antipathy rooted in a moment of childhood terror when he was dropped from Laura's arms into a rosebush far below, vanishes under the healing shock of Euthymia's ministrations. Kirkwood blooms, as does Myrtle Hazard, in the warm climate of endearments and embraces.
19. Writings, VI, 82, 115, 158.
20. Ibid., II, 15.
21. Ibid., III, 307.

VII. Whitman

1. The Complete Writings of Walt Whitman (10 vols.; New York and London: G. P. Putnam's Sons, 1902), V, 90.
2. Ibid., V, 99.
3. Ibid., V, 71.
4. Ibid., V, 152-54.
5. Ibid., V, 65.
6. The Uncollected Poetry and Prose of Walt Whitman, ed. Emory Holloway (2 vols.; New York: Doubleday, Page & Co., 1921), II, 6-7.
7. Complete Writings, V, 102.
8. Ibid., V, 103.
9. Ibid., V, 103.
10. Horace Traubel, With Walt Whitman in Camden (Vol. I, Boston,

1906; Vol. II, New York, 1908; Vol. III, New York, 1914), I, 145, 430.
11. Complete Writings, IV, vi, 112 ff.
12. Ibid., V, 188.
13. Ibid., IX, 5.
14. Ibid., VII, 70.
15. On the emphasis that should obtain on Whitman's supposed inversion, no one has written more justly than Newton Arvin (Whitman [New York: Macmillan Co., 1938]): "Not its obscure and private origins but its general and public bearing is the test of a great creative conception."
16. Complete Poetry, and Selected Prose and Letters, ed. Emory Holloway (New York: Random House, 1938), p. 1052.
17. Complete Writings, V, 131.
18. When D. H. Lawrence condemns Whitman's gravitating warmth in Studies in Classic American Literature, saying, "I find I can shake hands with a few people. But most I wouldn't touch with a long prop," he suggests himself as a truer representative than Whitman of the American mass man. The educated New Englander, the sophisticated city dweller, might feel this aloofness; but certainly not the average American either of Whitman's day or ours.
19. Traubel, op. cit., I, 429.
20. Complete Writings, V, 117.
21. Ibid., II, 118-19.
22. Ibid., IX, 181, 182, 183.
23. Ibid., V, 260.
24. Ibid., V, 271.
25. Ibid., V, 80.
26. Ibid., IX, 145.
27. Ibid., V, 166-67.
28. Ibid., V, 270.
39. John Burroughs, Birds and Poets (Boston, 1877), p. 188.
30. Complete Writings, VI, 290.
31. Interpretations of Poetry and Religion (New York, 1900), p. 182.

32. *Ibid.*, p. 177.
33. Traubel, *op. cit.*, I, 166.
34. *Complete Writings*, IX, 133.
35. *The Gathering of the Forces*, ed. Cleveland Rodgers and John Black (2 vols.; New York and London: G. P. Putnam's Sons, 1920), I, 128.
36. *Ibid.*, I, 132.
37. *Complete Writings*, V, 15.
38. *Ibid.*, V, 227.
39. *Forces*, I, 37-38.
40. *Complete Writings*, V, 95.
41. *Ibid.*, VI, 133.
42. *Ibid.*, VIII, 255.
43. *Complete Writings*, V, 101.
44. *Walt Whitman's Workshop*, ed. Clifton J. Furness (Cambridge: Harvard University Press, 1928), p. 93.
45. *Ibid.*, p. 74.
46. Traubel, *op. cit.*, II, 88.
47. *Complete Writings*, IX, 138-39.
48. *Walt Whitman's Workshop*, p. 83.
49. *Complete Writings*, VII, 43-44.
50. Traubel, *op. cit.*, I, 181.
51. *Complete Writings*, V, 57.
52. *ibid.*, V, 72.
53. "The fear of conflicting and irreconcilable interiors," wrote Whitman, "and the lack of a common skeleton, knitting all close, continually haunts me." (*Complete Writings*, V, 59.)
54. *Complete Writings*, V, 224.
55. *Forces*, II, 111-12.
56. *Ibid.*, I, 16.
57. *Complete Writings*, VIII, 265.
58. *Ibid.*, VIII, 264.
59. *Forces*, II, 286.
60. *Complete Writings*, V, 286.
61. *Ibid.*, V, 286.
62. *Ibid.*, VI, 291.
63. Traubel, *op. cit.*, I, 201.
64. *Complete Writings*, V, 254.

Vignette: 1885

1. Hamlin Garland, *Ulysses S. Grant* (New York, 1898), p. 524.
2. Adam Badeau, "The Last Days of Ulysses S. Grant," *Century Magazine*, October, 1885, p. 921.
3. *Century*, February, 1885, p. 598; *Personal Memoirs of U. S. Grant* (2 vols.; New York, 1885), I, 342-43.
4. *Century*, February, 1885, pp. 600, 603; *Memoirs*, I, 344, 349.
5. *Century*, October, 1885, p. 923.

VIII. Howells, Bellamy, George

1. Howells, *Years of My Youth* (New York, 1916), p. 23.
2. I am here following Harry Barnard, *"Eagle Forgotten"* (New York and Indianapolis: Bobbs-Merrill Co., 1938), pp. 97-114, 203-15. See Edgar Lee Masters' remarkable article on Altgeld in *American Mercury*, February, 1925, pp. 161-74.
3. *Life in Letters of William Dean Howells*, ed. Mildred Howells (2 vols.; Garden City, 1928), I, 399, 402.
4. *A Hazard of New Fortunes* (2 vols.; New York, 1890), II, 253-54; *The Quality of Mercy* (New York, 1892), p. 474. For biographical details I am indebted to Delmar Gross Cooke, *William Dean Howells* (New York, 1922); Everett Carter, *Howells and the Age of Realism* (Philadelphia: J. B. Lippincott Co., 1950); and Oscar W. Firkins, *William Dean Howells* (Cambridge, 1924). An invaluable guide to Howells' career may be found in *William Dean Howells*, by Clara and Rudolf Kirk (New York: American Book Co., 1950).
5. I am here following Arthur E. Morgan, *Edward Bellamy* (New York: Columbia University Press, 1944), pp. 8, 41, 50, 57 ff., 71, 204-44.
6. *Looking Backward* (Boston, 1917), p. 290.
7. *Ibid.*, p. 323.

8. Henry George, Jr., *The Life of Henry George* (New York, 1930), p. 192. I am indebted to this book for other biographical details. See also the delightful but less informative volume, *Henry George, Citizen of the World*, by Anna George De Mille (Chapel Hill: University of North Carolina Press, 1950).
9. *Progress and Poverty* (New York: Dutton, Everyman edition, 1911), p. 383.
10. *Ibid.*, p. 340.
11. *Ibid.*, p. 333.
12. *Ibid.*, p. 332.

IX. Mark Twain

1. *The Mysterious Stranger and Other Stories* (New York, 1922), p. 112.
2. *Mark Twain in Eruption*, ed. Bernard DeVoto (New York: Harper & Bros., 1940), p. 384.
3. Albert Bigelow Paine, *Mark Twain, A Biography* (3 vols.; New York, 1912), III, 1363.
4. *The Mysterious Stranger*, p. 90.
5. *Ibid.*, p. 118.
6. *Mark Twain in Eruption*, p. 72.
7. *The Mysterious Stranger*, p. 139.
8. *What Is Man?* (New York, 1917), pp. 12, 19.
9. *Ibid.*, pp. 43, 46.
10. *Pudd'nhead Wilson* (New York, 1899), pp. 123, 202.
11. *Mark Twain's Letters* (2 vols.; New York, 1917), II, 788-89; II, 757.
12. *A Connecticut Yankee in King Arthur's Court* (New York, 1917), p. 105.
13. *The Mysterious Stranger*, p. 132.
14. William Dean Howells, *My Mark Twain* (New York, 1910), pp. 100-101.
Note: An especially valuable recent book is Justin Kaplan's *Mr. Clemens and Mark Twain*. Mr. Kaplan has had access to unpublished documents, many of them from the Mark Twain

Papers in the University of California Library at Berkeley. Mr. Kaplan's narrative is especially rich in details of Mark's family life during the last unhappy years of Livy, Jean, and Susy. Other important recent books are the *Mark Twain–Howells Letters*, ed. Henry Nash Smith and William M. Gibson (Harvard University Press, 1960) and the *Autobiography*, ed Charles Neider (Harper and Brothers, 1959).

Vignette: 1895

1. *Heart of Burroughs's Journals*, ed. Clara Barrus (Boston, 1923), p. 189; Paine, *Mark Twain, A Biography*, II, 998; III, 1006-1007.
2. Robert H. Elias, *Dreiser: Apostle of Nature* (New York: Alfred A. Knopf, 1949), p. 86; Dreiser, "Mark Twain: Three Contacts," *Esquire*, October, 1935, pp. 22, 162.
3. E. K. Brown and Leon Edel, *Willa Cather: A Critical Biography* (New York: Alfred A. Knopf, 1953), pp. 75-76; James R. Shively, *Writings from Willa Cather's Campus Years* (Lincoln: University of Nebraska Press, 1950), pp. 21, 24.
4. *Heart of Burroughs's Journals*, pp. 189, 190, 195.
5. Ellen Glasgow, *The Woman Within* (New York: Harcourt, Brace & Co., 1954), pp. 72, 111-12, 152.

X. Henry Adams

1. William H. Jordy, *Henry Adams* (New Haven: Yale University Press, 1952), p. 125; Henry Adams, *History of the United States During the Administrations of Jefferson and Madison* (9 vols.; New York, 1889-91), IX, 224.
2. *History*, I, 159-60.
3. *Ibid.*, I, 160, 183.
4. *Ibid.*, I, 184.

5. *Democracy* (New York, 1880), p. 77; *Letters, 1858-1891,* ed. Worthington Chauncey Ford (Boston and New York, 1930), p. 302.
6. *History,* IX, 226, 238.
7. *The Education of Henry Adams* (New York, 1918), pp. 57-58 (Lee), p. 107 (Lincoln); *Letters, 1858-1891,* p. 66 (Lincoln).
8. In *Education,* however, written long before "The Rule of Phase in History," Adams had spoken in his chapter on "The Dynamo and the Virgin" of the sexual woman as "reproduction—the greatest and most mysterious of all energies; all she needed was to be fecund."
9. *The Tendency of History* (New York, 1928), pp. 8-48, 69-71.

XI. Brooks Adams

1. Henry Adams, *The Degradation of the Democratic Dogma* (New York, 1919), pp. vii-viii. See Arthur F. Beringause, *Brooks Adams, A Biography* (New York: Alfred A. Knopf, 1955), p. 373.
2. *The Emancipation of Massachusetts* (New York, 1919), p. 5; *Degradation* (1919), pp. 85, 105.
3. *The Law of Civilization and Decay* (New York: Vintage Books, 1955), pp. 16-17.
4. *Ibid.,* pp. 4-5.
5. *Ibid.,* p. 6.

XII. William James

1. "The Environment of Great Men," in *The Will to Believe* (New York, 1917), pp. 230, 243, 248, 249.
2. "The Genesis of Genius," *Atlantic Monthly,* March, 1881, pp. 373, 377.

Vignette: 1915

1. A. A. Hoehling and Mary Hoehling, *The Last Voyage of the Lusitania* (New York: Henry Holt & Co., 1956), pp. 33, 150, 169.
2. "Climate and Civilization," *Harper's Magazine,* February, 1915, pp. 366-73; "Is Civilization Determined by Climate?" May, 1915, pp. 943-51. See also Huntington's *Mainsprings of Civilization* (New York: John Wiley & Sons, 1945), pp. 80-88, 343-60; *Civilization and Climate* (3rd ed.; New Haven: Yale University Press, 1924), pp. 80-152; *Principles of Human Geography* (New York: John Wiley & Sons, 1940), pp. 496-509.

XIII. Darrow, Steffens, Broun

1. *The Autobiography of Lincoln Steffens* (New York: Harcourt, Brace & Co., 1931), p. 114.
2. *Ibid.,* pp. 408, 475, 478, *passim.*
3. *Ibid.,* p. 479.
4. *Crime, Its Cause and Treatment* (New York, 1922), pp. 30-31.
5. *Debate: Is Man a Machine?* (New York, 1927), pp 15, 16, 36, 80.
6. *Collected Edition of Heywood Broun,* ed. Heywood Hale Broun (New York: Harcourt, Brace & Co., 1941), p. 198.
7. *Ibid.,* pp. 495-96.
8. *Ibid.,* pp. 455-56.
9. Clarence Darrow, *A Persian Pearl and Other Essays* (Boston, 1931), p. 107.

Vignette: 1924

1. Clarence Darrow, *The Story of My Life* (New York: Charles Scribner's Sons, 1932), pp. 226-28; Francis Xavier Busch, *Prisoners at the Bar* (Indianapolis: Bobbs-Merrill Co., 1952), pp. 156-58.
2. Maureen McKernan, *The Amazing Crime and Trial of Leopold and Loeb* (Chicago: Plymouth Court Press, 1924), pp. 146-55.

3. *Ibid.*, pp. 155-63.
4. *Ibid.*, p. 143.
5. *Ibid.*, p. 144.
6. *Ibid.*, p. 147.
7. *Ibid.*, p. 150.
8. *Ibid.*, p. 251.
9. *Ibid.*, pp. 251-52.
10. *Ibid.*, p. 254.
11. *Ibid.*, p. 258.
12. *Ibid.*, p. 259.
13. *Ibid.*, p. 264.
14. Theodore Dreiser, *Dawn* (New York: Horace Liveright, 1931), p. 422.
15. Meyer Levin, *Compulsion* (New York: Simon & Schuster, 1956), p. 325.
16. Convicted of murder in the first degree, Loeb and Leopold were sentenced to life (plus ninety-nine years) and incarcerated in Stateville Prison, Joliet, Illinois. On January 29, 1936, Loeb was slashed to death in a shower stall by a fellow prisoner, James Day; Day claimed that he had acted in self-defense. He was acquitted on June 5. Leopold's conduct in prison proved exemplary. Thirty-three years after the crime, on February 21, 1958, Leopold was granted parole, and was released on March 14. The Illinois Parole Board permitted him to accept a position in the laboratory of the Church of the Brethren in Puerto Rico. On February 8, 1961, Leopold married. On July 11, 1961, the parole board was urged by three prominent citizens—Elmer Gertz, Dr. W. Harold Row, and Ralph Newman—to recommend a full pardon for Leopold. To this plea the parole board, however, made no response.

XIV. Veblen

1. Joseph Dorfman, *Thorstein Veblen and His America* (New York:
Viking Press, 1934), pp. 1-37, 40-44, 79-82, 87, 174 ff.
2. *Ibid.*, pp. 412, 449 ff., 503.
3. *Essays in Our Changing Order* (New York: Viking Press, 1934), p. 86; *The Instinct of Workmanship* (New York, 1914), pp. 25-26.
4. *The Theory of the Leisure Class* (New York: Modern Library, 1934), p. 223
5. *Essays in Our Changing Order*, pp. 209, 216.
6. *The Mind in the Making* (New York, 1921), pp. 68, 71.

XV. Dewey

1. I am indebted for these biographical details to Max Eastman, *Heroes I Have Known* (New York: Simon & Schuster, 1942), pp. 276, 279, 281; *The Philosophy of John Dewey*, ed. Paul A. Schilpp (Evanston: Northwestern University Press, 1939), pp. 7-13, 14-29, 29-35.
2. Waldo Frank, *Time Exposures* (New York, 1926), pp. 122, 124, 125.
3. *Human Nature and Conduct* (New York, 1922), pp. 90, 177.
4. *Problems of Men* (New York: Philosophical Library, 1946), p. 191.
5. *Human Nature and Conduct*, pp. 65, 97.
6. *Ibid.*, pp. 65-66, 97.
7. *Intelligence in the Modern World: John Dewey's Philosophy*, ed. Joseph Ratner (New York: Modern Library, 1939), p. 399.

XVI. Dreiser

1. *Dawn* (New York: Horace Liveright, 1931), p. 73.
2. *Ibid.*, p. 12.
3. *Ibid.*, p. 368.
4. *Ibid.*, p. 422.
5. *Hey, Rub-a-Dub-Dub* (New York: Boni & Liveright, 1920), p. 163.

6. *Ibid.*, p. 132.
7. *Ibid.*, p. 135.
8. *A Book about Myself* (New York: Boni & Liveright, 1922), p. 427.
9. *Hey, Rub-a-Dub-Dub,* p. 6.
10. *Ibid.*, p. 110.
11. *Ibid.*, p. 81.
12. *Ibid.*, p. 167.
13. *Progress and Poverty* (New York: Dutton, Everyman edition, 1911), p. 332.
14. *Hey, Rub-a-Dub-Dub,* p. 145.
15. *Ibid.*, p. 218.
16. *Dreiser Looks at Russia* (New York: Horace Liveright, 1928), p. 255.
17. Jacques Loeb, *The Mechanistic Conception of Life* (Chicago, 1912), p. 3.
18. George Washington Crile, *Man— An Adaptive Mechanism* (New York, 1916), p. 156.
19. George Washington Crile, *The Mechanistic Interpretation of War and Peace* (New York, 1915), p. 99.
20. *Ibid.*, p. 100.
21. Thomas Beer, *Stephen Crane* (New York: Alfred A. Knopf, 1923), p. 233.
22. *Jennie Gerhardt* (New York, 1911), p. 132.
23. *Ibid.*, pp. 141, 139.
24. *Ibid.*, p. 133.
25. *Free and Other Stories* (New York: Modern Library, 1925), p. 18.
26. *Ibid.*, p. 53.
27. In *Hey, Rub-a-Dub-Dub* Dreiser mentions Huxley's *Science and the Hebrew Tradition* and *Science and the Christian Tradition* with high approval.
28. *Jennie Gerhardt,* pp. 427, 428.
29. *Dawn,* p. 107.
30. *An American Tragedy* (2 vols.; New York: Boni & Liveright, 1925), I, 47.
31. Emerson, *The Conduct of Life,* essay on "Behavior."

32. *An American Tragedy,* I, 239.
33. *Ibid.*, I, 328.
34. *Ibid.*, I, 309.
35. *Ibid,* II, 45.
36. *Ibid.*, II, 77.
37. *Ibid.*, II, 389-90.
38. *Dawn,* p. 344.
39. *Ibid.*, p. 22.
40. *America Is Worth Saving* (New York: Modern Age Books, 1941), pp. 150, 271, 277, 280.
41. *The Bulwark* (New York: Doubleday, Doran & Co., 1946), pp. 318-19.
42. *Dawn,* p. 19.
43. *The Genius* (New York, 1915), p. 65.
44. Sherwood Anderson, *Horses and Men* (New York: Viking Press, 1923), pp. xi-xii.

Vignette: 1935

1. *Time,* January 7, 1935, p. 16.
2. *New Republic,* April 10, 1935, p. 237.
3. *Time,* January 7, 1935, p. 16.
4. *Franklin Delano Roosevelt: A Memorial* (New York: Pocket Books, 1945), p. 165.
5. *Consumer Incomes in the United States* (Washington, D. C.: Government Printing Office, 1938), p. 95.
6. *Harper's Magazine,* January, 1936, p. 200.
7. *Atlantic Monthly,* November, 1935, p. 527.
8. *Ibid.*, p. 526.
9. *Nation,* September 15, 1935, p. 344.
10. *Time,* January 14, 1935, p. 15.
11. *Time,* January 7, 1935.
12. *New Republic,* February 27, 1935, p. 62.
13. *Harper's Magazine,* January, 1936, pp. 148-59.
14. *Atlantic Monthly,* October, 1935, p. 413.
15. *Ibid.*, p. 420.
16. *Scribner's Magazine,* July, 1935, p. 9.
17. *Ibid.*, p. 10.

18. *Ibid.*, pp. 12-13.

XVII. Faulkner and Hemingway

1. William Faulkner, *Soldiers' Pay* (New York: Liveright, 1926), p. 295.
2. *William Faulkner: Two Decades of Criticism*, ed. Frederick J. Hoffman and Olga W. Vickery (East Lansing: Michigan State College Press, 1954), p. 244.
3. William Faulkner, *The Sound and the Fury & As I Lay Dying* (New York: Modern Library, 1946), p. 461.
4. *Ibid.*, pp. 461-62.
5. *Ibid.*, p. 467.
6. *Ibid.*, p. 467.
7. *The Faulkner Reader* (New York: Random House, 1954), p. 500.
8. *Ibid.*, p. 503. Cf. Faulkner's own comment on the relatively sexless hero and heroine of *Intruder in the Dust* (New York: Signet Books, 1949), p. 73: "It remained for them, a white youth of sixteen and a Negro one of the same and an old white spinster of seventy to elect and do at the same time . . . to violate the grave of one of its progeny in order to save a nigger murderer from its vengeance."
9. *Ibid.*, p. 514.
10. *Ibid.*, pp. 515-16.
11. William Faulkner, *Go Down, Moses* (New York: Modern Library, 1955), p. 374.
12. *Ibid.*, p. 347.
13. *Ibid.*, p. 354.
14. William Van O'Connor, *The Tangled Fire of William Faulkner* (Minneapolis: University of Minnesota Press, 1954), p. 43.
15. Ernest Hemingway, *The Sun Also Rises* (New York: Bantam Books, 1949), p. 7.
16. *The Short Stories of Ernest Hemingway* (New York: Modern Library, n.d.), p. 104.
17. Ernest Hemingway, *The Green*

Hills of Africa (New York: Permabooks, 1954), p. 125.
18. Thomas Wolfe, *You Can't Go Home Again* (New York: Sun Dial Press, 1942), p. 434.
19. *Ibid.*, p. 435.
20. *Ibid.*, p. 436.

Vignette: 1945

1. *Time*, April 2, 1945, pp. 15, 26.
2. *Time*, April 30, 1945, p. 40.
3. *Ibid.*, p. 43.
4. *Ibid.*, p. 46.
5. *Nation*, July 28, 1945, pp. 74-75.
6. *Time*, April 23, 1945, p. 18.
7. *Time*, April 30, 1945, p. 61.
8. *Newsweek*, May 14, 1945, p. 35.
9. *Harper's Magazine*, January, 1946, p. 3.
10. *Ibid.*
11. *Ibid.*
12. John Hersey, *Hiroshima* (New York: Alfred A. Knopf, 1946), p. 35.
13. *Ibid.*, p. 101.
14. *Time*, August 20, 1945, p. 29. As Secretary Stimson later pointed out ("The Decision to Use the Atomic Bomb," *Harper's Magazine*, February, 1947, p. 101), some atomic scientists wished only a technical demonstration of the power of the weapon with the idea of inducing surrender. Stimson's article gives an invaluable perspective on the recommendations of the scientists and the decisions leading to the use of the bomb. From his account it is plain that some of the scientists felt a much greater compunction about the use of the bomb than the President, the Secretary of War, and their advisers.
15. *New Republic*, August 20, 1945, p. 212.
16. *Time*, August 20, 1945, p. 36.

XVIII. Terman

1. Catharine M. Cox, *The Early*

Mental Traits of Three Hundred Geniuses (Stanford: Stanford University Press, 1926), pp. 90, 93, 96, 102, 105, 110, 113.

2. Lewis M. Terman, "The Intelligence Quotient of Francis Galton in Childhood," *American Journal of Psychology*, XXVIII (1917), 209-15.

3. Biographical information cited mainly by Cox, *Early Mental Traits*, pp. 216-17, 761-815 *passim*.

4. *Ibid.*, p. 218.

5. *Ibid.*, p. 219.

6. Terman, *Mental and Physical Traits of a Thousand Gifted Children* (Stanford: Stanford University Press, 1925), pp. vi, 19-28, 29-31; Terman, *The Gifted Child Grows Up* (Stanford: Stanford University Press, 1947), pp. 2, 5, 6, 11-14.

7. *The Gifted Child Grows Up*, pp. 20, 22, 23, 38-39, 55-57.

8. Harvey C. Lehman, *Age and Achievement* (Princeton: Princeton University Press, 1953).

9. *The Gifted Child Grows Up*, pp. 311, 316, 318, 320, 336, 349-52.

10. *Ibid.*, pp. 338-44.

11. *Ibid.*, pp. 330-32.

12. *Ibid.*, p. 314.

XIX. Biology

1. In the field of biology American science lags far behind British, its main fault its extreme specialization. T. H. Morgan we have produced, it is true, H. S. Jennings, and George Crile. But in social biology we have no one of stature comparable to Julian Huxley or Lancelot Hogben. In the field of anthropology, on the other hand, the Americans Morgan, Boas, Benedict, and Hooton have a superior place in the esteem of the scientific world.

2. Lancelot Hogben, *The Nature of Living Matter* (London, 1930),
pp. 206-7.

3. John E. Pfeiffer, *The Human Brain* (New York: Harper & Bros., 1955), p. 207. This volume is an invaluable guide for the layman to solved and unsolved problems.

4. Arthur Thomson, *What Is Man?* (London, 1924), p. 197.

5. *Nature and Nurture* (London, 1939), p. 91.

6. Thomson, *op. cit.*, p. 151.

7. T. H. Morgan, *The Scientific Basis of Evolution* (New York, 1932), pp. 70-90.

8. H. S. Jennings, *The Biological Basis of Human Nature*, p. 11.

9. It is significant that T. H. Morgan himself has made no claims whatever for the genetic inheritance of mental or moral traits. In *Evolution and Genetics* (1925) he wrote (p. 205): "Until we know how much environment is responsible for, I am inclined to think that the student of human heredity will do well to recommend more enlightenment as to the social causes of deficiencies . . . in the present deplorable state of our ignorance as to the causes of mental differences."

10. On the score of genetic determinism, Arnold Gesell's books represent important advances in biological science. To Gesell man's uniqueness in personality is inherent in his genetic patterns; and these are inseparable from his behavior, which manifests itself long before birth. The key to man's behavior is the unique pattern of his neuronic growth. Yet the identification of particular genetic units is still to come. See Gesell's illuminating *The Embryology of Behavior* (New York: Harper & Bros., 1945) and *Infant Development* (Harper & Bros., 1952). On genetic causes of schizophrenia, body build, and longevity, see *infra*, pp. 394-95, 407.

11. T. H. Morgan, *Evolution and Genetics* (Princeton: Princeton University Press, 1925), p. 201.
12. Floyd L. Ruch, *Psychology and Life* (New York: Scott, Foresman & Co., 1941), p. 504.
13. Mandel Sherman and Thomas R. Henry, *The Hollow Folk* (New York: Thomas Y. Crowell Co., 1933).
14. Louis Petroff, *Solitaries and Solitarization* (Los Angeles: University of Southern California Press, 1936). See Arnold Gesell, "The Biography of a Wolf-Child," *Harper's Magazine*, January, 1941, for a fascinating brief history. Gesell regards Kamala and Amala as further evidence of the extreme plasticity of the human organism.
15. *Negro Intelligence and Selective Migration* (New York: Columbia University Press, 1935).
16. Otto Klineberg, "Racial Psychology," *The Science of Man in the World Crisis* (New York: Columbia University Press, 1945), p. 69.
17. Researches of Dr. Hilda Knobloch and her colleagues show that infants tested by the Gesell Developmental Examination were much more nearly alike in potential of intelligence than formerly supposed. Pointing out that "the intactness of neuro-psychologic functioning is basic to later integration and learning, and as such offers a reliable estimate of intellectual potential," Dr. Knobloch concluded that for those infants born with undamaged brains "the range of normal human intellectual potential is much narrower than has been thought." The researchers found no differences in intelligence of infants according to race or socio-economic status. It is the early experiences of the child that separate him from the normal in intelligence, not his inherited neural constitution. See

"The Distribution of Intellectual Potential in an Infant Population," by Hilda Knobloch and others (Preliminary draft of a paper presented in New York, December 28, 1956). Dr. Knobloch is Director of the Clinic of Child Development, Children's Hospital, Columbus 5, Ohio.
18. *Twins: A Study of Heredity and Environment* (Chicago: University of Chicago Press, 1937), p. 341. For an able analysis of *A Study* and the prospect of further research on twins, see Robert C. Cook, *Human Fertility: The Modern Dilemma* (London: Gollancz, 1951), pp. 192-206 and 206-9. It is estimated that there are more than 2,500 pairs of identical twins in New York City schools alone.
19. Sir Francis Galton, *Essays in Eugenics* (London, 1909), p. 3.
20. Jennings, *op. cit.*, p. 173.
21. Even E. A. Hooton, in *Crime and the Man* (Cambridge: Harvard University Press, 1939), repudiates Lombroso, though holding in general that positive physical differences exist between criminals as a class and noncriminals.
22. Hogben, *op. cit.*, p. 210.
23. "Heredity," *Encyclopedia of the Social Sciences*.
24. "The son of a civilized man," asserts Linton (*The Study of Man*, p. 68), "if he grew up in complete isolation, would be nearer to an ape in his behavior than to his own father."
25. James Harvey Robinson, *The Mind in the Making*, p. 57.
26. Julian Huxley, *Man Stands Alone* (New York: Harper & Bros., 1941), p. 63.
27. *Ibid.*, p. 60.
28. I. V. Pavlov, *Conditioned Reflexes* (Oxford, 1927), p. 395.
29. In this description of the cortex I have followed Pfeiffer, *The Human Brain*, Linton, *The Study*

of Man, Pavlov, *Conditioned Reflexes*, Thomson, *What Is Man?*
30. Pavlov, *op. cit.*, p. 395.
31. *The Human Brain*, p. 61.
32. Gesell, *The Embryology of Behavior*, pp. 186-90.
33. See Alfred Kroeber's excellent analysis of Galton's estimate of the frequency of genius in his *Anthropology* (New York: Harcourt, Brace & Co., 1948), pp. 336-40.
34. Robert Ardrey, *African Genesis* (New York: Atheneum Publishers, 1963), p. 160.
35. *Ibid.*, p. 167.
36. *Man and Aggression*, ed. M. F. Ashley Montagu (New York: Oxford University Press, 1968), p. 78.
37. "A Script Written in the Bones," *New York Times Book Review*, September 11, 1966, p. 6.
38. Sigmund Freud, *Civilization and Its Discontents*, ed. James Strachey (New York: W. W. Norton & Company, Inc., 1962), p. 58.
39. *Ibid.*
40. Eiseley, *loc. cit.*
41. *Man and Aggression*, p. 53.
42. *Ibid.*, p. 151.
43. *Ibid.*, p. 86.

pp. 28-29.
3. *Time*, January 10, 1955, p. 11.
4. *Time*, January 3, 1955, p. 42.
5. *Statistical Abstract: 1956*, p. 209.
6. *Ibid.*, p. 116; *World Almanac, 1957*, p. 539.
7. Robert C. Wilson, "The Under-Educated: How We Have Neglected the Bright Child," *Atlantic Monthly*, May, 1955, p. 60. .
8. *Time*, January 17, 1955, p. 62.
9. *Statistical Abstract: 1956*, pp. 147, 150.
10. John E. Pfeiffer, *The Human Brain* (New York: Harper & Bros., 1955), p. 207.
11. *Ibid.*, p. 224.
12. Arnold Lorand, *Human Intelligence* (Philadelphia: F. A. Davis Co., 1927), p. 208.
13. Pfeiffer, *op. cit.*, p. 225.
14. *Ibid.*, p. 124.
15. *Ibid.*, p. 229.
16. Paul de Kruif, *A Man Against Insanity* (New York: Harcourt, Brace & Co., 1957), pp. 18-20.
17. *Time*, May 2, 1955, p. 50.
18. *Ibid.*, p. 54.
19. "On Privacy," *Harper's Magazine*, July, 1955, p. 38.

XX. Kinsey

1. *Sexual Behavior in the Human Male* (Philadelphia: W. B. Saunders Co., 1948), pp. 302, 325.
2. *Ibid.*, pp. 299, 301, 309, 569.
3. *Ibid.*, pp. 306-9.
4. *Ibid.*, pp. 305-7.

Vignette: 1955

1. U. S. Bureau of the Census, *Statistical Abstract of the United States: 1956* (Washington, D. C., 1956), p. 697.
2. *Harper's Magazine*, March, 1957,

XXI. Anthropology

1. For a valuable succinct history of schools of thought about the nature of man, see Ashley Montagu, *The Biosocial Nature of Man* (New York: Grove Press, 1956). Montagu's analysis of co-operation in the biological processes may be best examined in *Darwin, Competition and Cooperation* (New York: Henry Schuman, 1952).
2. Ruth Benedict, *Patterns of Culture* (Penguin Books, 1946), p. 2.
3. Franz Boas, *Anthropology and Modern Life* (London, 1930), p. 202.
4. W. M. Krogman, "The Concept

of Race," in *The Science of Man in the World Crisis* (New York, 1945), pp. 56-59.

5. *Changes in Bodily Form of Descendants of Immigrants* (Report of the Immigration Commission, Senate Document No. 208 [Washington, D. C.: Government Printing Office, 1911]), p. 5.

6. Krogman, *op. cit.*, p. 59.

7. Robert Redfield, "What Do We Know About Race?" *Scientific Monthly*, LVII (1943), 193-201.

8. Boas, *op. cit.*, p. 75.

9. See *Negro Intelligence and Selective Migration* (New York, 1935).

10. Melville J. Herskovits, *The Negro and the Intelligence Tests* (Hanover, 1928).

11. Franz Boas, *Race and Democratic Society* (New York, 1945), p. 37.

12. See Boas' analysis in his *General Anthropology* (1938), in the chapter titled "Methods of Research."

13. Franz Boas, *The Mind of Primitive Man* (1938), p. 252.

14. *Ibid.*, p. 141.

15. Margaret Mead, *Sex and Temperament in Three Primitive Societies* (New York: William Morrow & Co., 1935), p. 61.

16. *Ibid.*, p. xxii.

17. *Ibid.*, p. 287.

18. Benedict, *op. cit.*, p. 235.

19. Hocking, *Human Nature and Its Remaking* (New Haven: Yale University Press, 1918), pp. 9-10.

20. See *Personality in Nature, Society, and Culture*, ed. Clyde Kluckhohn and Henry A. Murray (Alfred A. Knopf, 1953), Chaps. 4 (Genetic Theory of Schizophrenia), 6 (Masculine Component), and 11 (Physique and Personality).

21. Amram Scheinfeld, *The New You and Heredity* (J. B. Lippincott Co., 1950), pp. 352 ff. This book summarizes objectively the evidence for and against inherited musical talent, genius, intelligence, longev-ity, etc.

Vignette: 1969

1. *The New York Times*, December 25, 1968, p. 1.

2. *The Other America* (Boston: Penguin Books, 1963), p. 88.

3. *Ibid.*, p. 3.

4. *Ibid.*, pp. 171-86.

5. *The New York Times*, January 16, 1969, p. 17.

6. *The New York Times*, January 17, 1969, p. 15.

7. *Ibid.*, p. 14.

8. *The New York Times*, April 21, 1969, p. 35.

9. *The New York Times*, April 24, 1969, p. 34.

10. *The New York Times*, May 2, 1969, pp. 1, 28.

11. *Ibid.*, p. 1.

12. *Ibid.*

13. *The New York Times*, May 2, 1969, p. 42.

14. *The New York Times*, April 28, 1969, p. 18.

15. *The Republic*, tr. Benjamin Jowett, VIII, 563 (New York: Modern Library, 1941), p. 319.

16. *The New York Times*, April 30, 1969, p. 20.

17. *Ibid.*

18. *The New York Times*, May 12, 1969, p. 41.

19. *Educational Directory, 1968–69*, Part III: *Higher Education* (Washington, D. C., 1968), p. 6.

20. *The New York Times*, July 21, 1969, p. 1; July 22, 1969, p. 1; July 23, 1969, p. 26.

XXII. Intelligence and Hunger

1. *The Republic*, tr. Benjamin Jowett, III, 415 (New York: Modern Library, 1941), p. 125.

2. "Statement by Charles Upton Lowe, M. D. . . . Before the Senate Select Committee on Nutrition and Related Human Needs," Jan-

uary 28, 1969, p. 6.
3. *Ibid.*, pp. 6-7.
4. *Ibid.*, p. 7.
5. *Ibid.*
6. *Ibid.*, pp. 8-9.
7. "Statement by Charles Upton Lowe, M. D. . . . Before the Committee on Agriculture, House of Representatives," April 24, 1969, p. 8.
8. *Ibid.*, p. 5.
9. Benjamin S. Bloom, *Stability and Change in Human Characteristics* (New York: John Wiley & Sons, 1964), p. 88.
10. Charles Upton Lowe, "Statement . . . ," January 28, 1969, p. 12.
11. *Ibid.*, pp. 12-13.
12. *Ibid.*, pp. 16-17.
13. *The New York Times*, February 16, 1969, p. 56.
14. *Hunger, U.S.A.*, ed. Benjamin E. Mays and Leslie W. Dunbar (Boston: Beacon Press, 1968), pp. 95-96.
15. *Ibid.*, p. 38.
16. *Ibid.*, p. 7.
17. *The New York Times*, February 20, 1969, p. 33.
18. Lowe, "Statement . . . ," April 24, 1969, p. 2.
19. *The New York Times*, November 13, 1968, p. 29.

XXIII. Plastic Mind

1. William R. Thompson and Ronald Melzack, "Early Environment," *Scientific American*, CXCIV (January, 1956), 40, 42.
2. Hilda Knobloch and others, "The Distribution of Intellectual Potential in an Infant Population" (delivered as "Epidemiology of Mental Disorder" to the American Psychiatric Association and American Public Health Association, December 28, 1956), p. 2.

Bibliography

Introduction

ARISTOTLE. *Ethics.* New York: Dutton, Everyman edition, 1911.

BOAS, FRANZ. *Anthropology and Modern Life.* London, 1930.

Clarke Papers, ed. CHARLES FIRTH. 4 vols. Camden Society Publication, 1891-1901.

GEORGE, HENRY. *Progress and Poverty.* New York: Dutton, Everyman edition, 1911.

HOBBES, THOMAS. *The Leviathan.* New York: Dutton, Everyman edition, 1914.

LINCOLN, ABRAHAM. *Letters and Speeches.* New York: Dutton, Everyman edition, 1907.

MACHIAVELLI, NICCOLÒ. *The Prince and The Discourses.* New York: Modern Library, 1940.

MILTON, JOHN. *Samson Agonistes. (English Poems,* ed. R. C. BROWNE, Vol. II.) Oxford: Clarendon Press, 1894.

MONTAGU, M. F. ASHLEY. *The Biosocial Nature of Man.* New York: Grove Press, 1956.

———. *Darwin, Competition and Cooperation.* New York: Henry Schuman, 1952.

New York Times Magazine, July 6, 1947.

NEWMAN, H. H., FREEMAN, F. N., and HOLZINGER, K. J. *Twins: A Study of Heredity and Environment.* Chicago: University of Chicago Press, 1937.

OWEN, ROBERT. *A New View of Society.* New York: Dutton, Everyman edition, 1927.

PAINE, THOMAS. *Selections from the Writings of Thomas Paine,* ed. CARL VAN DOREN. New York: Modern Library, n.d.

PLATO. *The Republic.* New York: Modern Library, 1941.

I. Jefferson and the Science of Man

ADAMS, JOHN. *Life and Works*, ed. CHARLES FRANCIS ADAMS. 8 vols. Boston, 1851.

CABANIS, PIERRE JEAN GEORGES. *Oeuvres Complètes.* 5 vols. Paris, 1824.

CONDORCET, MARQUIS DE. *Outlines of an Historical View of the Progress of the Human Mind.* Baltimore, 1802.

Federalist, The.

GODWIN, WILLIAM. *Enquiry Concerning Political Justice.* 3rd ed., 2 vols. London, 1798.

HAMILTON, ALEXANDER. *Works*, ed. HENRY CABOT LODGE. 12 vols. New York, 1904.

HUME, DAVID. *A Treatise of Human Nature*, ed. A. D. LINDSAY. 2 vols. London, 1911.

JEFFERSON, THOMAS. *Correspondence . . . Du Pont de Nemours.* With an Introduction by GILBERT CHINARD. Baltimore: Johns Hopkins University Press, 1931.

———. *Life and Selected Writings*, ed. ADRIENNE KOCH and WILLIAM PEDEN. New York: Random House, 1944.

———. *Notes on the State of Virginia.* Philadelphia, 1788.

———. *Writings*, ed. PAUL LEICESTER FORD. 10 vols. New York, 1892-99.

———. *Writings.* Memorial ed. 20 vols. Washington, D. C., 1923.

———. *Writings*, ed. H. A. WASHINGTON. 9 vols. New York, 1859.

KIMBALL, MARIE. *Jefferson: The Road to Glory.* New York: Coward-McCann, 1943.

KOCH, ADRIENNE. *The Philosophy of Jefferson.* New York: Columbia University Press, 1943.

LOCKE, JOHN. *An Essay Concerning Human Understanding*, ed. A. S. PRINGLE PATTISON. Oxford: Oxford University Press, 1950.

MALONE, DUMAS. *Jefferson and His Time.* 2 vols. Boston: Little, Brown & Co., 1948-51.

PADOVER, SAUL K. *Jefferson.* London: Jonathan Cape, 1942.

PRIESTLEY, JOSEPH. *Lectures on History, and General Policy.* 2 vols. Philadelphia, 1803.

RANDALL, HENRY S. *The Life of Thomas Jefferson.* 3 vols. New York, 1858.

TRACY, DESTUTT DE. *A Treatise on Political Economy.* Georgetown, 1817.

TURGOT, ANNE ROBERT JACQUES. *Notes on Universal History,* in *Life and Writings,* ed. W. WALKER STEPHENS. London, 1895.

II. The Plastic Mind: Tocqueville and Horace Mann

CURTI, MERLE. *The Social Ideas of American Educators.* New York: Charles Scribner's Sons, 1935.

MANN, HORACE. *Life and Works,* ed. MARY TYLER MANN. 5 vols. Boston, 1891.

MANN, MARY TYLER. *Life of Horace Mann.* Boston, 1904.

MAYER, J. P. *Prophet of the Mass Age.* London: J. M. Dent & Sons, 1939.

PIERSON, GEORGE W. *Tocqueville and Beaumont in America.* New York: Oxford University Press, 1938.

TOCQUEVILLE, ALEXIS DE. *Democracy in America.* Translated by HENRY REEVE and revised by FRANCIS BOWEN. 2 vols. Cambridge, 1863.

————. *Memoir, Letters, and Remains,* ed. GUSTAVE DE BEAUMONT. 2 vols. Boston, 1862.

Vignette: 1835

ALCOTT, AMOS BRONSON. *Journals,* ed. ODELL SHEPARD. Boston: Little, Brown & Co., 1938.

ALLEN, GAY WILSON. *The Solitary Singer.* New York: Macmillan Co., 1955.

ALLEN, HERVEY. *Israfel.* New York: Farrar and Rinehart, 1934.

EMERSON, RALPH WALDO. *Journals.* 10 vols. Boston and New York, 1909-14.

GILMAN, WILLIAM H. *Melville's Early Life and Redburn.* New York: New York University Press, 1951; London: Oxford University Press, 1951.

HERNDON, WILLIAM H. *Life of Lincoln.* Cleveland: World Publishing Co., 1942.

HOWARD, LEON. *Herman Melville.* Berkeley and Los Angeles: University of California Press, 1951.

METCALF, ELEANOR MELVILLE. *Herman Melville: Cycle and Epicycle.* Cambridge: Harvard University Press, 1953.

SANDBURG, CARL. *Abraham Lincoln: The Prairie Years.* 2 vols. New York: Harcourt, Brace & Co., 1926.

WOODBERRY, GEORGE E. *Nathaniel Hawthorne.* ("American Men of Letters Series.") New York, 1902. (Woodberry cites "The Devil in Manuscript," which was in manuscript early in 1835, as representing in the character of Oberon Hawthorne's feelings, feelings too intimate to be entered in the early passages of his *Notebooks.*)

III. Perfection A Priori: Ralph Waldo Emerson

ALCOTT, AMOS BRONSON. *Journals,* ed. ODELL SHEPARD. Boston: Little, Brown & Co., 1938.

BROOKS, VAN WYCK. *The Flowering of New England, 1815-1865.* New York: E. P. Dutton & Co., 1936.

————. *The Life of Emerson.* New York: Literary Guild, 1932.

EMERSON, RALPH WALDO. *Complete Works,* ed. EDWARD W. EMERSON. 14 vols. Boston and New York, 1903-4.

————. *Complete Writings.* New York: William H. Wise & Co., 1929.

————. *Journals.* 10 vols. Boston and New York, 1909-14.

————. *Letters,* ed. RALPH L. RUSK. 6 vols. New York: Columbia University Press, 1939.

Vignette: 1855

ADAMS, HENRY. *The Degradation of the Democratic Dogma.* New York, 1919.

Atlantic Monthly. 1855.

Bizarre. 1855.

Census, The Seventh, of the United States. J. D. B. De Bow, Superintendent. Washington, 1853.

Christian Examiner. 1855.

EMERSON, RALPH WALDO. *Letters,* ed. RALPH L. RUSK. 6 vols. New York: Columbia University Press, 1939.

FITZHUGH, GEORGE. *Sociology for the South.* Richmond, 1854.

Fraser's Magazine. 1855.

GODWIN, PARKE. *Political Essays.* New York, 1856.
Graham's Magazine. 1855.
Harper's Magazine. 1855.
HOLMES, OLIVER WENDELL. *Writings.* 14 vols. Cambridge, 1891-92.
LERNER, MAX. *The Mind and Faith of Justice Holmes.* Boston: Little, Brown & Co., 1943.
Living Age. 1855.
MATTHIESSEN, F. O. *American Rennaissance.* London and New York: Oxford University Press, 1941.
New Englander. 1855.
New York Quarterly. 1855.
Orestes Brownson's Quarterly Review. 1855.
OSSOLI, MARGARET FULLER. *Woman in the Nineteenth Century.* Boston, 1845.
People's Organ. 1855.
PERRY, RALPH BARTON. *The Thought and Character of William James.* 2 vols. Boston: Little, Brown & Co., 1935.
Putnam's Monthly. 1855.
Republican Quarterly Review. 1855.
SANDBURG, CARL. *Abraham Lincoln: The Prairie Years and the War Years.* New York: Harcourt, Brace & Co., 1954.
Southern Literary Messenger. 1855.
THOREAU, HENRY DAVID. *Writings.* 14 vols. Boston and New York, 1906.
U.S. Democratic Review. 1855.
U.S. Magazine of Science, Art, Manufactures, Agriculture, Commerce, and Trade. 1855.
U.S. Review. 1855.
Western Journal and Civilian. 1855.

IV. A Contrast in Democratic Temper: Lincoln and Emerson

EMERSON, RALPH W. *Complete Works,* ed. EDWARD W. EMERSON. 14 vols. Boston and New York, 1903-4.
———. *Journals.* 10 vols. Boston and New York, 1909-14.
Hidden Lincoln, The, ed. EMANUEL HERTZ. New York: Viking Press, 1938.
LINCOLN, ABRAHAM. *Autobiography,* ed. N. W. STEPHENSON. Indianapolis, 1926.

V. Lincoln: Human Nature in America's Crucible

HERNDON, WILLIAM H. *Life of Lincoln.* Cleveland: World Publishing Co., 1942.
Hidden Lincoln, The, ed. EMANUEL HERTZ. New York: Viking Press, 1938.
LINCOLN, ABRAHAM. *Complete Works,* ed. JOHN G. NICOLAY and JOHN HAY. 2 vols. New York, 1922.
————. *Speeches and Letters, 1832-65.* New York: Dutton, Everyman edition, 1907.

Vignette: 1865

Abraham Lincoln Quarterly. March, 1941.
ADAMS, HENRY. *The Degradation of the Democratic Dogma.* New York, 1919.
Atlantic Monthly. 1865.
BEARD, CHARLES A. *The American Spirit.* New York: Macmillan Co., 1942.
————, and BEARD, MARY R. *The Rise of American Civilization.* New York: Macmillan Co., 1933.
Christian Examiner. 1865.
COMTE, AUGUSTE. *The Positive Philosophy.* Translated by HARRIET MARTINEAU. New York, 1855.
CONWAY, MONCURE DANIEL. *Addresses and Reprints, 1850-1907.* New York, 1909.
————. *Autobiography.* Boston and New York, 1904.
GODWIN, WILLIAM. *Caleb Williams.* London and New York, 1794.
HALE, WILLIAM H. *Horace Greeley.* New York: Harper & Bros., 1950.
Harper's Magazine. 1865.
Independent, April 27, 1865; May 4, 1865; May 11, 1865.
LERNER, MAX. *The Mind and Faith of Justice Holmes.* Boston: Little, Brown & Co., 1943.
Living Age. 1865.
New Englander. 1865.
New Nation. 1865.
New York Tribune, January 2, 1865; February 7, 1865; March 9, 1865; April 10, 1865; April 13, 1865; April 15, 1865.

North American Review. 1865.
NOTT, J. C., and GLIDDON, G. R. *Types of Mankind.* Philadelphia, 1865.
READE, WINWOOD. *The Martyrdom of Man.* New York, 1887.
SPENCER, HERBERT. *Social Statics.* New York, 1865 (London, 1850).

VI. Of Crime and Responsibility: Oliver Wendell Holmes

HOLMES, OLIVER WENDELL. *Life and Letters,* ed. JOHN T. MORSE. 2 vols. Boston, 1896.
———. *Writings.* 14 vols. Cambridge, 1891-92.

Vignette: 1875

ABBOTT, N. W., M.D. "The Origin of Crime," *Inland Magazine,* VIII (July, 1876), 921-29.
ALCOTT, AMOS BRONSON. *Journals,* ed. ODELL SHEPARD. Boston: Little, Brown & Co., 1938.
Annual Record of Science and Industry. 1874.
Atlantic Monthly. 1875.
BURGH, JAMES. *The Dignity of Human Nature.* Hartford, 1802.
CUBBERLEY, ELLWOOD P. *Public Education in the United States.* New York and Chicago, 1919.
DUNNE, EDMUND F. *Our Public Schools: Are They Free for All, or Are They Not?* New York, 1875.
FISKE, JOHN. *Outlines of Cosmic Philosophy.* Boston, 1874.
———. *Outlines of Organic Philosophy.* Boston, 1875.
Harper's Magazine. 1875.
HARRIS, W. T. "Relation of Physical Science to Human Life," *Western,* I (January, 1875), 20-29.
———. "Thoughts on Pessimism," *Western,* I (May, 1875), 304-11.
HARTE, BRET. *Gabriel Conroy: Bohemian Papers, Stories of and for the Young.* Boston and New York, 1871.
———. *Letters,* ed. GEOFFREY BRET HARTE. New York, 1926.
———. *Tales of the Argonauts.* New York, 1872.
HITTELL, JOHN S. *A History of the Mental Growth of Mankind.* San Francisco, 1889.
HOLMES, OLIVER WENDELL. *Life and Letters,* ed. JOHN T. MORSE. 2 vols. Boston, 1896.

472 THE IMAGE OF MAN IN AMERICA

HOWELLS, WILLIAM DEAN. *A Foregone Conclusion.* Boston, 1875.
———. *Life in Letters,* ed. MILDRED HOWELLS. 2 vols. Garden City, 1928.
INGERSOLL, CHARLES. *Fears for Democracy Regarded from the American Point of View.* Philadelphia, 1875.
LANIER, SIDNEY. *Letters: Selections from His Correspondence, 1866-1881.* With an Introduction by WILLIAM R. THAYER. New York, 1899.
Living Age. 1875.
LYELL, SIR CHARLES. *Principles of Geology.* London, 1837.
MILL, JOHN STUART. *Auguste Comte and Positivism.* Reprinted from the *Westminster Review.* London, 1882.
———. *Considerations on Representative Government.* New York, 1874.
———. *The Contest in America.* Reprinted from *Fraser's Magazine.* Boston, 1862.
———. *Socialism.* New York, 1890.
National Quarterly Review. June, 1875.
New Englander. 1875.
New York Tribune. January 4, 1875; January 5, 1875; January 7, 1875; January 9, 1875; February 4, 1875; April 10, 1875.
New Orleans Monthly Review. 1874.
NICHOLS, THOMAS L. *Forty Years of American Life.* London, 1874.
NORDHOFF, CHARLES. *Communistic Communities of the United States.* New York, 1875.
North American Review. 1875.
Overland Monthly. 1875.
PAINE, ALBERT BIGELOW. *Mark Twain, A Biography.* 3 vols. New York, 1912.
PEABODY, ELIZABETH P. *Record of a School: Exemplifying the General Principles of Spiritual Culture.* Boston, 1835.
SANDBURG, CARL. *Abraham Lincoln: The Prairie Years and the War Years.* New York: Harcourt, Brace & Co., 1954.
Scribner's Magazine. 1875.
STARKE, AUBREY H. *Sidney Lanier.* Chapel Hill: University of North Carolina Press, 1933.
Unitarian Review. 1875.
WILLIAMS, JOHN M. *Nullification and Compromise.* New York, 1863.

VII. Whitman and the Ideal Man

ALLEN, GAY WILSON. *The Solitary Singer*. New York: Macmillan Co., 1955.

———. *Walt Whitman Handbook*. Chicago: Packard & Co., 1946.

ARVIN, NEWTON. *Whitman*. New York: Macmillan Co., 1938.

BROOKS, VAN WYCK. *The Times of Melville and Whitman*. New York: E. P. Dutton & Co., 1947.

BUCKE, RICHARD M. *Walt Whitman*. Philadelphia, 1883.

BURROUGHS, JOHN. *Birds and Poets*. Boston, 1877.

CANBY, HENRY SEIDEL. *Walt Whitman*. New York: Literary Classics, 1943.

GLICKSBERG, CHARLES I. *Walt Whitman and the Civil War*. Philadelphia: University of Pennsylvania Press, 1933.

JAMES, HENRY. "Mr. Walt Whitman," *Nation*, I, 20 (November 16, 1865) 625-26. (From *Views and Reviews*, Boston, 1908).

LAWRENCE, D. H. *Studies in Classic American Literature*. New York, 1923.

MASTERS, EDGAR LEE. *Whitman*. New York: Charles Scribner's Sons, 1937.

SANTAYANA, GEORGE. *Interpretations of Poetry and Religion*. New York, 1900.

TRAUBEL, HORACE. *With Walt Whitman in Camden*. 3 vols. Boston and New York, 1906-14.

WHITMAN, WALT. *Calamus*, ed. DR. MAURICE BUCKE. Boston, 1897.

———. *Complete Poetry, and Selected Prose and Letters*, ed. EMORY HOLLOWAY. New York: Random House, 1938.

———. *Complete Writings*. 10 vols. New York and London, 1902.

———. *Diary in Canada*, ed. WILLIAM SLOANE KENNEDY. Boston, 1904.

———. *The Gathering of the Forces*, ed. CLEVELAND RODGERS and JOHN BLACK. 2 vols. New York and London, 1920.

———. *Uncollected Poetry and Prose*, ed. EMORY HOLLOWAY. New York, 1921.

———. *Workshop*, ed. CLIFTON J. FURNESS. Cambridge, Massachusetts, 1928.

Vignette: 1885

Atlantic Monthly, 1885.

Century Magazine. 1885.
GARLAND, HAMLIN. *Ulysses S. Grant.* New York, 1898.
GRANT, ULYSSES S. *Personal Memoirs.* 2 vols. New York, 1885.
Harper's Magazine. 1885.
MELVILLE, HERMAN. *Works.* 16 vols. London, 1922-24.
North American Review. 1885.

VIII. Utopian Dissent and Affirmation: Howells, Bellamy, and George

American Mercury. February, 1925.
BARNARD, HARRY. *"Eagle Forgotten."* New York and Indianapolis: Bobbs-Merrill Co., 1938.
BELLAMY, EDWARD. *Looking Backward.* Boston, 1917.
———. *Philosophy,* ed. ARTHUR E. MORGAN. New York: King's Crown Press, 1945.
CARTER, EVERETT. *Howells and the Age of Realism.* Philadelphia: J. B. Lippincott Co., 1950.
COOKE, DELMAR GROSS. *William Dean Howells.* New York, 1922.
DE MILLE, ANNA GEORGE. *Henry George, Citizen of the World.* Chapel Hill: University of North Carolina Press, 1950.
FIRKINS, OSCAR W. *William Dean Howells.* Cambridge, 1924.
GEORGE, HENRY. *Progress and Poverty.* Dutton, Everyman edition. New York, 1911.
GEORGE, HENRY, JR. *The Life of Henry George.* New York, 1930.
HOWELLS, WILLIAM DEAN. *A Hazard of New Fortunes.* New York, 1890.
———. *Life in Letters,* ed. MILDRED HOWELLS. 2 vols. Garden City, 1928.
———. *The Quality of Mercy.* New York, 1892.
———. *A Traveler from Alturia.* New York, 1894.
———. *Years of My Youth.* New York, 1916.
KIRK, CLARA and RUDOLF. *William Dean Howells.* New York: American Book Co., 1950.
MORGAN, ARTHUR E. *Edward Bellamy.* New York, 1944.

IX. Mark Twain: On the Bitter Root of the Human Tree

BROOKS, VAN WYCK. *The Ordeal of Mark Twain.* New York: E. P. Dutton & Co., 1933.

HOWELLS, WILLIAM DEAN. *My Mark Twain*. New York, 1910.

KAPLAN, JUSTIN. *Mr. Clemens and Mark Twain*. New York: Simon and Schuster, Inc., 1966.

Mark Twain–Howells Letters, ed. HENRY NASH SMITH and WILLIAM M. GIBSON. Cambridge, Mass.: Harvard University Press, 1960.

Mark Twain in Eruption, ed. BERNARD DEVOTO. New York, 1940.

PAINE, ALBERT BIGELOW. *Mark Twain, A Biography*. 3 vols. New York, 1912.

TWAIN, MARK. *Autobiography*, ed. CHARLES NEIDER. New York: Harper and Brothers, 1959.

———. *The Celebrated Jumping Frog of Calaveras County, and Other Sketches*. New York, 1867.

———. *A Connecticut Yankee in King Arthur's Court*. New York, 1917.

———. *Letters*, ed. ALBERT BIGELOW PAINE. 2 vols. New York, 1917.

———. *The Gilded Age*. New York, 1873-74.

———. *Innocents Abroad*. New York, 1869.

———. *The Mysterious Stranger and Other Stories*. New York, 1922.

———. *Pudd'nhead Wilson*. New York, 1899.

———. *Roughing It*. New York, 1872.

———. *Sketches New and Old*. New York, 1875.

———. *Speeches*. New York, 1923.

———. *A True Story*. New York, 1877.

———. *What Is Man?* New York, 1917.

Vignette: 1895

Atlantic Monthly. 1895.

BELLAMY, EDWARD. "Christians in the Year 2000," *Ladies Home Journal*, XII (January, 1895), 6.

BENNETT, MILDRED. *The World of Willa Cather*. New York: Dodd, Mead & Co., 1951.

BROWN, E. K. and EDEL, LEON. *Willa Cather: A Critical Biography*. New York: Alfred A. Knopf, 1953.

DREISER, THEODORE. "Mark Twain: Three Contacts." *Esquire*, IV (October, 1935), 22.

ELIAS, ROBERT H. *Dreiser: Apostle of Nature*. New York: Alfred A. Knopf, 1949.

GLASGOW, ELLEN. *The Woman Within*. New York: Harcourt, Brace & Co., 1954.

Harper's Magazine. 1895.

Heart of Burroughs's Journals, ed. CLARA BARRUS. Boston, 1923.

JAMES, HENRY. *Letters,* ed. PERCY LUBBOCK. 2 vols. London and New York, 1920.

MORGAN, ARTHUR E. *Edward Bellamy.* New York, 1944.

Nation. 1895.

New York Times, March 14-21, 1895.

North American Review. 1895.

Overland Monthly. 1890.

PAINE, ALBERT BIGELOW. *Mark Twain, A Biography.* 3 vols. New York, 1912.

ROOSEVELT, THEODORE. *The Winning of the West.* 4 vols. New York, 1889-96.

Scribner's Magazine. 1895.

SHIVELY, JAMES R. *Writings from Willa Cather's Campus Years.* Lincoln: University of Nebraska Press, 1950.

TWAIN, MARK. *Letters,* ed. ALBERT BIGELOW PAINE. 2 vols. New York, 1917.

WHARTON, EDITH. "The Lamp of Psyche," *Scribner's,* XVIII (October, 1895), 418-28.

X. Henry Adams and the Direction of Human Energies

ADAMS, HENRY. *The Degradation of the Democratic Dogma.* New York, 1919.

———. *Democracy.* New York, 1880.

———. *The Education of Henry Adams.* New York, 1918.

———. *History of the United States during the Administrations of Jefferson and Madison.* 9 vols. New York, 1889-91.

———. *Letters, 1858-1891,* ed. WORTHINGTON CHAUNCEY FORD. Boston and New York, 1930.

———. *Mont-Saint-Michel and Chartres.* Cambridge, 1904.

———. *The Tendency of History.* New York, 1928.

BRADFORD, GAMALIEL. *American Portraits.* Boston and New York, 1922.

HUME, ROBERT ARTHUR. *Runaway Star.* Ithaca: Cornell University Press, 1951.

JORDY, WILLIAM H. *Henry Adams.* New Haven: Yale University Press, 1952.

XI. Brooks Adams: Human Nature in the Decay of Civilization

ADAMS, BROOKS. *America's Economic Supremacy*. New York and London, 1900.

———. *The Emancipation of Massachusetts*. New York, 1919.

———. *The Law of Civilization and Decay*. New York: Vintage Books, 1955.

———. *The New Empire*. New York, 1902.

———. *The Theory of Social Revolutions*. New York, 1913.

———. "Title to Property." Address before New Jersey State Bar Association, June 13, 1914.

ADAMS, HENRY. *The Degradation of the Democratic Dogma*. New York, 1919.

BERINGAUSE, ARTHUR F. *Brooks Adams, A Biography*. New York: Alfred A. Knopf, 1955.

XII. On the Genesis of Great Men: William James

ALLEN, GRANT. "The Genesis of Genius," *Atlantic Monthly*, XLVII (March, 1881), 371-81.

———. "Hellas and Civilisation," *Gentleman's Magazine*, CCXLV (August, 1878), 156-70.

———. "Nation Making," *Gentleman's Magazine*, CCXLV (November, 1878), 580-91.

FISKE, JOHN. "Sociology and Hero-Worship," in *Excursions of an Evolutionist*. Boston and New York, 1891.

JAMES, HENRY. *Notes of a Son and Brother*. New York, 1914.

———. *A Small Boy and Others*. New York, 1913.

JAMES, WILLIAM. *Essays in Radical Empiricism*, ed. RALPH BARTON PERRY. New York, 1912.

———. *Letters*, ed. HENRY JAMES. 2 vols. Boston, 1920.

———. *Memories and Studies*, New York, 1911.

———. *The Philosophy of William James*, ed. HORACE M. KALLEN. New York: Modern Library, n.d.

———. *Pragmatism*. New York, 1907.

———. *Principles of Psychology*. 2 vols. New York and London, 1890.

———. *Talks to Teachers*. New York and London, 1899.
———. *The Will to Believe*. New York, 1917.
PERRY, RALPH BARTON. *The Thought and Character of William James*. Boston: Little, Brown & Co., 1935.

                              Vignette: 1915

Atlantic Monthly. 1915.
DAVENPORT, CHARLES B. *Heredity in Relation to Eugenics*. New York, 1911.
DU BOIS, W. E. B. "The African Roots of War," *Atlantic Monthly*, CXV (May, 1915), 707-14.
Harper's Magazine. 1915.
HOEHLING, A. A. and MARY. *The Last Voyage of the Lusitania*. New York: Henry Holt & Co., 1956.
HUNTINGTON, ELLSWORTH. *Civilization and Climate*. New Haven: Yale University Press, 1924.
———. *Mainsprings of Civilization*. New York: John Wiley & Sons, 1945.
———. *Principles of Human Geography*. New York: John Wiley & Sons, 1940.
MORGAN, GERALD. "The Matter with Russia," *New Republic*, IV (September 18, 1915), 175-76.
New Republic. 1915.
WISTER, OWEN. "Quack Novels and Democracy," *Atlantic Monthly*, CXV (June, 1915), 721-34.

XIII. On the Ways of Man: Darrow, Steffens, and Broun

BROUN, HEYWOOD. *Collected Edition*, ed. HEYWOOD HALE BROUN. New York: Harcourt, Brace & Co., 1941.
DARROW, CLARENCE. *Crime, Its Cause and Treatment*. New York, 1922.
———. *Debate: Is Man a Machine?* New York, 1927.
———. *A Persian Pearl and Other Essays*. Boston, 1931.
———. *Resist Not Evil*. Chicago, 1904.
———. *The Story of My Life*. New York, 1932.
STEFFENS, LINCOLN. *Autobiography*. New York, 1931.

Vignette: 1924

BUSCH, FRANCIS X. *Prisoners at the Bar.* Indianapolis: Bobbs-Merrill Co., 1952.

COBB, IVO GEIKE, M.D. *The Glands of Destiny.* London, 1927.

DARROW, CLARENCE A. *Crime and Criminals.* Chicago, 1910.

———. *Farmington.* Chicago, 1904.

———. *Resist Not Evil.* Chicago, 1904.

———. *The Story of My Life.* New York, 1932.

DREISER, THEODORE. *Dawn.* New York, 1931.

HOSKINS, ROY G., M.D. *The Tides of Life.* New York: W. W. Norton Co., 1933.

KERNAN, MAUREEN. *The Amazing Crime and Trial of Leopold and Loeb.* Chicago: Plymouth Court Press, 1924.

LEVIN, MEYER. *Compulsion.* New York: Simon & Schuster, 1956.

MARTIN, JOHN BARTLOW. "Nathan Leopold's Thirty Desperate Years," *Saturday Evening Post,* CCXXVII (April 2, 1955), 17-19+; (April 9, 1955), 32-33+; (April 16, 1955), 36+; (April 23, 1955), 28+.

PINCUS, GREGORY, and THIRMANN, KENNETH V. (eds.). *The Hormones.* New York: Academic Press, 1955.

XIV. Veblen and the Mystery of Behavior

DORFMAN, JOSEPH. *Thorstein Veblen and His America.* New York: Viking Press, 1934.

ROBINSON, JAMES HARVEY. *The Mind in the Making.* New York, 1921.

VEBLEN, THORSTEIN. *The Engineers and the Price System.* New York, 1921.

———. *Essays in Our Changing Order.* New York, 1934.

———. *Imperial Germany and the Industrial Revolution.* New York, 1915.

———. *The Instinct of Workmanship.* New York, 1914.

———. *The Portable Veblen,* ed. MAX LERNER. New York: Viking Press, 1948.

———. *The Theory of the Leisure Class.* New York: Modern Library, 1934.

XV. John Dewey and the Plasticity of Impulse

DEWEY, JOHN. *Democracy and Education.* New York, 1922.

———. *Human Nature and Conduct.* New York, 1922.

———. *Philosophy,* ed. PAUL A. SCHILPP. Evanston: Northwestern University Press, 1939.

———. *Problems of Men.* New York: Philosophical Library, 1946.

EASTMAN, MAX. *Heroes I Have Known.* New York: Simon & Schuster, 1942.

FRANK, WALDO. *Time Exposures.* New York, 1926.

RATNER, JOSEPH (ed.). *Intelligence in the Modern World: John Dewey's Philosophy.* New York: Modern Library, 1939.

XVI. Theodore Dreiser and the Human Enigma

ANDERSON, SHERWOOD. *Horses and Men.* New York, 1923.

BEER, THOMAS. *Stephen Crane.* New York: Alfred A. Knopf, 1923.

CRILE, GEORGE WASHINGTON. *Man—An Adaptive Mechanism.* New York, 1916.

———. *The Mechanistic Interpretation of War and Peace.* New York, 1915.

DREISER, THEODORE. *America Is Worth Saving.* New York: Modern Age Books, 1941.

———. *An American Tragedy.* New York, 1925.

———. *A Book about Myself.* New York, 1922.

———. *The Bulwark.* New York: Doubleday, Doran & Co., 1946.

———. *Dawn.* New York, 1931.

———. *Dreiser Looks at Russia.* New York, 1928.

———. *Free and Other Stories.* New York: Modern Library, 1925.

———. *The Genius.* New York, 1915.

———. *Hey, Rub-a-Dub-Dub.* New York, 1920.

———. *Jennie Gerhardt.* New York, 1911.

EMERSON, RALPH WALDO. *The Conduct of Life.* Boston, 1860.

GEISMAR, MAXWELL. *Rebels and Ancestors.* Boston: Houghton Mifflin Co., 1953.

GEORGE, HENRY. *Progress and Poverty.* New York: Dutton, Everyman edition, 1911.

LOEB, JACQUES. *The Mechanistic Conception of Life.* Chicago, 1912.

MATTHIESSEN, F. O. *Theodore Dreiser.* New York: William Sloane Associates, 1951.

Vignette: 1935

Atlantic Monthly. 1935.
Franklin Delano Roosevelt: A Memorial. New York: Pocket Books, 1945.
Harper's Magazine. 1935, 1936.
Nation. 1935.
New Republic. 1935.
Scribner's Magazine. 1935.
Time. 1935.

XVII. Faulkner and Hemingway: Image of Man's Desolation

BAKER, CARLOS. *Hemingway: The Writer as Artist*. Princeton: Princeton University Press, 1952.
FAULKNER, WILLIAM. *Absalom, Absalom!* New York: Modern Library, 1951.
———. *The Sound and the Fury & As I Lay Dying*. New York: Modern Library, 1946.
———. *Go Down, Moses*. New York: Modern Library, 1955.
———. *Intruder in the Dust*. New York: Signet Books, 1949.
———. *Light in August*. New York: Smith and Haas, 1932.
———. *The Portable Faulkner*, ed. MALCOLM COWLEY. New York: Viking Press, 1946.
———. *Reader*. New York: Random House, 1954.
———. *Sanctuary and Requiem for a Nun*. New York: New American Library, 1954.
———. *Soldiers' Pay*. New York, 1926.
HEMINGWAY, ERNEST. *A Farewell to Arms*, ed. ROBERT PENN WARREN. Charles Scribner's Sons, 1953.
———. *For Whom the Bell Tolls*. New York: Charles Scribner's Sons, 1940.
———. *The Green Hills of Africa*. New York: Permabooks, 1954.
———. *In Our Time*. New York: Charles Scribner's Sons, 1930.
———. *The Old Man and the Sea*. New York: Charles Scribner's Sons, 1952.
———. *Short Stories*. New York: Modern Library, n.d.
———. *The Sun Also Rises*. New York: Bantam Books, 1949.
HOFFMAN, FREDERICK J. and VICKERY, OLGA W. (eds.) *William*

Faulkner: Two Decades of Criticism. East Lansing: Michigan State College Press, 1954.
O'CONNOR, WILLIAM VAN. *The Tangled Fire of William Faulkner.* Minneapolis: University of Minnesota Press, 1954.
WOLFE, THOMAS. *You Can't Go Home Again.* New York: Sun Dial Press, 1942.

Vignette: 1945

Harper's Magazine. 1945.
HERSEY, JOHN. *Hiroshima.* New York: Alfred A. Knopf, 1946.
Nation. 1945.
Newsweek. 1945.
STIMSON, HENRY L. "The Decision to Use the Atomic Bomb," *Harper's Magazine,* CXCIV (February, 1947), 97-107.
Time. 1945.

XVIII. Terman and the Definition of Genius

BURKS, BARBARA, and Others. *The Promise of Youth.* Stanford: Stanford University Press, 1930.
COX, CATHARINE M., and Others. *The Early Mental Traits of Three Hundred Geniuses.* Stanford: Stanford University Press, 1926.
LEHMAN, HARVEY C. *Age and Achievement.* Princeton: Princeton University Press, 1953.
TERMAN, LEWIS M. "The Intelligence Quotient of Francis Galton in Childhood," *American Journal of Psychology,* XXVIII (April, 1917), 209-15.
———. and Others. *The Gifted Child Grows Up.* Stanford: Stanford University Press, 1947.
———. *The Gifted Group at Mid-Life.* Stanford: Stanford University Press, 1959.
———. *Mental and Physical Traits of a Thousand Gifted Children.* Stanford: Stanford University Press, 1925.

XIX. Biology and the Quest for Certainty

ARDREY, ROBERT. *African Genesis.* New York: Atheneum Publishers, 1963.

————. *The Territorial Imperative.* New York: Atheneum Publishers, 1967.

EISELEY, LOREN. "A Script Written in the Bones," *New York Times Book Review* (September 11, 1966).

FARIS, ELLSWORTH. *The Nature of Human Nature.* New York and London: McGraw-Hill Book Company, Inc., 1937.

FREUD, SIGMUND. *Civilization and Its Discontents,* ed. JAMES STRACHEY. New York: W. W. Norton and Company, Inc., 1962.

GALTON, SIR FRANCIS. *Essays in Eugenics.* London, 1909.

————. *Hereditary Genius.* 1891 edition. London, 1869.

————. *Inquiries into Human Faculty.* London, 1883.

————. *Memories of My Life.* London, 1908.

GESELL, ARNOLD. *The Embryology of Behavior.* New York: Harper & Bros., 1945.

————. *Infant Development.* New York: Harper & Bros., 1952.

GLASS, BENTLEY. *Genes and the Man.* New York: Teachers College Press, 1943.

"Heredity," *Encyclopedia of the Social Sciences* (1930-35), VII, 328-35.

HOGBEN, LANCELOT. *The Nature of Living Matter.* London, 1930.

HOOTON, E. A. *Crime and the Man.* Cambridge: Harvard University Press, 1939.

HUNTINGTON, ELLSWORTH. *Civilization and Climate.* New Haven: Yale University Press, 1924.

————. *Mainsprings of Civilization.* New York: John Wiley & Sons, 1945.

JENNINGS, H. S. *The Biological Basis of Human Nature.* New York: W. W. Norton & Co., 1930.

KLINEBERG, OTTO. *Negro Intelligence and Selective Migration.* New York: Columbia University Press, 1935.

————. "Racial Psychology," *The Science of Man in the World Crisis.* New York: Columbia University Press, 1945.

KNOBLOCH, HILDA. "The Distribution of Intellectual Potential in an Infant Population." Preliminary draft of paper presented in New York, December 28, 1956.

McDOUGALL, WILLIAM. *Psychology.* New York, 1912.

MONTAGU, M. F. ASHLEY. *The Biosocial Nature of Man.* New York: Grove Press, 1956.

————. *Darwin, Competition and Cooperation.* New York: Henry Schuman, 1952.

————. *Man and Aggression.* New York: Oxford University Press, 1968.

MORGAN, T. H. *Evolution and Adaptation.* New York, 1903.

————. *Evolution and Genetics.* Princeton, 1925.

————. *The Physical Basis of Heredity.* Philadelphia and London, 1919.

————. *The Scientific Basis of Evolution.* New York, 1932.

————, and Others. *The Mechanism of Mendelian Heredity.* New York, 1915.

Nature and Nurture. London, 1939.

PEARSON, KARL. *The Grammar of Science.* London: J. M. Dent & Sons, 1937.

PETROFF, LOUIS. *Solitaries and Solitarization.* Los Angeles: University of Southern California Press, 1936.

PFEIFFER, JOHN E. *The Human Brain.* New York: Harper & Bros., 1955.

RUCH, FLOYD L. *Psychology and Life.* New York, 1941.

ROBINSON, JAMES HARVEY. *The Mind in the Making.* New York, 1921.

SHERMAN, MANDEL, and HENRY, THOMAS R. *The Hollow Folk.* New York, 1933.

THOMSON, ARTHUR. *What Is Man?* London, 1924.

XX. Heredity and Sexual Behavior: Alfred Kinsey

KINSEY, ALFRED W. *Sexual Behavior in the Human Male.* Philadelphia: W. B. Saunders Co., 1948.

Vignette: 1955

Atlantic Monthly. 1955.

DE KRUIF, PAUL. *A Man Against Insanity.* New York: Harcourt, Brace & Co., 1957.

DRUCKER, PETER. "America's Next Twenty Years," *Harper's Magazine,* CCX (March-June, 1955), 27-32, 39-44, 41-47, 52-59.

FAULKNER, WILLIAM. "On Privacy, the American Dream: What Happened to It," *Harper's Magazine,* CCXI (July, 1955), 33-38.

Harper's Magazine. 1955.

LORAND, ARNOLD. *Human Intelligence.* Philadelphia, 1927.

PFEIFFER, JOHN E. *The Human Brain.* New York: Harper & Bros., 1955.

Statistical Abstract of the United States: 1956. Compiled by the U.S. Department of Commerce and Bureau of the Census. Washington, D. C.: Government Printing Office, 1956.

Time. 1955.

World Almanac and Book of Facts for 1957. New York: World Telegram and Sun, 1957.

XXI. Anthropology and Man's Changing Image

BENEDICT, RUTH. *Patterns of Culture.* New York: Penguin Books, 1946.

BOAS, FRANZ. *Anthropology and Modern Life.* London, 1930.

———. *General Anthropology.* New York: Macmillan Co., 1938.

———. *The Mind of Primitive Man.* New York: Macmillan Co., 1938.

———. *Race and Democratic Society.* New York:. J. J. Augustin, 1945.

CARREL, ALEXIS. *Man the Unknown.* New York: Harper & Bros., 1935.

Changes in Bodily Form of Descendants of Immigrants. (Report of the Immigration Commission. Senate Document No. 208.) Washington, D. C., 1911.

ELDERTON, ETHEL M. *The Relative Strength of Nature and Nurture.* London, 1909.

FITZHUGH, GEORGE. *Cannibals All.* Richmond, 1857.

GESELL, ARNOLD. "The Biography of a Wolf-Child." *Harper's Magazine,* CLXXXII (January, 1941), 183-93.

GODDARD, HENRY H. *Human Efficiency and Levels of Intelligence.* Princeton, 1920.

HERSKOVITZ, MELVILLE J. *The American Negro.* New York: Alfred A. Knopf, 1928.

———. *Dahomey, an Ancient West African Kingdom.* 2 vols. New York: J. J. Augustin, 1938.

———. *The Negro and the Intelligence Tests.* Hanover, 1928.

HOCKING, WILLIAM E. *Human Nature and Its Remaking.* New Haven, 1918.

HOGBEN, LANCELOT. *Nature and Nurture.* London: Unwin, 1933, 1939.

———. *The Nature of Living Matter.* London, 1930.
HOOTON, EARNEST A. *Crime and the Man.* Cambridge: Harvard University Press, 1939.
HUNTINGTON, ELLSWORTH. *Civilization and Climate.* New Haven, 1924.
HUXLEY, JULIAN. *Man Stands Alone.* New York: Harper & Bros., 1941.
KLUCKHOHN, CLYDE, and MURRAY, HENRY A. (eds). *Personality in Nature, Society, and Culture.* New York: Alfred A. Knopf, 1953.
KROEBER, ALFRED. *Anthropology.* New York: Harcourt, Brace & Co., 1948.
———. *Configurations of Culture Growth.* Berkeley: University of California Press, 1944.
LINTON, RALPH. *The Study of Man.* New York: Appleton-Century Co., 1936.
———. (ed.) *The Science of Man in the World Crisis.* New York: Columbia University Press, 1945.
MEAD, MARGARET. *Sex and Temperament in Three Primitive Societies.* New York: William Morrow & Co., 1935.
MONTAGU, M. F. ASHLEY. *Darwin, Competition and Cooperation.* New York: Henry Schuman, 1952.
MORGAN, THOMAS H. *Evolution and Adaptation.* New York, 1903.
———. *Evolution and Genetics.* Princeton, 1925.
———. *The Scientific Basis of Evolution.* New York: W. W. Norton & Co., 1932.
MUMFORD, LEWIS. *The Condition of Man.* New York: Harcourt, Brace & Co., 1944.
MYRDAL, GUNNAR. *An American Dilemma.* 2 vols. New York: Harper & Bros., 1944.
NEWMAN, HORATIO, and Others. *Twins: A Study of Heredity and Environment.* Chicago: University of Chicago Press, 1937.
PAVLOV, I. V. *Conditioned Reflexes.* Oxford, 1927.
PEARSON, KARL. *National Life from the Standpoint of Science.* London, 1901.
REDFIELD, ROBERT. "What Do We Know About Race?" *Scientific Monthly,* LVII (September, 1943), 193-201.
SCHEINFELD, AMRAM. *The New You and Heredity.* Philadelphia: J. B. Lippincott Co., 1950.

SHERMAN, MANDEL, and HENRY, THOMAS R. *The Hollow Folk.* New York: Thomas Y. Crowell Co., 1933.
SINGH, REV. J. A. L., and ZINGG, ROBERT M. *Wolf-Children and Feral Man.* New York and London: Harper & Bros., 1942.
SUMNER, WILLIAM GRAHAM. *Folkways.* New York: Ginn & Co., 1940.

Vignette: 1969

Educational Directory, 1968–69, Part III: *Higher Education.* Washington, D. C., 1968.
HARRINGTON, MICHAEL. *The Other America.* Boston: Penguin Books, 1963.
The New York Times (December 25, 1968; January 16-17, 1969; April 21-30, 1969; May 2-12, 1969; July 21-23, 1969).
PLATO. *The Republic,* tr. BENJAMIN JOWETT. New York: Modern Library, 1941.

XXII. Intelligence and the Conquest of Hunger

BLOOM, BENJAMIN S. *Stability and Change in Human Characteristics.* New York: John Wiley & Sons, 1964.
LOWE, CHARLES UPTON. "Statement . . . Before the Committee on Agriculture, House of Representatives," April 24, 1969.
————. "Statement . . . Before the Senate Select Committee on Nutrition and Related Human Needs," January 28, 1969.
MAYS, BENJAMIN E., and DUNBAR, LESLIE W. (eds.). *Hunger, U.S.A.* Boston: Beacon Press, 1968.
The New York Times (November 13, 1968; February 20, 1969).
PLATO. *The Republic,* tr. BENJAMIN JOWETT. New York: Modern Library, 1941.

XXIII. Conclusion

KNOBLOCH, HILDA, and Others. "The Distribution of Intellectual Potential in an Infant Population." Preliminary draft of "Epidemiology of Mental Disorder," presented before the American Psychiatric Association and the American Public Health Association, December 27-28, 1956.
THOMPSON, WILLIAM R., and MELZACK, RONALD. "Early Environment," *Scientific American,* CLXCIV (January, 1956), 38-42.

Index

(For illustrations see list on page xiii.)

489